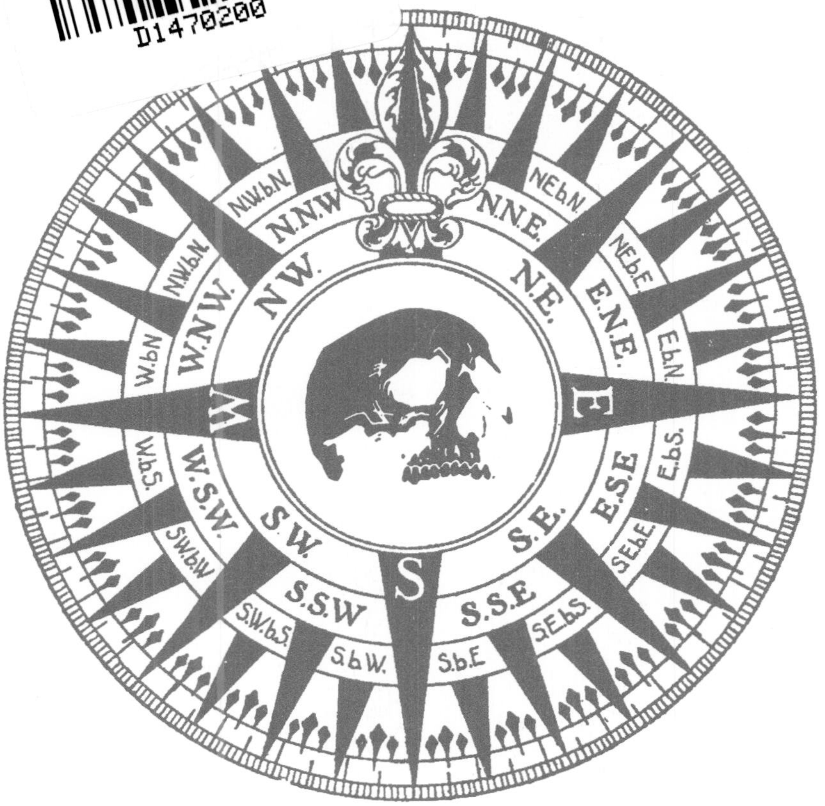
N.W.b.N.
N.N.W.
N.N.E.
N.E.b.N.
N.W.b.N.
N.W.
N.E.
N.E.b.E.
W.N.W.
E.N.E.
W.b.N.
E.b.N.
W
E
W.b.S.
E.b.S.
W.S.W.
E.S.E.
S.W.
S.E.
S.W.b.W.
S.E.b.E.
S.S.W.
S.S.E.
S
S.W.b.S.
S.E.b.S.
S.b.W.
S.b.E.

VOLUME ONE:

TOP HAT, WHITE LIES, AND TALES

THE MERCENARY SEA

WRITTEN BY **KEL SYMONS**
ART AND COLORS BY **MATHEW REYNOLDS**
LETTERING AND DESIGN BY **PAT BROSSEAU**
STORY EDITOR **SEBASTIAN GIRNER**

FOLLOW OUR CREW ON TWITTER:
@kelsymons @batfish73 @droog811 @sgirner

For updates on events, signings and exlusive previews of upcoming art, like our page
on Facebook and follow us on Tumblr and Instagram.

SEND YOUR COMMENTS AND QUESTIONS TO US AT
themercenarysea@gmail.com

OR MAIL US AT
The Mercenary Sea
c/o Kel Symons
P.O. Box 481301
Los Angeles, CA 90048

Be sure to inlude an SASE with your letter, and we'll send you back a
Merceary Sea sticker!

IMAGE COMICS, INC.
Robert Kirkman – Chief Operating Officer
Erik Larsen – Chief Financial Officer
Todd McFarlane – President
Marc Silvestri – Chief Executive Officer
Jim Valentino – Vice-President

Eric Stephenson – Publisher
Ron Richards – Director of Business Development
Jennifer de Guzman – Director of Trade Book Sales
Kat Salazar – Director of PR & Marketing
Jeremy Sullivan – Director of Digital Sales
Emilio Bautista – Sales Assistant
Branwyn Bigglestone – Senior Accounts Manager
Emily Miller – Accounts Manager
Jessica Ambriz – Administrative Assistant
Tyler Shainline – Events Coordinator
David Brothers – Content Manager
Jonathan Chan – Production Manager
Drew Gill – Art Director
Meredith Wallace – Print Manager
Monica Garcia – Senior Production Artist
Jenna Savage – Production Artist
Addison Duke – Production Artist
Tricia Ramos – Production Assistant
IMAGECOMICS.COM

THE MERCENARY SEA. Vol. 1, September 2014.
ISBN: 978-1-63215-108-7
Published by Image Comics, Inc. Office of Publication:
2001 Center Street, Sixth Floor, Berkeley, CA 94704. THE
MERCENARY SEA ™ & © 2014 Kel Symons and Mathew
Reynolds. Originally published in single magazine form as
THE MERCENARY SEA #1-6. "The Mercenary Sea," the The
Mercenary Sea logos and the likeness of all featured characters
are trademarks of Kel Symons and Mathew Reynolds. All
rights reserved. Image Comics ® and its logos are registered
trademarks of Image Comics, Inc. Any resemblance to actual
persons (living or dead), events, institutions, or locales, without
satiric intent, is coincidental. No portion of this publication may
be reproduced or transmitted, in any form or by any means,
without the express written permission of Kel Symons and
Mathew Reynolds. Printed in the U.S.A. For information
regarding the CPSIA on this printed material call: 203-595-
3636 and provide reference # RICH – 573560. For foreign
licensing and international rights contact: foreignlicensing@
imagecomics.com

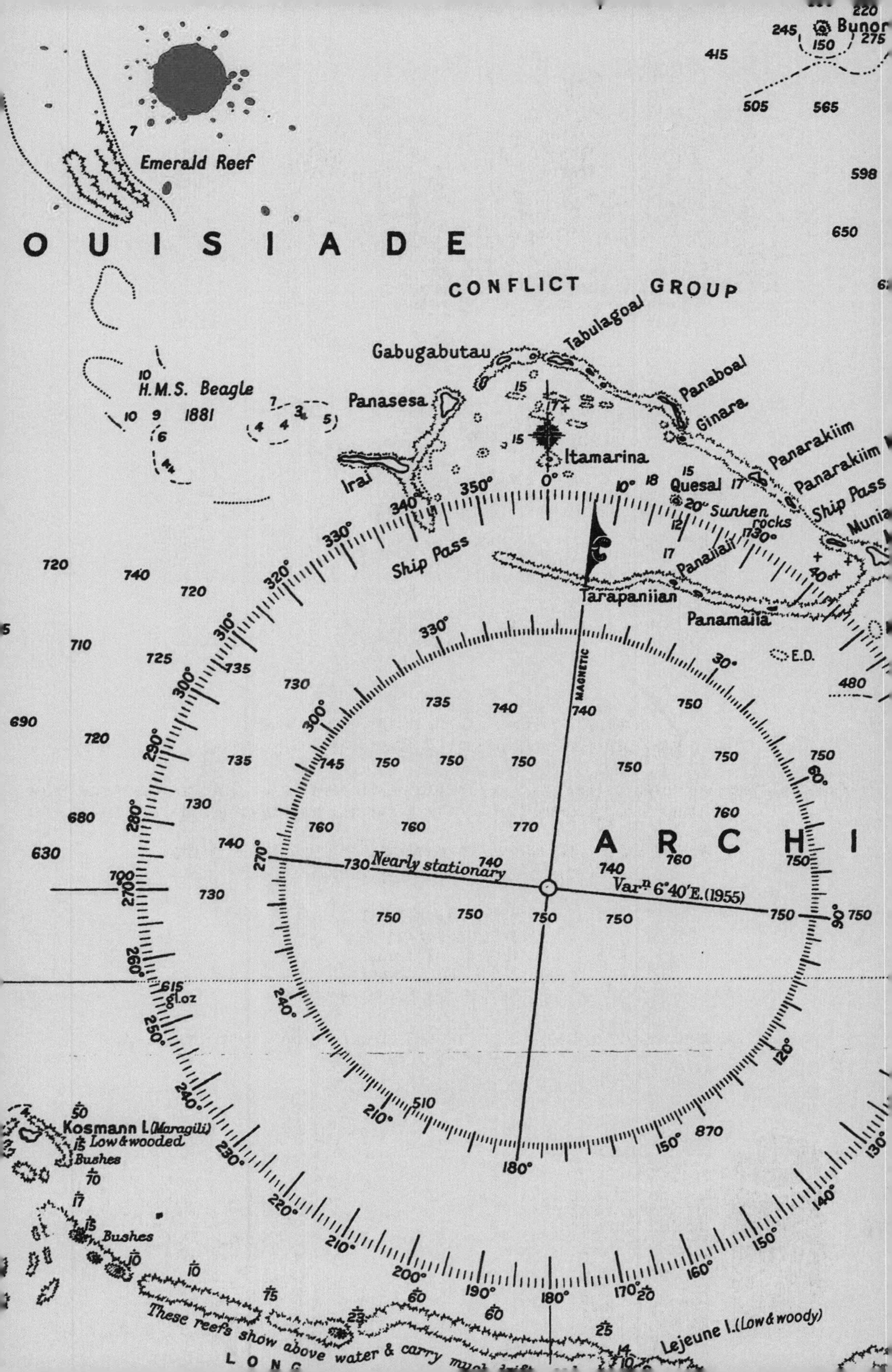

Emerald Reef
OUISIADE
CONFLICT GROUP
Tabulagoal
Gabugabutau
Panaboal
Panasesa
Ginara
H.M.S. Beagle
1881
Itamarina
Panarakiim
Irai
Quesal
Sunken rocks
Ship Pass
Munia
Panaiiaii
Tarapaniian
Panamaiia
E.D.
MAGNETIC
ARCHI
Nearly stationary
Varn 6°40′E. (1955)
gl.oz
Kosmann I. (Maragili)
Low & wooded
Bushes
These reefs show above water & carry much drift
Lejeune I. (Low & woody)
LONG
Bunor

Nice Work If You Can Get It

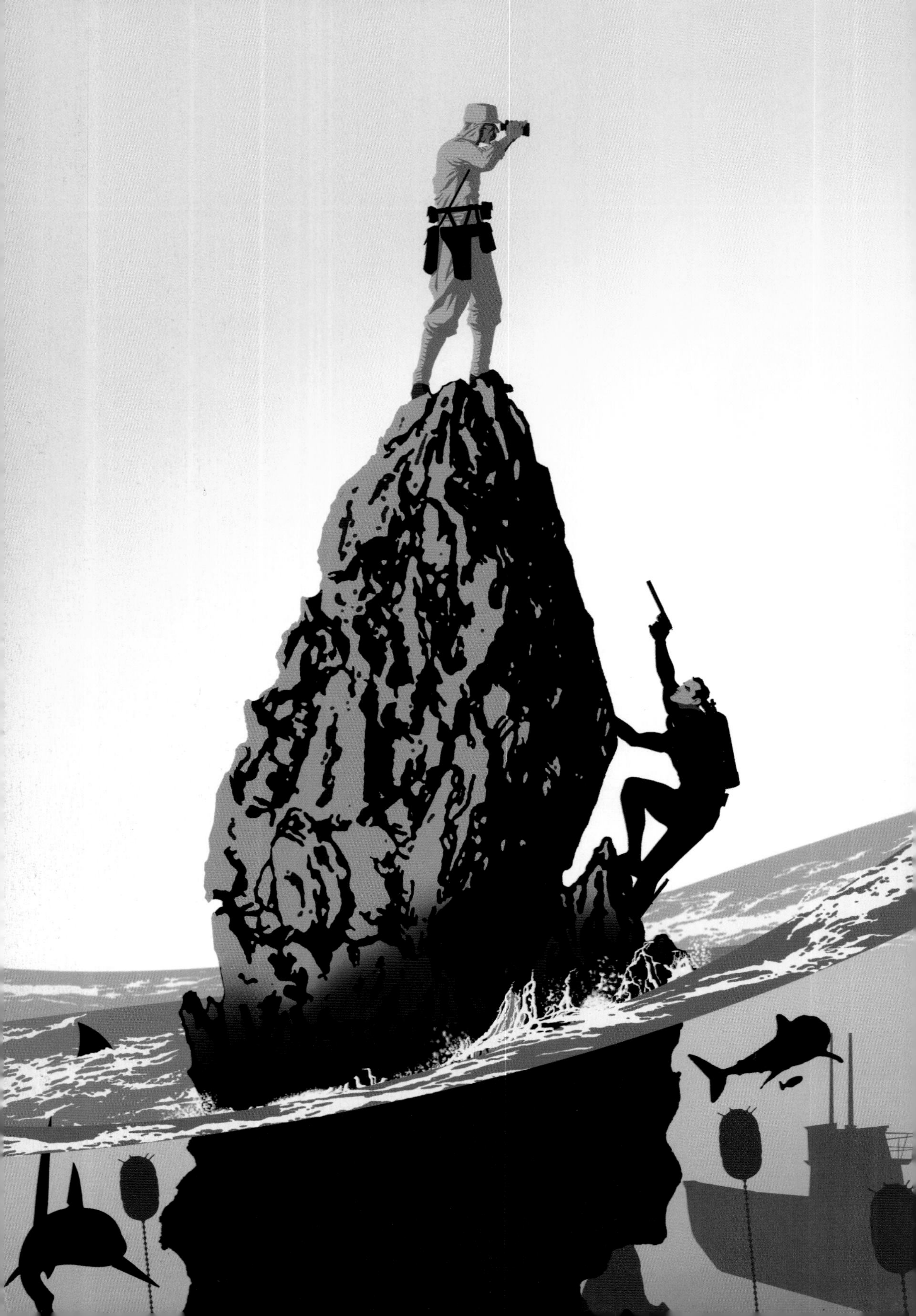

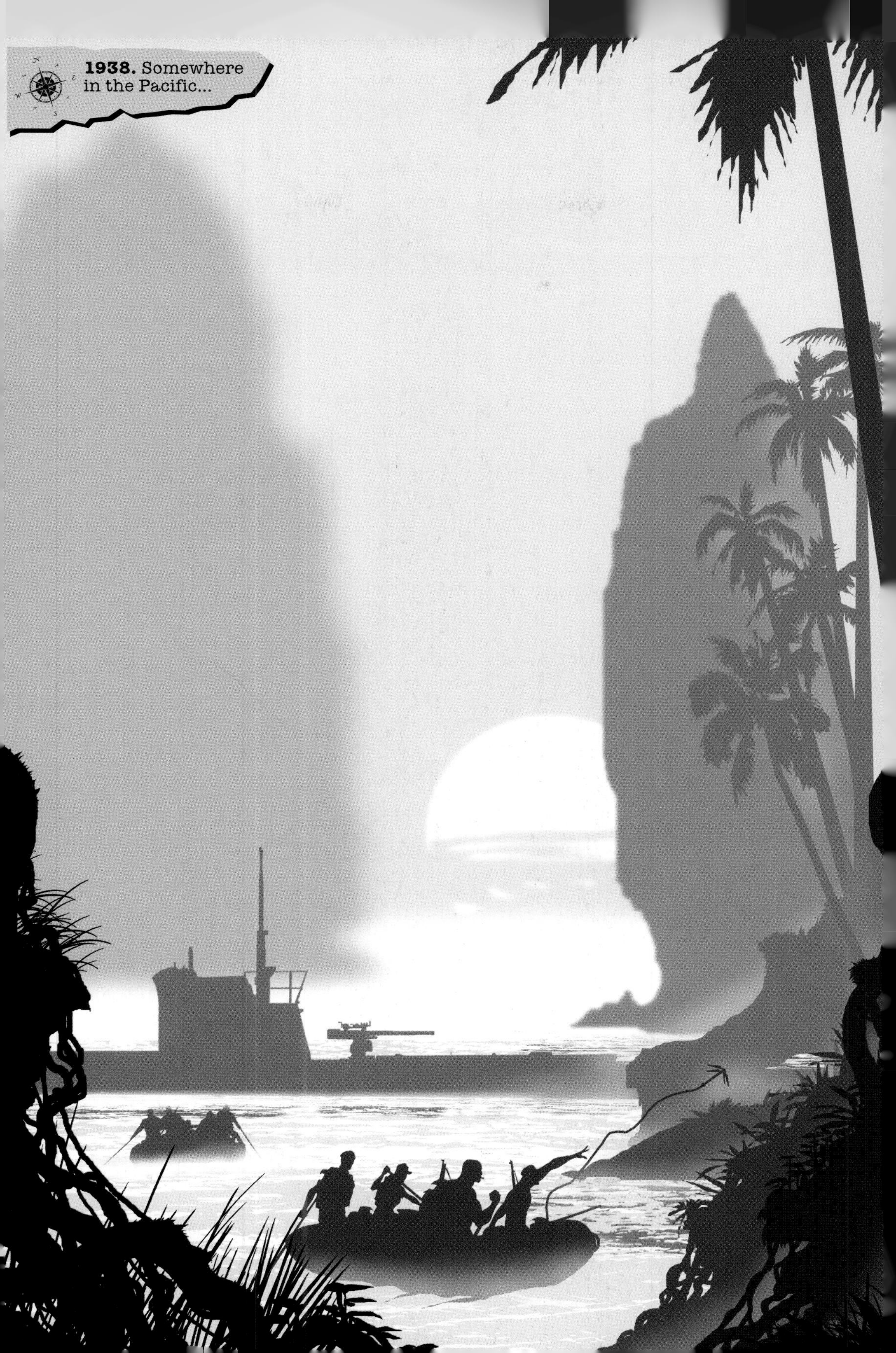
1938. Somewhere in the Pacific...

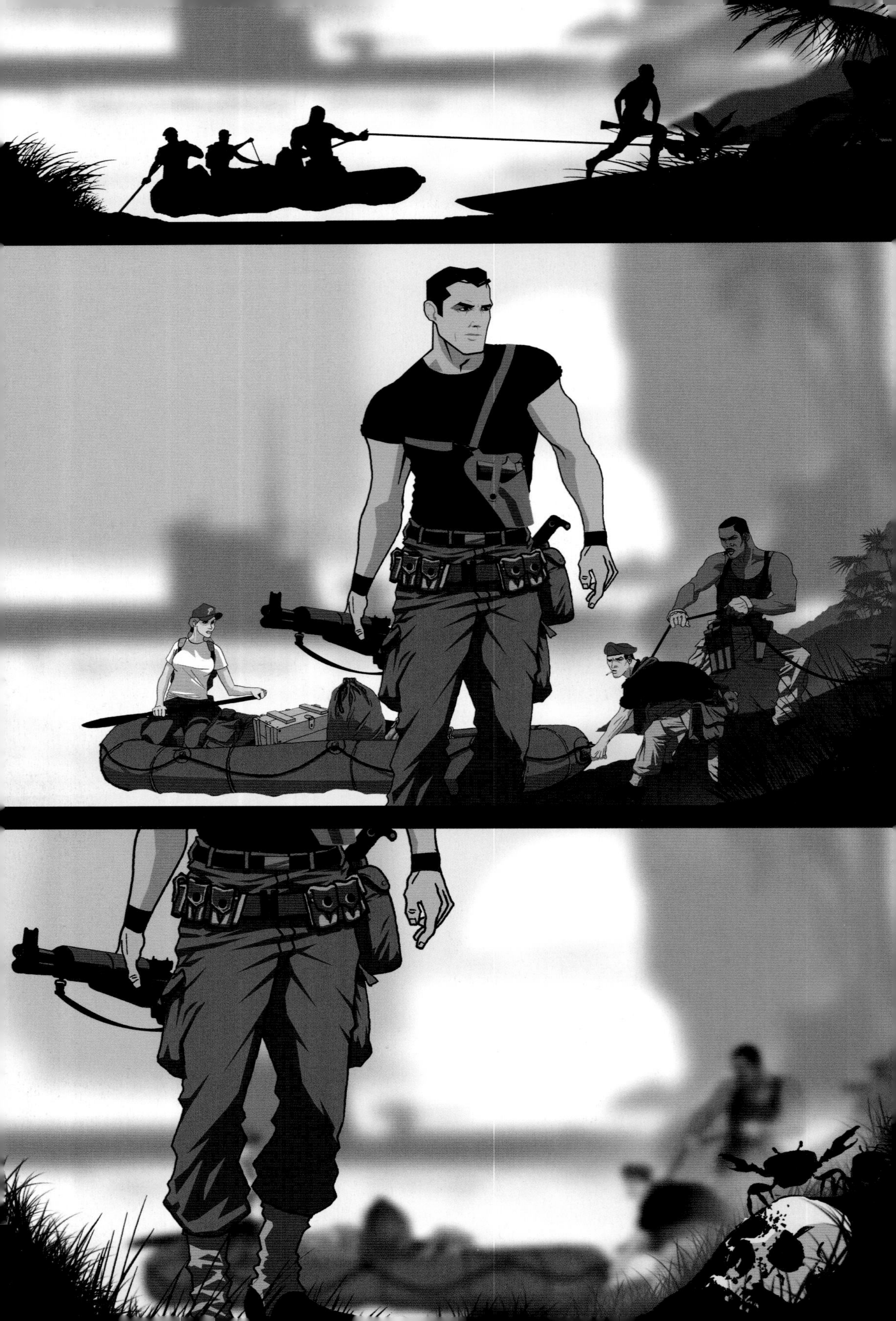

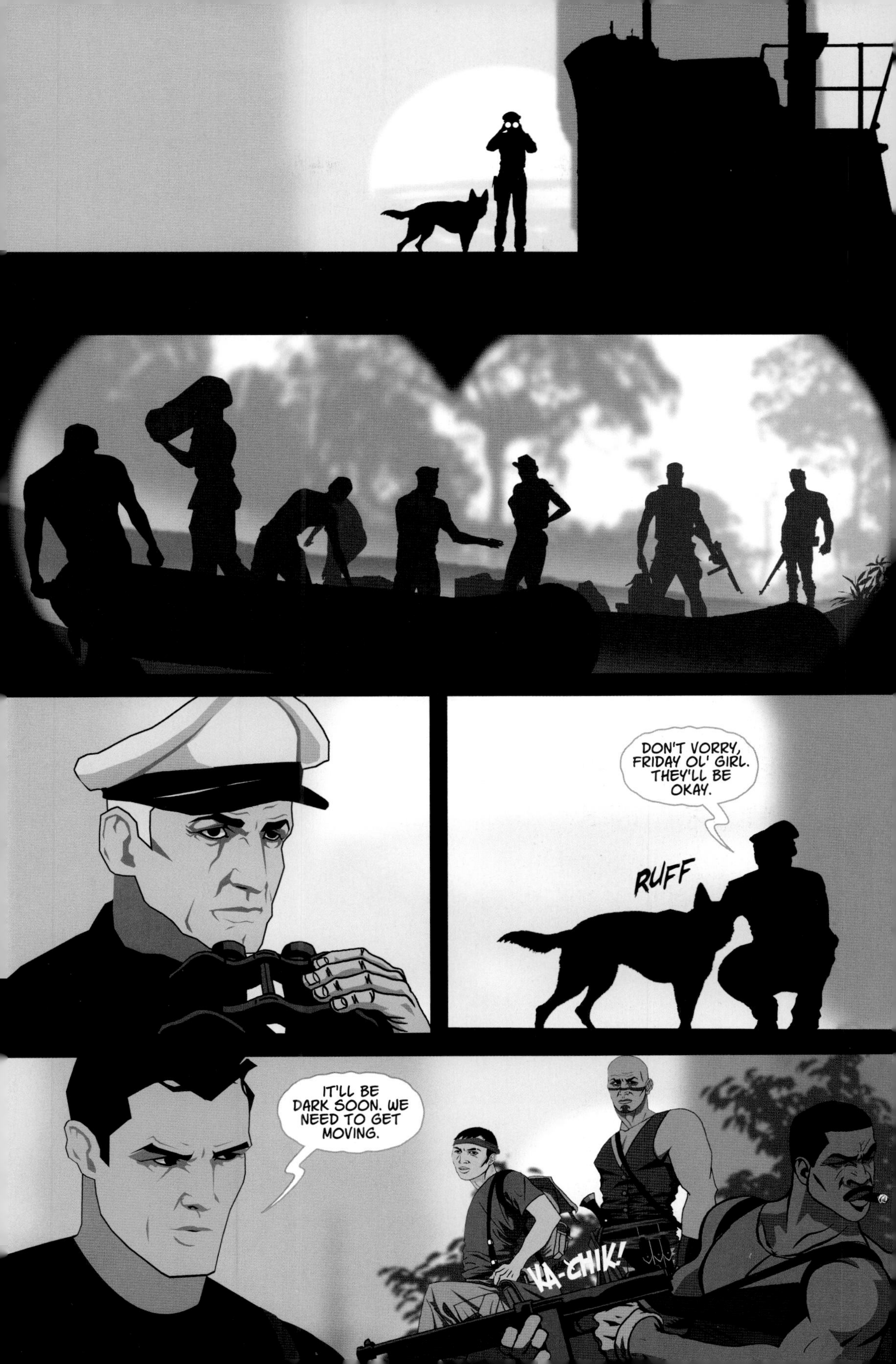
DON'T VORRY, FRIDAY OL' GIRL. THEY'LL BE OKAY.
RUFF
IT'LL BE DARK SOON. WE NEED TO GET MOVING.
KA-CHIK!

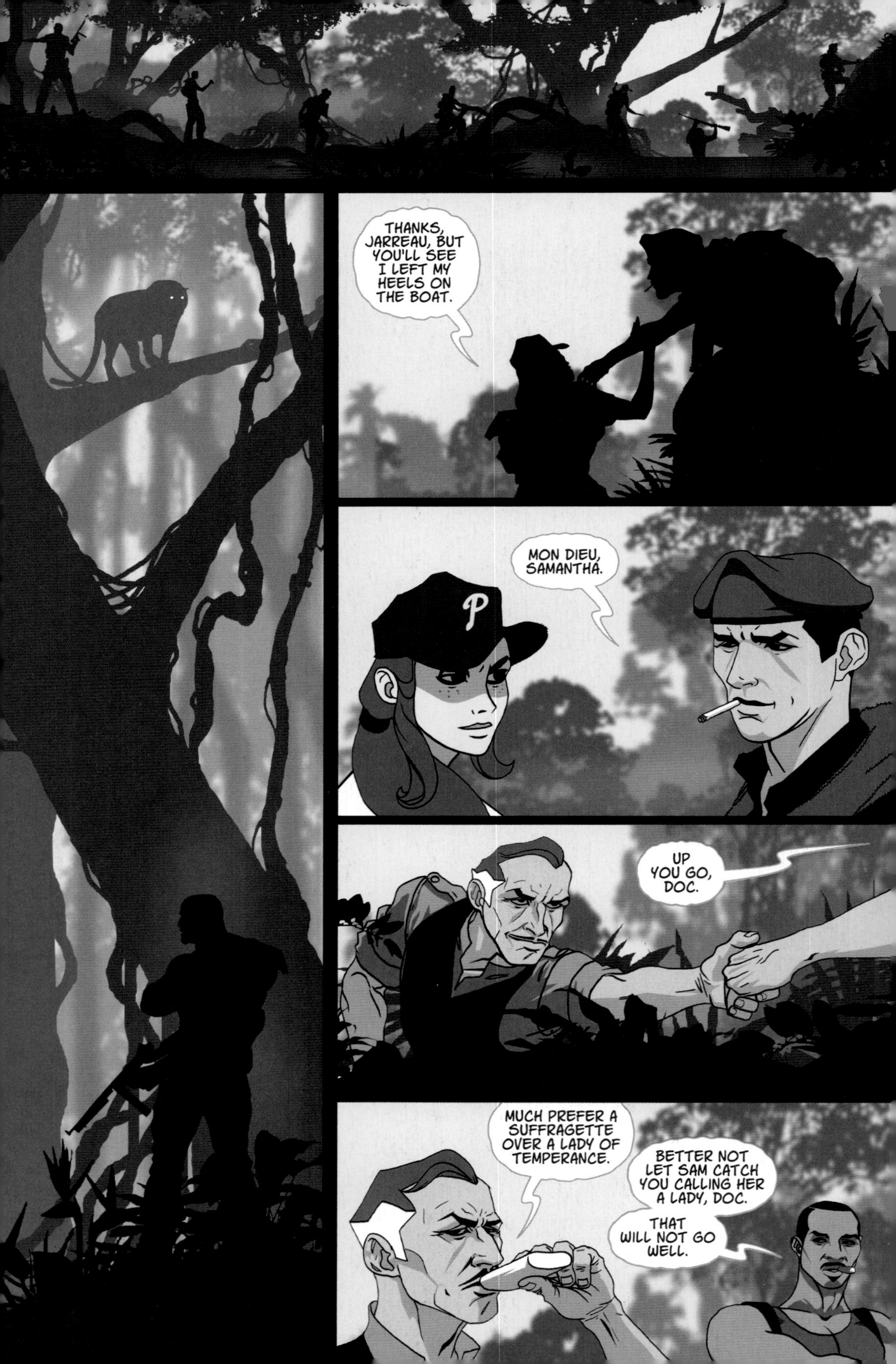
THANKS, JARREAU, BUT YOU'LL SEE I LEFT MY HEELS ON THE BOAT.
MON DIEU, SAMANTHA.
UP YOU GO, DOC.
MUCH PREFER A SUFFRAGETTE OVER A LADY OF TEMPERANCE.
BETTER NOT LET SAM CATCH YOU CALLING HER A LADY, DOC.
THAT WILL NOT GO WELL.

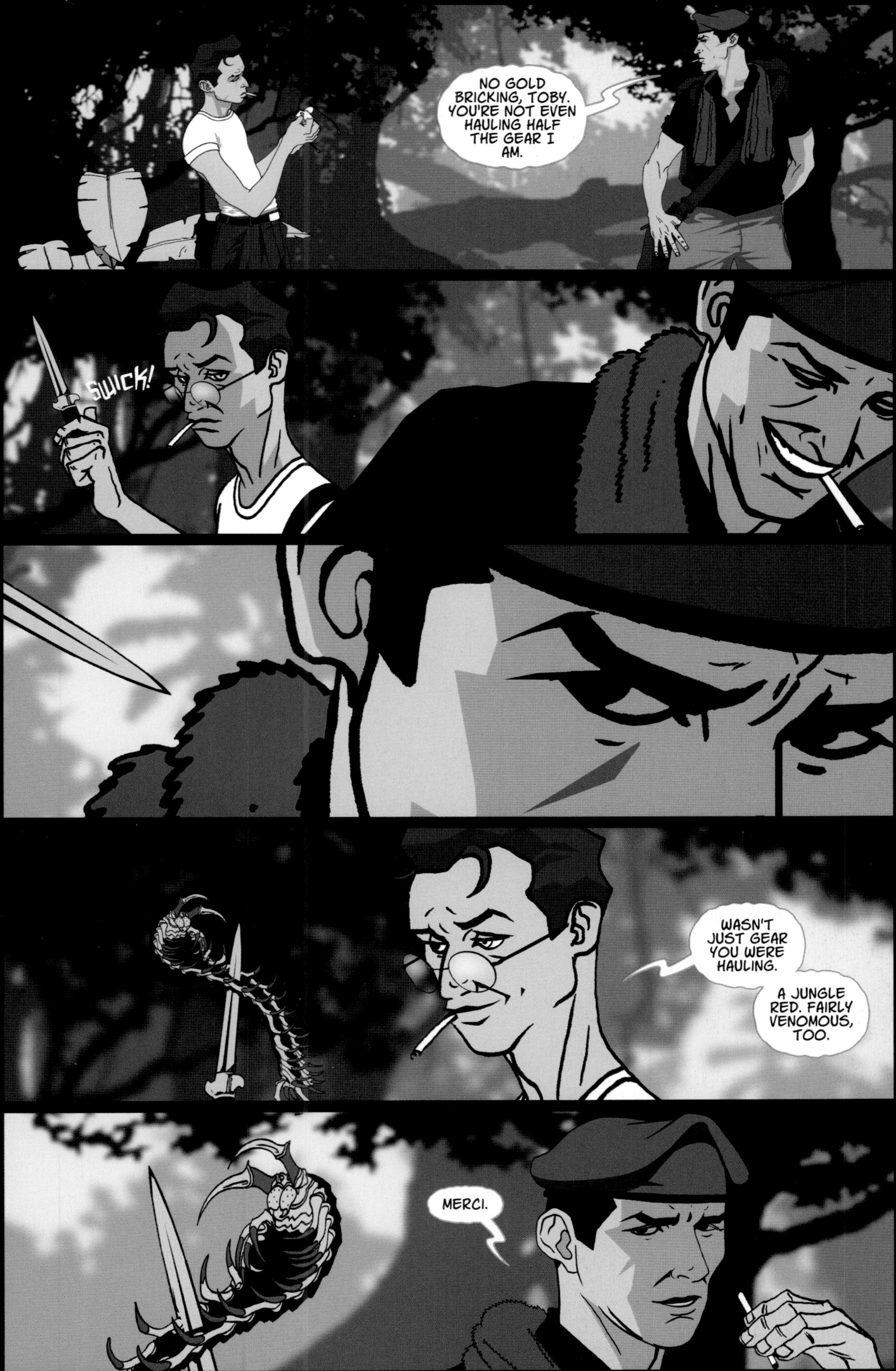
NO GOLD BRICKING, TOBY. YOU'RE NOT EVEN HAULING HALF THE GEAR I AM.
SWICK!
WASN'T JUST GEAR YOU WERE HAULING.
A JUNGLE RED. FAIRLY VENOMOUS, TOO.
MERCI.

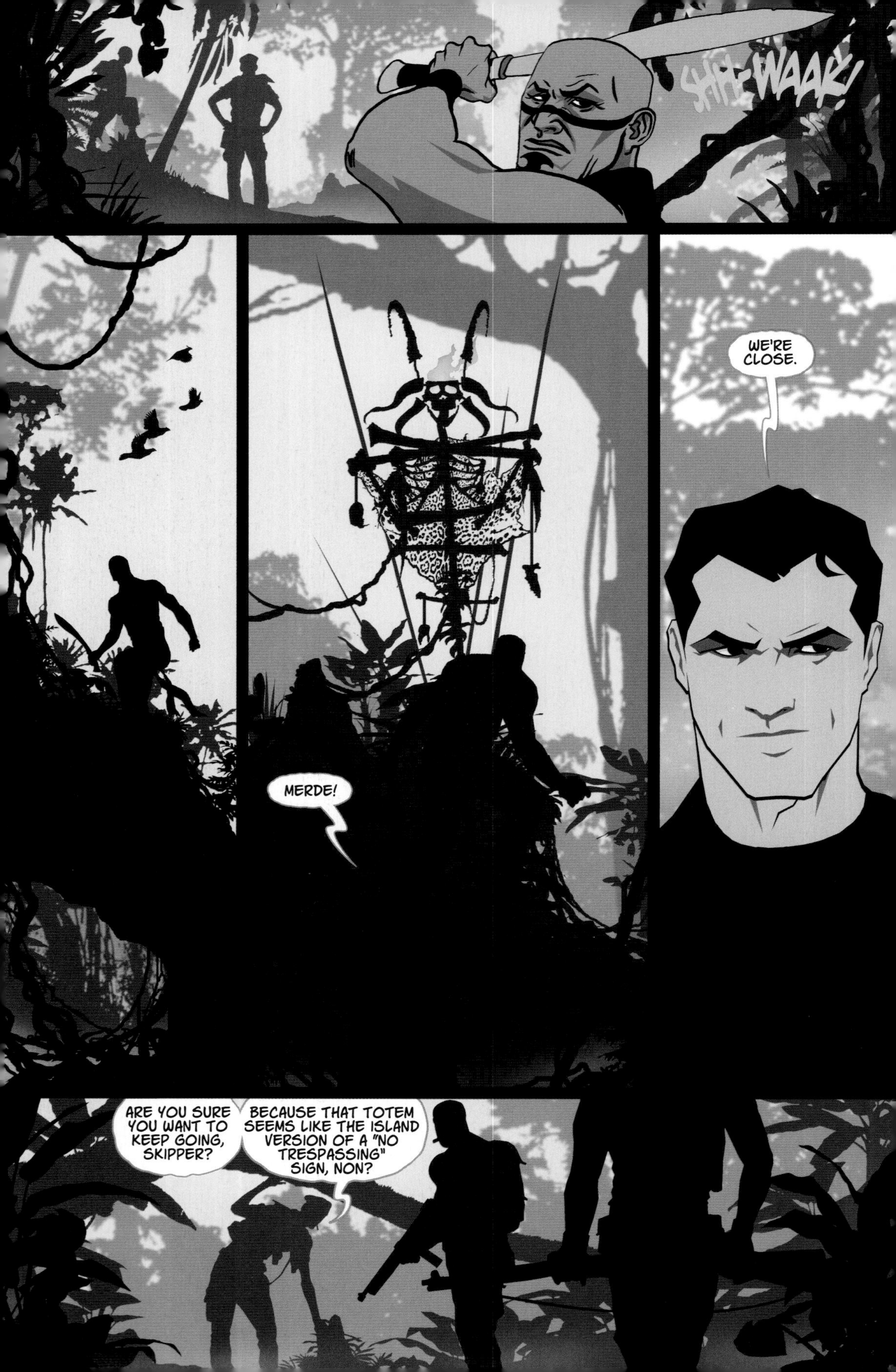
SHH-WAAK!
WE'RE CLOSE.
MERDE!
ARE YOU SURE YOU WANT TO KEEP GOING, SKIPPER?
BECAUSE THAT TOTEM SEEMS LIKE THE ISLAND VERSION OF A "NO TRESPASSING" SIGN, NON?

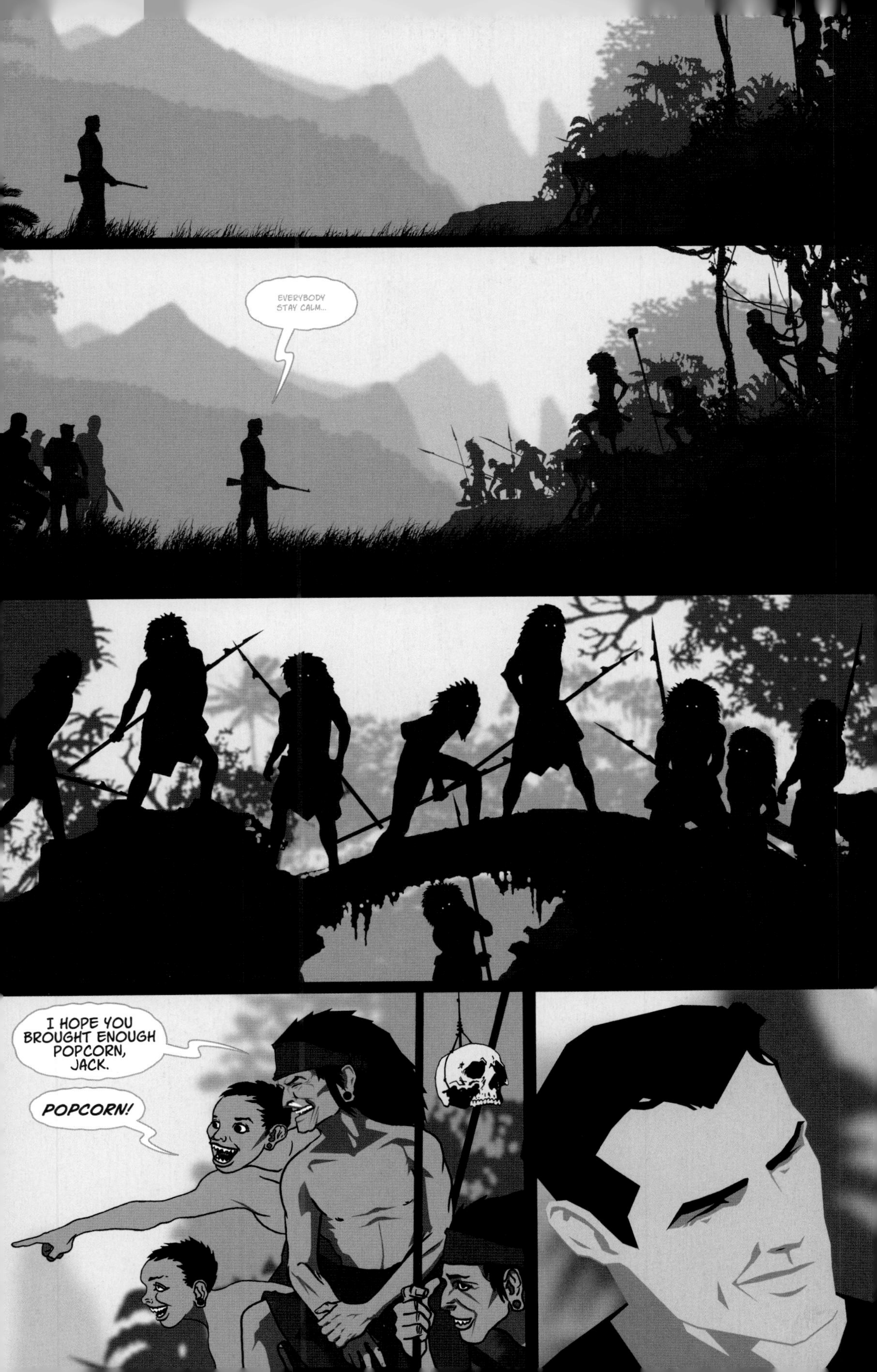
EVERYBODY STAY CALM...
I HOPE YOU BROUGHT ENOUGH POPCORN, JACK.
POPCORN!

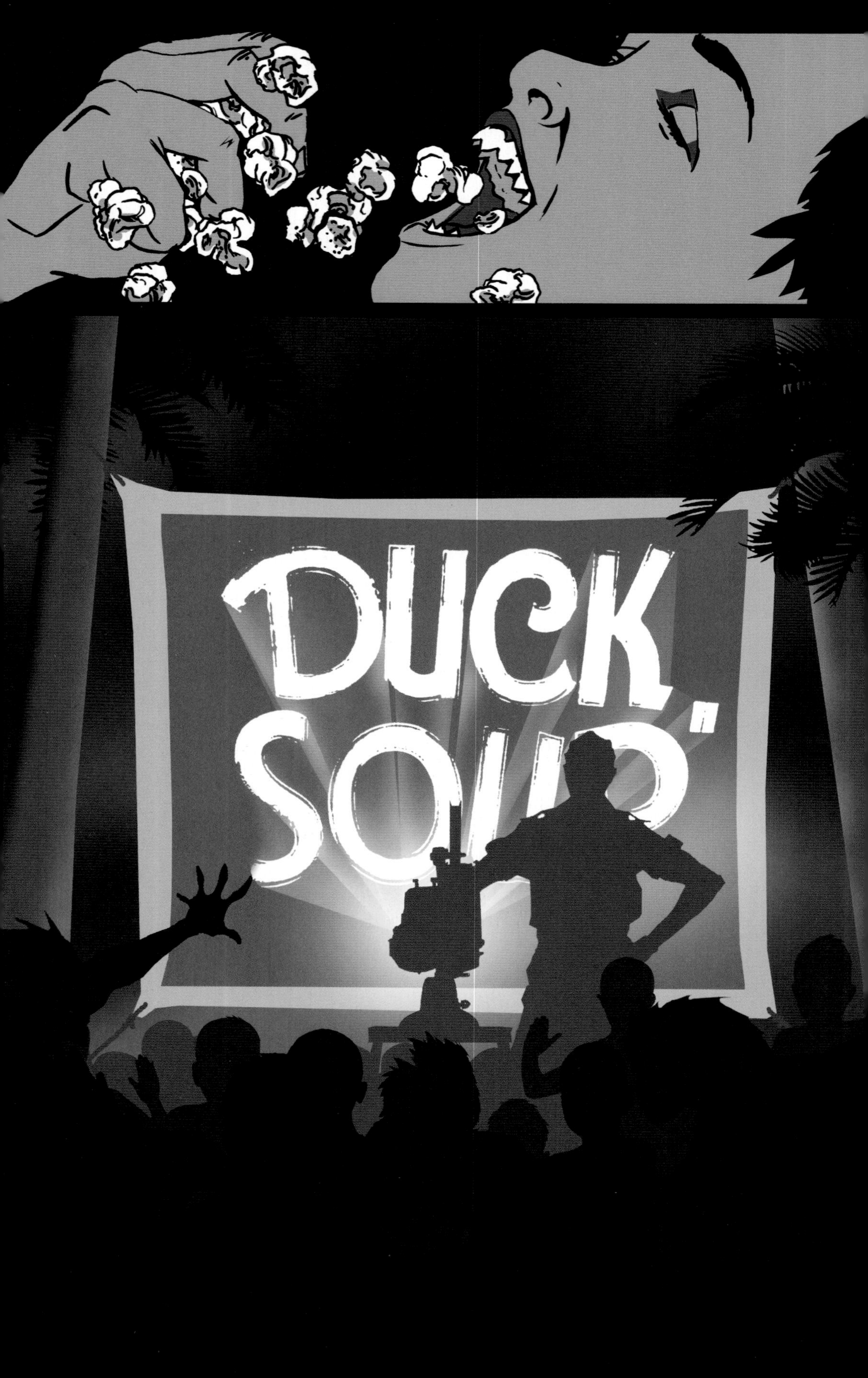
DUCK

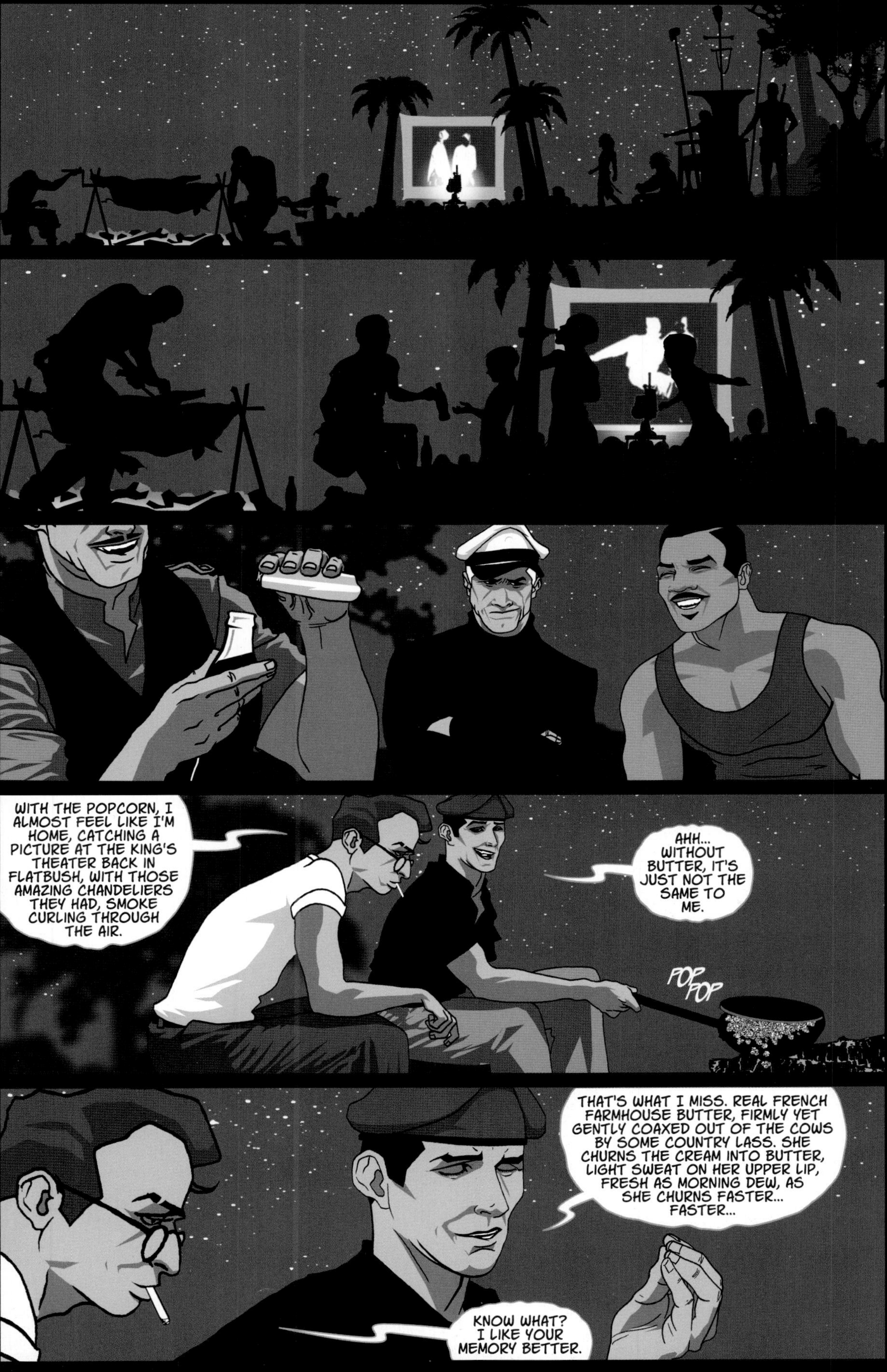
WITH THE POPCORN, I ALMOST FEEL LIKE I'M HOME, CATCHING A PICTURE AT THE KING'S THEATER BACK IN FLATBUSH, WITH THOSE AMAZING CHANDELIERS THEY HAD, SMOKE CURLING THROUGH THE AIR.
AHH... WITHOUT BUTTER, IT'S JUST NOT THE SAME TO ME.
POP POP
THAT'S WHAT I MISS. REAL FRENCH FARMHOUSE BUTTER, FIRMLY YET GENTLY COAXED OUT OF THE COWS BY SOME COUNTRY LASS. SHE CHURNS THE CREAM INTO BUTTER, LIGHT SWEAT ON HER UPPER LIP, FRESH AS MORNING DEW, AS SHE CHURNS FASTER... FASTER...
KNOW WHAT? I LIKE YOUR MEMORY BETTER.

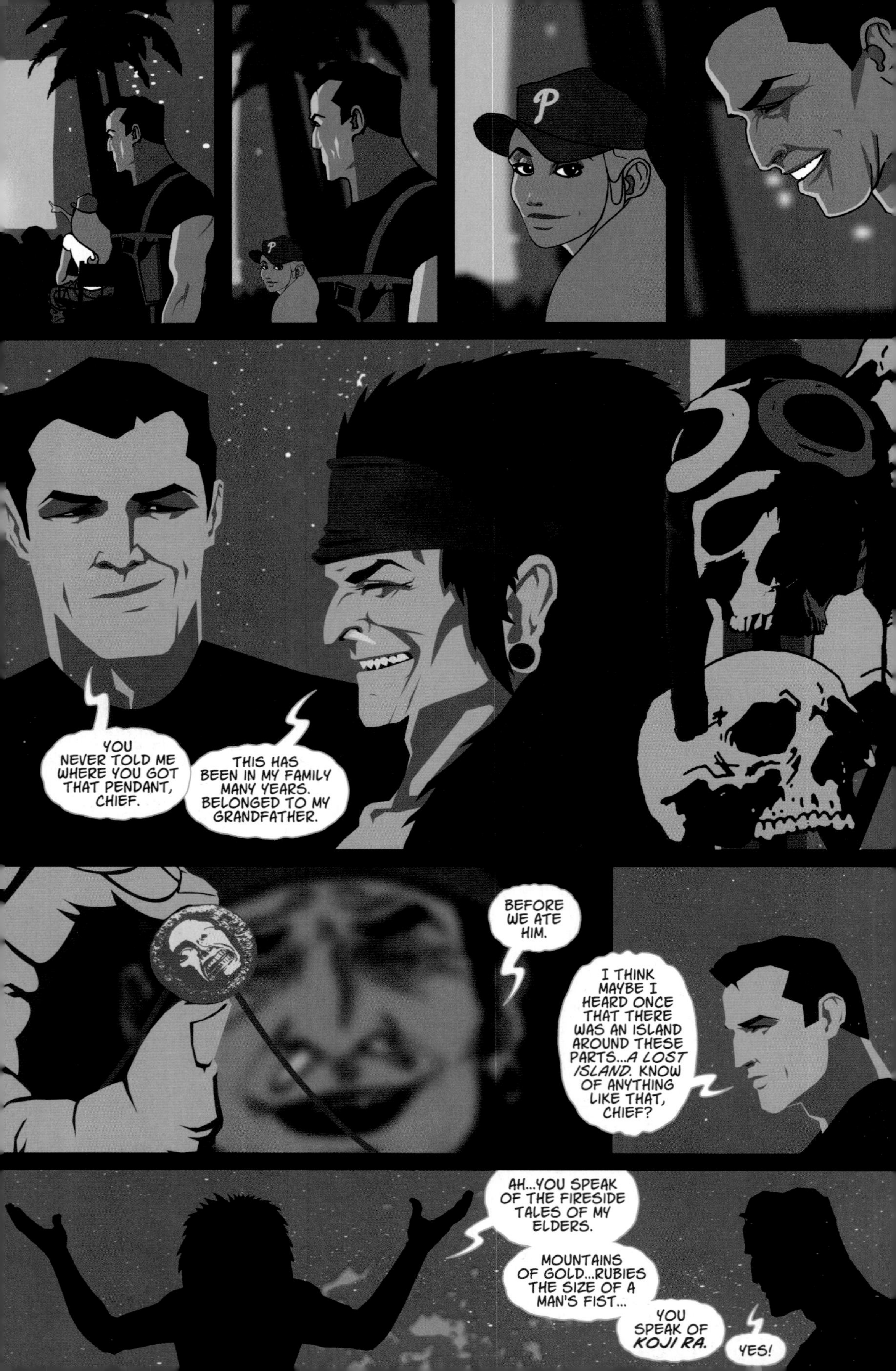
YOU NEVER TOLD ME WHERE YOU GOT THAT PENDANT, CHIEF.
THIS HAS BEEN IN MY FAMILY MANY YEARS. BELONGED TO MY GRANDFATHER.
BEFORE WE ATE HIM.
I THINK MAYBE I HEARD ONCE THAT THERE WAS AN ISLAND AROUND THESE PARTS...*A LOST ISLAND*. KNOW OF ANYTHING LIKE THAT, CHIEF?
AH...YOU SPEAK OF THE FIRESIDE TALES OF MY ELDERS.
MOUNTAINS OF GOLD...RUBIES THE SIZE OF A MAN'S FIST...
YOU SPEAK OF *KOJI RA*.
YES!

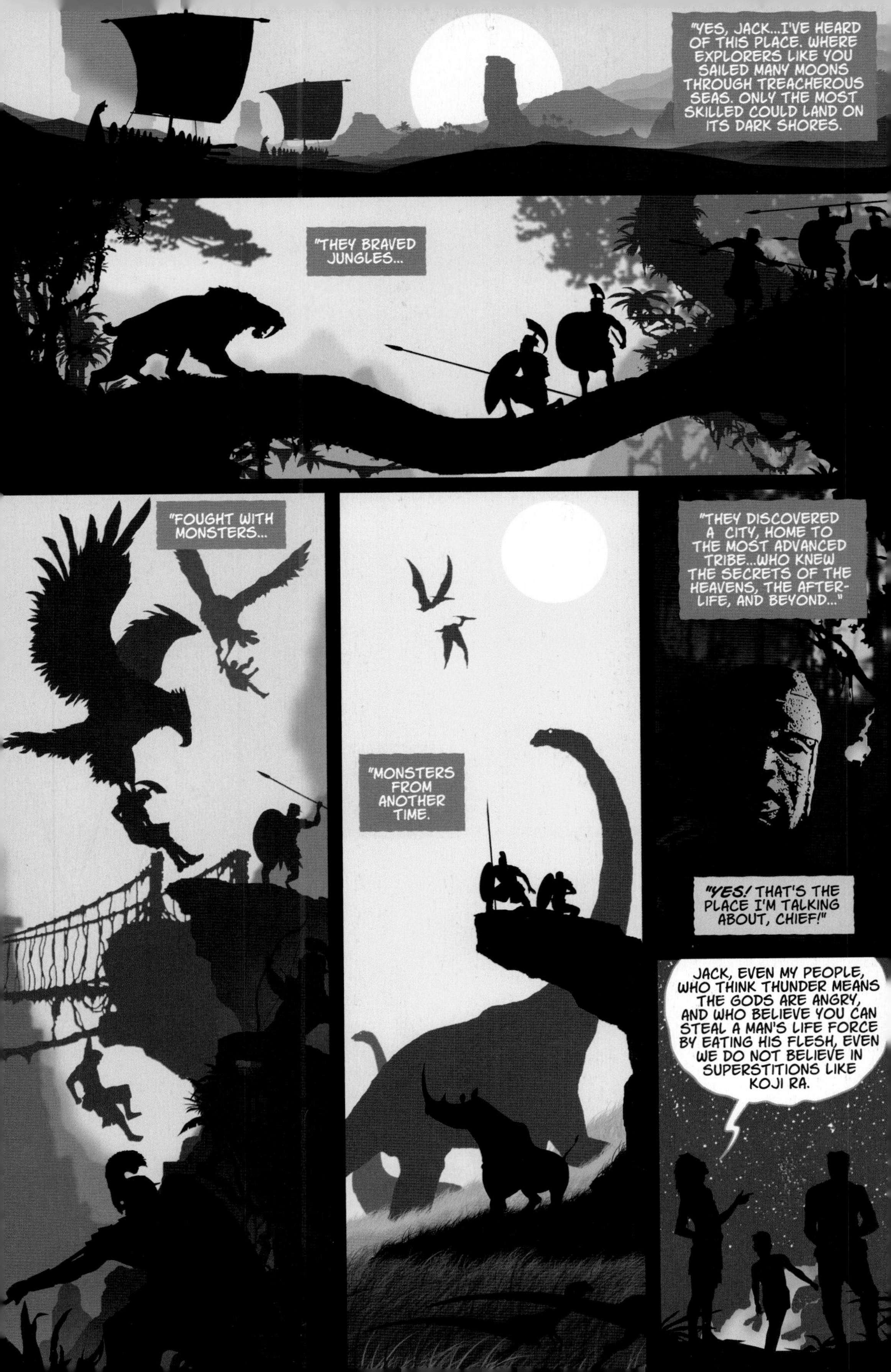
"YES, JACK...I'VE HEARD OF THIS PLACE. WHERE EXPLORERS LIKE YOU SAILED MANY MOONS THROUGH TREACHEROUS SEAS. ONLY THE MOST SKILLED COULD LAND ON ITS DARK SHORES.
"THEY BRAVED JUNGLES...
"FOUGHT WITH MONSTERS...
"MONSTERS FROM ANOTHER TIME.
"THEY DISCOVERED A CITY, HOME TO THE MOST ADVANCED TRIBE...WHO KNEW THE SECRETS OF THE HEAVENS, THE AFTER-LIFE, AND BEYOND..."
"YES! THAT'S THE PLACE I'M TALKING ABOUT, CHIEF!"
JACK, EVEN MY PEOPLE, WHO THINK THUNDER MEANS THE GODS ARE ANGRY, AND WHO BELIEVE YOU CAN STEAL A MAN'S LIFE FORCE BY EATING HIS FLESH, EVEN WE DO NOT BELIEVE IN SUPERSTITIONS LIKE KOJI RA.

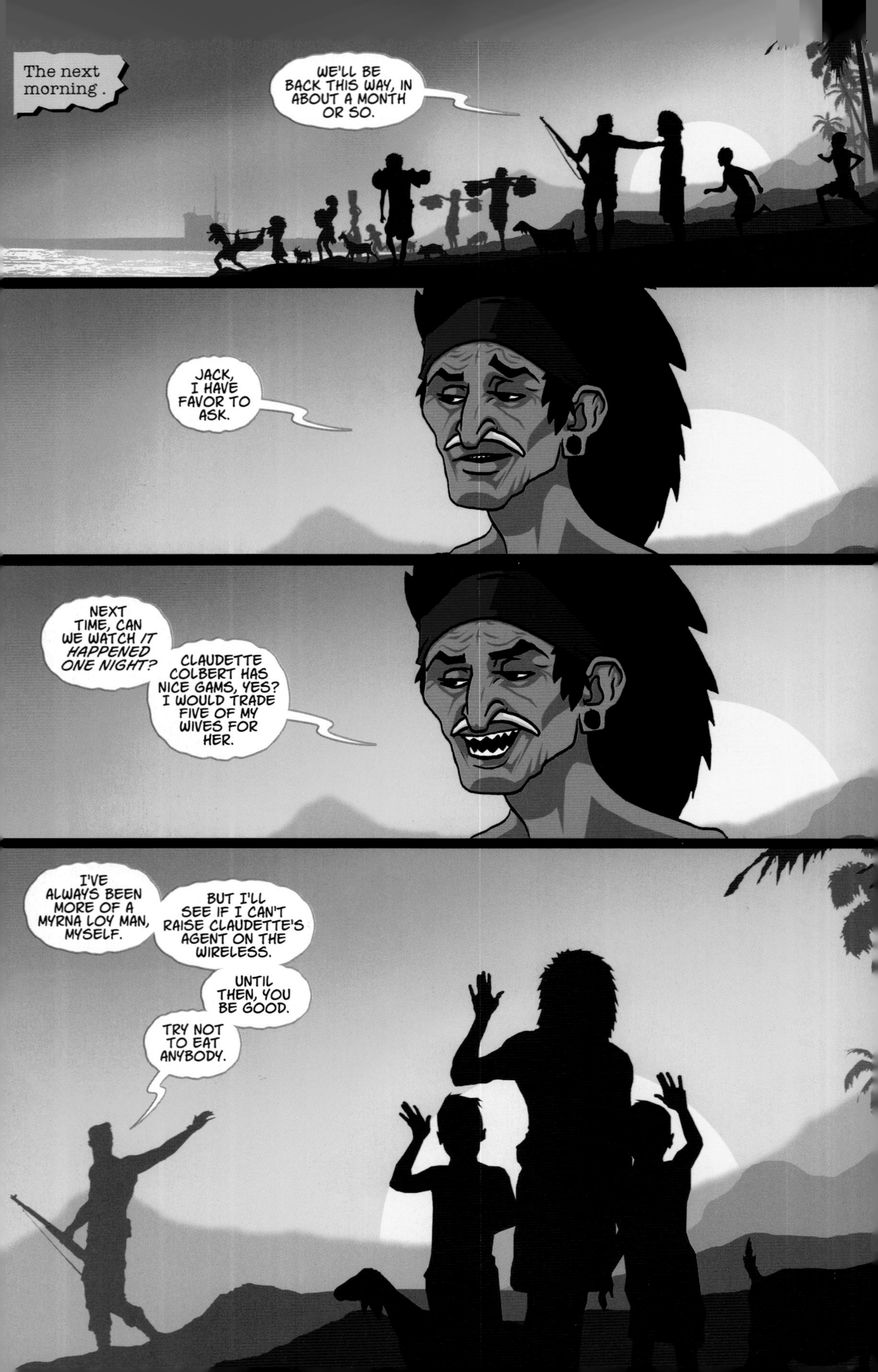

The next morning.
WE'LL BE BACK THIS WAY, IN ABOUT A MONTH OR SO.
JACK, I HAVE FAVOR TO ASK.
NEXT TIME, CAN WE WATCH *IT HAPPENED ONE NIGHT*?
CLAUDETTE COLBERT HAS NICE GAMS, YES? I WOULD TRADE FIVE OF MY WIVES FOR HER.
I'VE ALWAYS BEEN MORE OF A MYRNA LOY MAN, MYSELF.
BUT I'LL SEE IF I CAN'T RAISE CLAUDETTE'S AGENT ON THE WIRELESS.
UNTIL THEN, YOU BE GOOD.
TRY NOT TO EAT ANYBODY.

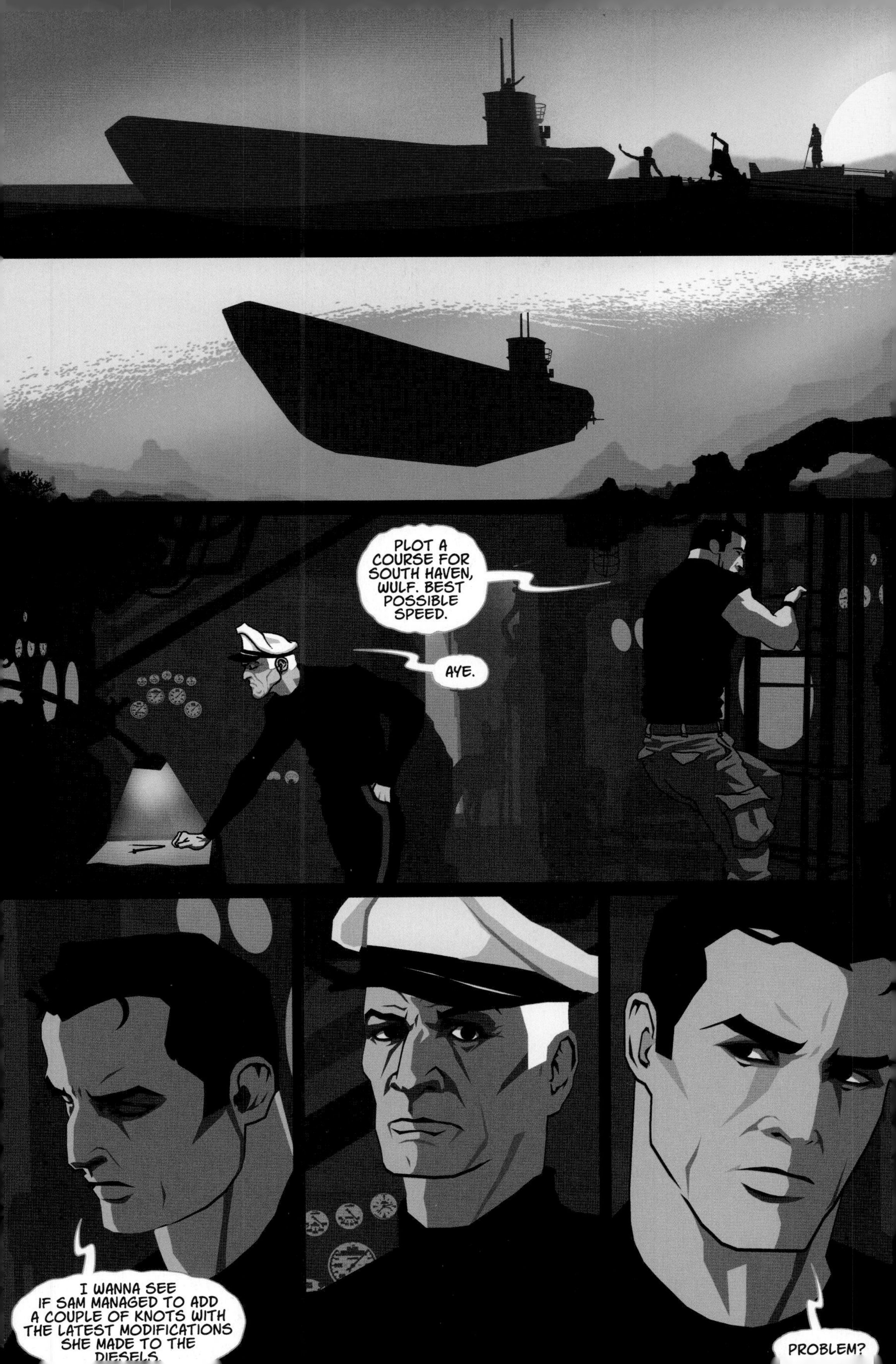
PLOT A COURSE FOR SOUTH HAVEN, WULF. BEST POSSIBLE SPEED.
AYE.
I WANNA SEE IF SAM MANAGED TO ADD A COUPLE OF KNOTS WITH THE LATEST MODIFICATIONS SHE MADE TO THE DIESELS.
PROBLEM?

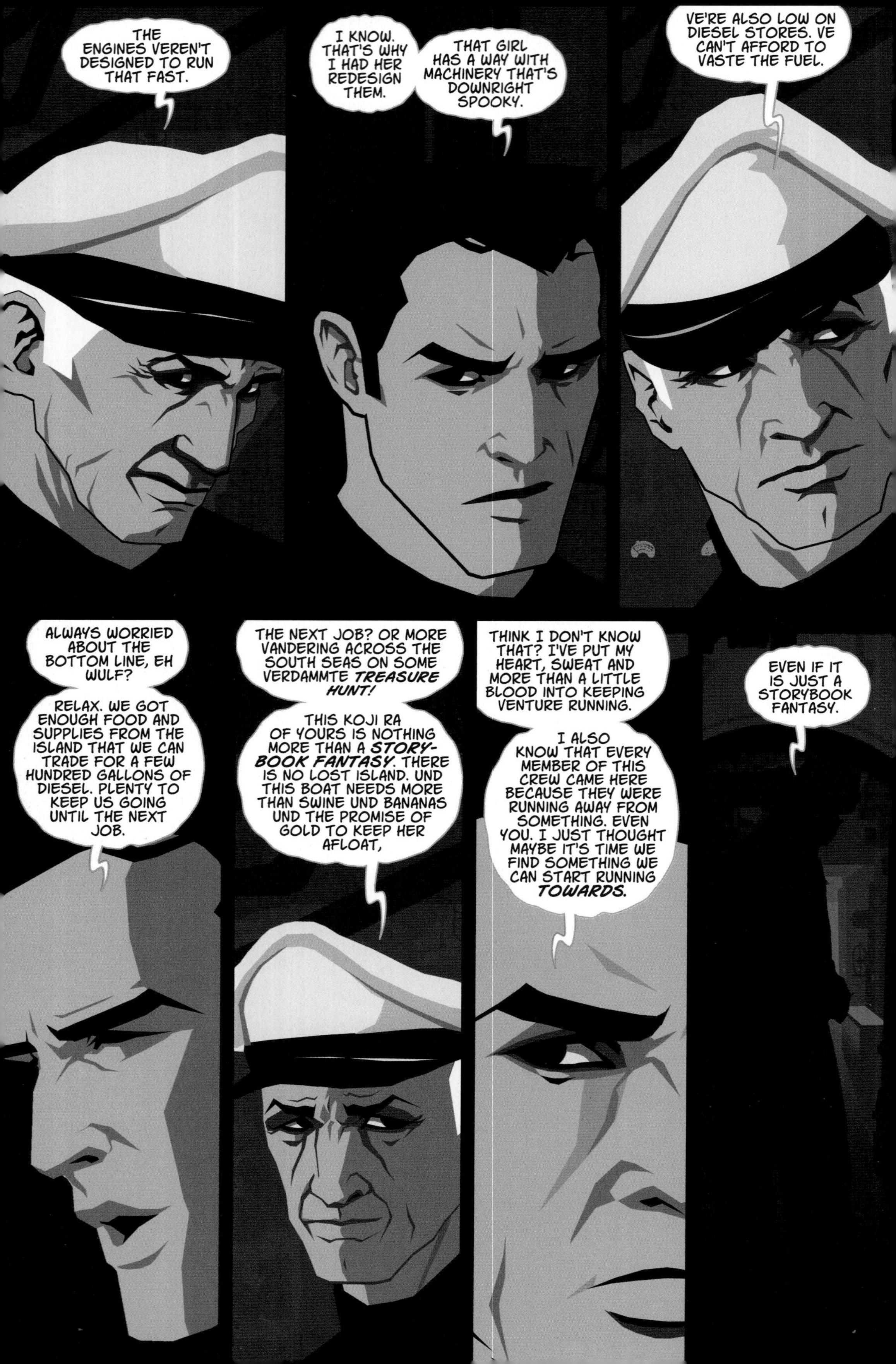
THE ENGINES VEREN'T DESIGNED TO RUN THAT FAST.
I KNOW. THAT'S WHY I HAD HER REDESIGN THEM.
THAT GIRL HAS A WAY WITH MACHINERY THAT'S DOWNRIGHT SPOOKY.
VE'RE ALSO LOW ON DIESEL STORES. VE CAN'T AFFORD TO VASTE THE FUEL.
ALWAYS WORRIED ABOUT THE BOTTOM LINE, EH WULF?
RELAX. WE GOT ENOUGH FOOD AND SUPPLIES FROM THE ISLAND THAT WE CAN TRADE FOR A FEW HUNDRED GALLONS OF DIESEL. PLENTY TO KEEP US GOING UNTIL THE NEXT JOB.
THE NEXT JOB? OR MORE VANDERING ACROSS THE SOUTH SEAS ON SOME VERDAMMTE *TREASURE HUNT!*
THIS KOJI RA OF YOURS IS NOTHING MORE THAN A *STORY-BOOK FANTASY*. THERE IS NO LOST ISLAND. UND THIS BOAT NEEDS MORE THAN SWINE UND BANANAS UND THE PROMISE OF GOLD TO KEEP HER AFLOAT,
THINK I DON'T KNOW THAT? I'VE PUT MY HEART, SWEAT AND MORE THAN A LITTLE BLOOD INTO KEEPING VENTURE RUNNING.
I ALSO KNOW THAT EVERY MEMBER OF THIS CREW CAME HERE BECAUSE THEY WERE RUNNING AWAY FROM SOMETHING. EVEN YOU. I JUST THOUGHT MAYBE IT'S TIME WE FIND SOMETHING WE CAN START RUNNING *TOWARDS.*
EVEN IF IT IS JUST A STORYBOOK FANTASY.

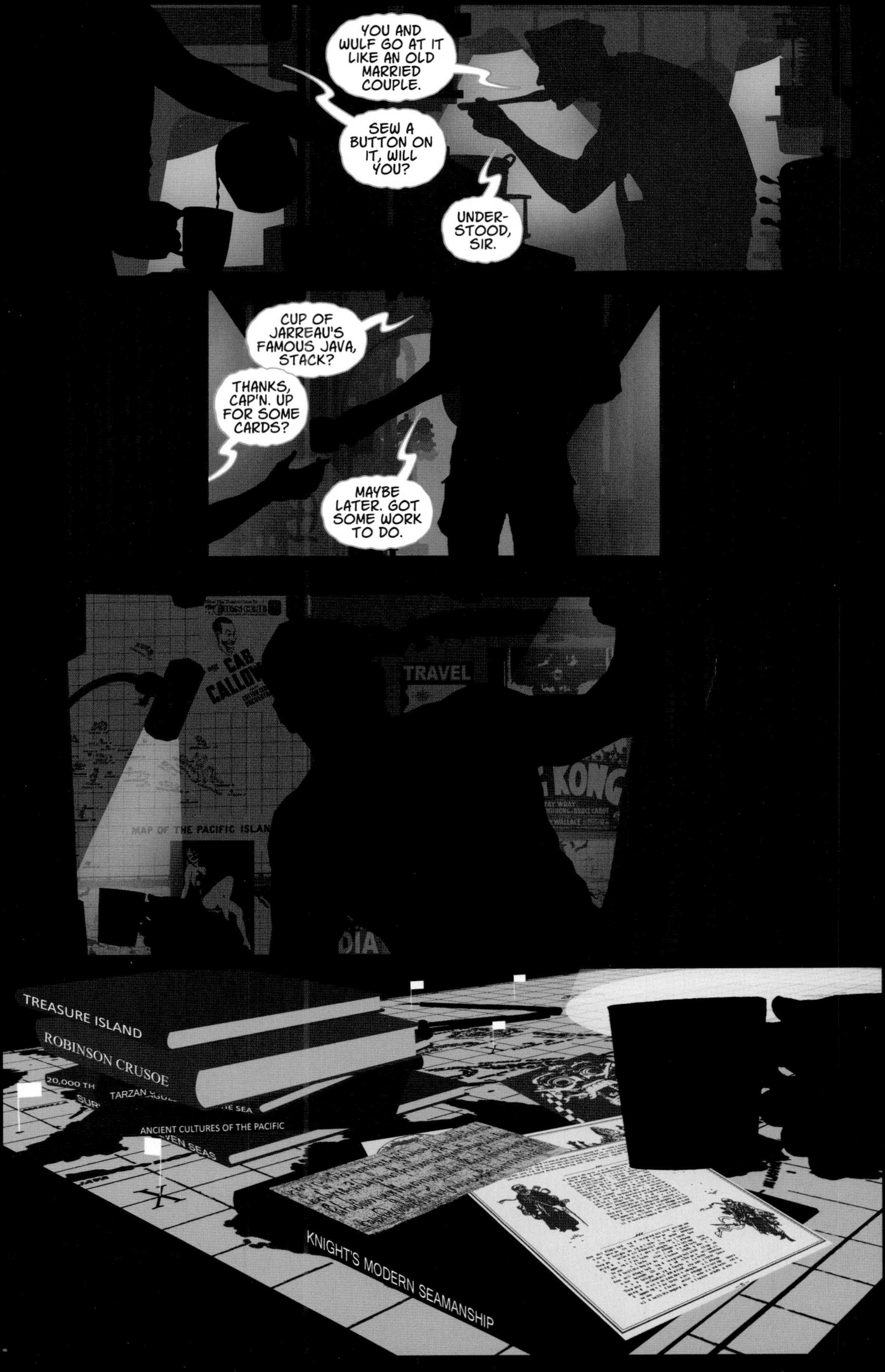
YOU AND WULF GO AT IT LIKE AN OLD MARRIED COUPLE.
SEW A BUTTON ON IT, WILL YOU?
UNDER-STOOD, SIR.
CUP OF JARREAU'S FAMOUS JAVA, STACK?
THANKS, CAP'N. UP FOR SOME CARDS?
MAYBE LATER. GOT SOME WORK TO DO.
TRAVEL
TREASURE ISLAND
ROBINSON CRUSOE
ANCIENT CULTURES OF THE PACIFIC
KNIGHT'S MODERN SEAMANSHIP

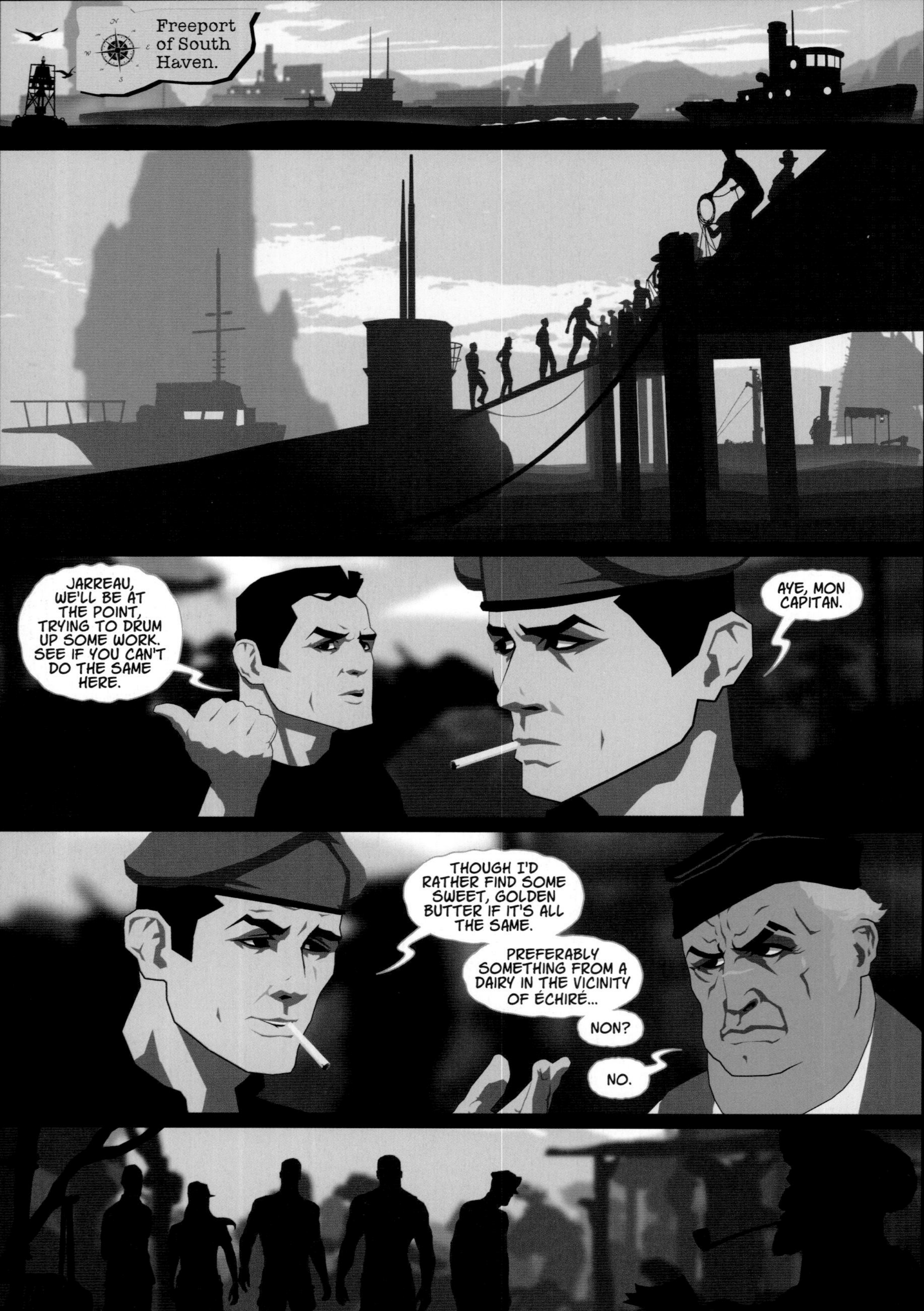
Freeport of South Haven.
JARREAU, WE'LL BE AT THE POINT, TRYING TO DRUM UP SOME WORK. SEE IF YOU CAN'T DO THE SAME HERE.
AYE, MON CAPITAN.
THOUGH I'D RATHER FIND SOME SWEET, GOLDEN BUTTER IF IT'S ALL THE SAME.
PREFERABLY SOMETHING FROM A DAIRY IN THE VICINITY OF ÉCHIRÉ...
NON?
NO.

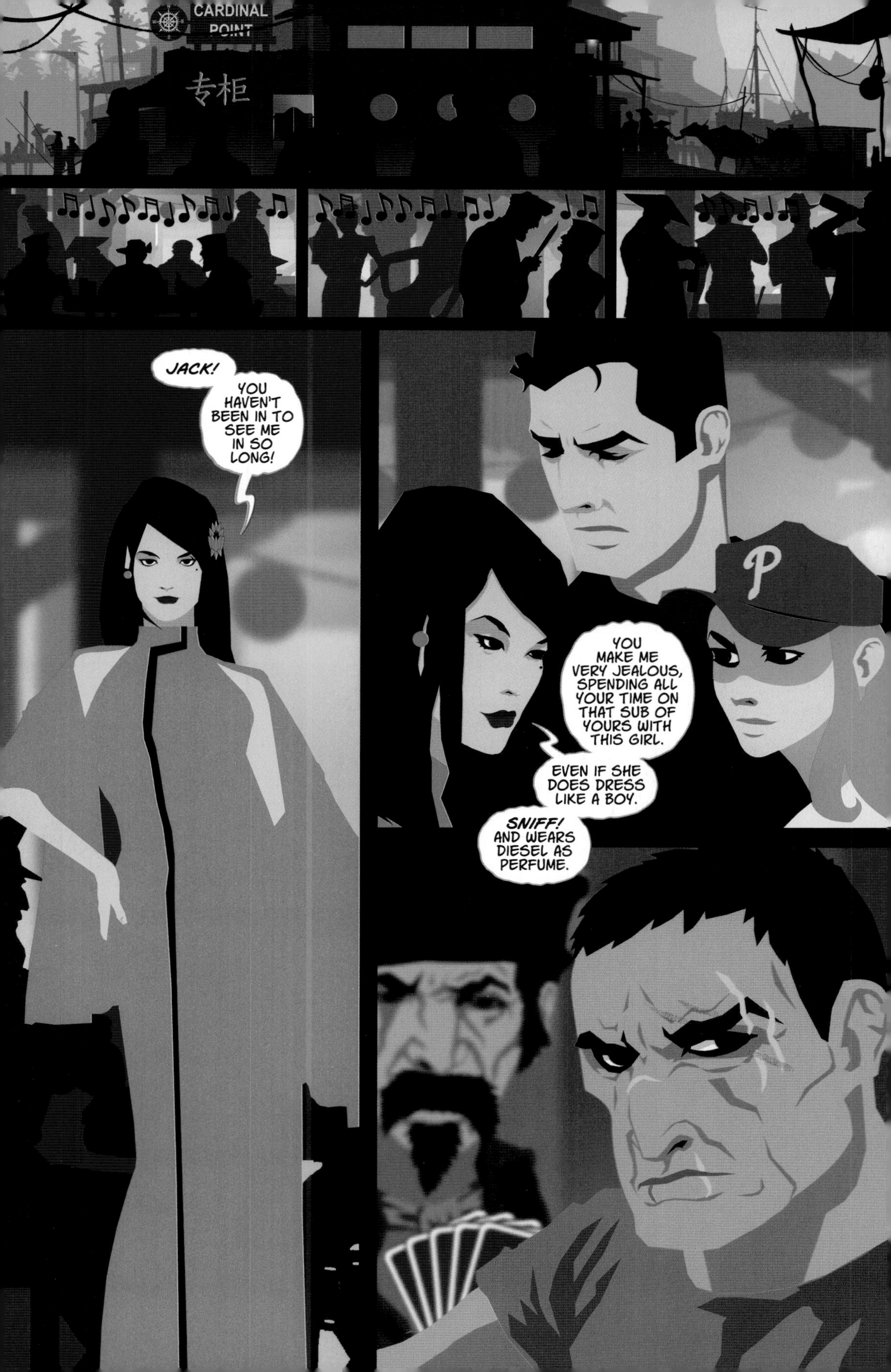

CARDINAL POINT
专柜
JACK!
YOU HAVEN'T BEEN IN TO SEE ME IN SO LONG!
YOU MAKE ME VERY JEALOUS, SPENDING ALL YOUR TIME ON THAT SUB OF YOURS WITH THIS GIRL.
EVEN IF SHE DOES DRESS LIKE A BOY.
SNIFF! AND WEARS DIESEL AS PERFUME.

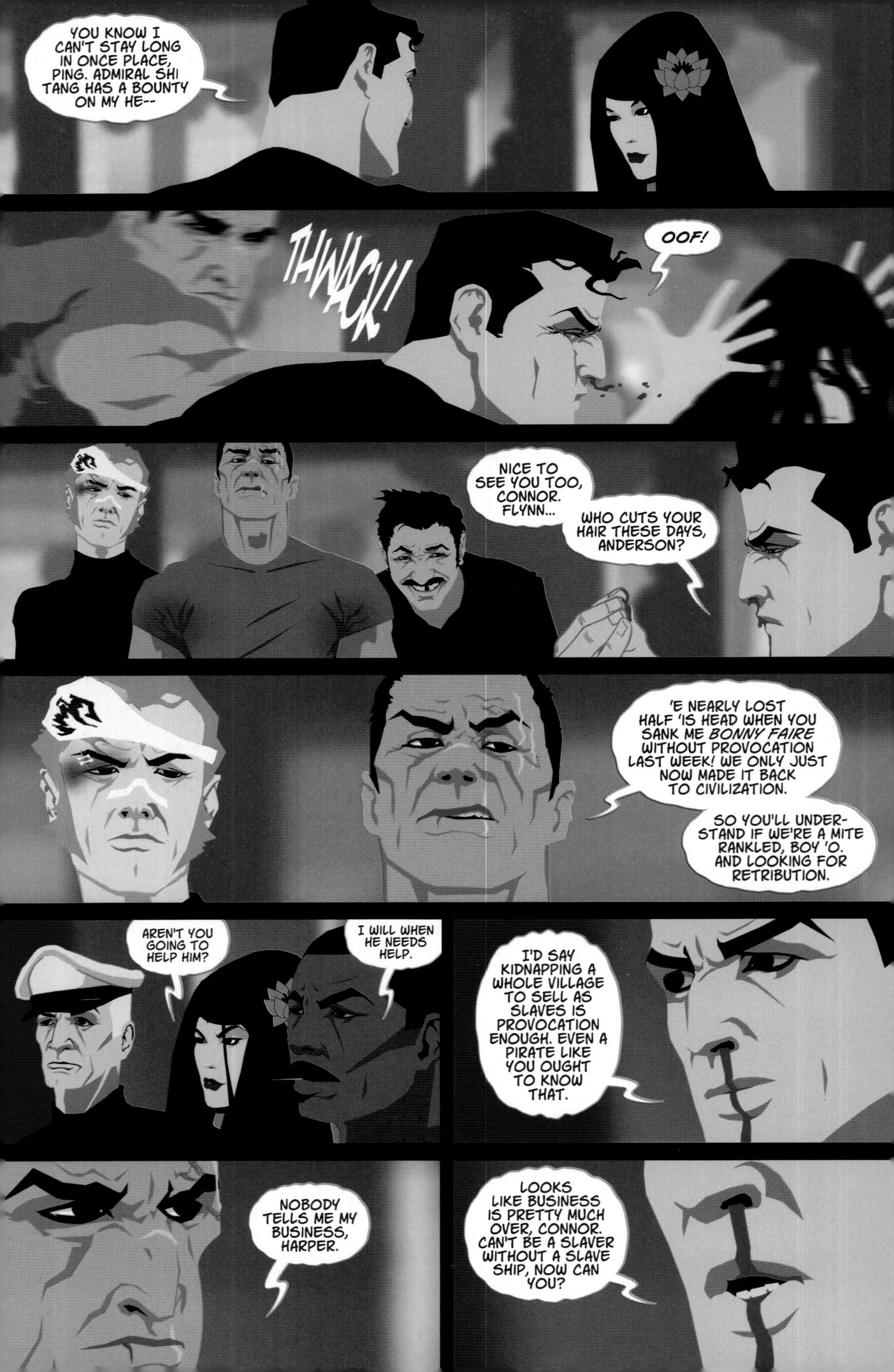
YOU KNOW I CAN'T STAY LONG IN ONCE PLACE, PING. ADMIRAL SHI TANG HAS A BOUNTY ON MY HE--
THWACK!!
OOF!
NICE TO SEE YOU TOO, CONNOR. FLYNN...
WHO CUTS YOUR HAIR THESE DAYS, ANDERSON?
'E NEARLY LOST HALF 'IS HEAD WHEN YOU SANK ME *BONNY FAIRE* WITHOUT PROVOCATION LAST WEEK! WE ONLY JUST NOW MADE IT BACK TO CIVILIZATION.
SO YOU'LL UNDERSTAND IF WE'RE A MITE RANKLED, BOY 'O. AND LOOKING FOR RETRIBUTION.
AREN'T YOU GOING TO HELP HIM?
I WILL WHEN HE NEEDS HELP.
I'D SAY KIDNAPPING A WHOLE VILLAGE TO SELL AS SLAVES IS PROVOCATION ENOUGH. EVEN A PIRATE LIKE YOU OUGHT TO KNOW THAT.
NOBODY TELLS ME MY BUSINESS, HARPER.
LOOKS LIKE BUSINESS IS PRETTY MUCH OVER, CONNOR. CAN'T BE A SLAVER WITHOUT A SLAVE SHIP, NOW CAN YOU?

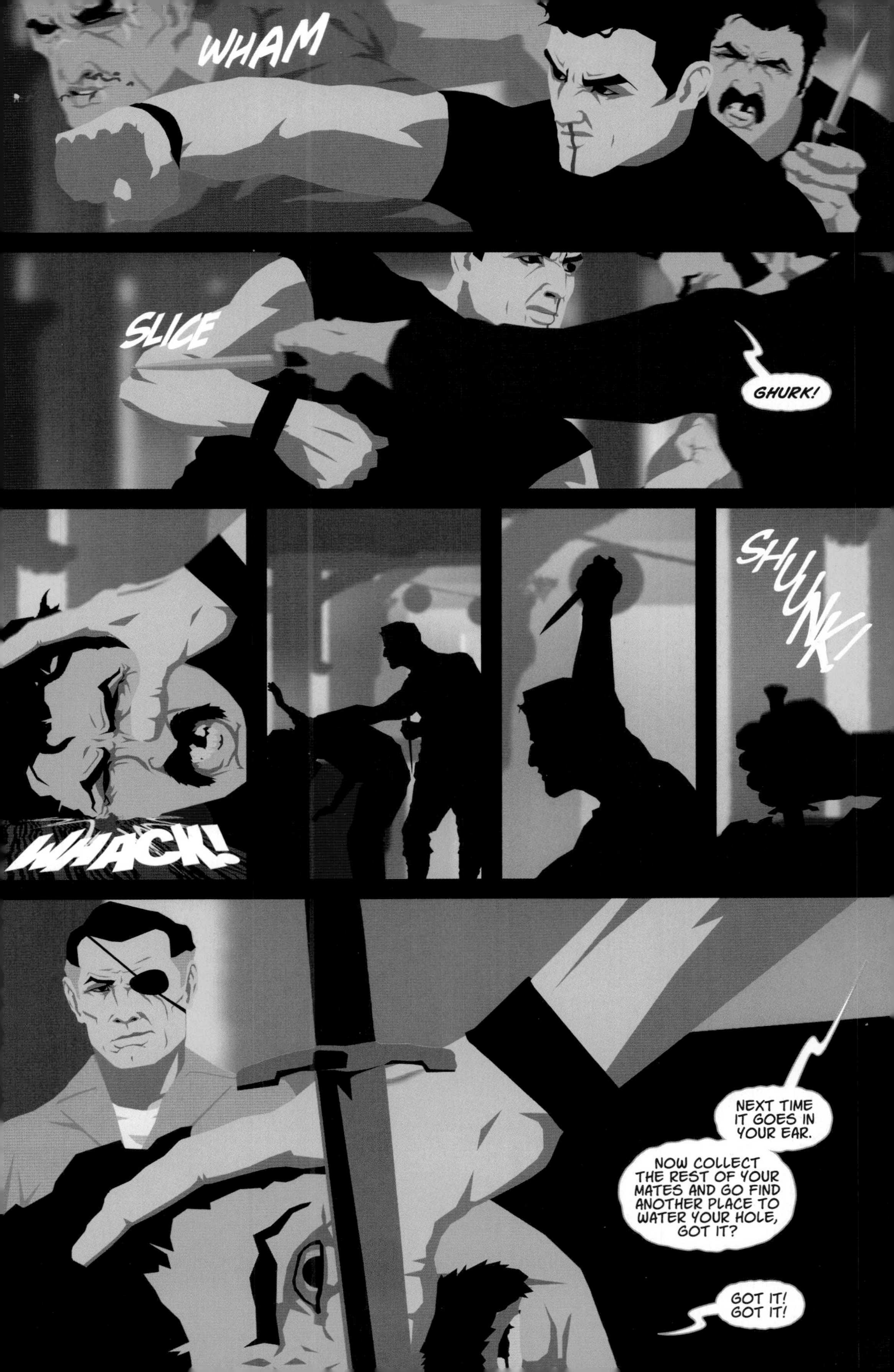
WHAM
SLICE
GHURK!
WHACK!
SHUUNK!
NEXT TIME IT GOES IN YOUR EAR.
NOW COLLECT THE REST OF YOUR MATES AND GO FIND ANOTHER PLACE TO WATER YOUR HOLE, GOT IT?
GOT IT! GOT IT!

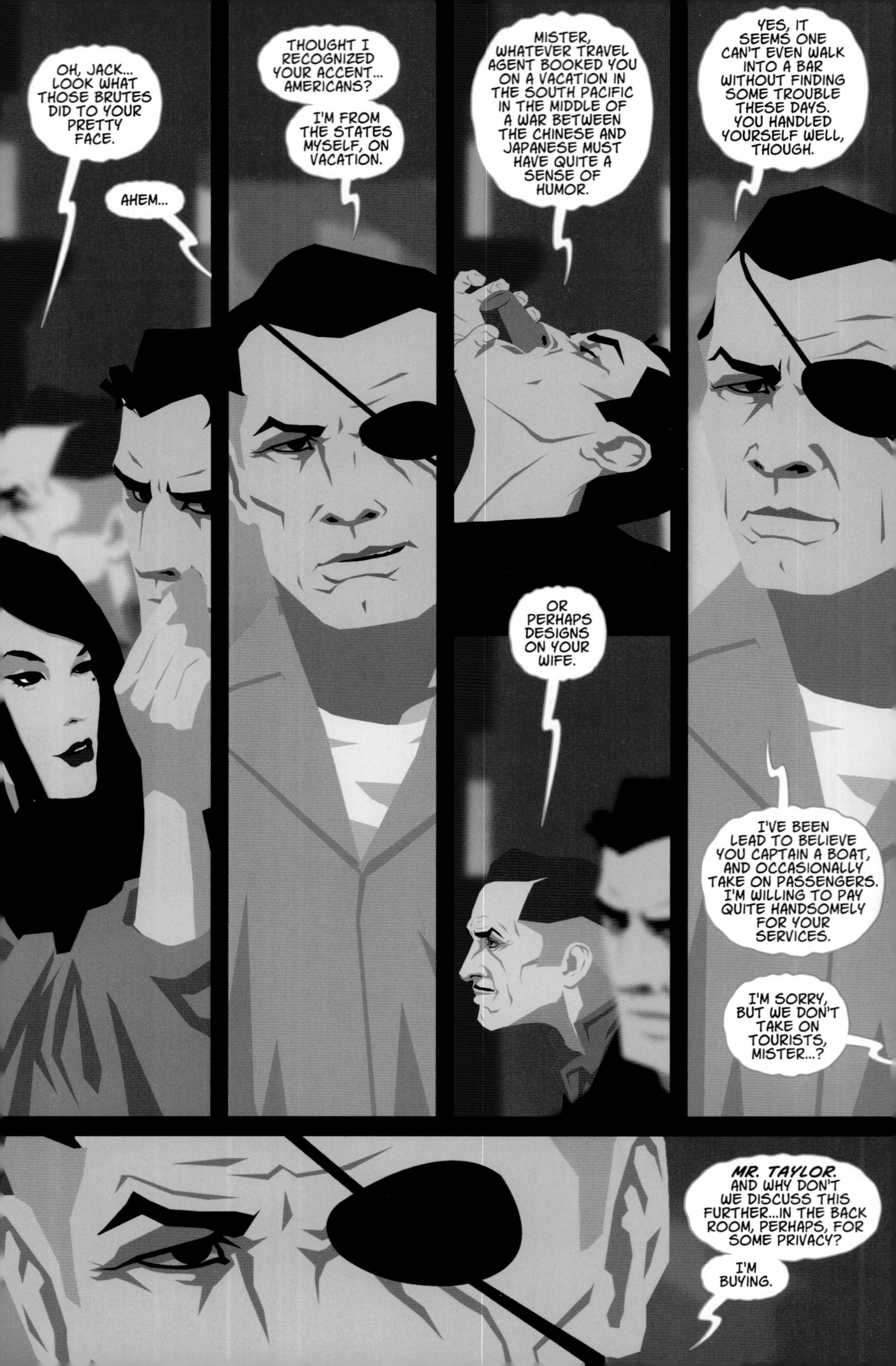
OH, JACK... LOOK WHAT THOSE BRUTES DID TO YOUR PRETTY FACE.
AHEM...
THOUGHT I RECOGNIZED YOUR ACCENT... AMERICANS?
I'M FROM THE STATES MYSELF, ON VACATION.
MISTER, WHATEVER TRAVEL AGENT BOOKED YOU ON A VACATION IN THE SOUTH PACIFIC IN THE MIDDLE OF A WAR BETWEEN THE CHINESE AND JAPANESE MUST HAVE QUITE A SENSE OF HUMOR.
OR PERHAPS DESIGNS ON YOUR WIFE.
YES, IT SEEMS ONE CAN'T EVEN WALK INTO A BAR WITHOUT FINDING SOME TROUBLE THESE DAYS. YOU HANDLED YOURSELF WELL, THOUGH.
I'VE BEEN LEAD TO BELIEVE YOU CAPTAIN A BOAT, AND OCCASIONALLY TAKE ON PASSENGERS. I'M WILLING TO PAY QUITE HANDSOMELY FOR YOUR SERVICES.
I'M SORRY, BUT WE DON'T TAKE ON TOURISTS, MISTER...?
MR. TAYLOR. AND WHY DON'T WE DISCUSS THIS FURTHER...IN THE BACK ROOM, PERHAPS, FOR SOME PRIVACY?
I'M BUYING.

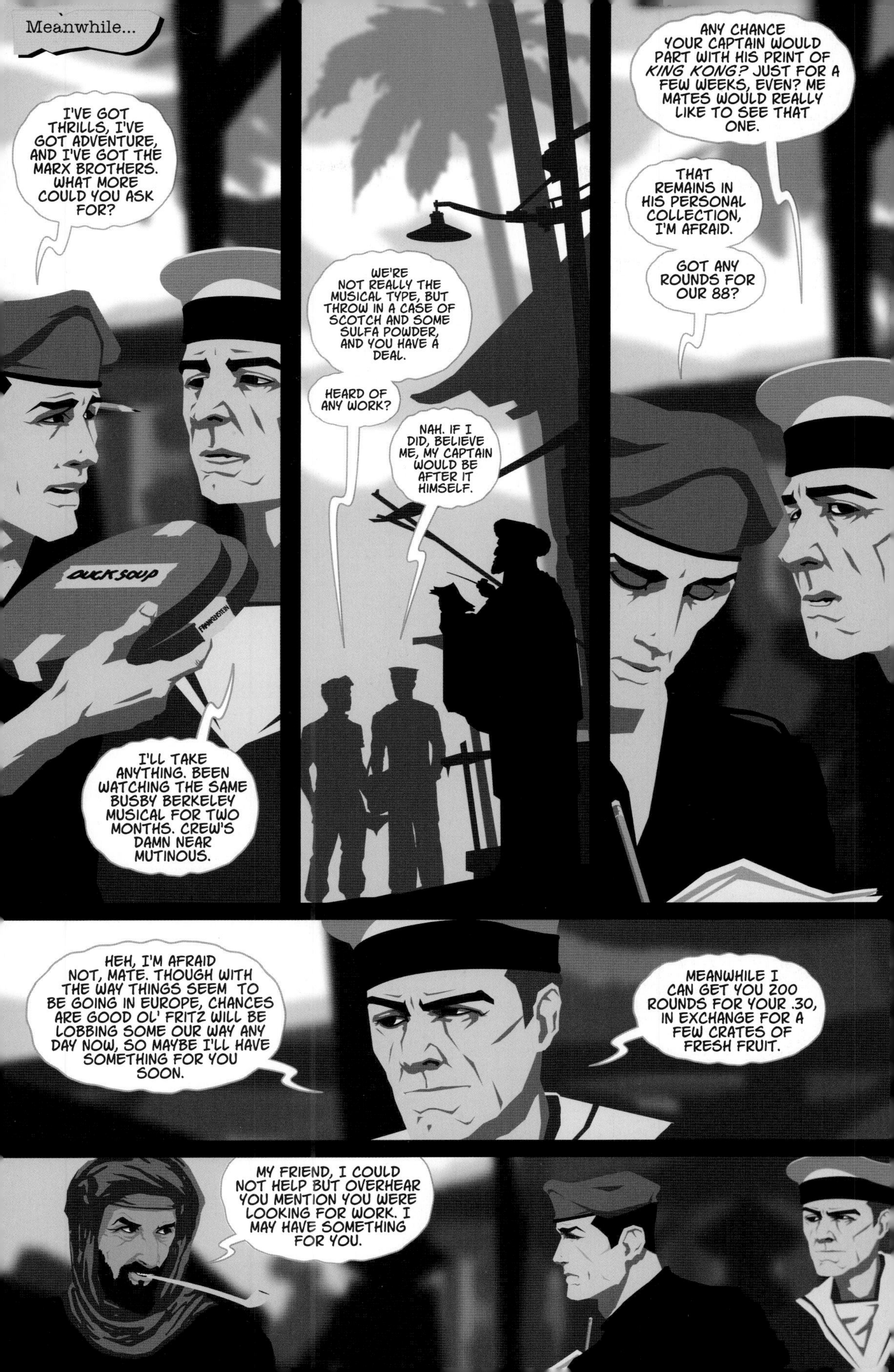
Meanwhile...
I'VE GOT THRILLS, I'VE GOT ADVENTURE, AND I'VE GOT THE MARX BROTHERS. WHAT MORE COULD YOU ASK FOR?
DUCK SOUP
FRANKENSTEIN
I'LL TAKE ANYTHING. BEEN WATCHING THE SAME BUSBY BERKELEY MUSICAL FOR TWO MONTHS. CREW'S DAMN NEAR MUTINOUS.
WE'RE NOT REALLY THE MUSICAL TYPE, BUT THROW IN A CASE OF SCOTCH AND SOME SULFA POWDER, AND YOU HAVE A DEAL.
HEARD OF ANY WORK?
NAH. IF I DID, BELIEVE ME, MY CAPTAIN WOULD BE AFTER IT HIMSELF.
ANY CHANCE YOUR CAPTAIN WOULD PART WITH HIS PRINT OF KING KONG? JUST FOR A FEW WEEKS, EVEN? ME MATES WOULD REALLY LIKE TO SEE THAT ONE.
THAT REMAINS IN HIS PERSONAL COLLECTION, I'M AFRAID.
GOT ANY ROUNDS FOR OUR 88?
HEH, I'M AFRAID NOT, MATE. THOUGH WITH THE WAY THINGS SEEM TO BE GOING IN EUROPE, CHANCES ARE GOOD OL' FRITZ WILL BE LOBBING SOME OUR WAY ANY DAY NOW, SO MAYBE I'LL HAVE SOMETHING FOR YOU SOON.
MEANWHILE I CAN GET YOU 200 ROUNDS FOR YOUR .30, IN EXCHANGE FOR A FEW CRATES OF FRESH FRUIT.
MY FRIEND, I COULD NOT HELP BUT OVERHEAR YOU MENTION YOU WERE LOOKING FOR WORK. I MAY HAVE SOMETHING FOR YOU.

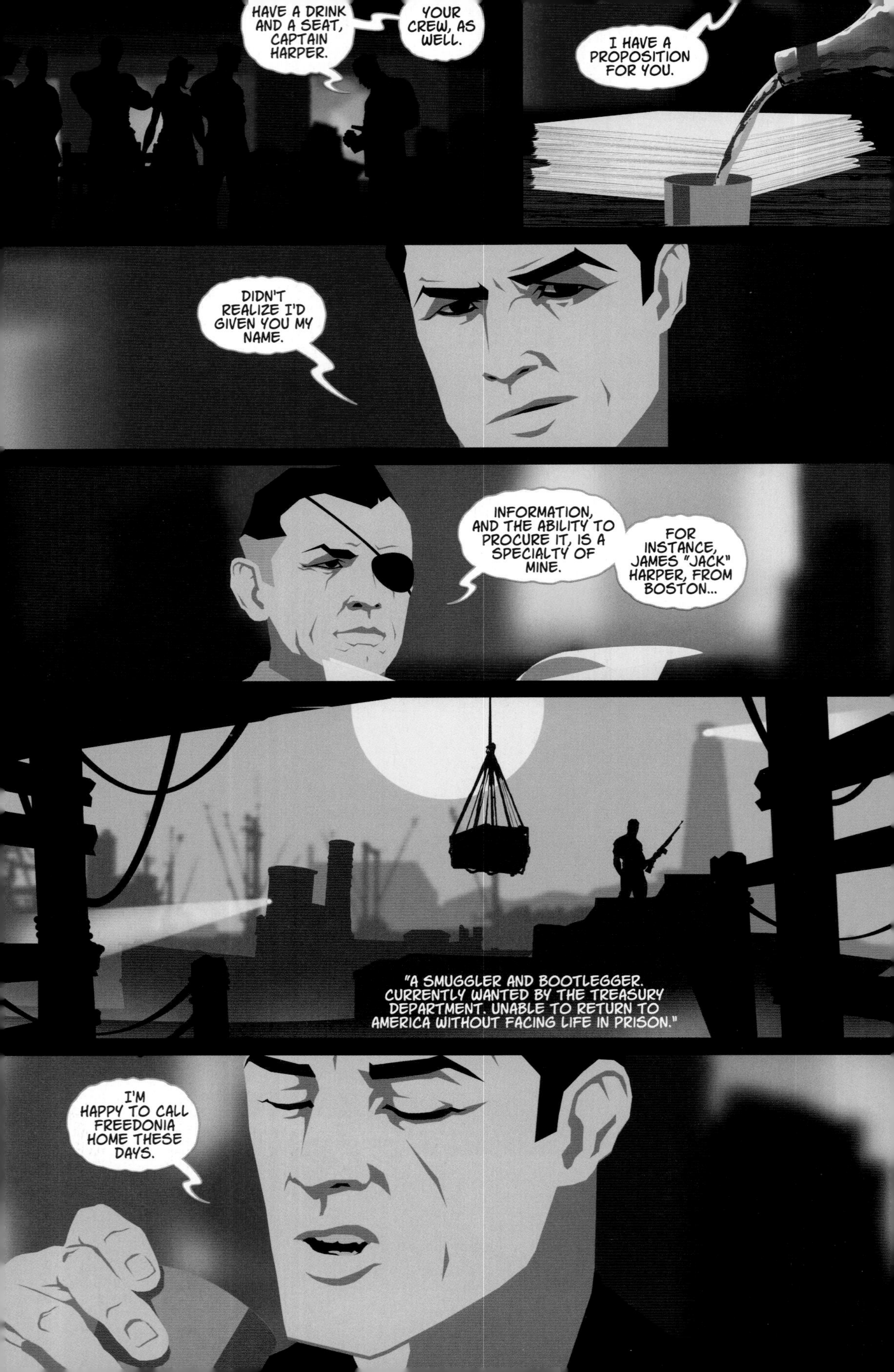
HAVE A DRINK AND A SEAT, CAPTAIN HARPER.
YOUR CREW, AS WELL.
I HAVE A PROPOSITION FOR YOU.
DIDN'T REALIZE I'D GIVEN YOU MY NAME.
INFORMATION, AND THE ABILITY TO PROCURE IT, IS A SPECIALTY OF MINE.
FOR INSTANCE, JAMES "JACK" HARPER, FROM BOSTON...
"A SMUGGLER AND BOOTLEGGER. CURRENTLY WANTED BY THE TREASURY DEPARTMENT. UNABLE TO RETURN TO AMERICA WITHOUT FACING LIFE IN PRISON."
I'M HAPPY TO CALL FREEDONIA HOME THESE DAYS.

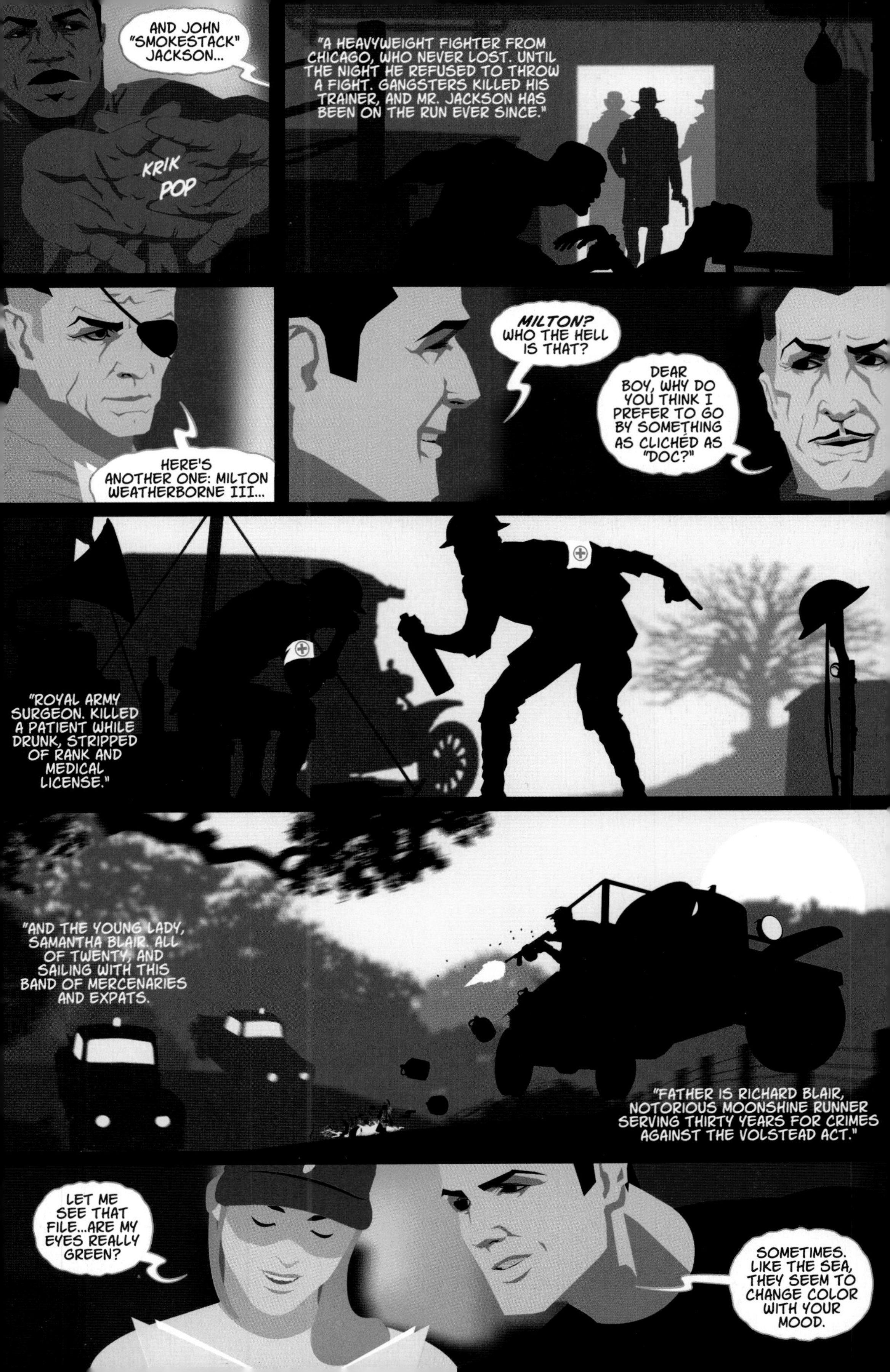
AND JOHN "SMOKESTACK" JACKSON...
KRIK
POP
"A HEAVYWEIGHT FIGHTER FROM CHICAGO, WHO NEVER LOST. UNTIL THE NIGHT HE REFUSED TO THROW A FIGHT. GANGSTERS KILLED HIS TRAINER, AND MR. JACKSON HAS BEEN ON THE RUN EVER SINCE."
HERE'S ANOTHER ONE: MILTON WEATHERBORNE III...
MILTON? WHO THE HELL IS THAT?
DEAR BOY, WHY DO YOU THINK I PREFER TO GO BY SOMETHING AS CLICHÉD AS "DOC?"
"ROYAL ARMY SURGEON. KILLED A PATIENT WHILE DRUNK, STRIPPED OF RANK AND MEDICAL LICENSE."
"AND THE YOUNG LADY, SAMANTHA BLAIR. ALL OF TWENTY, AND SAILING WITH THIS BAND OF MERCENARIES AND EXPATS.
"FATHER IS RICHARD BLAIR, NOTORIOUS MOONSHINE RUNNER SERVING THIRTY YEARS FOR CRIMES AGAINST THE VOLSTEAD ACT."
LET ME SEE THAT FILE...ARE MY EYES REALLY GREEN?
SOMETIMES. LIKE THE SEA, THEY SEEM TO CHANGE COLOR WITH YOUR MOOD.

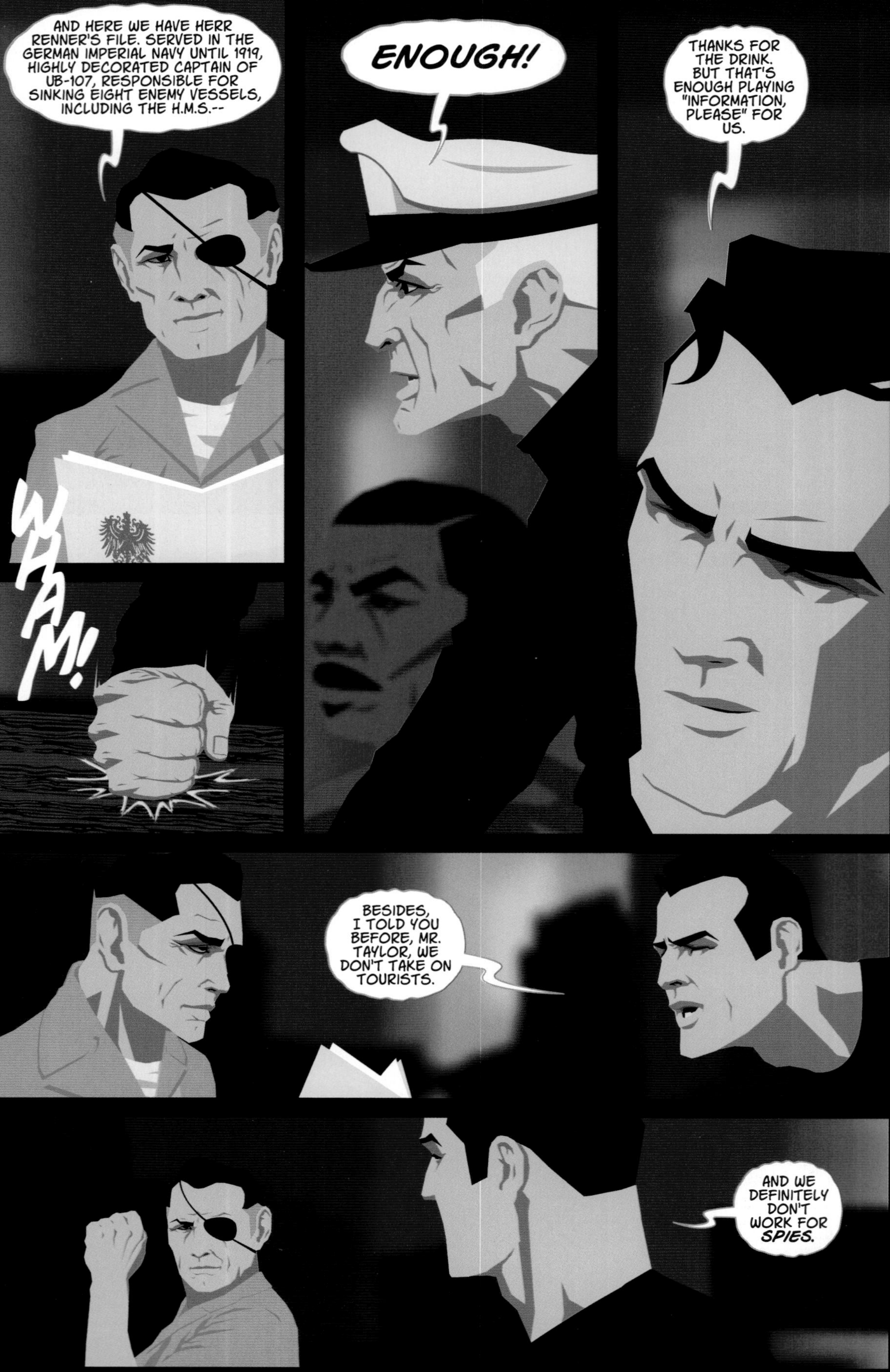

AND HERE WE HAVE HERR RENNER'S FILE. SERVED IN THE GERMAN IMPERIAL NAVY UNTIL 1919, HIGHLY DECORATED CAPTAIN OF UB-107, RESPONSIBLE FOR SINKING EIGHT ENEMY VESSELS, INCLUDING THE H.M.S.--
WHAM!
ENOUGH!
THANKS FOR THE DRINK. BUT THAT'S ENOUGH PLAYING "INFORMATION, PLEASE" FOR US.
BESIDES, I TOLD YOU BEFORE, MR. TAYLOR, WE DON'T TAKE ON TOURISTS.
AND WE DEFINITELY DON'T WORK FOR *SPIES*.

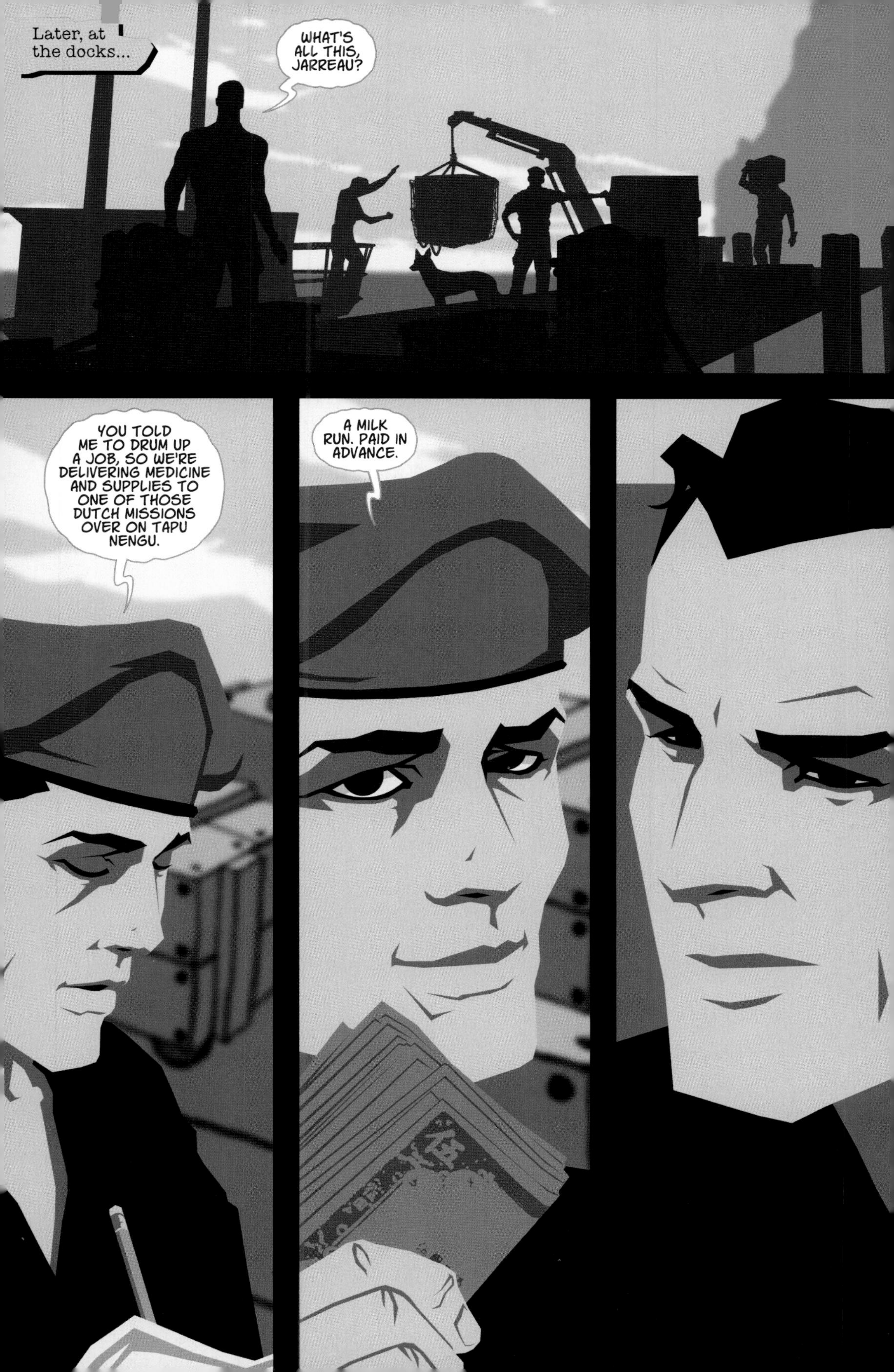
Later, at the docks...
WHAT'S ALL THIS, JARREAU?
YOU TOLD ME TO DRUM UP A JOB, SO WE'RE DELIVERING MEDICINE AND SUPPLIES TO ONE OF THOSE DUTCH MISSIONS OVER ON TAPU NENGU.
A MILK RUN. PAID IN ADVANCE.

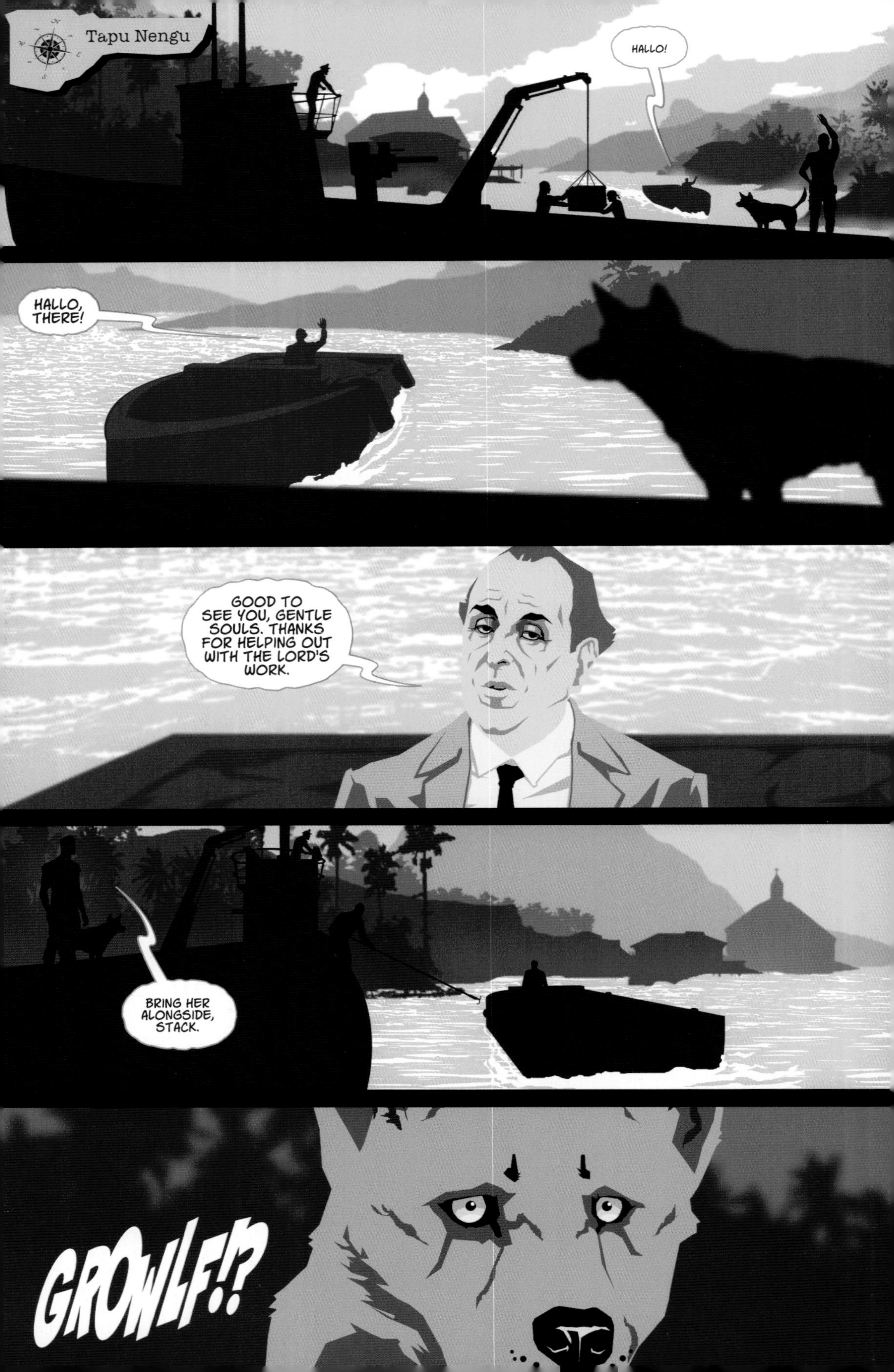
Tapu Nengu
HALLO!
HALLO, THERE!
GOOD TO SEE YOU, GENTLE SOULS. THANKS FOR HELPING OUT WITH THE LORD'S WORK.
BRING HER ALONGSIDE, STACK.
GROWLF!?

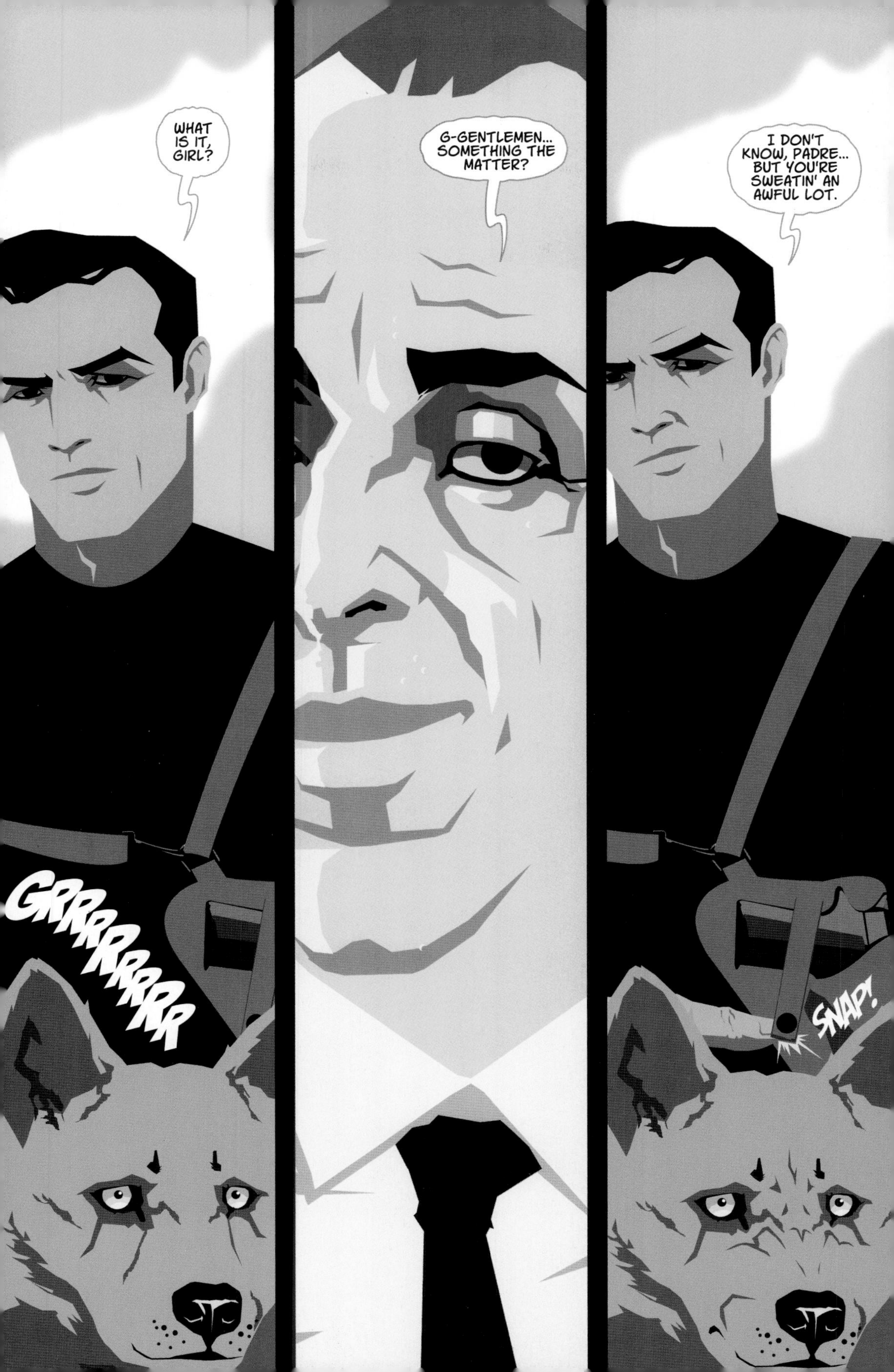
WHAT IS IT, GIRL?
GRRRRRRRR
G-GENTLEMEN... SOMETHING THE MATTER?
I DON'T KNOW, PADRE... BUT YOU'RE SWEATIN' AN AWFUL LOT.
SNAP!

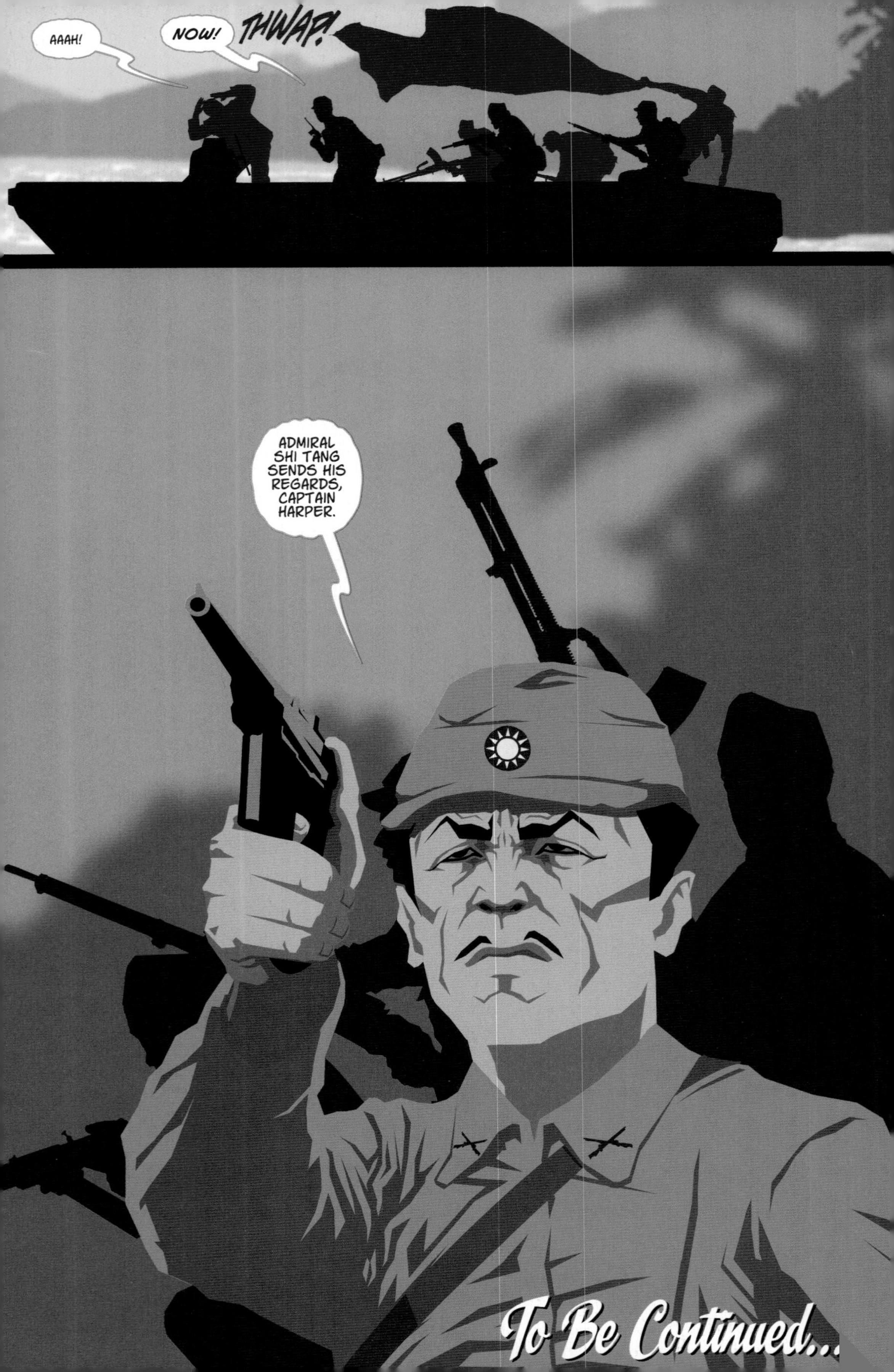
AAAH!
NOW!
THWAP!
ADMIRAL SHI TANG SENDS HIS REGARDS, CAPTAIN HARPER.
To Be Continued...

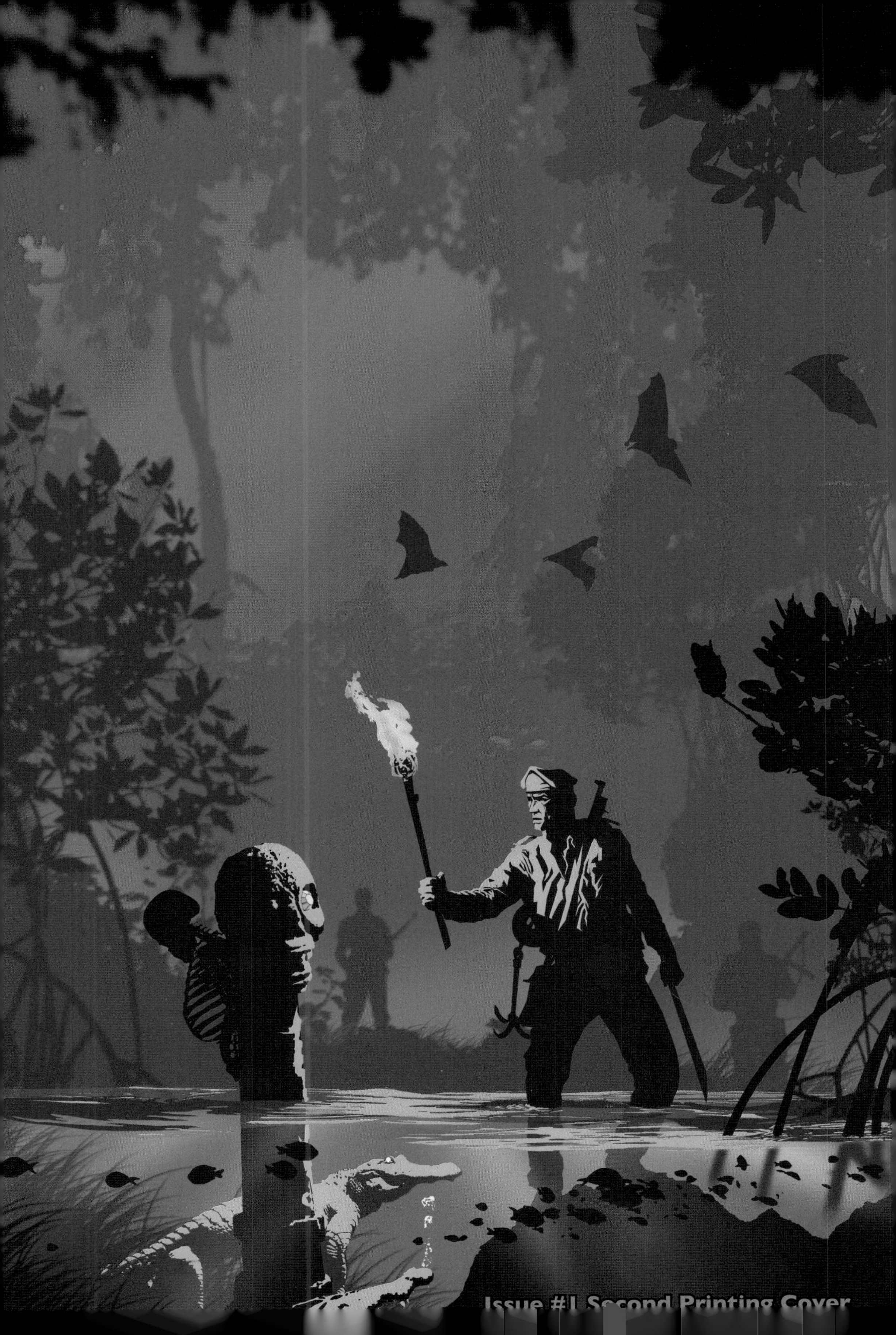

Issue #1 Second Printing Cover

Red Sails At Sunset

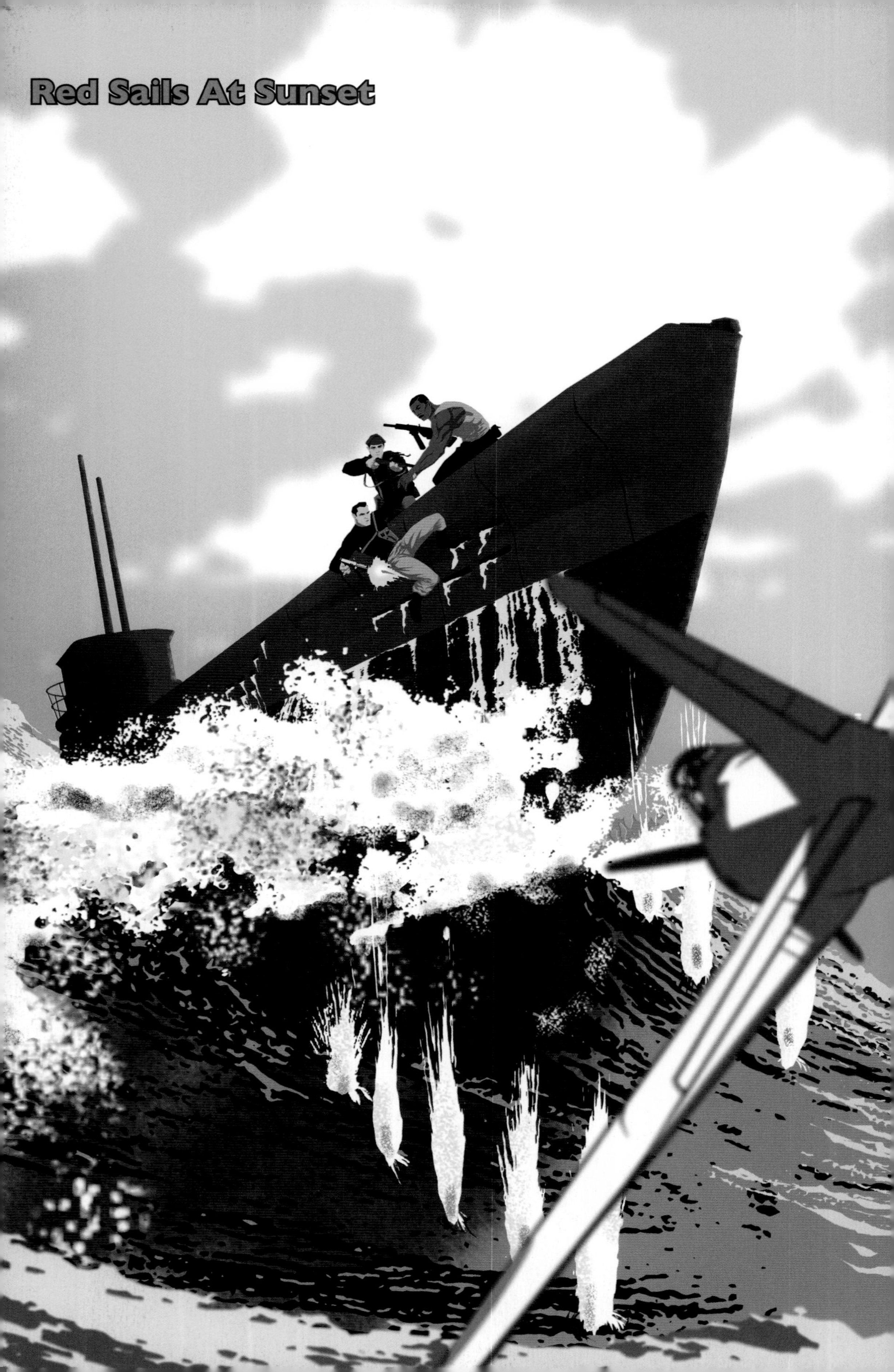

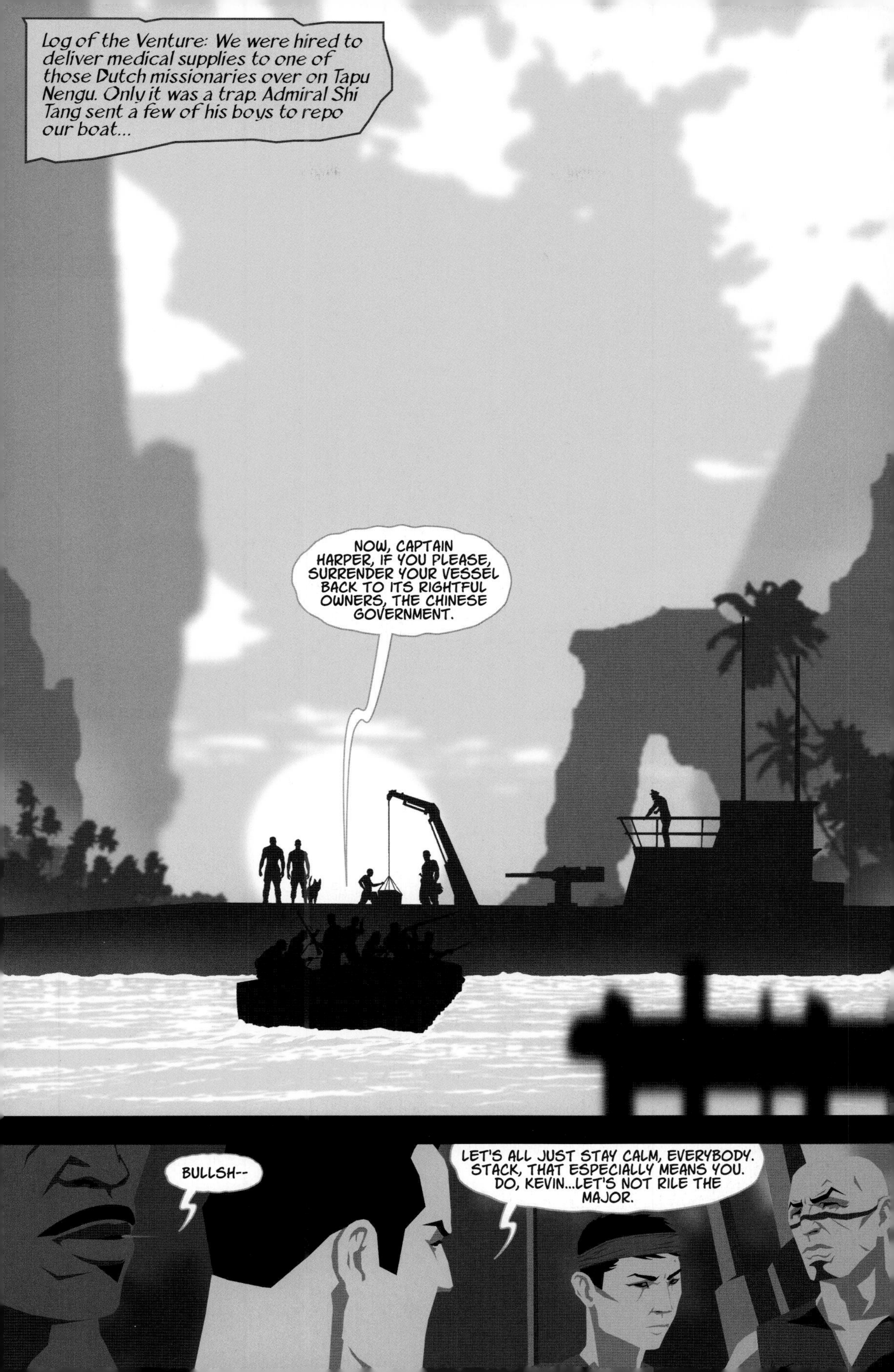
Log of the Venture: We were hired to deliver medical supplies to one of those Dutch missionaries over on Tapu Nengu. Only it was a trap. Admiral Shi Tang sent a few of his boys to repo our boat...
NOW, CAPTAIN HARPER, IF YOU PLEASE, SURRENDER YOUR VESSEL BACK TO ITS RIGHTFUL OWNERS, THE CHINESE GOVERNMENT.
BULLSH--
LET'S ALL JUST STAY CALM, EVERYBODY. STACK, THAT ESPECIALLY MEANS YOU. DO, KEVIN...LET'S NOT RILE THE MAJOR.

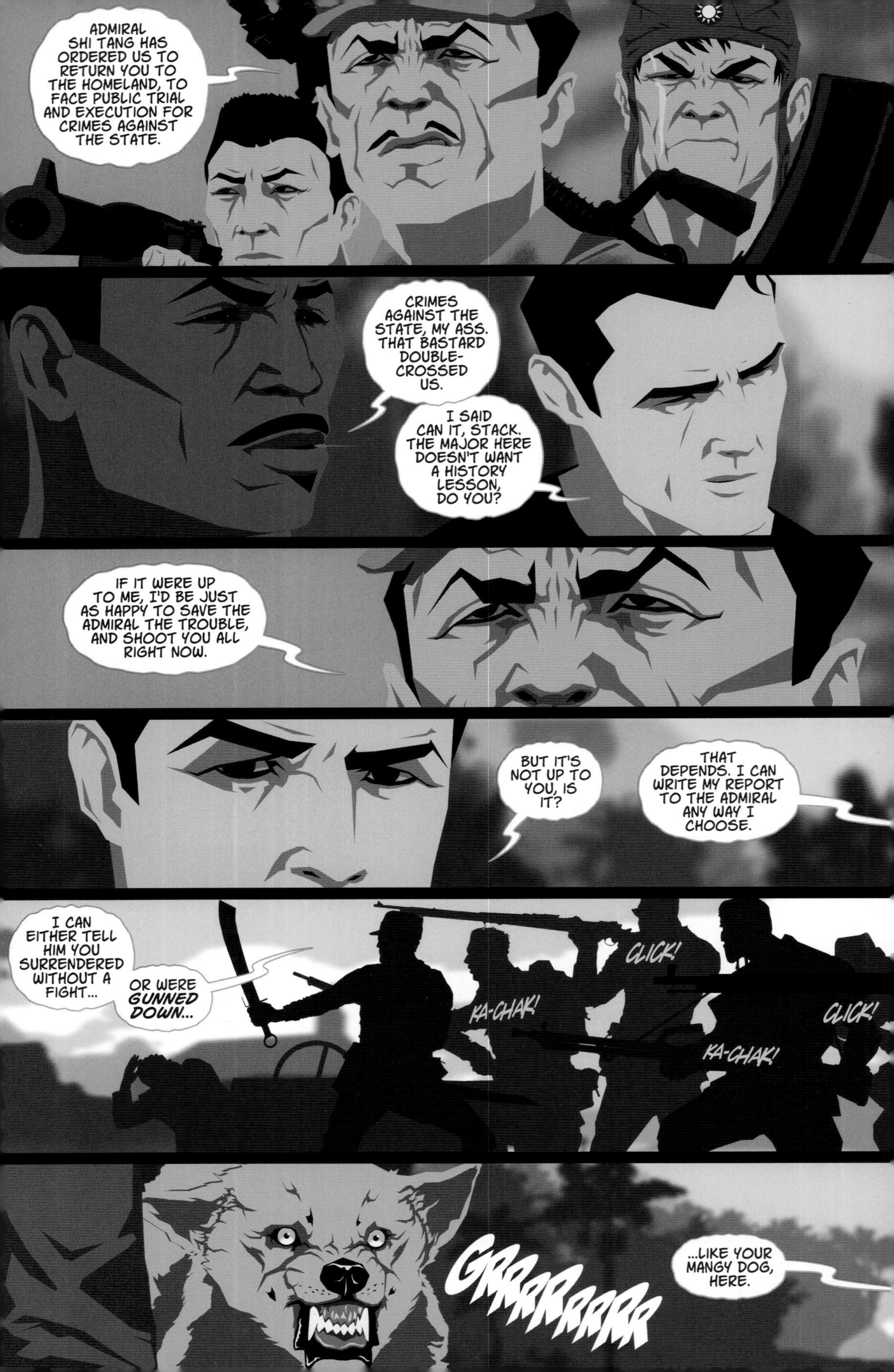
ADMIRAL SHI TANG HAS ORDERED US TO RETURN YOU TO THE HOMELAND, TO FACE PUBLIC TRIAL AND EXECUTION FOR CRIMES AGAINST THE STATE.
CRIMES AGAINST THE STATE, MY ASS. THAT BASTARD DOUBLE-CROSSED US.
I SAID CAN IT, STACK. THE MAJOR HERE DOESN'T WANT A HISTORY LESSON, DO YOU?
IF IT WERE UP TO ME, I'D BE JUST AS HAPPY TO SAVE THE ADMIRAL THE TROUBLE, AND SHOOT YOU ALL RIGHT NOW.
BUT IT'S NOT UP TO YOU, IS IT?
THAT DEPENDS. I CAN WRITE MY REPORT TO THE ADMIRAL ANY WAY I CHOOSE.
I CAN EITHER TELL HIM YOU SURRENDERED WITHOUT A FIGHT...
OR WERE GUNNED DOWN...
CLICK!
KA-CHAK!
CLICK!
KA-CHAK!
GRRRRRRRR
...LIKE YOUR MANGY DOG, HERE.

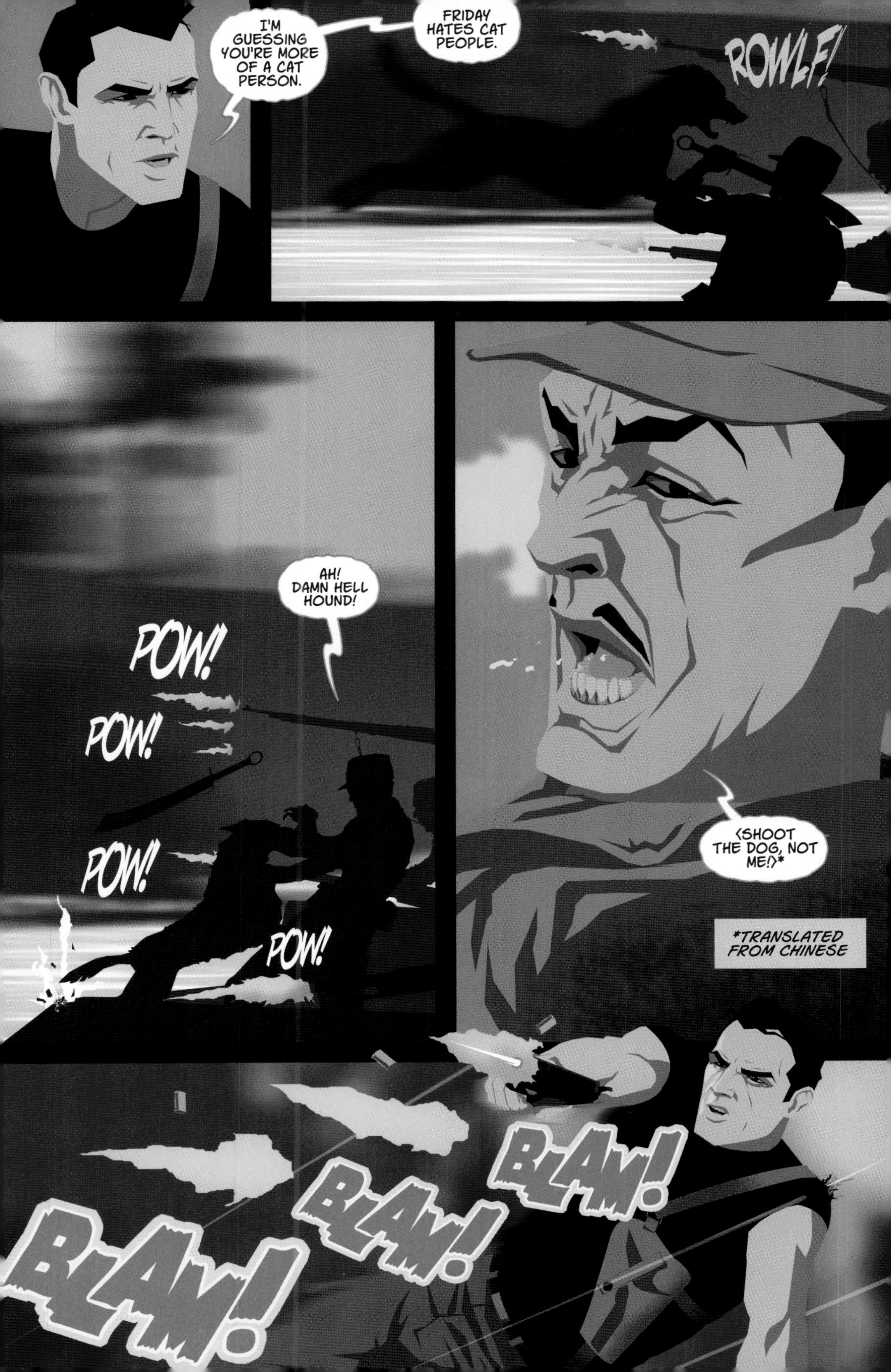
I'M GUESSING YOU'RE MORE OF A CAT PERSON.
FRIDAY HATES CAT PEOPLE.
ROWLF!
AH! DAMN HELL HOUND!
POW!
POW!
POW!
POW!
‹SHOOT THE DOG, NOT ME!›*
*TRANSLATED FROM CHINESE
BLAM!
BLAM!
BLAM!

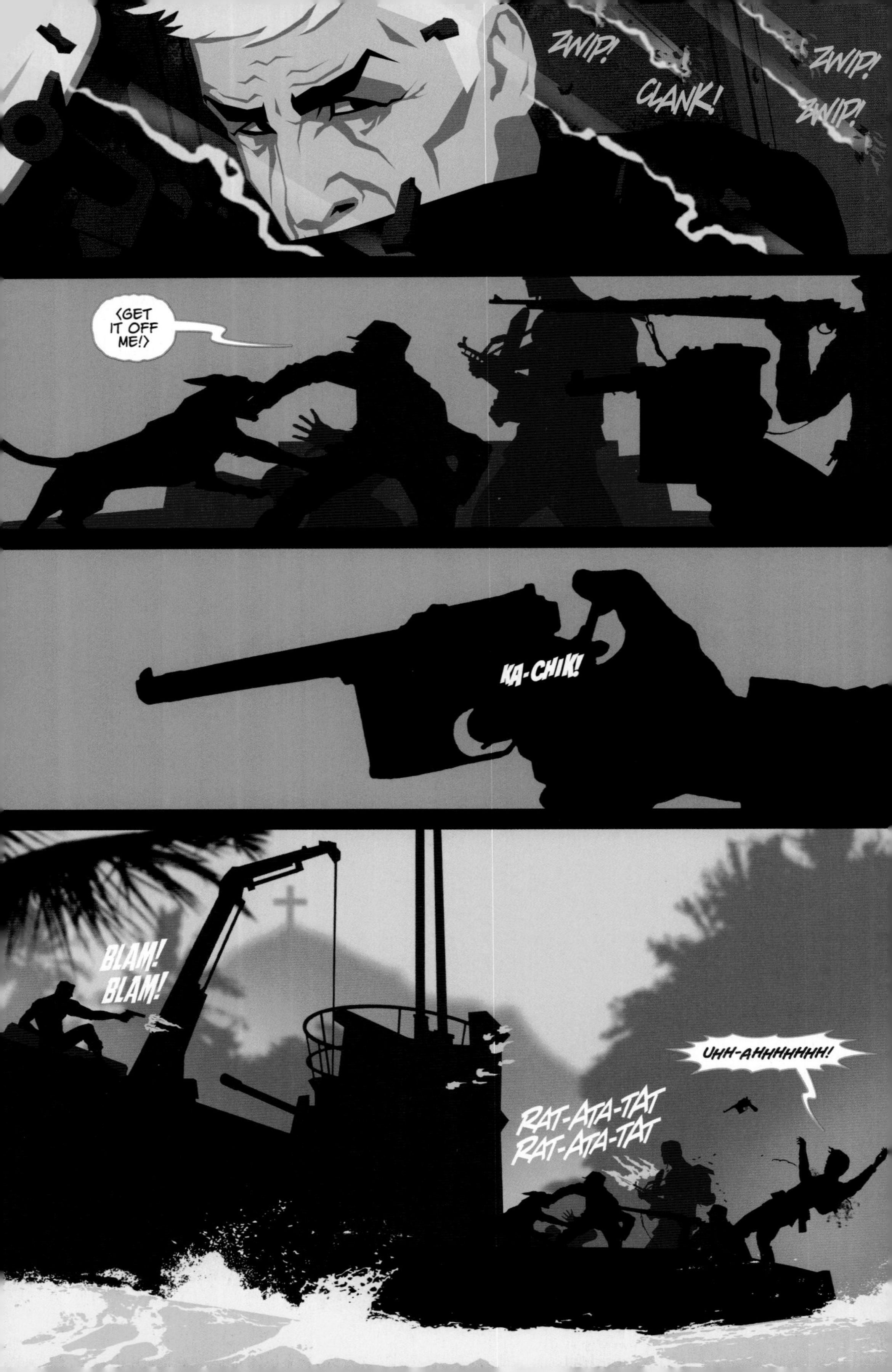
ZWIP!
CLANK!
ZWIP!
ZWIP!
<GET IT OFF ME!>
KA-CHIK!
BLAM! BLAM!
UHH-AHHHHHHH!
RAT-ATA-TAT
RAT-ATA-TAT

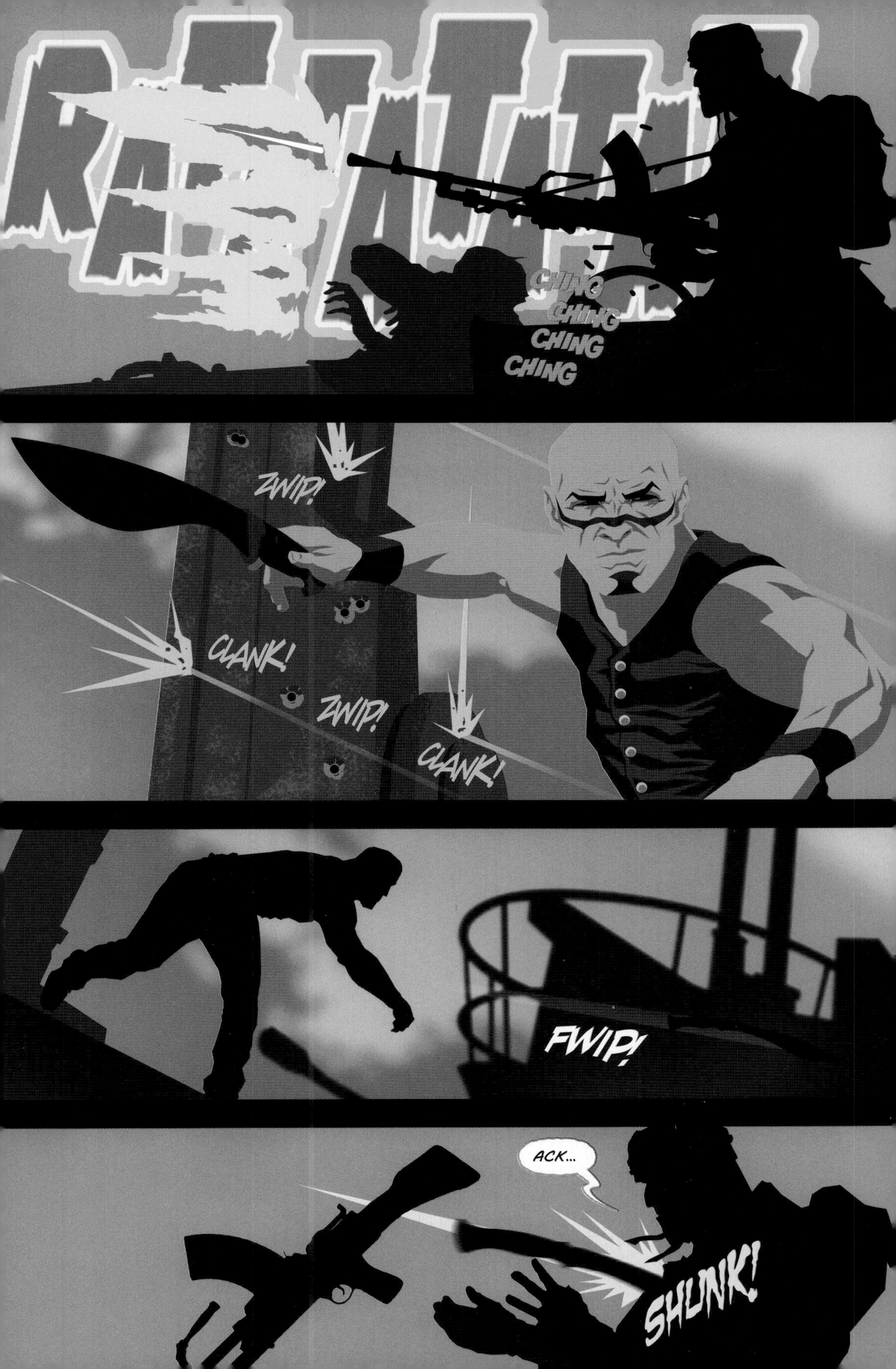
CHING
CHING
CHING
CHING
ZWIP!
CLANK!
ZWIP!
CLANK!
FWIP!
ACK...
SHUNK!

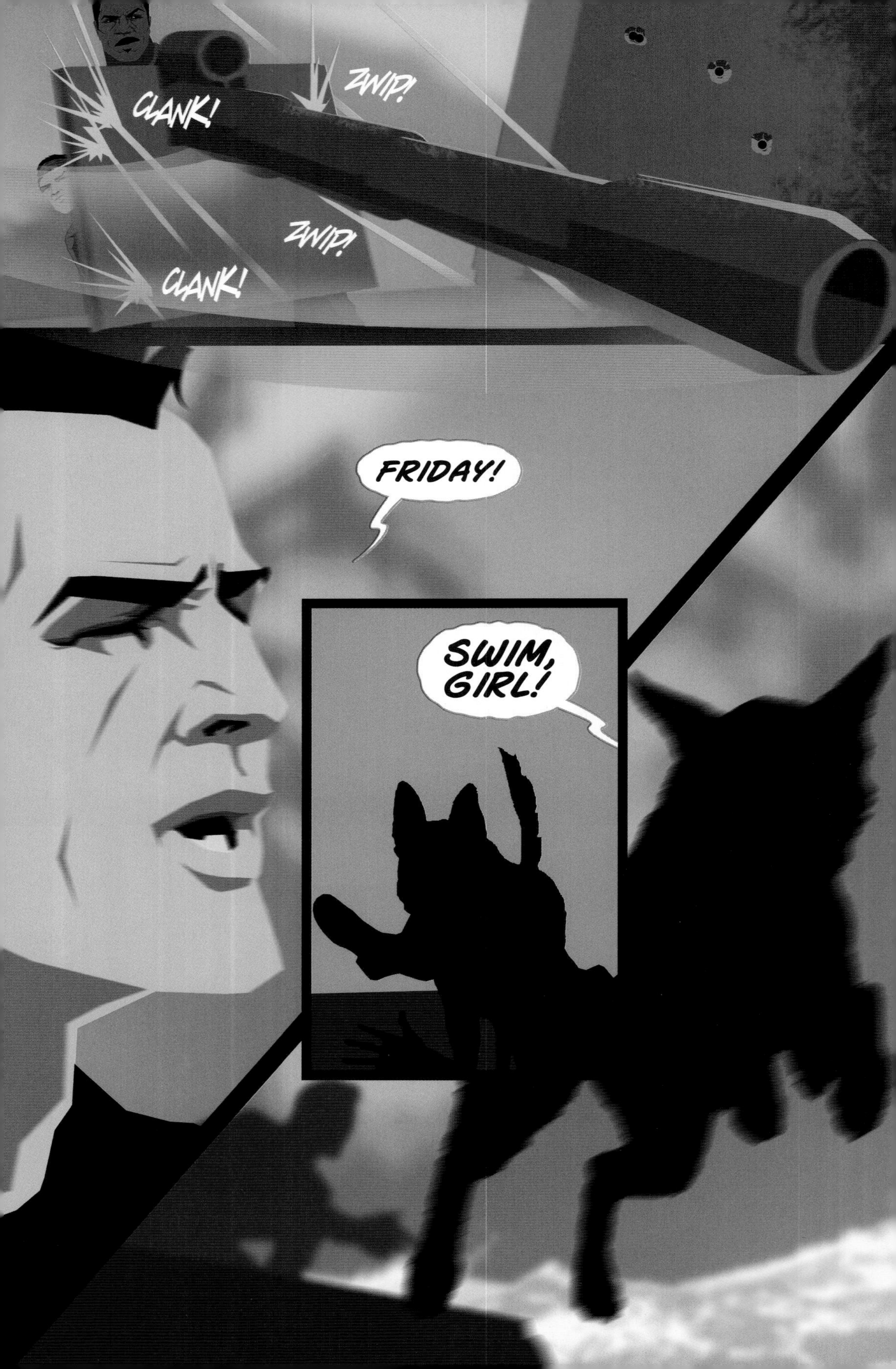
CLANK!
ZWIP!
ZWIP!
CLANK!
FRIDAY!
SWIM, GIRL!

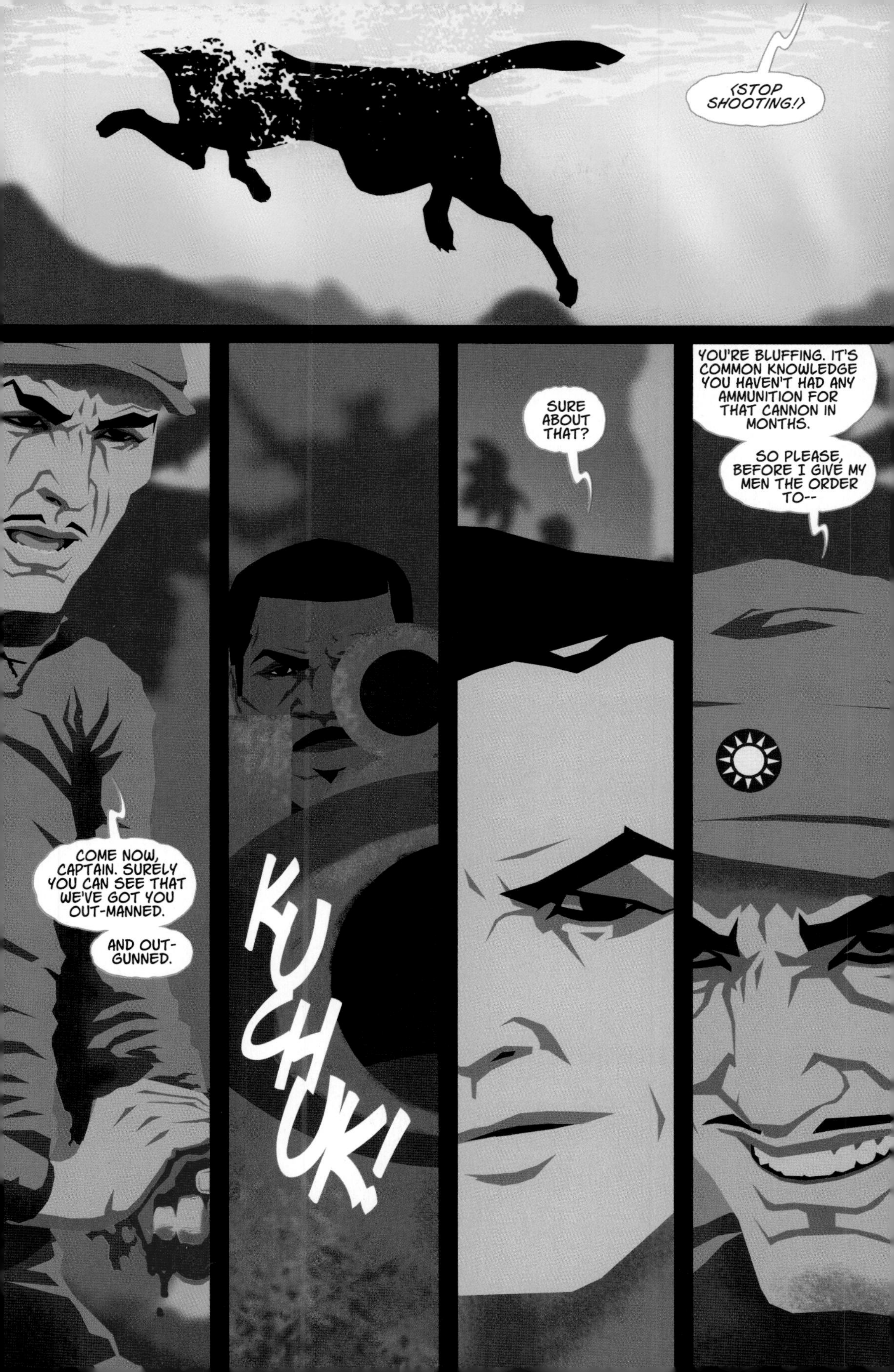
<STOP SHOOTING!>
COME NOW, CAPTAIN. SURELY YOU CAN SEE THAT WE'VE GOT YOU OUT-MANNED.
AND OUT-GUNNED.
KUCHUK!
SURE ABOUT THAT?
YOU'RE BLUFFING. IT'S COMMON KNOWLEDGE YOU HAVEN'T HAD ANY AMMUNITION FOR THAT CANNON IN MONTHS.
SO PLEASE, BEFORE I GIVE MY MEN THE ORDER TO--

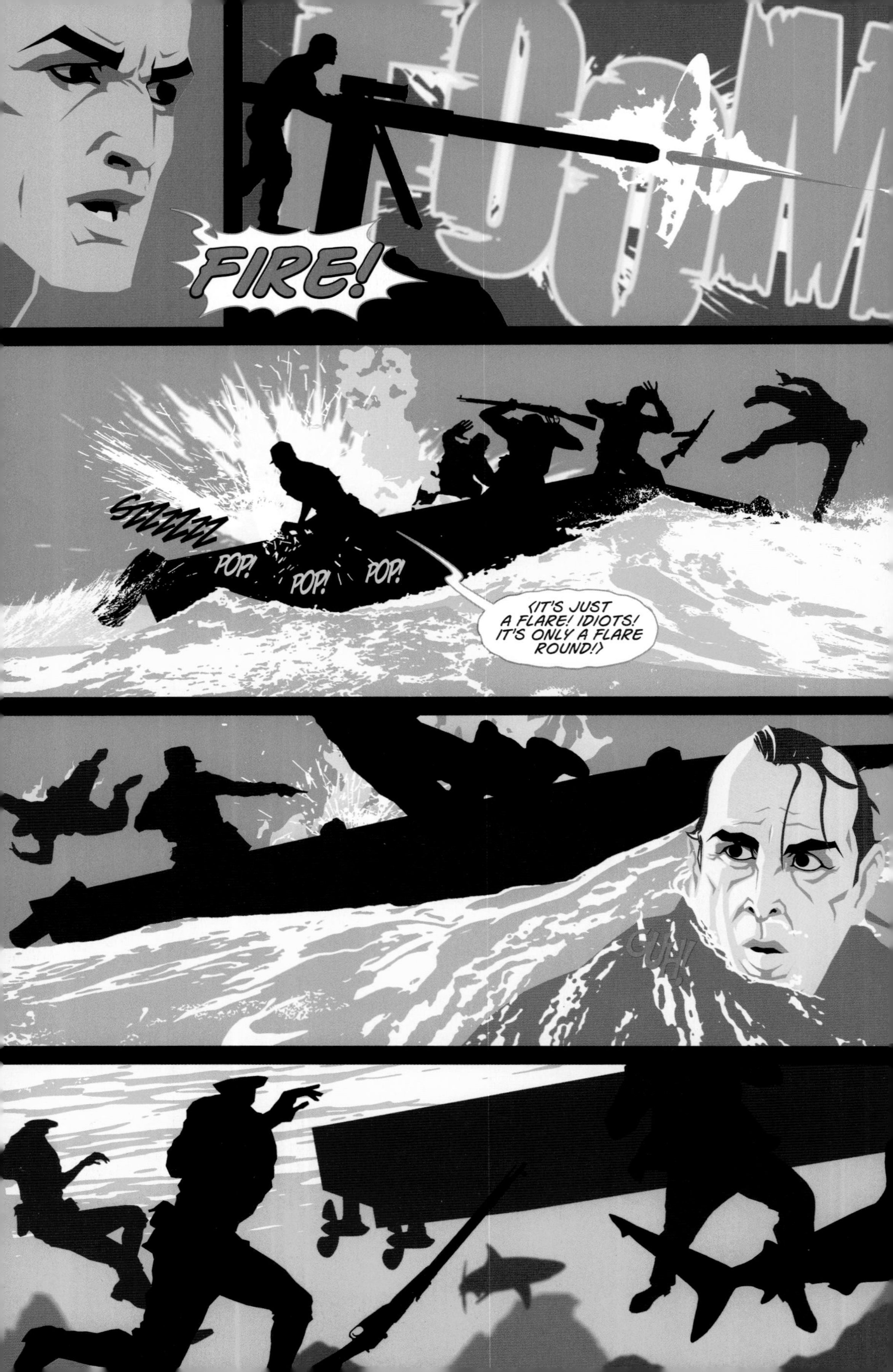
FIRE!
POP!
POP!
POP!
⟨IT'S JUST A FLARE! IDIOTS! IT'S ONLY A FLARE ROUND!⟩

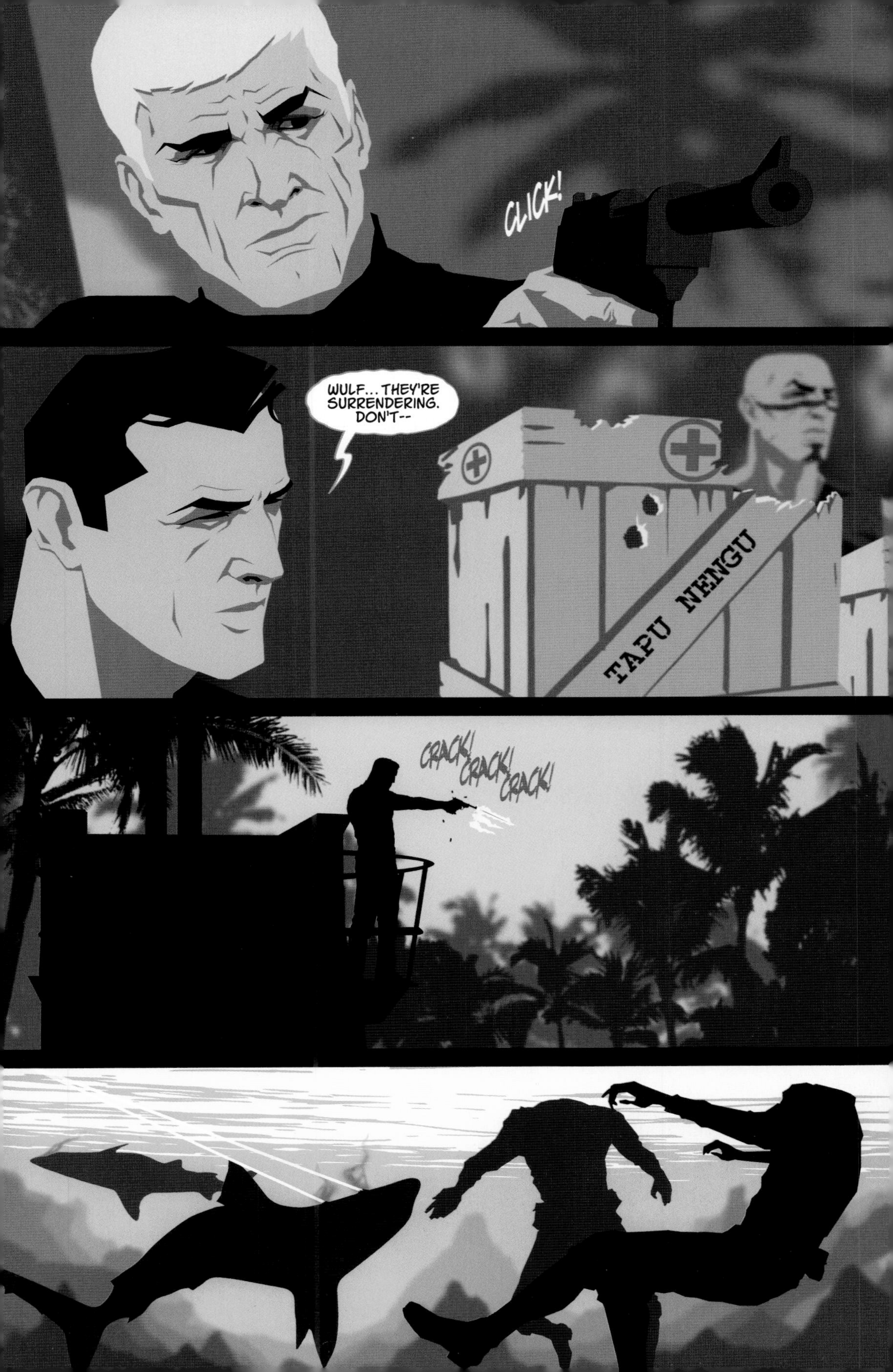
CLICK!
WULF... THEY'RE SURRENDERING. DON'T--
TAPU NENGU
CRACK! CRACK! CRACK!

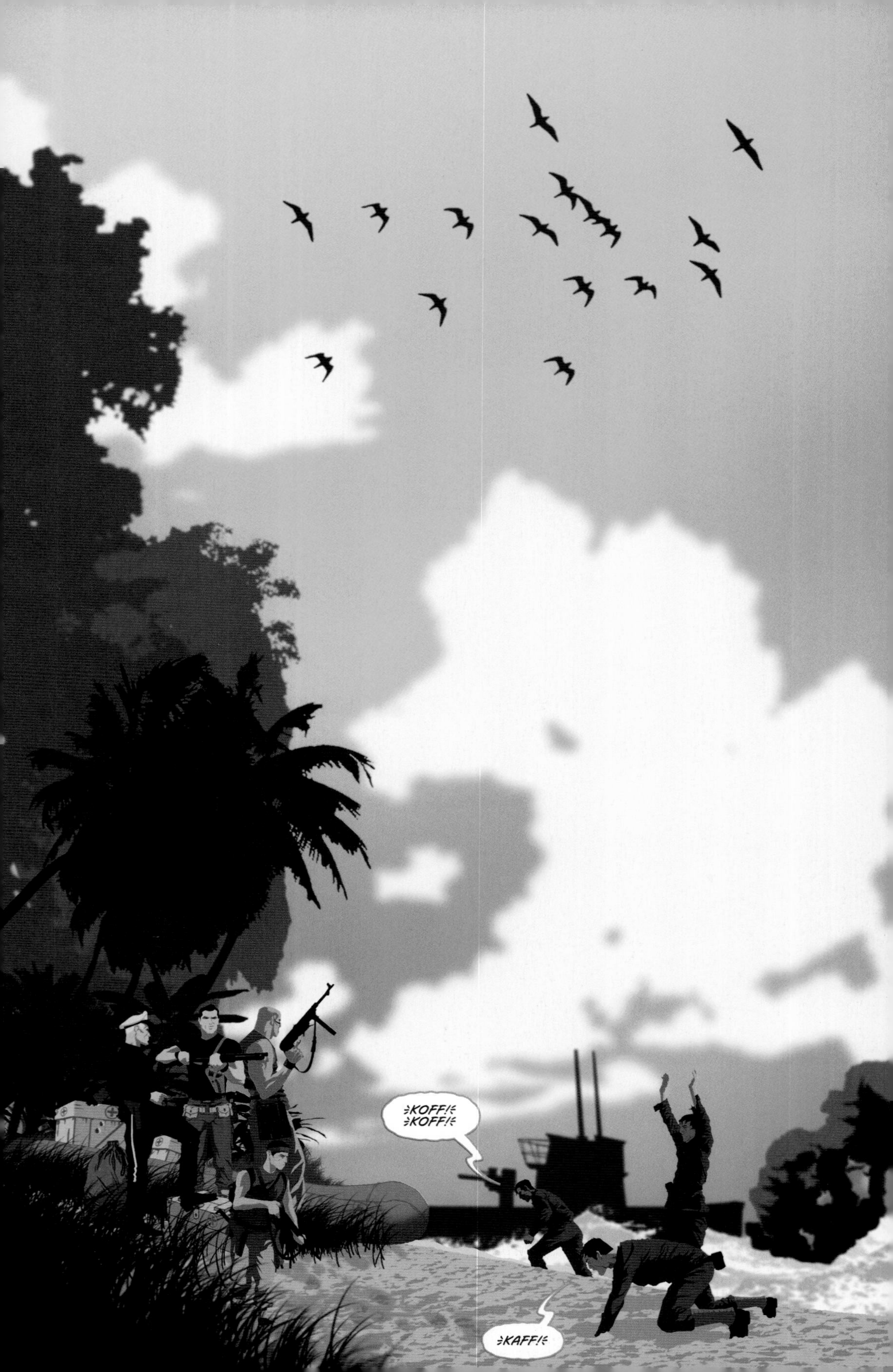

KOFF! KOFF!
KAFF!

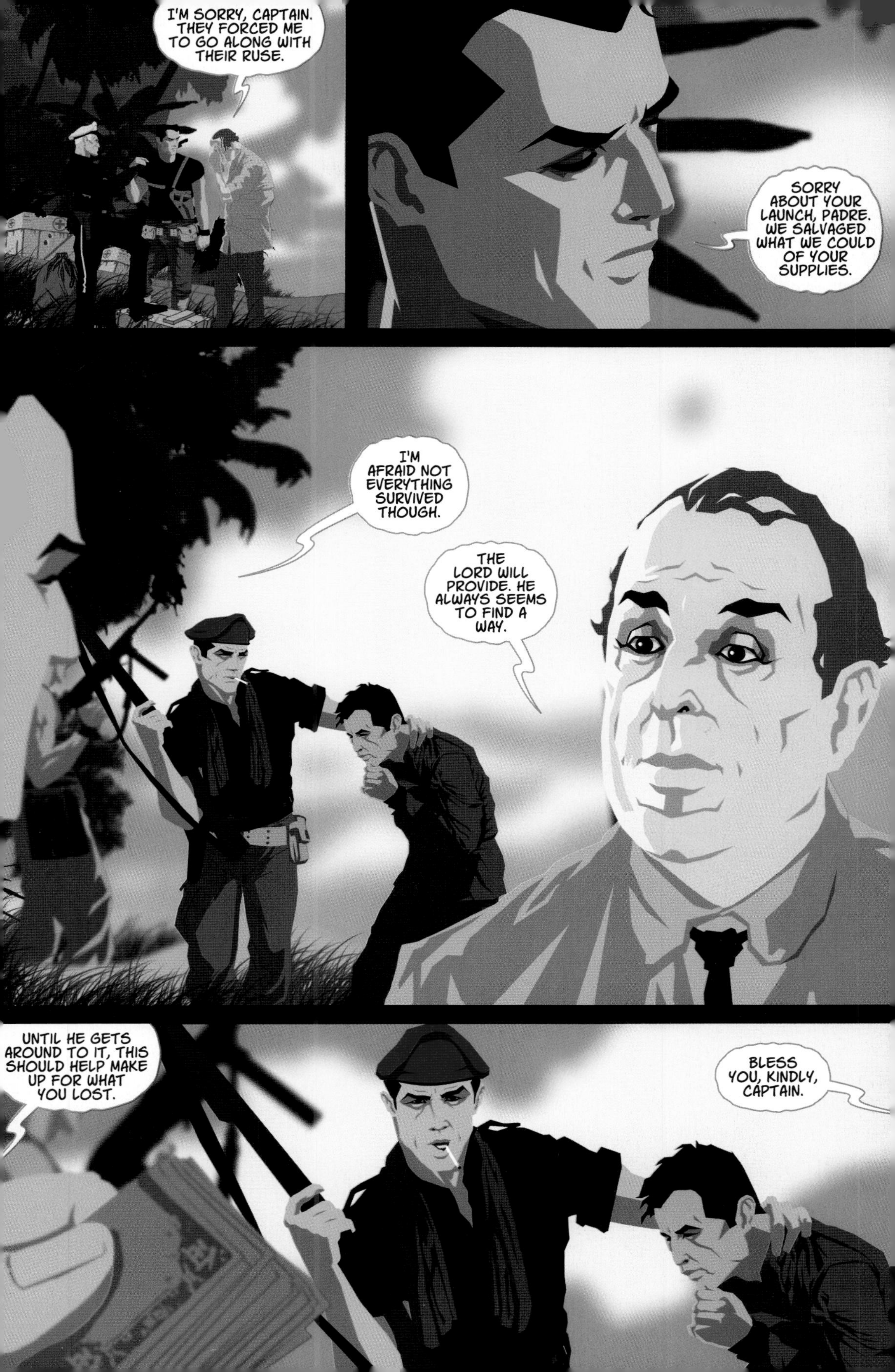
I'M SORRY, CAPTAIN. THEY FORCED ME TO GO ALONG WITH THEIR RUSE.
SORRY ABOUT YOUR LAUNCH, PADRE. WE SALVAGED WHAT WE COULD OF YOUR SUPPLIES.
I'M AFRAID NOT EVERYTHING SURVIVED THOUGH.
THE LORD WILL PROVIDE. HE ALWAYS SEEMS TO FIND A WAY.
UNTIL HE GETS AROUND TO IT, THIS SHOULD HELP MAKE UP FOR WHAT YOU LOST.
BLESS YOU, KINDLY, CAPTAIN.

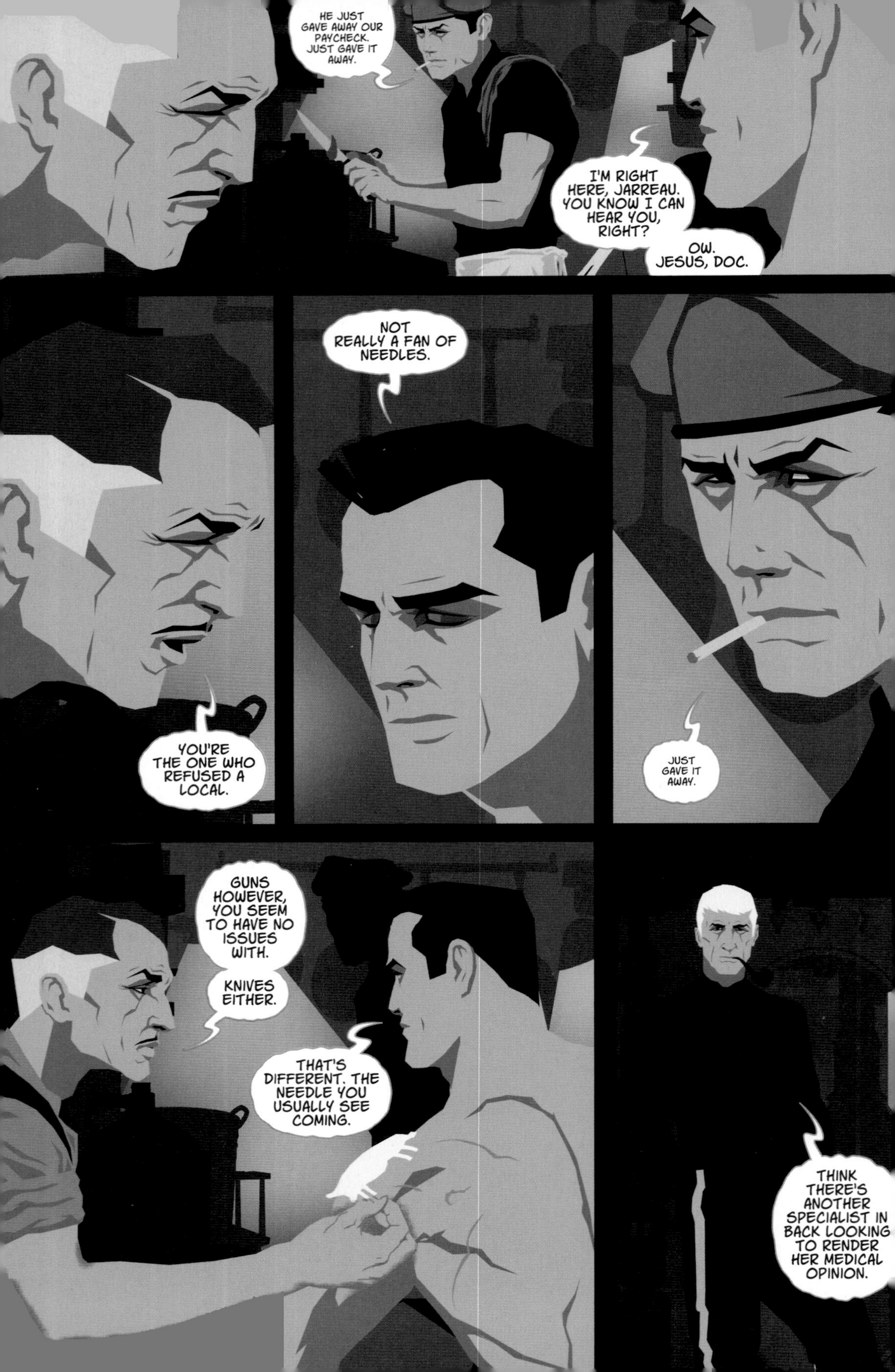
HE JUST GAVE AWAY OUR PAYCHECK. JUST GAVE IT AWAY.
I'M RIGHT HERE, JARREAU. YOU KNOW I CAN HEAR YOU, RIGHT?
OW. JESUS, DOC.
YOU'RE THE ONE WHO REFUSED A LOCAL.
NOT REALLY A FAN OF NEEDLES.
JUST GAVE IT AWAY.
GUNS HOWEVER, YOU SEEM TO HAVE NO ISSUES WITH.
KNIVES EITHER.
THAT'S DIFFERENT. THE NEEDLE YOU USUALLY SEE COMING.
THINK THERE'S ANOTHER SPECIALIST IN BACK LOOKING TO RENDER HER MEDICAL OPINION.

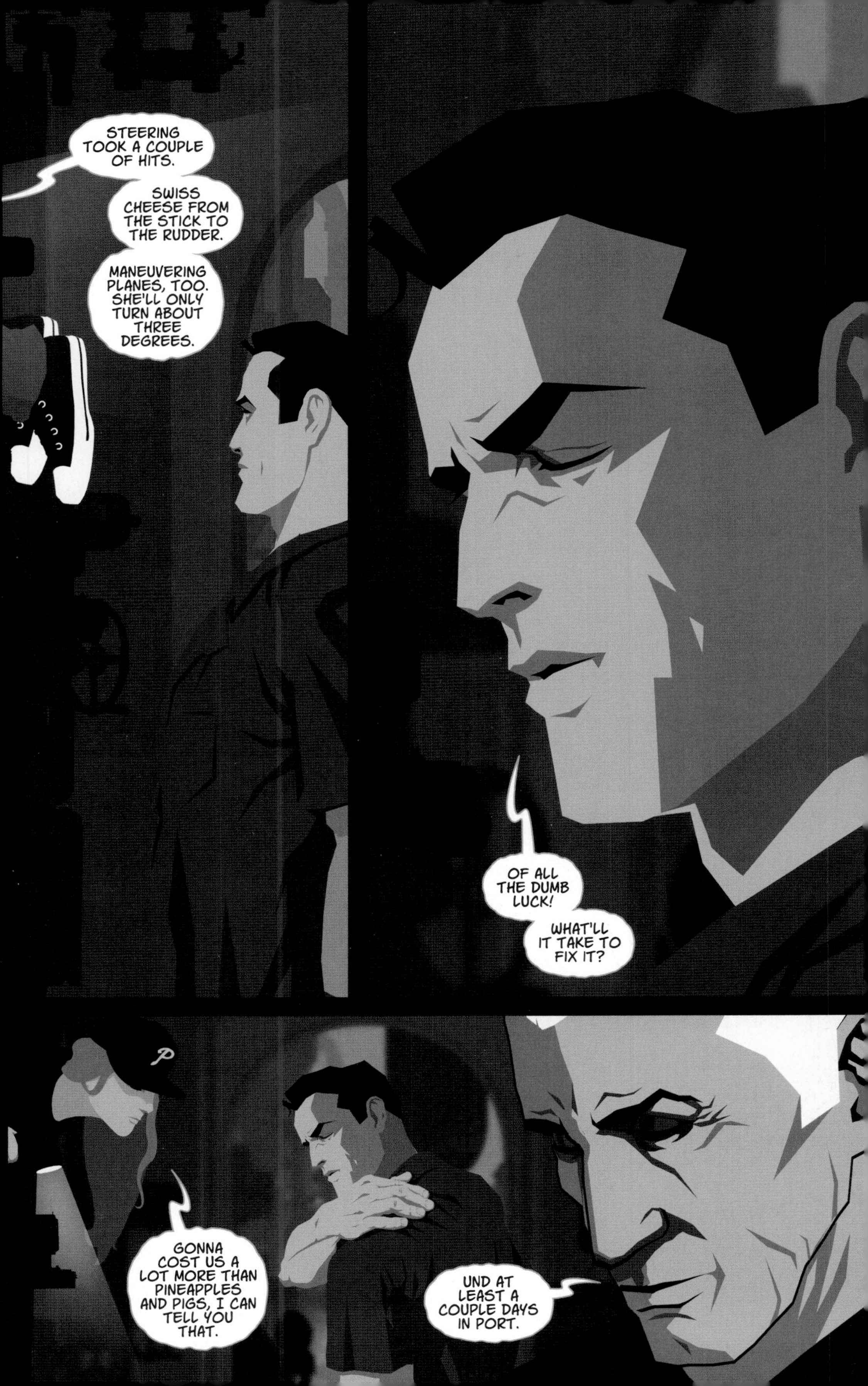
STEERING TOOK A COUPLE OF HITS.
SWISS CHEESE FROM THE STICK TO THE RUDDER.
MANEUVERING PLANES, TOO. SHE'LL ONLY TURN ABOUT THREE DEGREES.
OF ALL THE DUMB LUCK!
WHAT'LL IT TAKE TO FIX IT?
GONNA COST US A LOT MORE THAN PINEAPPLES AND PIGS, I CAN TELL YOU THAT.
UND AT LEAST A COUPLE DAYS IN PORT.

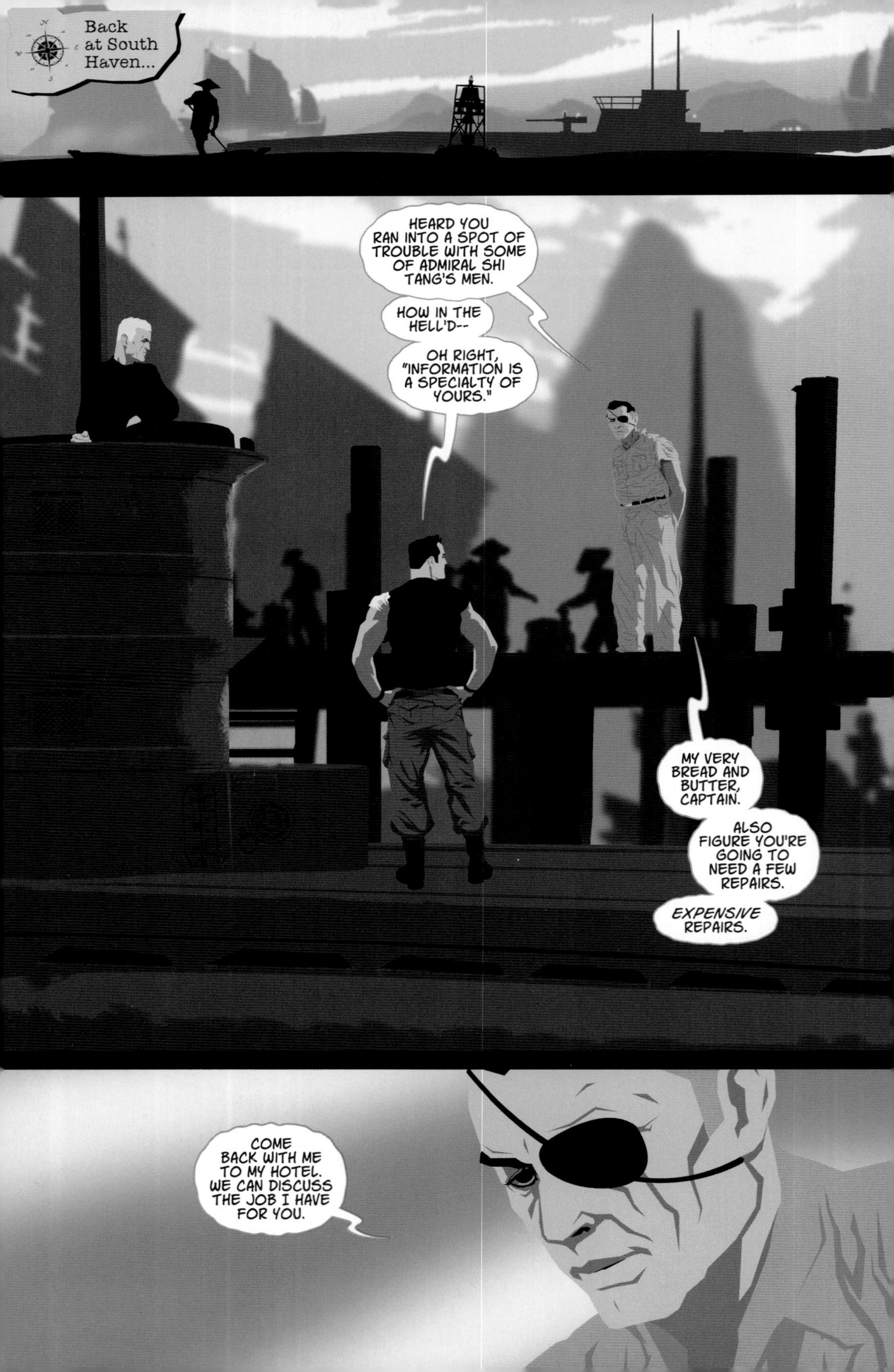
Back at South Haven...
HEARD YOU RAN INTO A SPOT OF TROUBLE WITH SOME OF ADMIRAL SHI TANG'S MEN.
HOW IN THE HELL'D--
OH RIGHT, "INFORMATION IS A SPECIALTY OF YOURS."
MY VERY BREAD AND BUTTER, CAPTAIN.
ALSO FIGURE YOU'RE GOING TO NEED A FEW REPAIRS.
EXPENSIVE REPAIRS.
COME BACK WITH ME TO MY HOTEL. WE CAN DISCUSS THE JOB I HAVE FOR YOU.

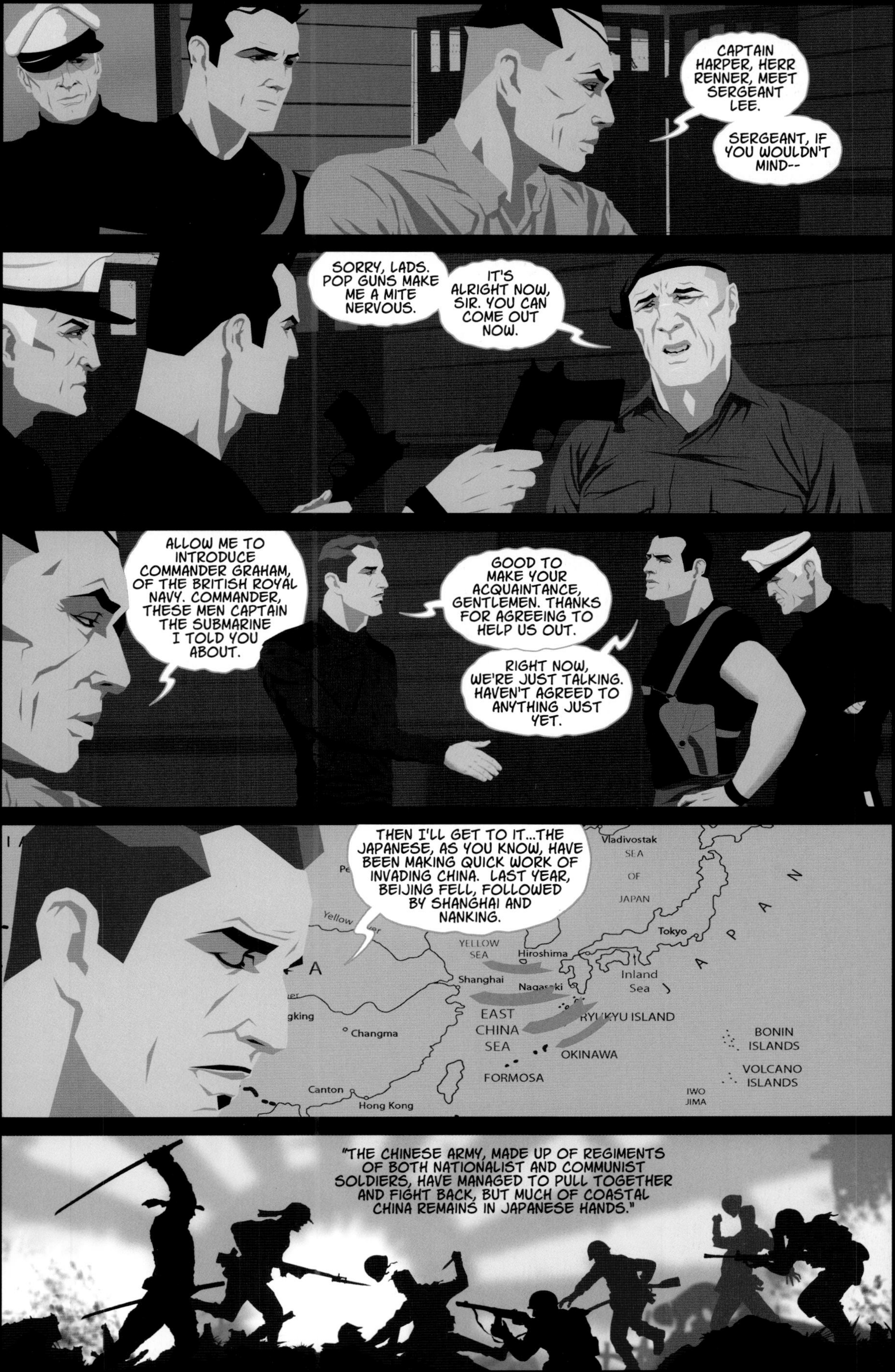
CAPTAIN HARPER, HERR RENNER, MEET SERGEANT LEE.
SERGEANT, IF YOU WOULDN'T MIND--
SORRY, LADS. POP GUNS MAKE ME A MITE NERVOUS.
IT'S ALRIGHT NOW, SIR. YOU CAN COME OUT NOW.
ALLOW ME TO INTRODUCE COMMANDER GRAHAM, OF THE BRITISH ROYAL NAVY. COMMANDER, THESE MEN CAPTAIN THE SUBMARINE I TOLD YOU ABOUT.
GOOD TO MAKE YOUR ACQUAINTANCE, GENTLEMEN. THANKS FOR AGREEING TO HELP US OUT.
RIGHT NOW, WE'RE JUST TALKING. HAVEN'T AGREED TO ANYTHING JUST YET.
THEN I'LL GET TO IT...THE JAPANESE, AS YOU KNOW, HAVE BEEN MAKING QUICK WORK OF INVADING CHINA. LAST YEAR, BEIJING FELL, FOLLOWED BY SHANGHAI AND NANKING.
Vladivostak
SEA OF JAPAN
J A P A N
Tokyo
YELLOW SEA
Hiroshima
Shanghai
Nagasaki
Inland Sea
EAST CHINA SEA
RYUKYU ISLAND
Changma
BONIN ISLANDS
OKINAWA
VOLCANO ISLANDS
FORMOSA
Canton
Hong Kong
IWO JIMA
"THE CHINESE ARMY, MADE UP OF REGIMENTS OF BOTH NATIONALIST AND COMMUNIST SOLDIERS, HAVE MANAGED TO PULL TOGETHER AND FIGHT BACK, BUT MUCH OF COASTAL CHINA REMAINS IN JAPANESE HANDS."

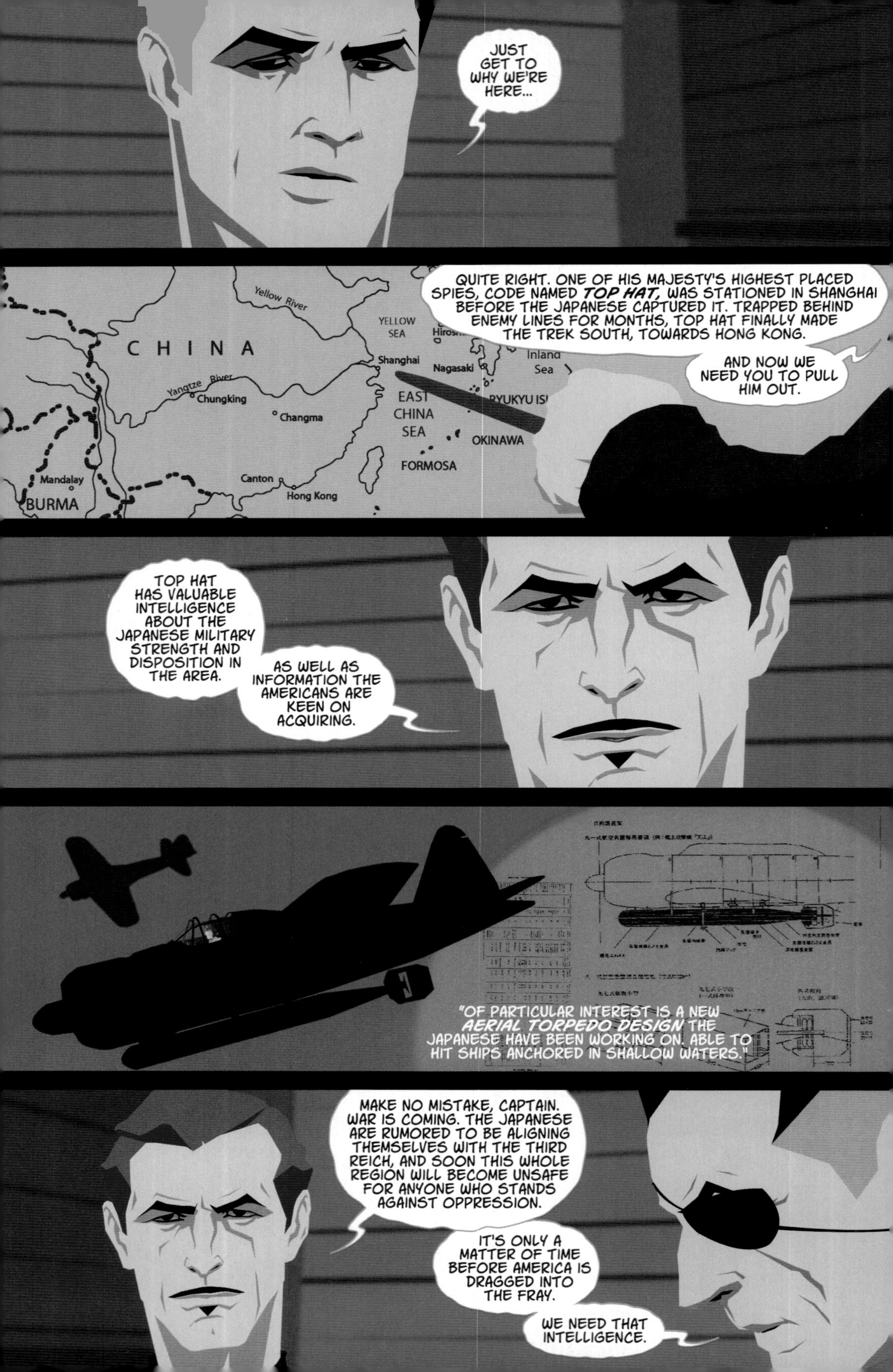
JUST GET TO WHY WE'RE HERE...
QUITE RIGHT. ONE OF HIS MAJESTY'S HIGHEST PLACED SPIES, CODE NAMED *TOP HAT,* WAS STATIONED IN SHANGHAI BEFORE THE JAPANESE CAPTURED IT. TRAPPED BEHIND ENEMY LINES FOR MONTHS, TOP HAT FINALLY MADE THE TREK SOUTH, TOWARDS HONG KONG.
AND NOW WE NEED YOU TO PULL HIM OUT.
Yellow River
YELLOW SEA
CHINA
Shanghai
Nagasaki
Inland Sea
Yangtze River
Chungking
Changma
EAST CHINA SEA
OKINAWA
FORMOSA
Mandalay
BURMA
Canton
Hong Kong
TOP HAT HAS VALUABLE INTELLIGENCE ABOUT THE JAPANESE MILITARY STRENGTH AND DISPOSITION IN THE AREA.
AS WELL AS INFORMATION THE AMERICANS ARE KEEN ON ACQUIRING.
"OF PARTICULAR INTEREST IS A NEW *AERIAL TORPEDO DESIGN* THE JAPANESE HAVE BEEN WORKING ON. ABLE TO HIT SHIPS ANCHORED IN SHALLOW WATERS."
MAKE NO MISTAKE, CAPTAIN. WAR IS COMING. THE JAPANESE ARE RUMORED TO BE ALIGNING THEMSELVES WITH THE THIRD REICH, AND SOON THIS WHOLE REGION WILL BECOME UNSAFE FOR ANYONE WHO STANDS AGAINST OPPRESSION.
IT'S ONLY A MATTER OF TIME BEFORE AMERICA IS DRAGGED INTO THE FRAY.
WE NEED THAT INTELLIGENCE.

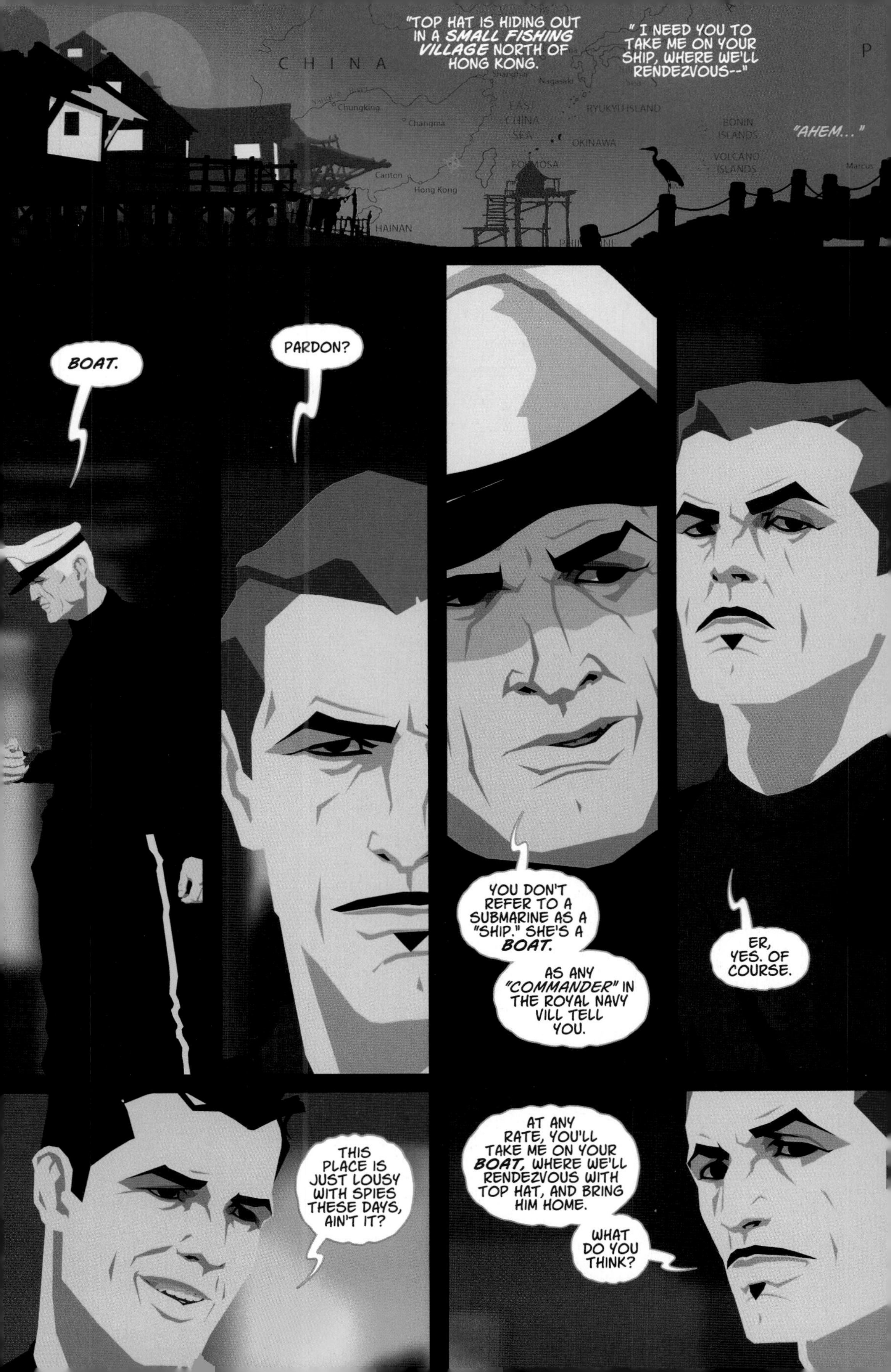
"TOP HAT IS HIDING OUT IN A *SMALL FISHING VILLAGE* NORTH OF HONG KONG.
" I NEED YOU TO TAKE ME ON YOUR SHIP, WHERE WE'LL RENDEZVOUS--"
"AHEM..."
CHINA
Chungking
Canton
Hong Kong
HAINAN
EAST CHINA SEA
RYUKYU ISLAND
OKINAWA
FORMOSA
BONIN ISLANDS
VOLCANO ISLANDS
Marcus
BOAT.
PARDON?
YOU DON'T REFER TO A SUBMARINE AS A "SHIP." SHE'S A *BOAT*.
AS ANY *"COMMANDER"* IN THE ROYAL NAVY VILL TELL YOU.
ER, YES. OF COURSE.
THIS PLACE IS JUST LOUSY WITH SPIES THESE DAYS, AIN'T IT?
AT ANY RATE, YOU'LL TAKE ME ON YOUR *BOAT,* WHERE WE'LL RENDEZVOUS WITH TOP HAT, AND BRING HIM HOME.
WHAT DO YOU THINK?

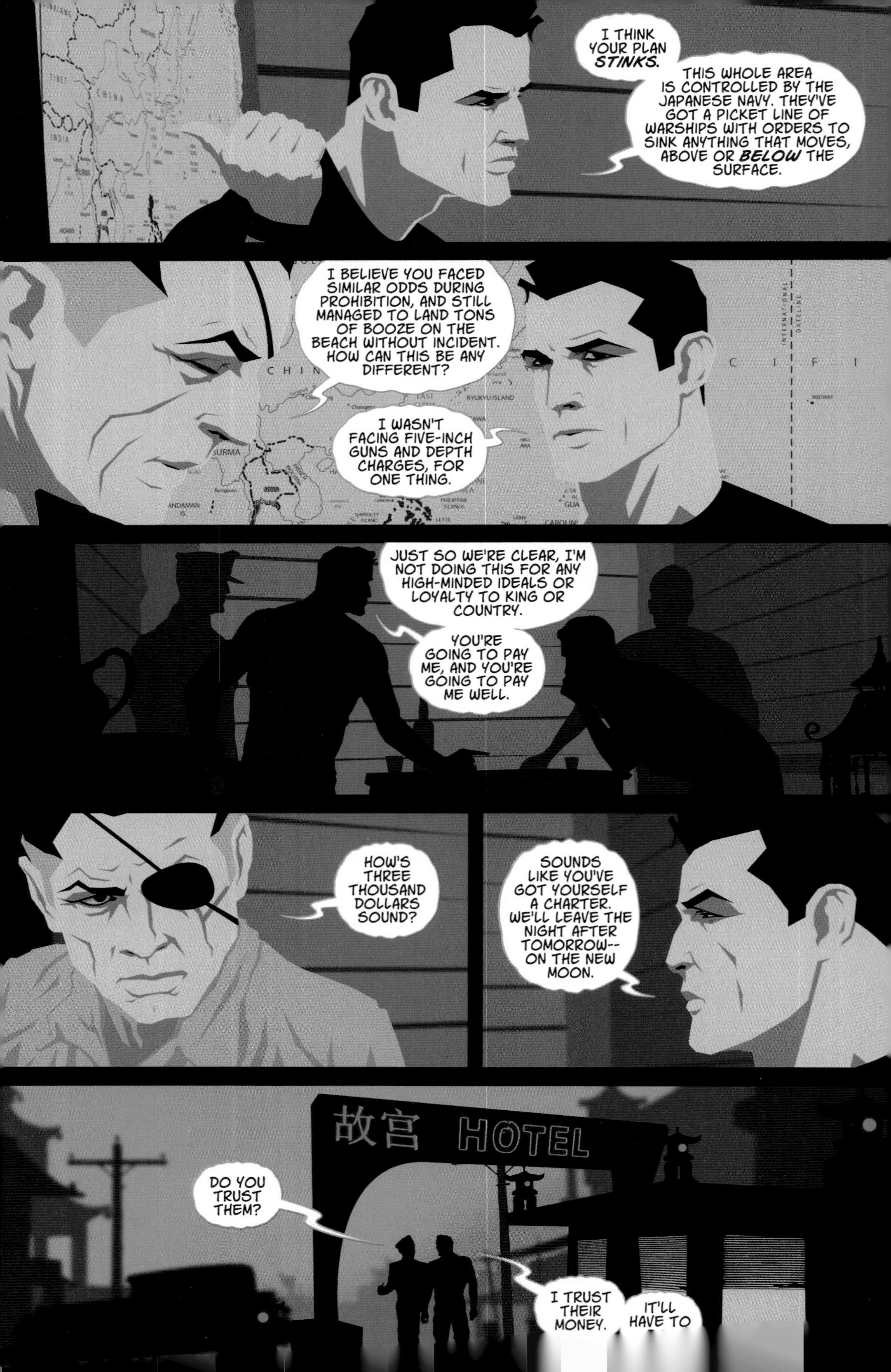
I THINK YOUR PLAN STINKS.
THIS WHOLE AREA IS CONTROLLED BY THE JAPANESE NAVY. THEY'VE GOT A PICKET LINE OF WARSHIPS WITH ORDERS TO SINK ANYTHING THAT MOVES, ABOVE OR BELOW THE SURFACE.
I BELIEVE YOU FACED SIMILAR ODDS DURING PROHIBITION, AND STILL MANAGED TO LAND TONS OF BOOZE ON THE BEACH WITHOUT INCIDENT. HOW CAN THIS BE ANY DIFFERENT?
I WASN'T FACING FIVE-INCH GUNS AND DEPTH CHARGES, FOR ONE THING.
JUST SO WE'RE CLEAR, I'M NOT DOING THIS FOR ANY HIGH-MINDED IDEALS OR LOYALTY TO KING OR COUNTRY.
YOU'RE GOING TO PAY ME, AND YOU'RE GOING TO PAY ME WELL.
HOW'S THREE THOUSAND DOLLARS SOUND?
SOUNDS LIKE YOU'VE GOT YOURSELF A CHARTER. WE'LL LEAVE THE NIGHT AFTER TOMORROW-- ON THE NEW MOON.
故宮 HOTEL
DO YOU TRUST THEM?
I TRUST THEIR MONEY.
IT'LL HAVE TO

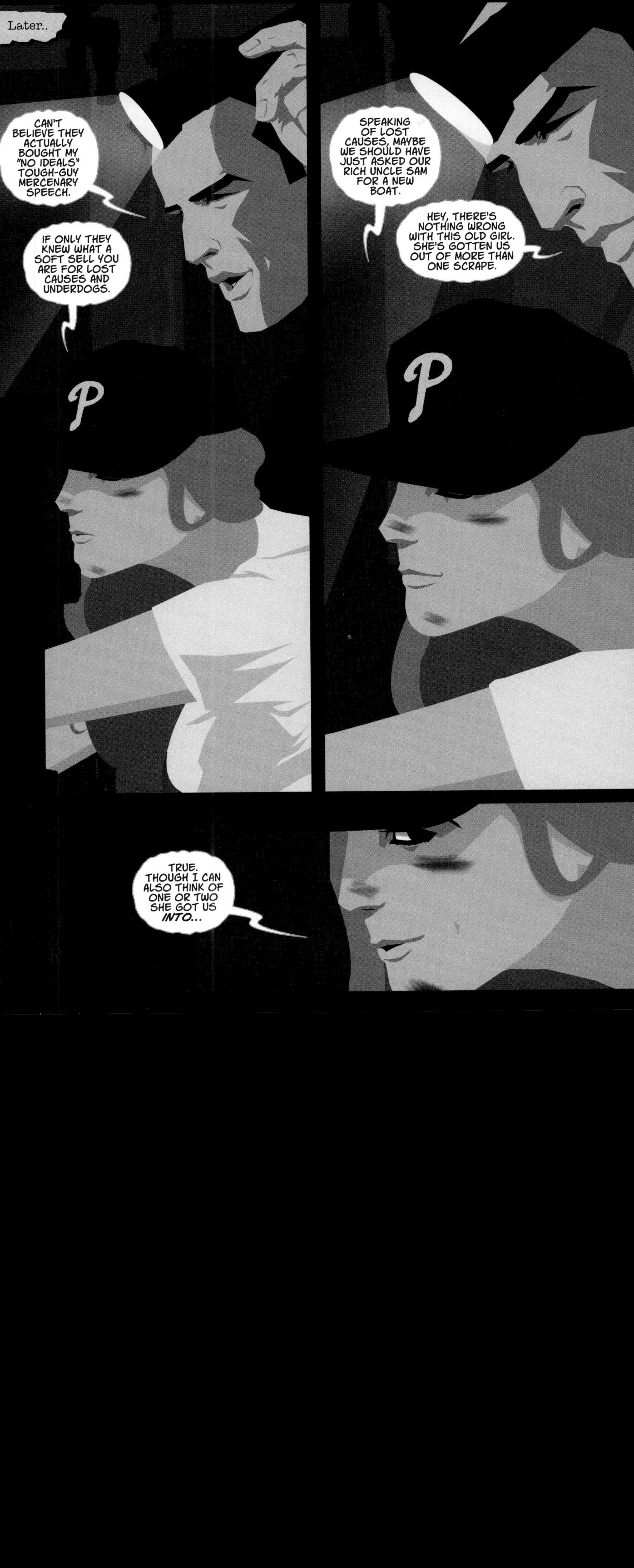
Later..
CAN'T BELIEVE THEY ACTUALLY BOUGHT MY "NO IDEALS" TOUGH-GUY MERCENARY SPEECH.
IF ONLY THEY KNEW WHAT A SOFT SELL YOU ARE FOR LOST CAUSES AND UNDERDOGS.
SPEAKING OF LOST CAUSES, MAYBE WE SHOULD HAVE JUST ASKED OUR RICH UNCLE SAM FOR A NEW BOAT.
HEY, THERE'S NOTHING WRONG WITH THIS OLD GIRL. SHE'S GOTTEN US OUT OF MORE THAN ONE SCRAPE.
TRUE. THOUGH I CAN ALSO THINK OF ONE OR TWO SHE GOT US *INTO*...

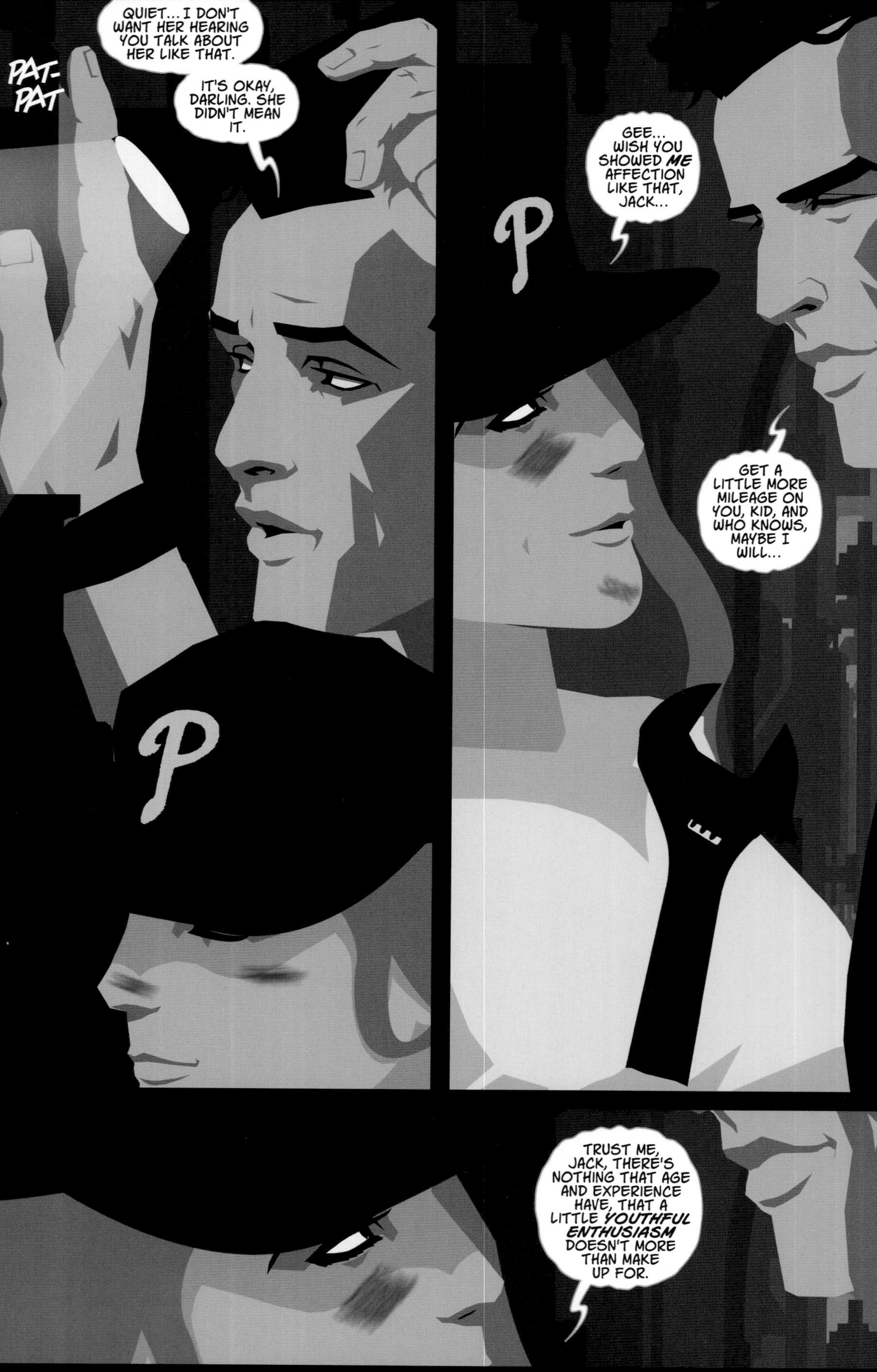
PAT-PAT
QUIET... I DON'T WANT HER HEARING YOU TALK ABOUT HER LIKE THAT.
IT'S OKAY, DARLING. SHE DIDN'T MEAN IT.
GEE... WISH YOU SHOWED ME AFFECTION LIKE THAT, JACK...
GET A LITTLE MORE MILEAGE ON YOU, KID, AND WHO KNOWS, MAYBE I WILL...
TRUST ME, JACK, THERE'S NOTHING THAT AGE AND EXPERIENCE HAVE, THAT A LITTLE YOUTHFUL ENTHUSIASM DOESN'T MORE THAN MAKE UP FOR.

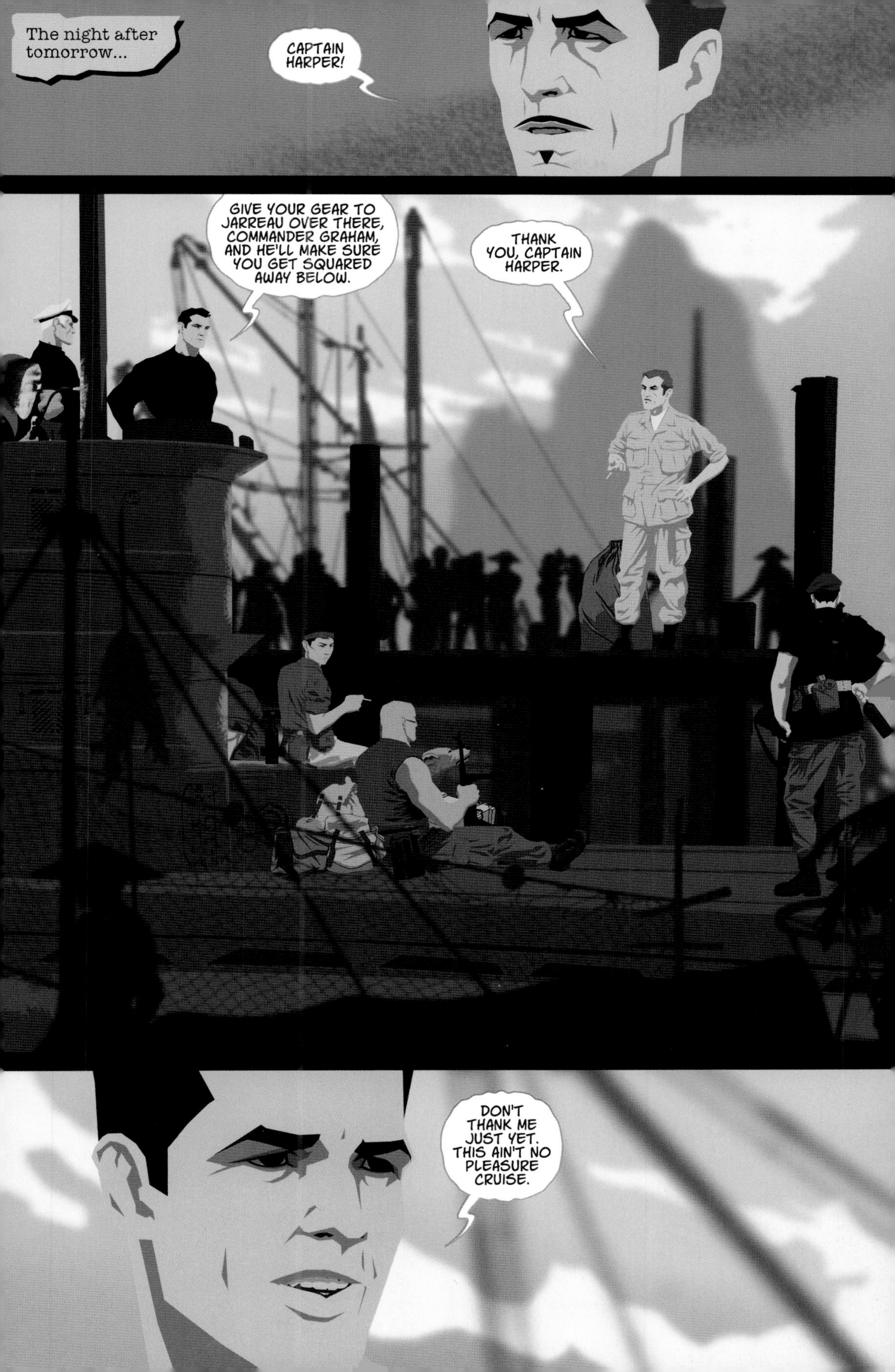
The night after tomorrow...
CAPTAIN HARPER!
GIVE YOUR GEAR TO JARREAU OVER THERE, COMMANDER GRAHAM, AND HE'LL MAKE SURE YOU GET SQUARED AWAY BELOW.
THANK YOU, CAPTAIN HARPER.
DON'T THANK ME JUST YET. THIS AIN'T NO PLEASURE CRUISE.

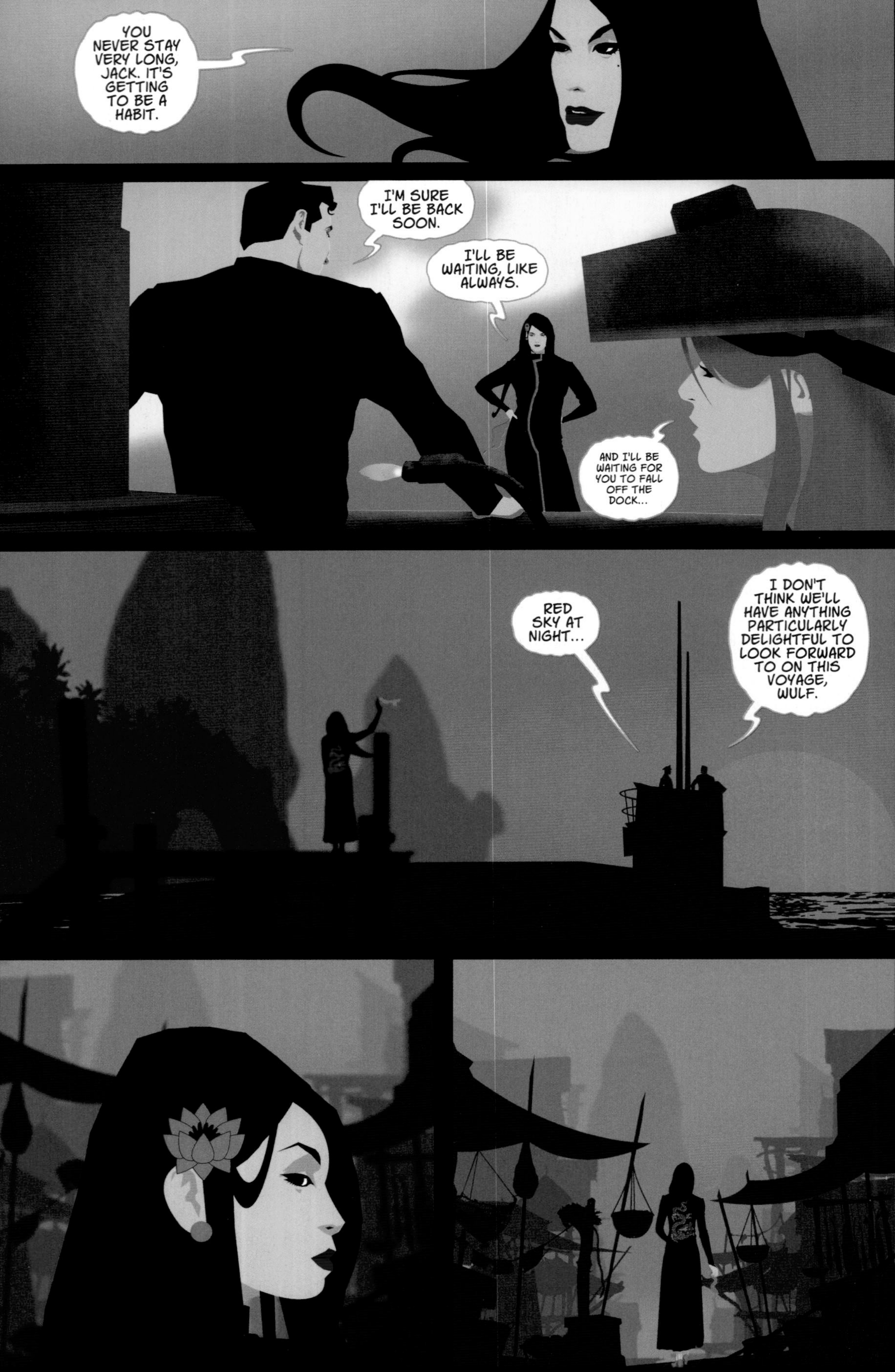
YOU NEVER STAY VERY LONG, JACK. IT'S GETTING TO BE A HABIT.
I'M SURE I'LL BE BACK SOON.
I'LL BE WAITING, LIKE ALWAYS.
AND I'LL BE WAITING FOR YOU TO FALL OFF THE DOCK...
RED SKY AT NIGHT...
I DON'T THINK WE'LL HAVE ANYTHING PARTICULARLY DELIGHTFUL TO LOOK FORWARD TO ON THIS VOYAGE, WULF.

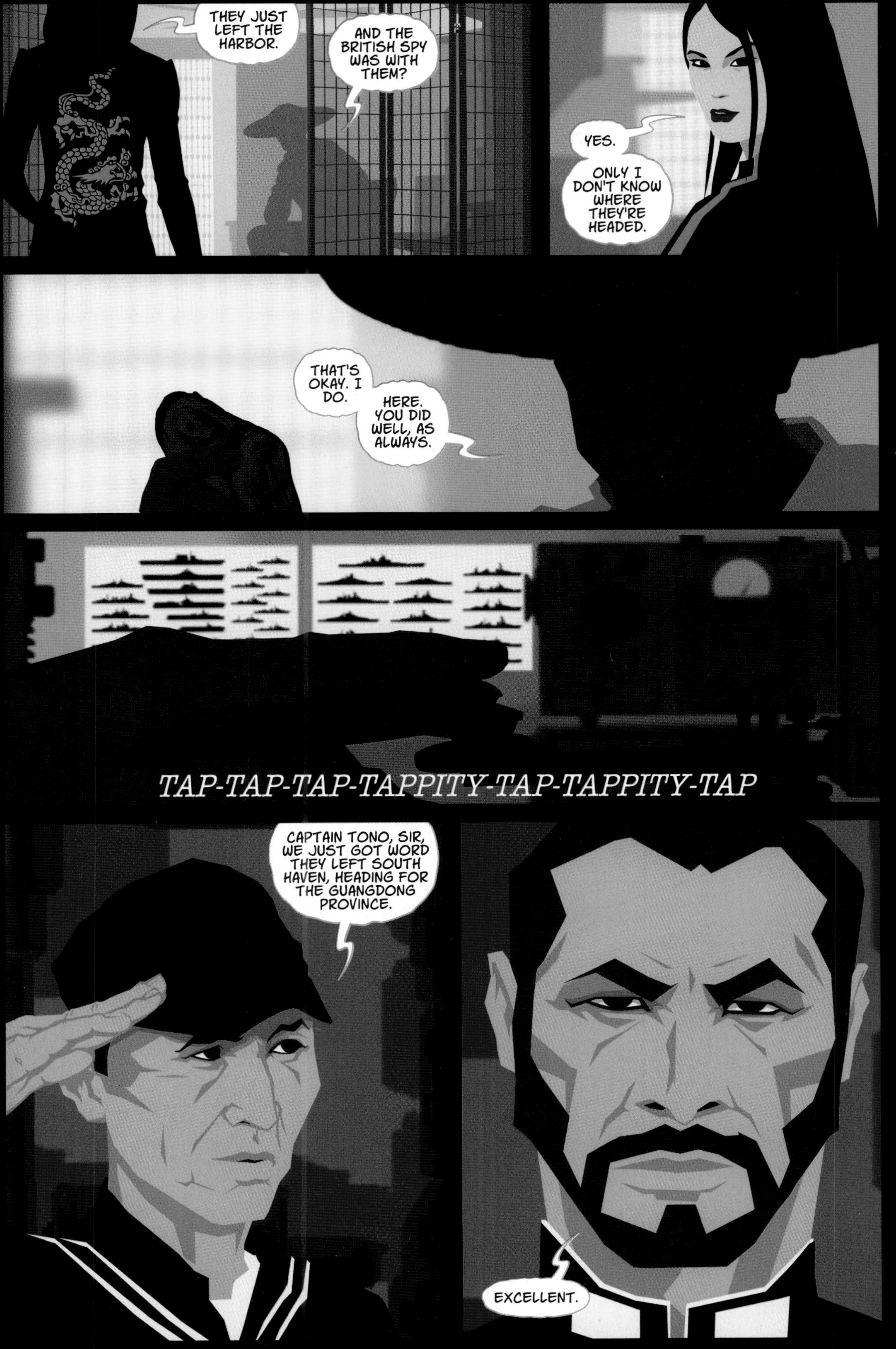
THEY JUST LEFT THE HARBOR.
AND THE BRITISH SPY WAS WITH THEM?
YES.
ONLY I DON'T KNOW WHERE THEY'RE HEADED.
THAT'S OKAY. I DO.
HERE. YOU DID WELL, AS ALWAYS.
TAP-TAP-TAP-TAPPITY-TAP-TAPPITY-TAP
CAPTAIN TONO, SIR, WE JUST GOT WORD THEY LEFT SOUTH HAVEN, HEADING FOR THE GUANGDONG PROVINCE.
EXCELLENT.

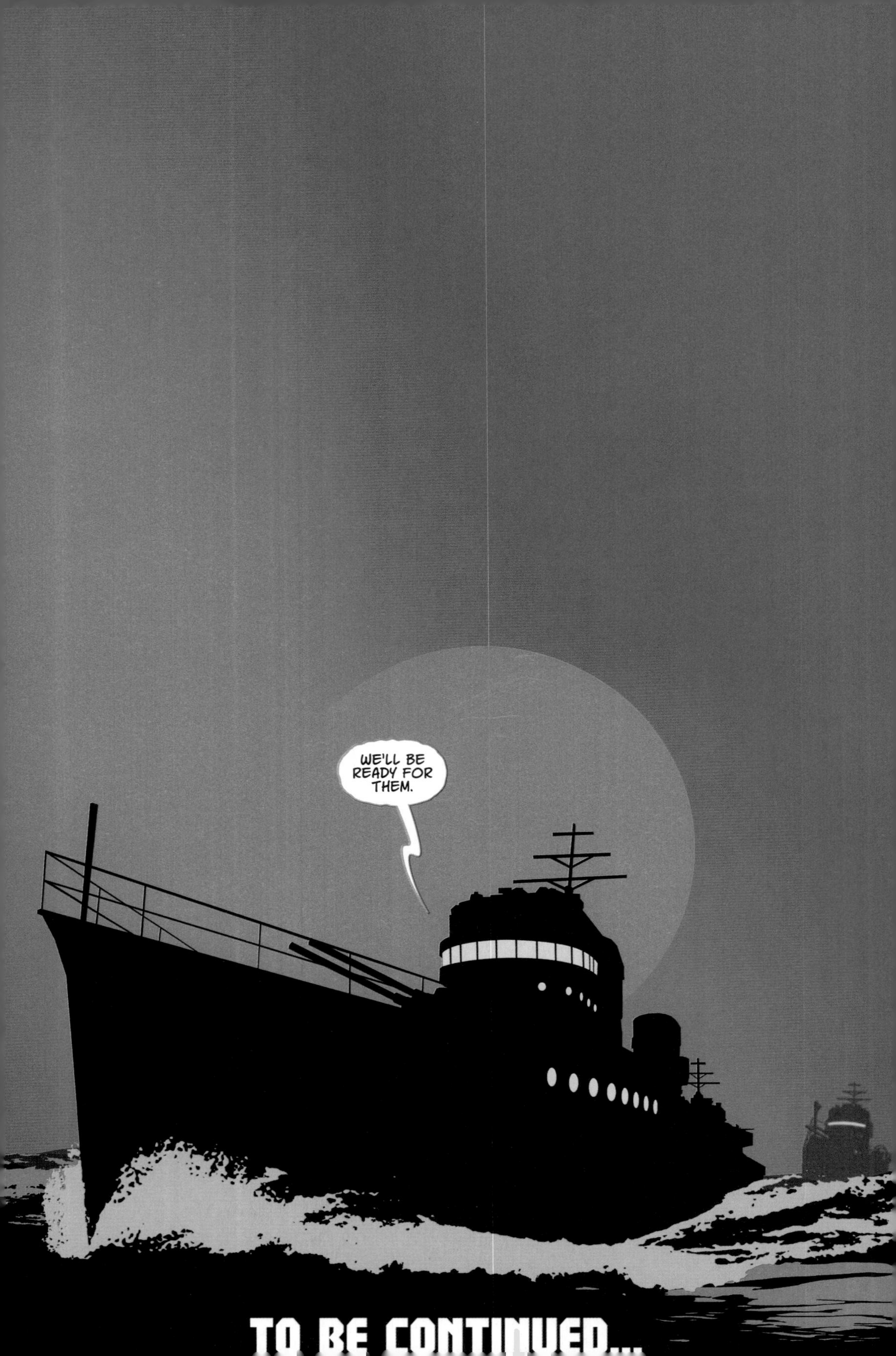
WE'LL BE READY FOR THEM.
TO BE CONTINUED...

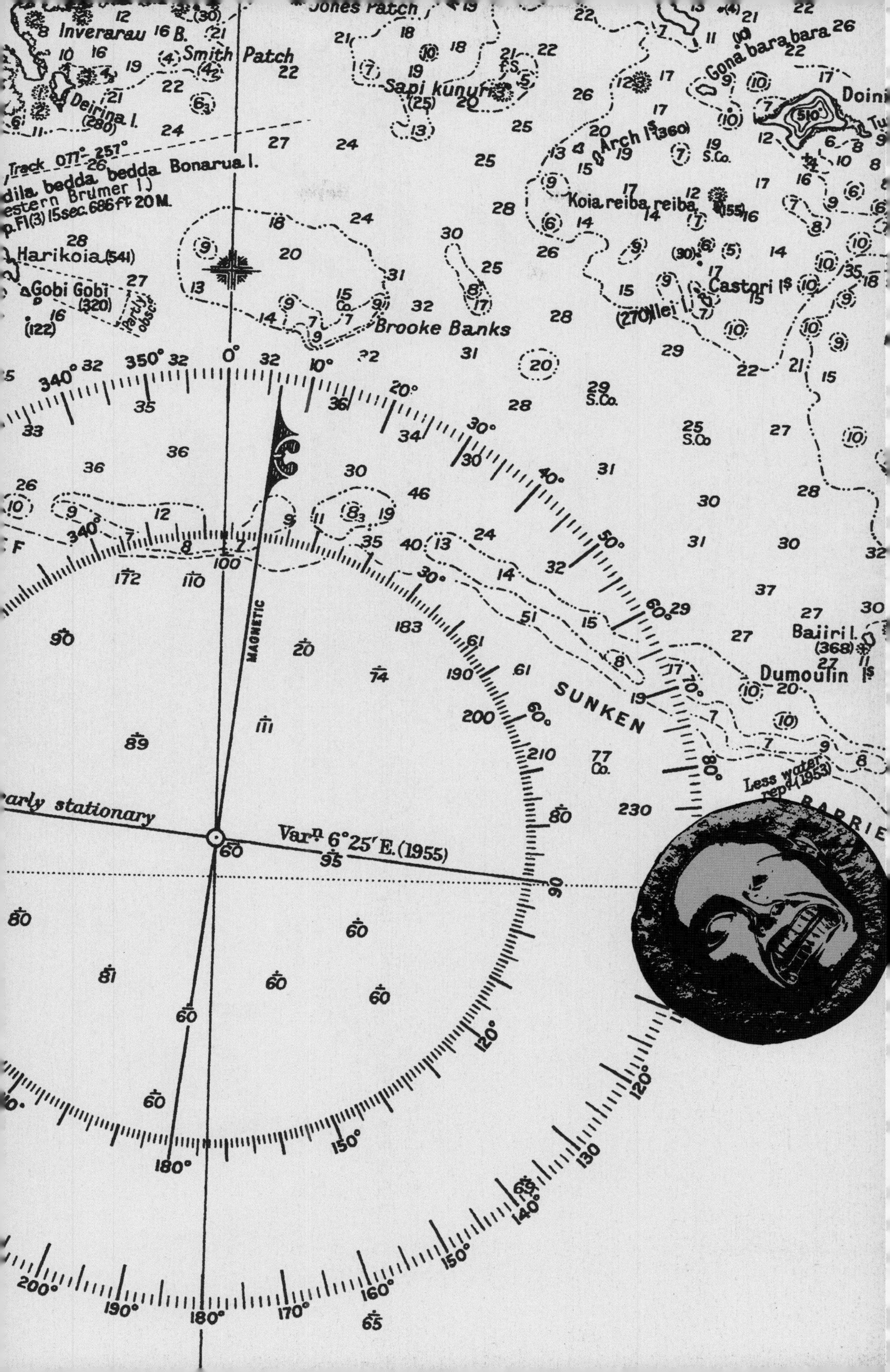
Jones Patch
Inverarau
Smith Patch
Deirina I.
(280)
Track 077°-257°
dila bedda bedda Bonarua I.
estern Brumer I.)
p.Fl(3) 15sec. 686 ft 20 M.
Harikoia (541)
Gobi Gobi (320)
Partly obscd
Sapi kunuri
Brooke Banks
Arch Is (360)
Koia reiba reiba
Gona bara bara
Doini
Castori Is
(270) Ilei I.
MAGNETIC
SUNKEN
Baiiri I. (368)
Dumoulin Is
Less water repd (1953)
BARRIE
arly stationary
Varn 6°25′ E. (1955)

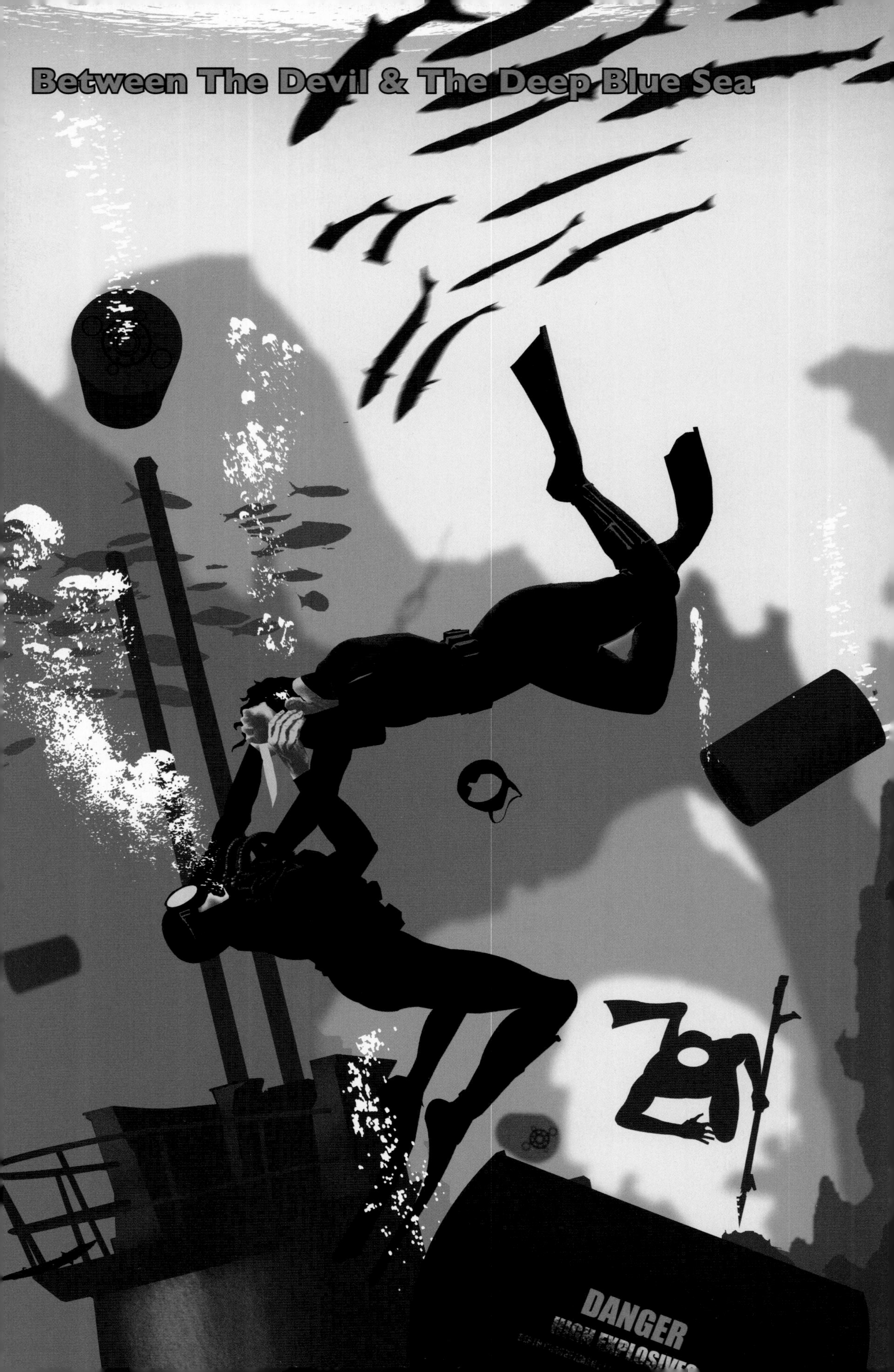
Between The Devil & The Deep Blue Sea
DANGER

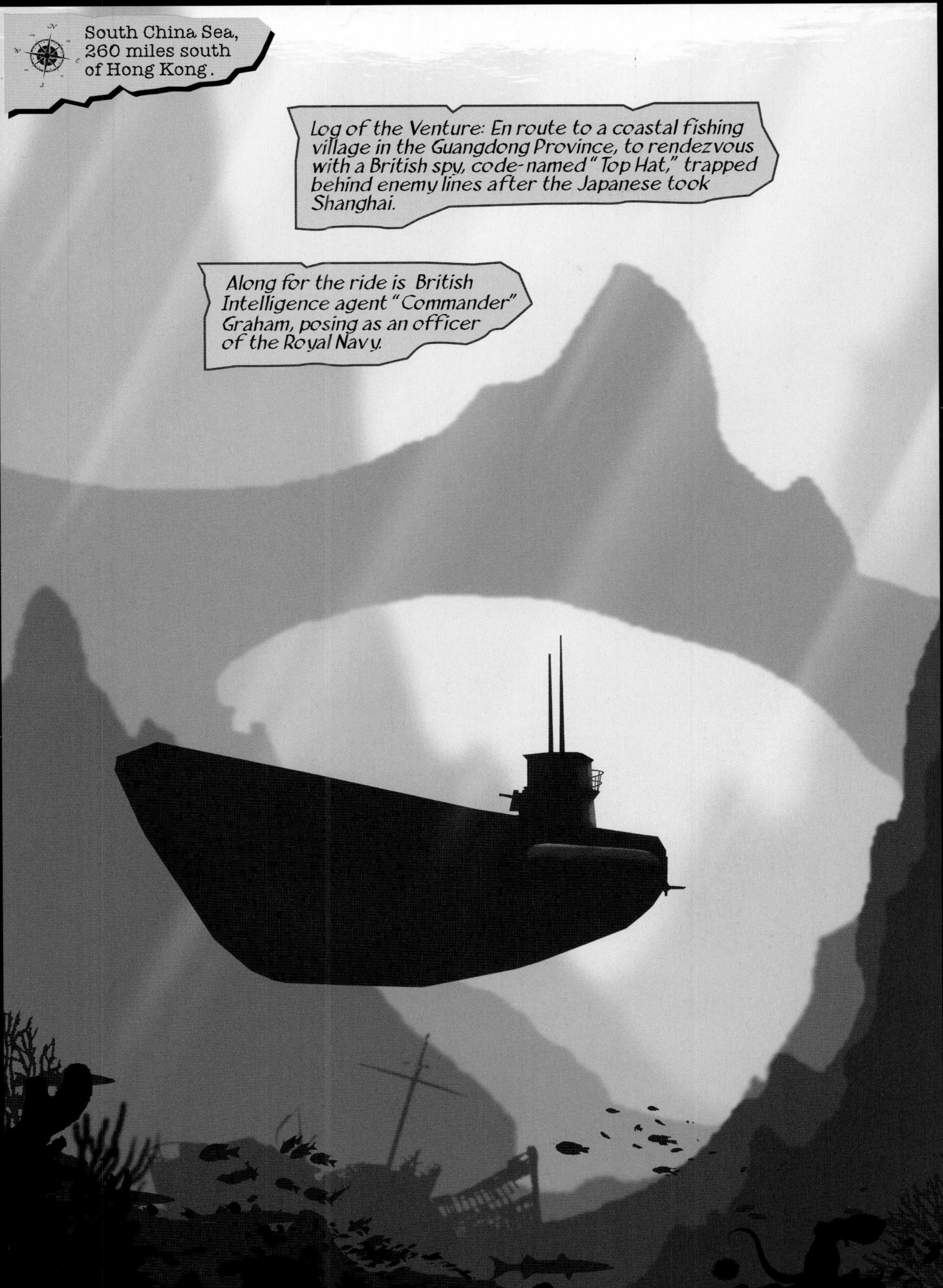
South China Sea, 260 miles south of Hong Kong.
Log of the Venture: En route to a coastal fishing village in the Guangdong Province, to rendezvous with a British spy, code-named "Top Hat," trapped behind enemy lines after the Japanese took Shanghai.
Along for the ride is British Intelligence agent "Commander" Graham, posing as an officer of the Royal Navy.

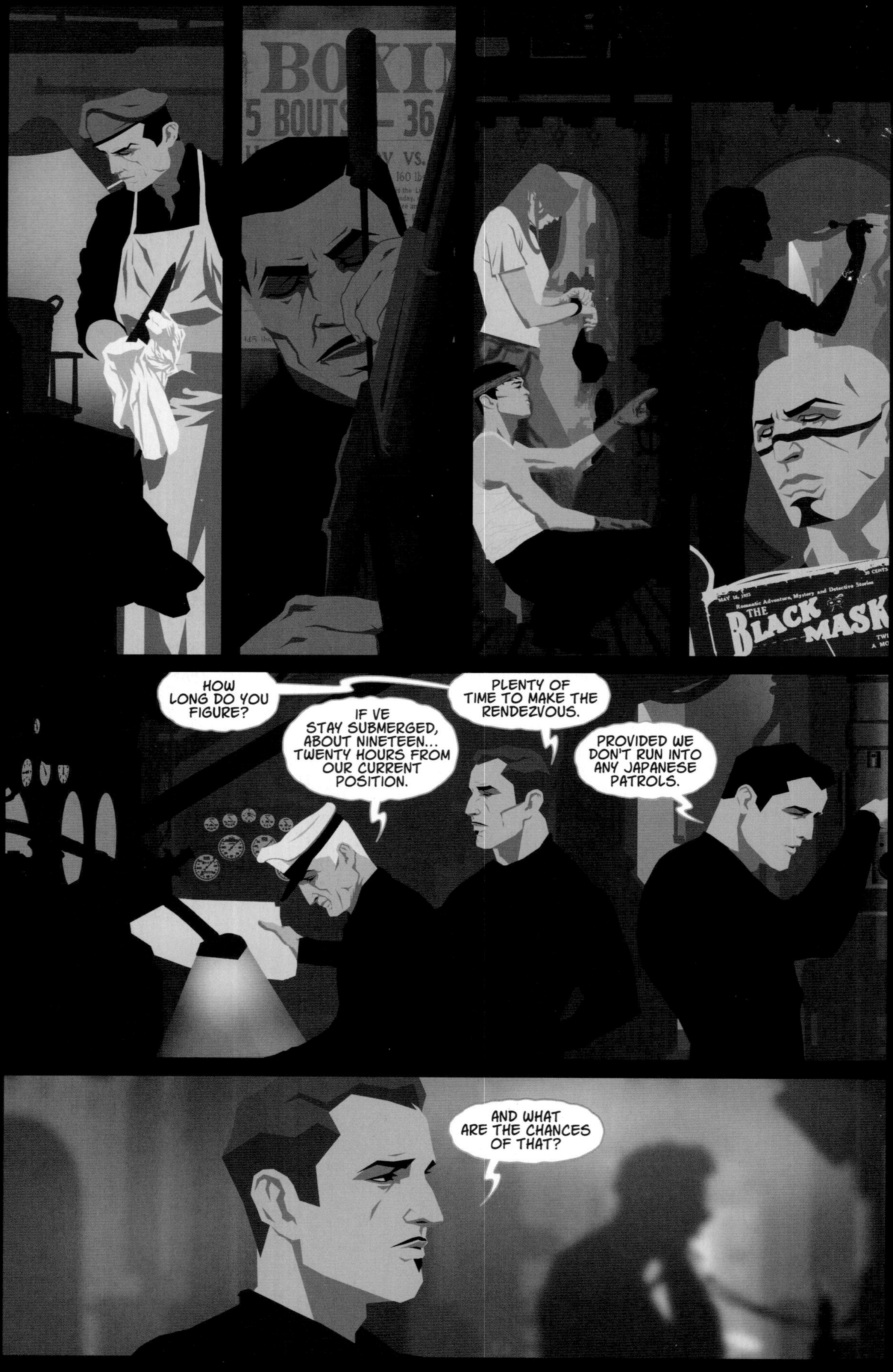
Romantic Adventure, Mystery and Detective Stories
THE BLACK MASK
HOW LONG DO YOU FIGURE?
IF VE STAY SUBMERGED, ABOUT NINETEEN... TWENTY HOURS FROM OUR CURRENT POSITION.
PLENTY OF TIME TO MAKE THE RENDEZVOUS.
PROVIDED WE DON'T RUN INTO ANY JAPANESE PATROLS.
AND WHAT ARE THE CHANCES OF THAT?

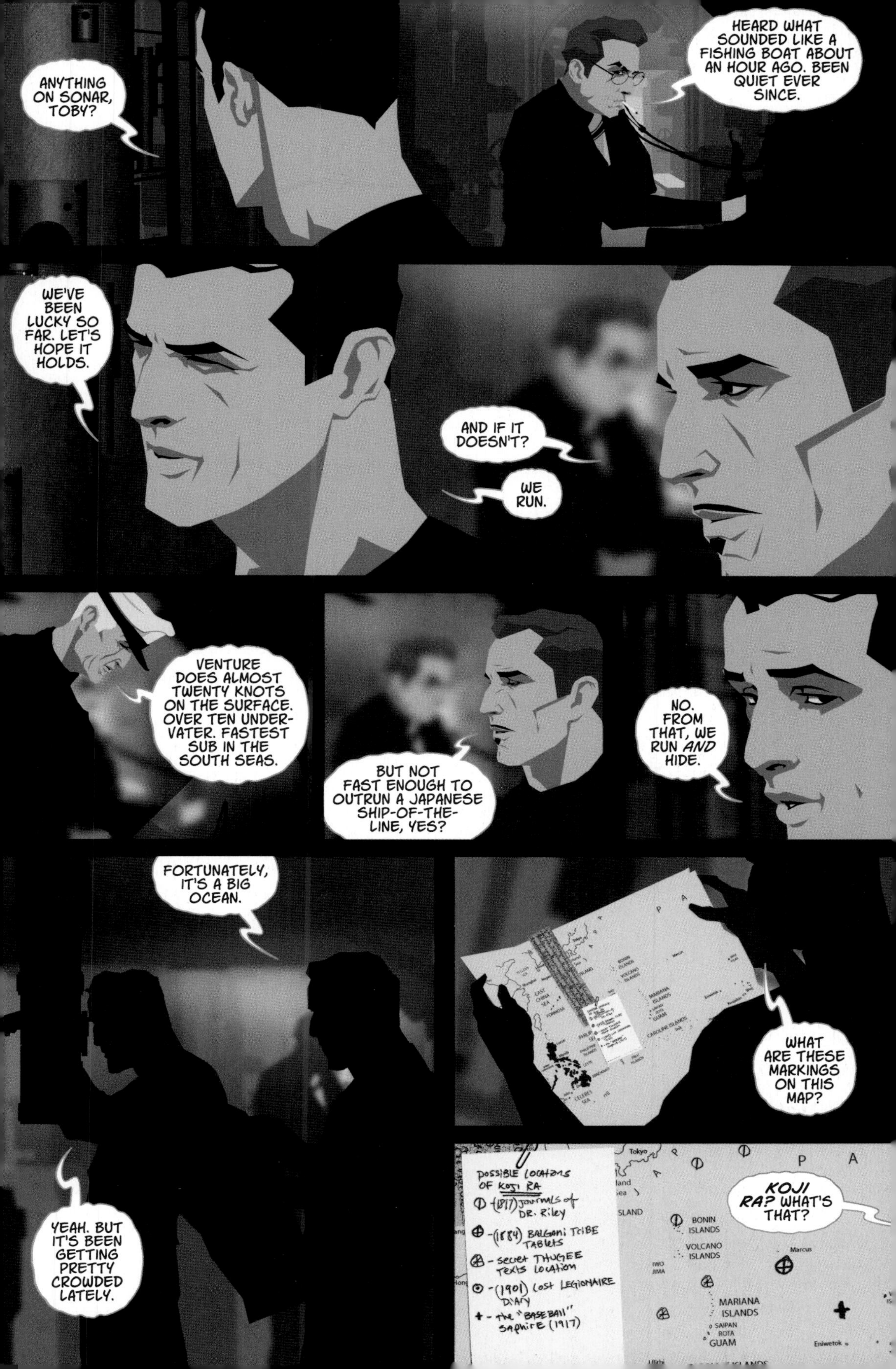
ANYTHING ON SONAR, TOBY?
HEARD WHAT SOUNDED LIKE A FISHING BOAT ABOUT AN HOUR AGO. BEEN QUIET EVER SINCE.
WE'VE BEEN LUCKY SO FAR. LET'S HOPE IT HOLDS.
AND IF IT DOESN'T?
WE RUN.
VENTURE DOES ALMOST TWENTY KNOTS ON THE SURFACE. OVER TEN UNDER-VATER. FASTEST SUB IN THE SOUTH SEAS.
BUT NOT FAST ENOUGH TO OUTRUN A JAPANESE SHIP-OF-THE-LINE, YES?
NO. FROM THAT, WE RUN *AND* HIDE.
FORTUNATELY, IT'S A BIG OCEAN.
YEAH. BUT IT'S BEEN GETTING PRETTY CROWDED LATELY.
WHAT ARE THESE MARKINGS ON THIS MAP?
Possible locations of Koji Ra
-(1817) journals of Dr. Riley
-(1884) Balgani Tribe Tablets
- secret THUGEE Texts location
-(1901) Lost LEGIONAIRE Diary
- the "BASEBALL" Saphire (1917)
Tokyo
BONIN ISLANDS
VOLCANO ISLANDS
Marcus
MARIANA ISLANDS
SAIPAN
ROTA
GUAM
Eniwetok
KOJI RA? WHAT'S THAT?

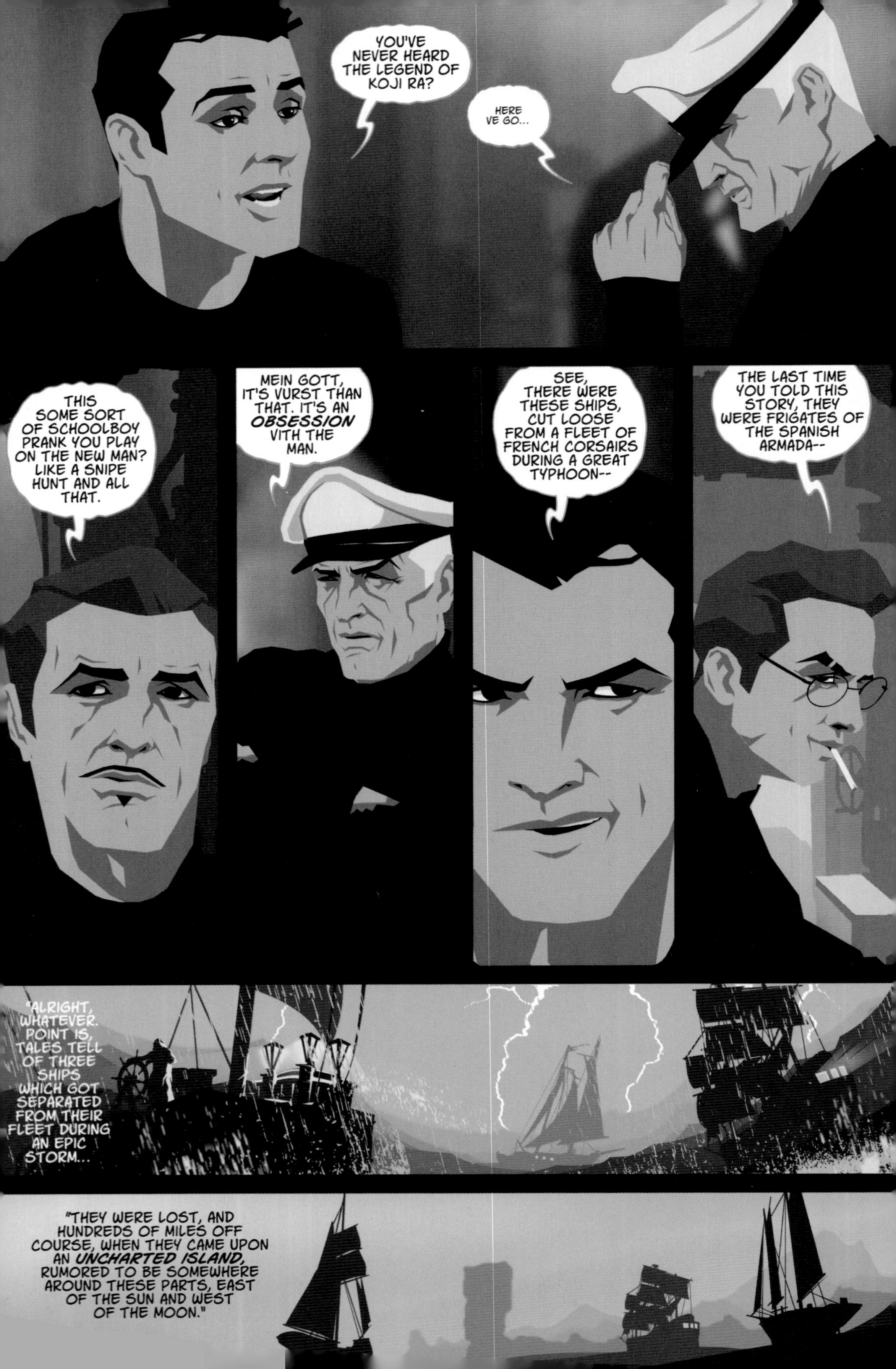
YOU'VE NEVER HEARD THE LEGEND OF KOJI RA?
HERE VE GO...
THIS SOME SORT OF SCHOOLBOY PRANK YOU PLAY ON THE NEW MAN? LIKE A SNIPE HUNT AND ALL THAT.
MEIN GOTT, IT'S VURST THAN THAT. IT'S AN OBSESSION VITH THE MAN.
SEE, THERE WERE THESE SHIPS, CUT LOOSE FROM A FLEET OF FRENCH CORSAIRS DURING A GREAT TYPHOON--
THE LAST TIME YOU TOLD THIS STORY, THEY WERE FRIGATES OF THE SPANISH ARMADA--
"ALRIGHT, WHATEVER. POINT IS, TALES TELL OF THREE SHIPS WHICH GOT SEPARATED FROM THEIR FLEET DURING AN EPIC STORM...
"THEY WERE LOST, AND HUNDREDS OF MILES OFF COURSE, WHEN THEY CAME UPON AN UNCHARTED ISLAND, RUMORED TO BE SOMEWHERE AROUND THESE PARTS, EAST OF THE SUN AND WEST OF THE MOON."

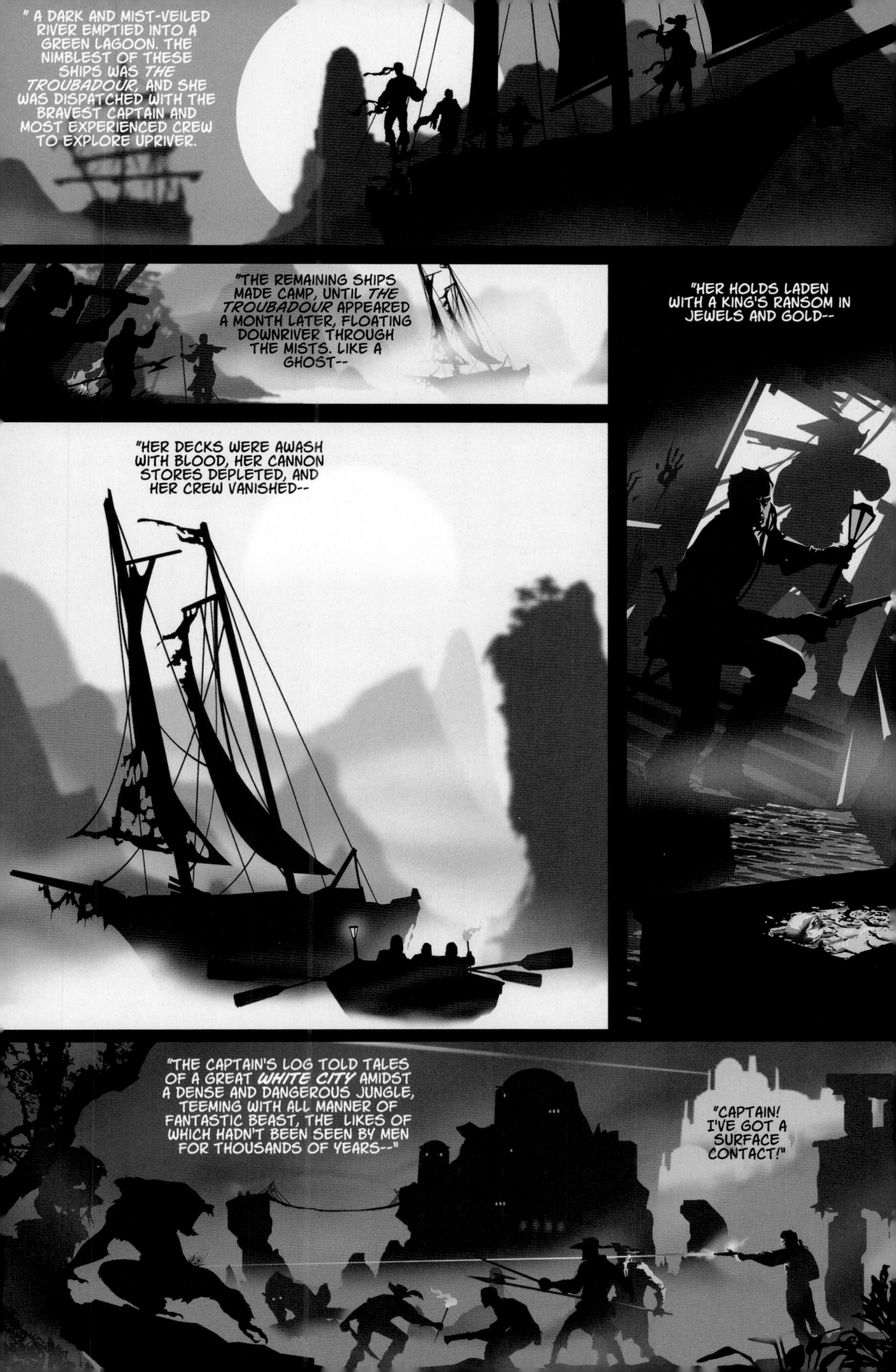
" A DARK AND MIST-VEILED RIVER EMPTIED INTO A GREEN LAGOON. THE NIMBLEST OF THESE SHIPS WAS *THE TROUBADOUR,* AND SHE WAS DISPATCHED WITH THE BRAVEST CAPTAIN AND MOST EXPERIENCED CREW TO EXPLORE UPRIVER.
"THE REMAINING SHIPS MADE CAMP, UNTIL *THE TROUBADOUR* APPEARED A MONTH LATER, FLOATING DOWNRIVER THROUGH THE MISTS. LIKE A GHOST--
"HER DECKS WERE AWASH WITH BLOOD, HER CANNON STORES DEPLETED, AND HER CREW VANISHED--
"HER HOLDS LADEN WITH A KING'S RANSOM IN JEWELS AND GOLD--
"THE CAPTAIN'S LOG TOLD TALES OF A GREAT *WHITE CITY* AMIDST A DENSE AND DANGEROUS JUNGLE, TEEMING WITH ALL MANNER OF FANTASTIC BEAST, THE LIKES OF WHICH HADN'T BEEN SEEN BY MEN FOR THOUSANDS OF YEARS--"
"CAPTAIN! I'VE GOT A SURFACE CONTACT!"

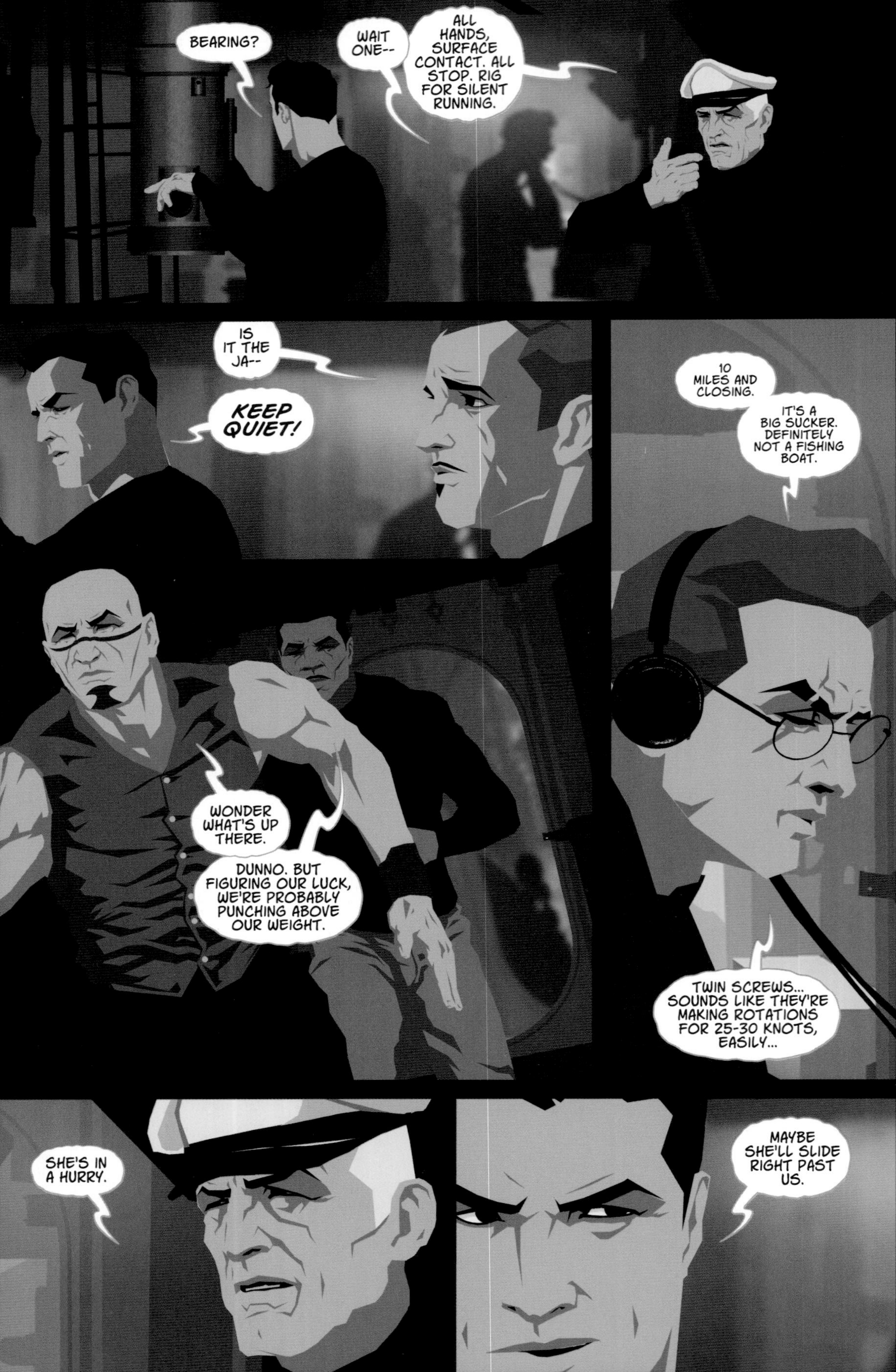
BEARING?
WAIT ONE--
ALL HANDS, SURFACE CONTACT. ALL STOP. RIG FOR SILENT RUNNING.
IS IT THE JA--
KEEP QUIET!
10 MILES AND CLOSING.
IT'S A BIG SUCKER. DEFINITELY NOT A FISHING BOAT.
WONDER WHAT'S UP THERE.
DUNNO. BUT FIGURING OUR LUCK, WE'RE PROBABLY PUNCHING ABOVE OUR WEIGHT.
TWIN SCREWS... SOUNDS LIKE THEY'RE MAKING ROTATIONS FOR 25-30 KNOTS, EASILY...
SHE'S IN A HURRY.
MAYBE SHE'LL SLIDE RIGHT PAST US.

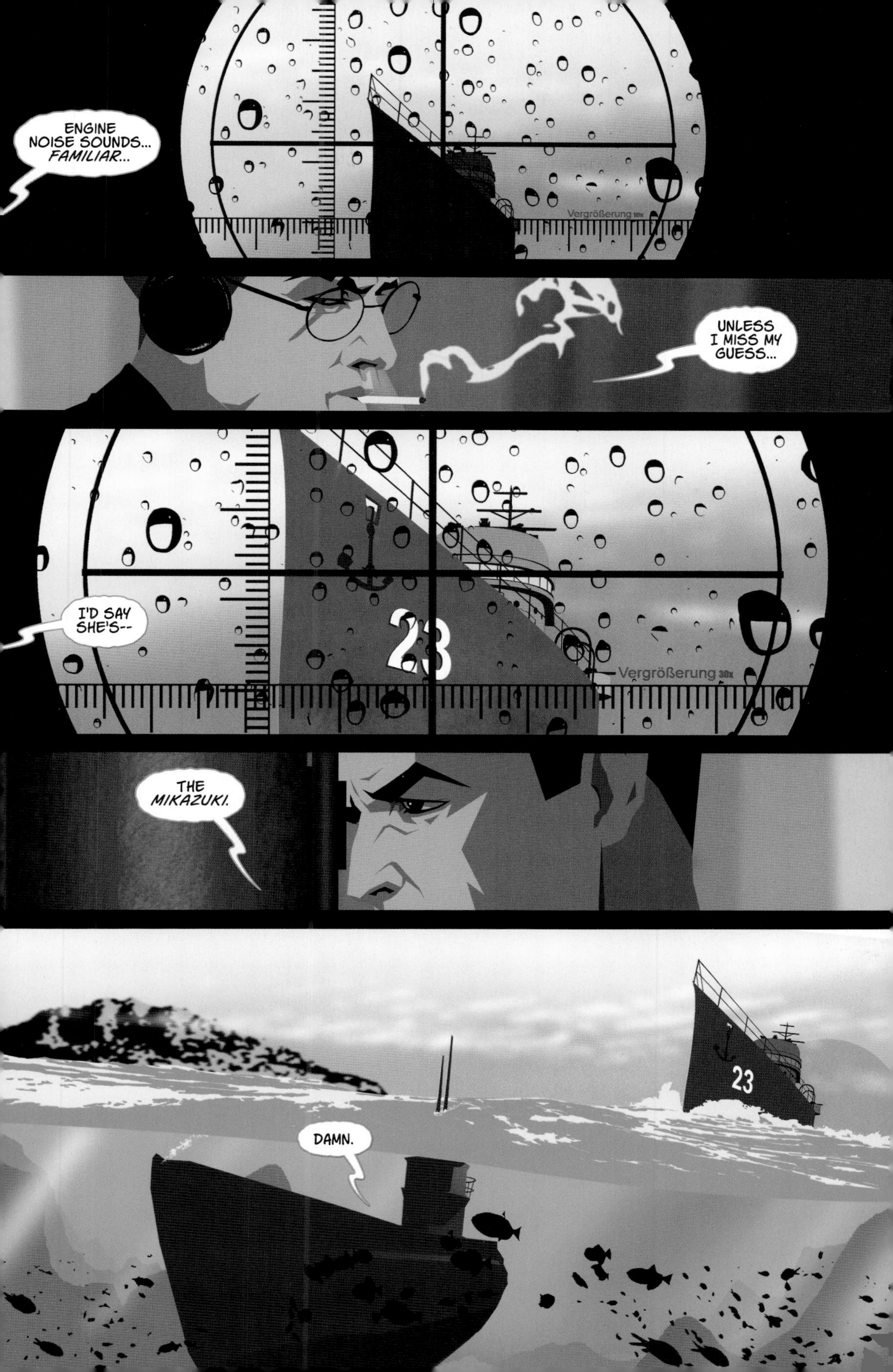
ENGINE NOISE SOUNDS... FAMILIAR...
Vergrößerung 10x
UNLESS I MISS MY GUESS...
I'D SAY SHE'S--
23
Vergrößerung 30x
THE MIKAZUKI.
23
DAMN.

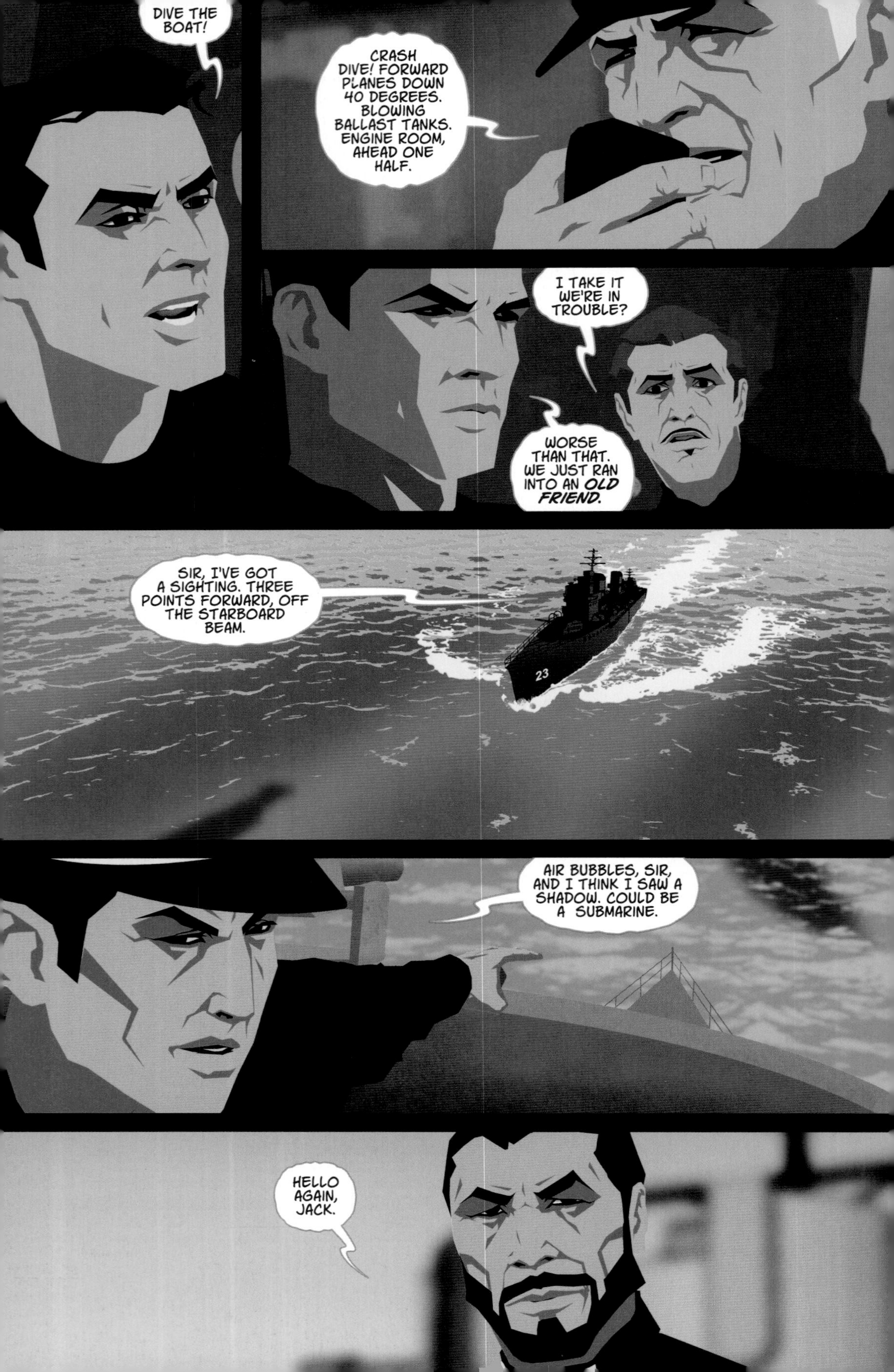
DIVE THE BOAT!
CRASH DIVE! FORWARD PLANES DOWN 40 DEGREES. BLOWING BALLAST TANKS. ENGINE ROOM, AHEAD ONE HALF.
I TAKE IT WE'RE IN TROUBLE?
WORSE THAN THAT. WE JUST RAN INTO AN *OLD FRIEND*.
SIR, I'VE GOT A SIGHTING. THREE POINTS FORWARD, OFF THE STARBOARD BEAM.
23
AIR BUBBLES, SIR, AND I THINK I SAW A SHADOW. COULD BE A SUBMARINE.
HELLO AGAIN, JACK.

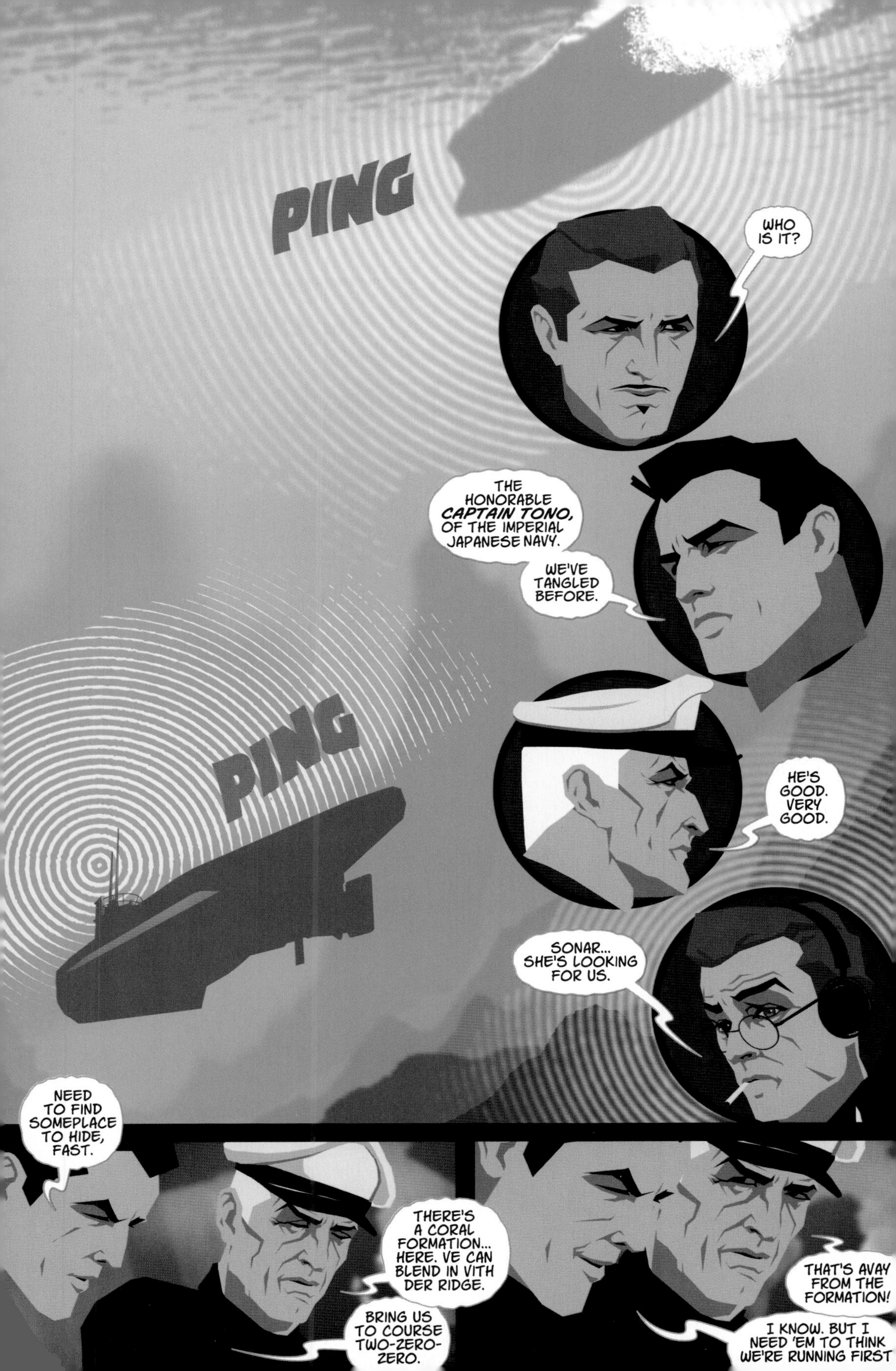
PING
WHO IS IT?
THE HONORABLE CAPTAIN TONO, OF THE IMPERIAL JAPANESE NAVY.
WE'VE TANGLED BEFORE.
PING
HE'S GOOD. VERY GOOD.
SONAR... SHE'S LOOKING FOR US.
NEED TO FIND SOMEPLACE TO HIDE, FAST.
THERE'S A CORAL FORMATION... HERE. VE CAN BLEND IN VITH DER RIDGE.
BRING US TO COURSE TWO-ZERO-ZERO.
THAT'S AVAY FROM THE FORMATION!
I KNOW. BUT I NEED 'EM TO THINK WE'RE RUNNING FIRST

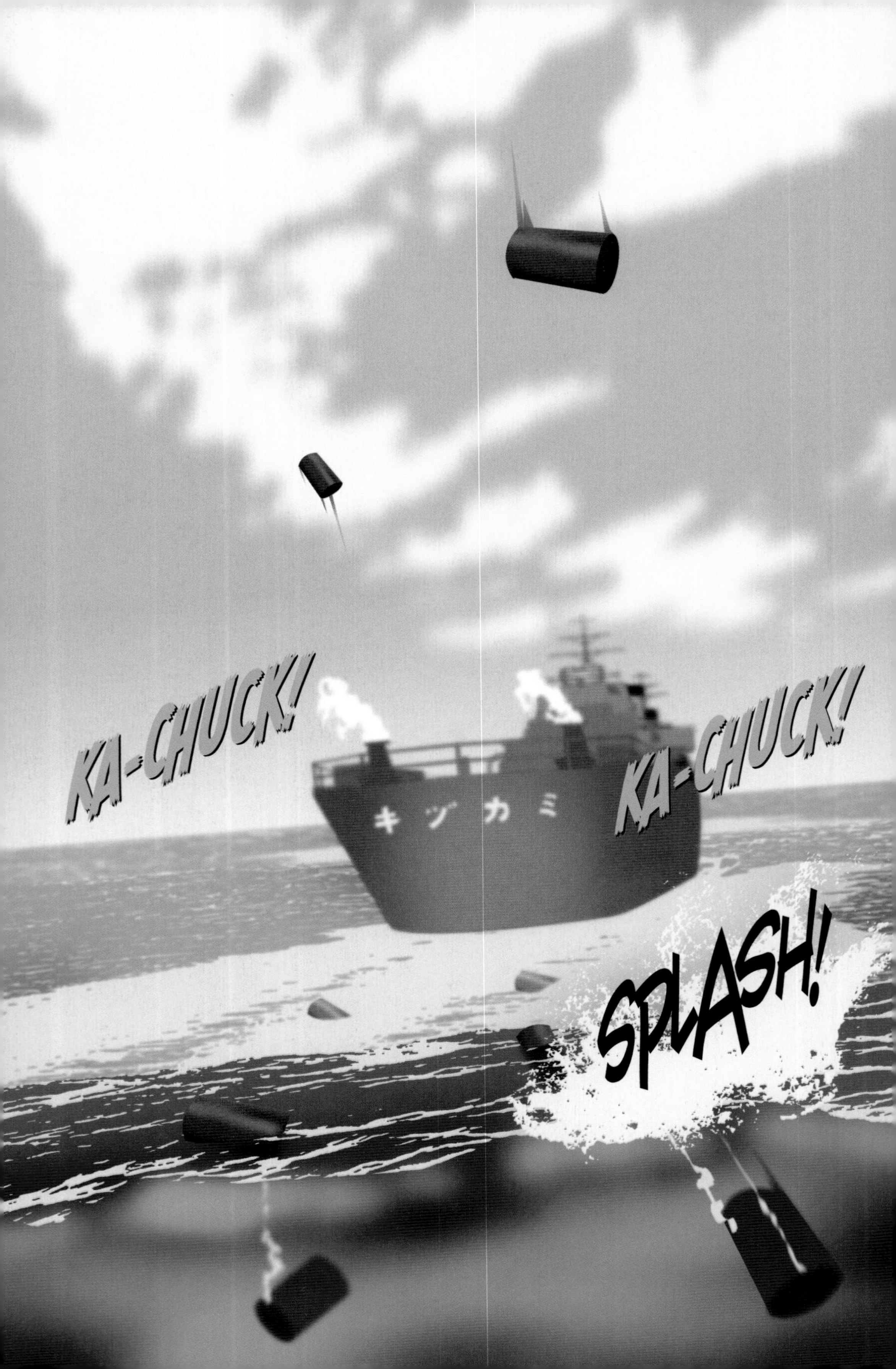

KA-CHUCK!
キヅカミ
KA-CHUCK!
SPLASH!

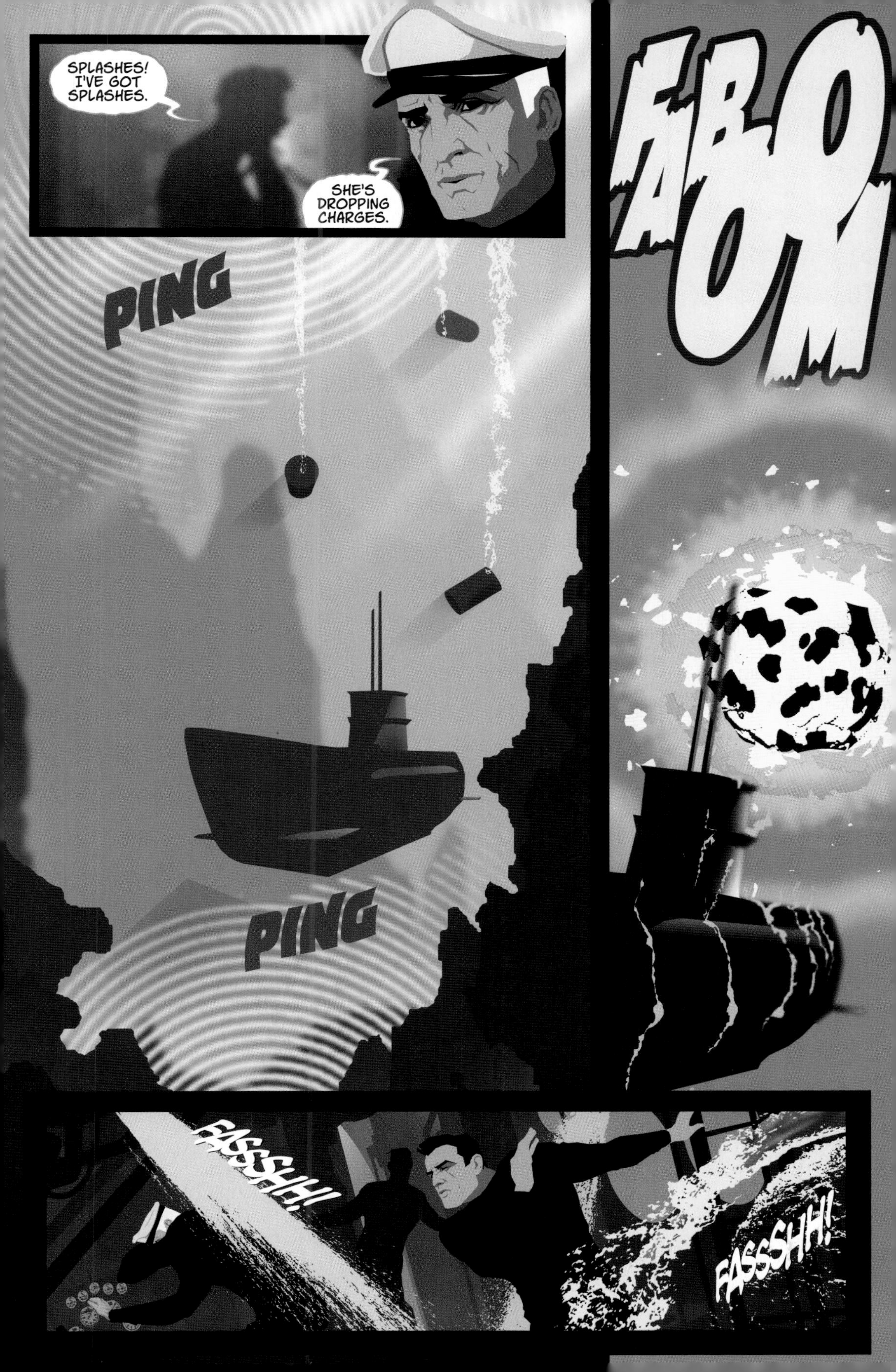

SPLASHES! I'VE GOT SPLASHES.
SHE'S DROPPING CHARGES.
PING
PING
KA-BOOM
FASSSHH!
FASSSHH!

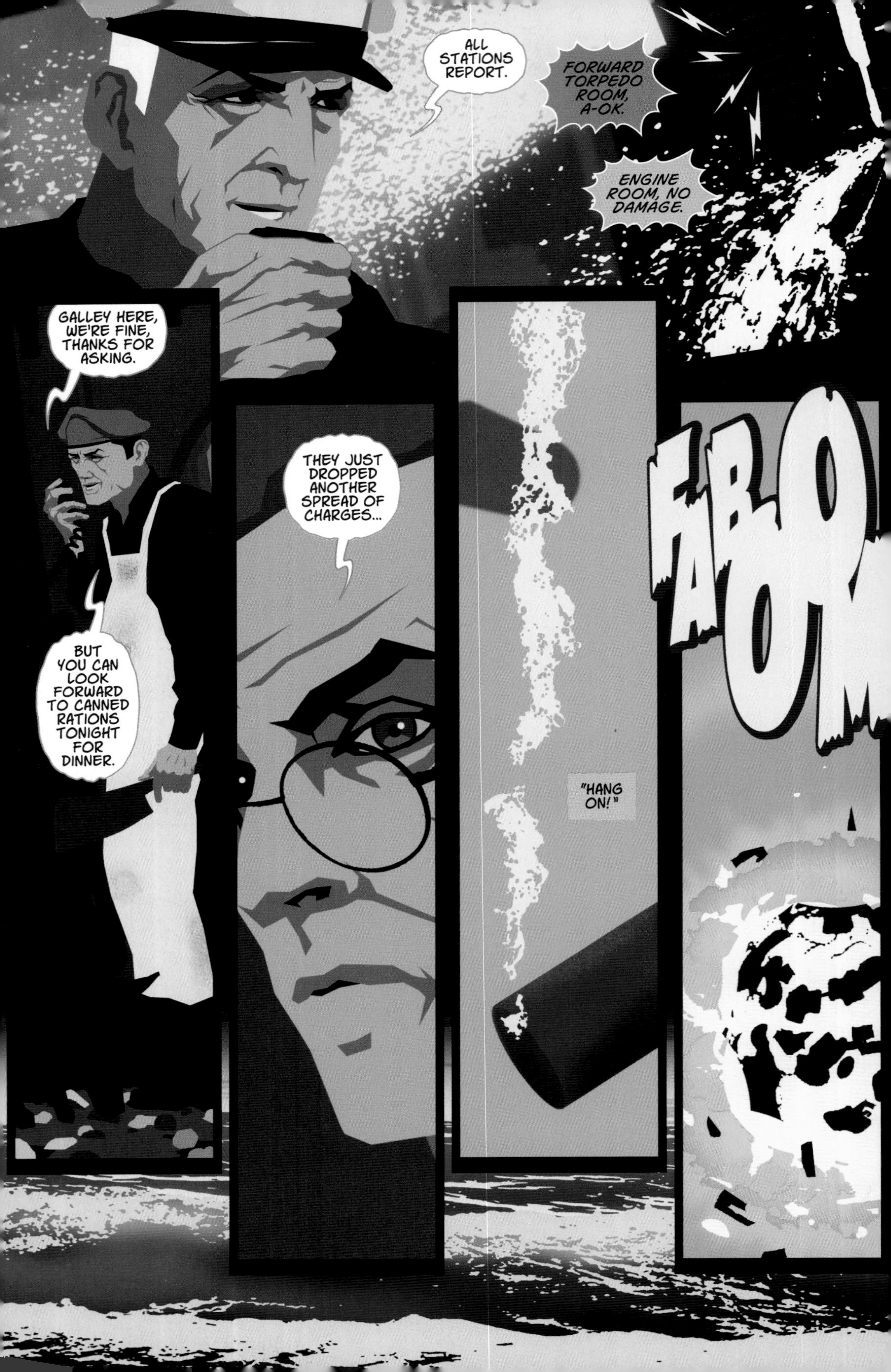
ALL STATIONS REPORT.
FORWARD TORPEDO ROOM, A-OK.
ENGINE ROOM, NO DAMAGE.
GALLEY HERE, WE'RE FINE, THANKS FOR ASKING.
BUT YOU CAN LOOK FORWARD TO CANNED RATIONS TONIGHT FOR DINNER.
THEY JUST DROPPED ANOTHER SPREAD OF CHARGES...
"HANG ON!"
FABOOM

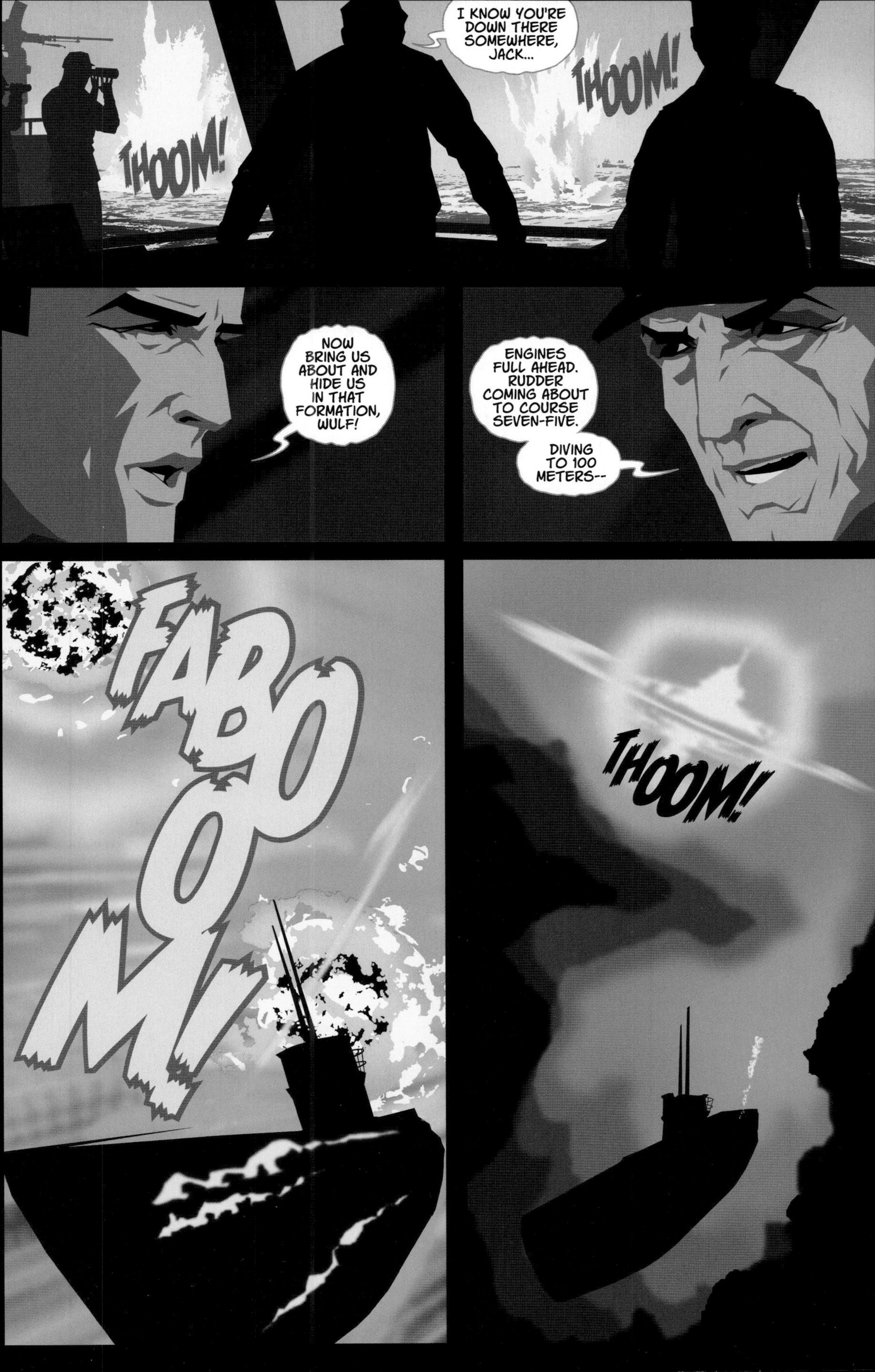

THOOM!
I KNOW YOU'RE DOWN THERE SOMEWHERE, JACK...
THOOM!
NOW BRING US ABOUT AND HIDE US IN THAT FORMATION, WULF!
ENGINES FULL AHEAD. RUDDER COMING ABOUT TO COURSE SEVEN-FIVE.
DIVING TO 100 METERS--
FABOOM!
THOOM!

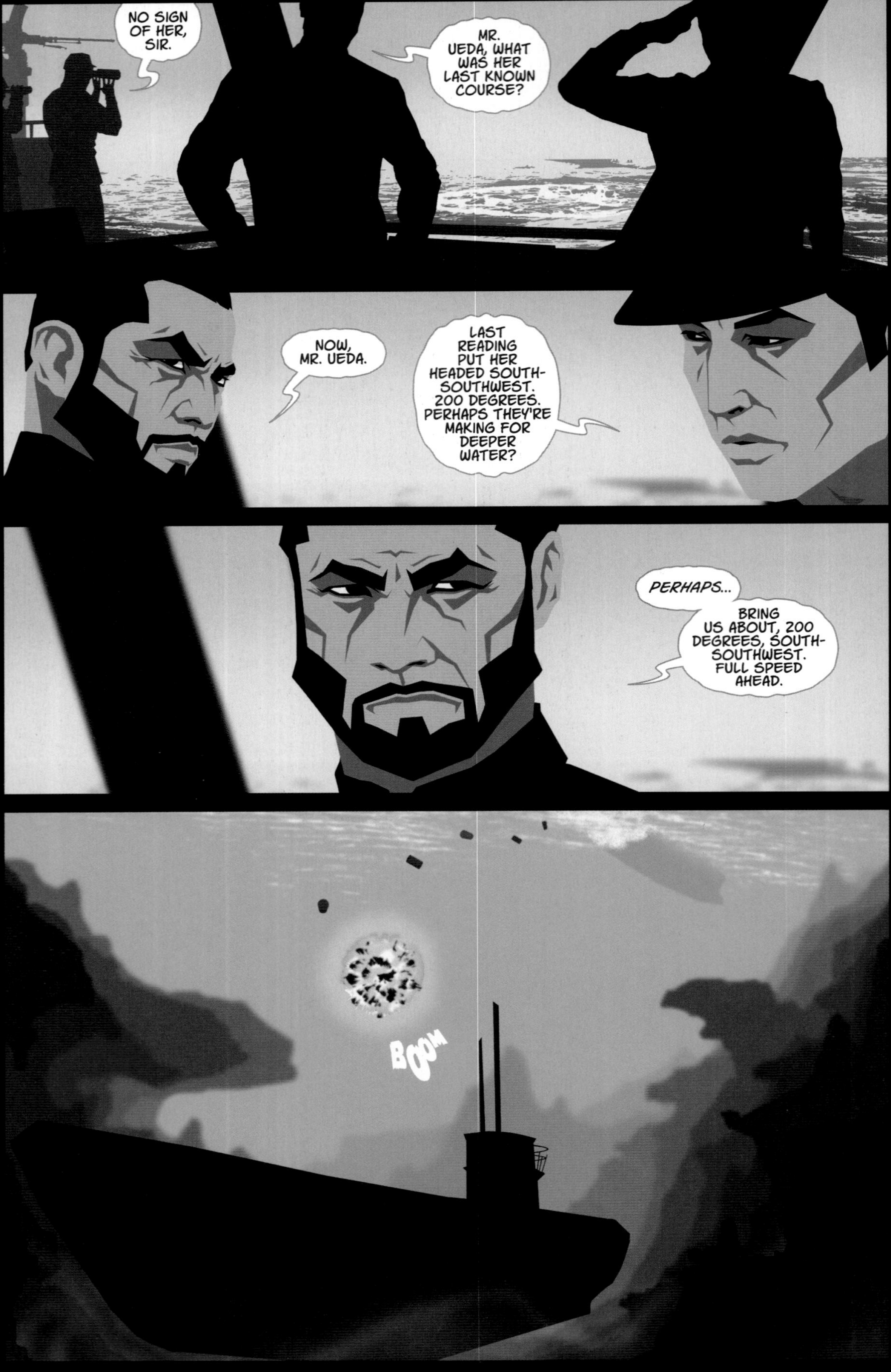
NO SIGN OF HER, SIR.
MR. UEDA, WHAT WAS HER LAST KNOWN COURSE?
NOW, MR. UEDA.
LAST READING PUT HER HEADED SOUTH-SOUTHWEST. 200 DEGREES. PERHAPS THEY'RE MAKING FOR DEEPER WATER?
PERHAPS...
BRING US ABOUT, 200 DEGREES, SOUTH-SOUTHWEST. FULL SPEED AHEAD.
BOOM

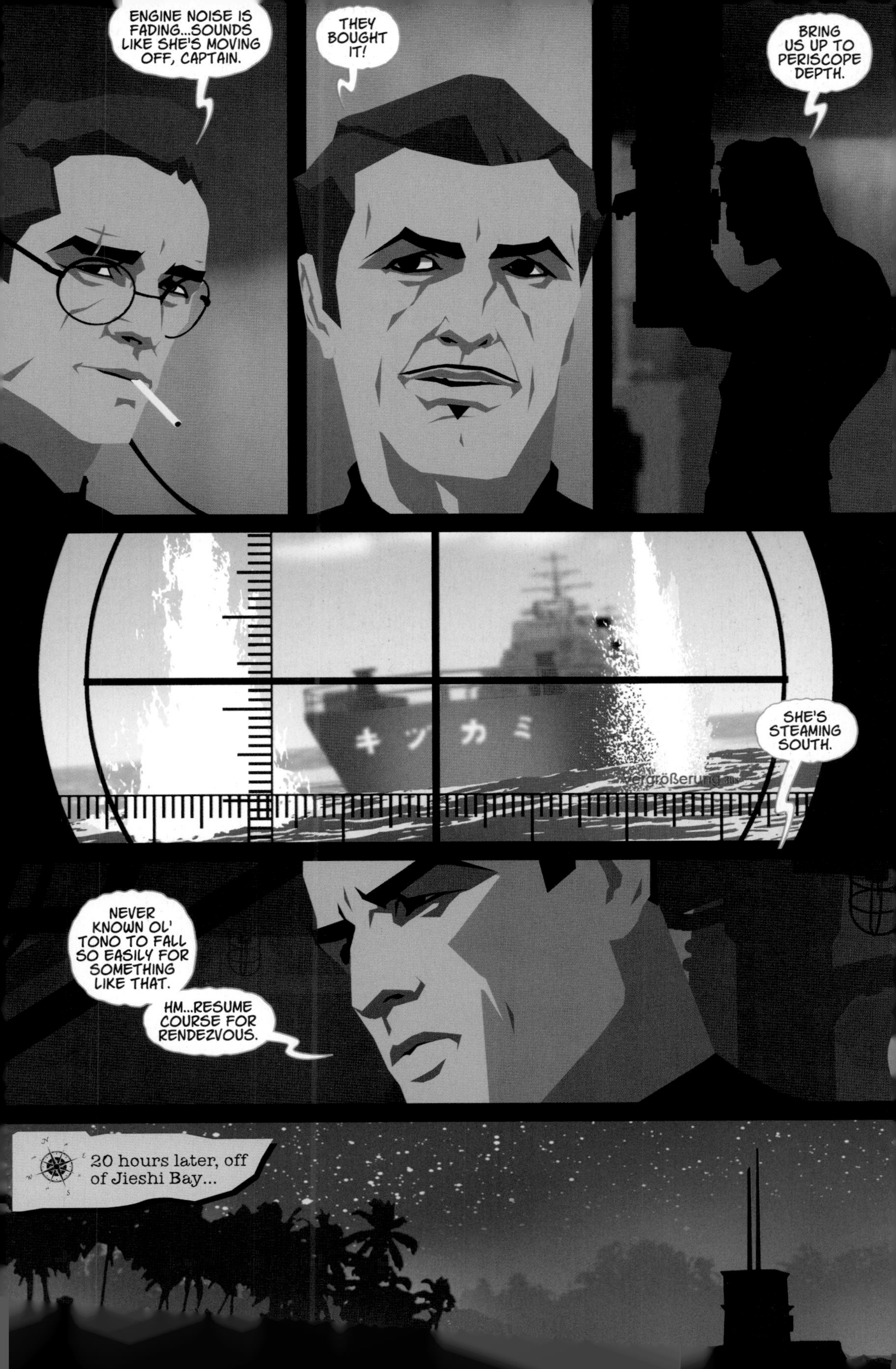
ENGINE NOISE IS FADING...SOUNDS LIKE SHE'S MOVING OFF, CAPTAIN.
THEY BOUGHT IT!
BRING US UP TO PERISCOPE DEPTH.
キツカミ
Vergrößerung
SHE'S STEAMING SOUTH.
NEVER KNOWN OL' TONO TO FALL SO EASILY FOR SOMETHING LIKE THAT.
HM...RESUME COURSE FOR RENDEZVOUS.
20 hours later, off of Jieshi Bay...

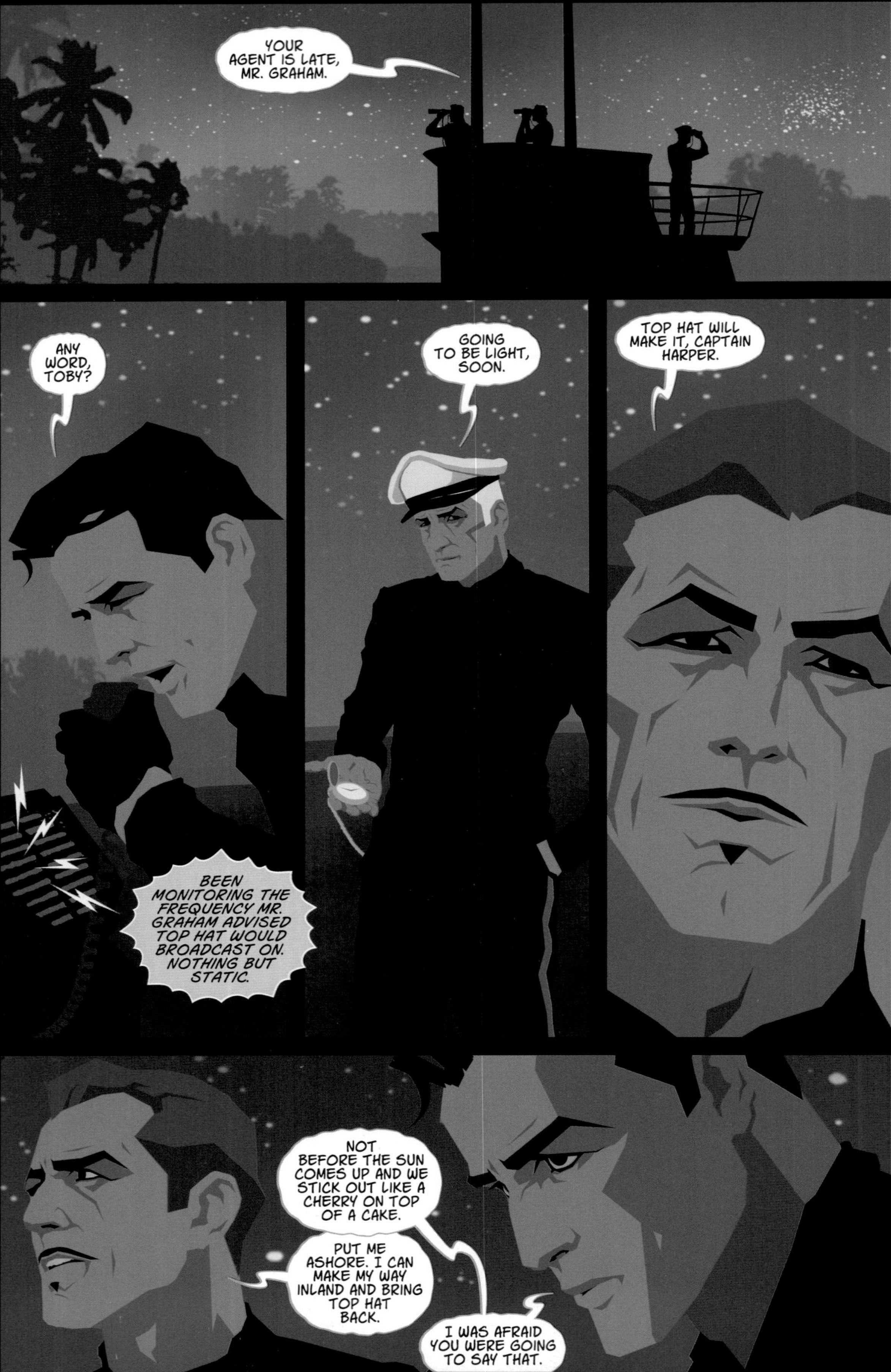
YOUR AGENT IS LATE, MR. GRAHAM.
ANY WORD, TOBY?
BEEN MONITORING THE FREQUENCY MR. GRAHAM ADVISED TOP HAT WOULD BROADCAST ON. NOTHING BUT STATIC.
GOING TO BE LIGHT, SOON.
TOP HAT WILL MAKE IT, CAPTAIN HARPER.
NOT BEFORE THE SUN COMES UP AND WE STICK OUT LIKE A CHERRY ON TOP OF A CAKE.
PUT ME ASHORE. I CAN MAKE MY WAY INLAND AND BRING TOP HAT BACK.
I WAS AFRAID YOU WERE GOING TO SAY THAT.

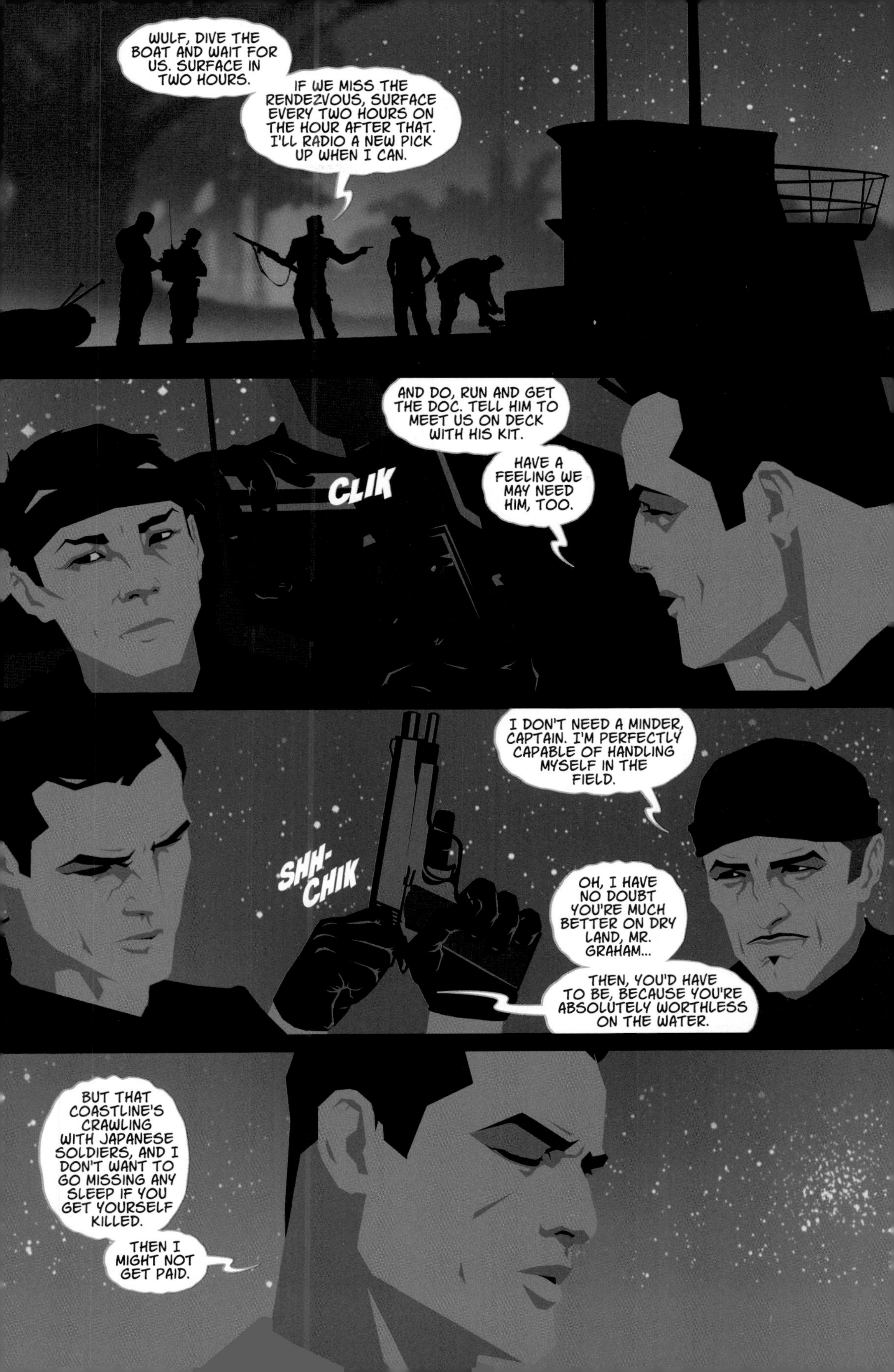
WULF, DIVE THE BOAT AND WAIT FOR US. SURFACE IN TWO HOURS.
IF WE MISS THE RENDEZVOUS, SURFACE EVERY TWO HOURS ON THE HOUR AFTER THAT. I'LL RADIO A NEW PICK UP WHEN I CAN.
AND DO, RUN AND GET THE DOC. TELL HIM TO MEET US ON DECK WITH HIS KIT.
HAVE A FEELING WE MAY NEED HIM, TOO.
CLIK
I DON'T NEED A MINDER, CAPTAIN. I'M PERFECTLY CAPABLE OF HANDLING MYSELF IN THE FIELD.
SHH-CHIK
OH, I HAVE NO DOUBT YOU'RE MUCH BETTER ON DRY LAND, MR. GRAHAM...
THEN, YOU'D HAVE TO BE, BECAUSE YOU'RE ABSOLUTELY WORTHLESS ON THE WATER.
BUT THAT COASTLINE'S CRAWLING WITH JAPANESE SOLDIERS, AND I DON'T WANT TO GO MISSING ANY SLEEP IF YOU GET YOURSELF KILLED.
THEN I MIGHT NOT GET PAID.

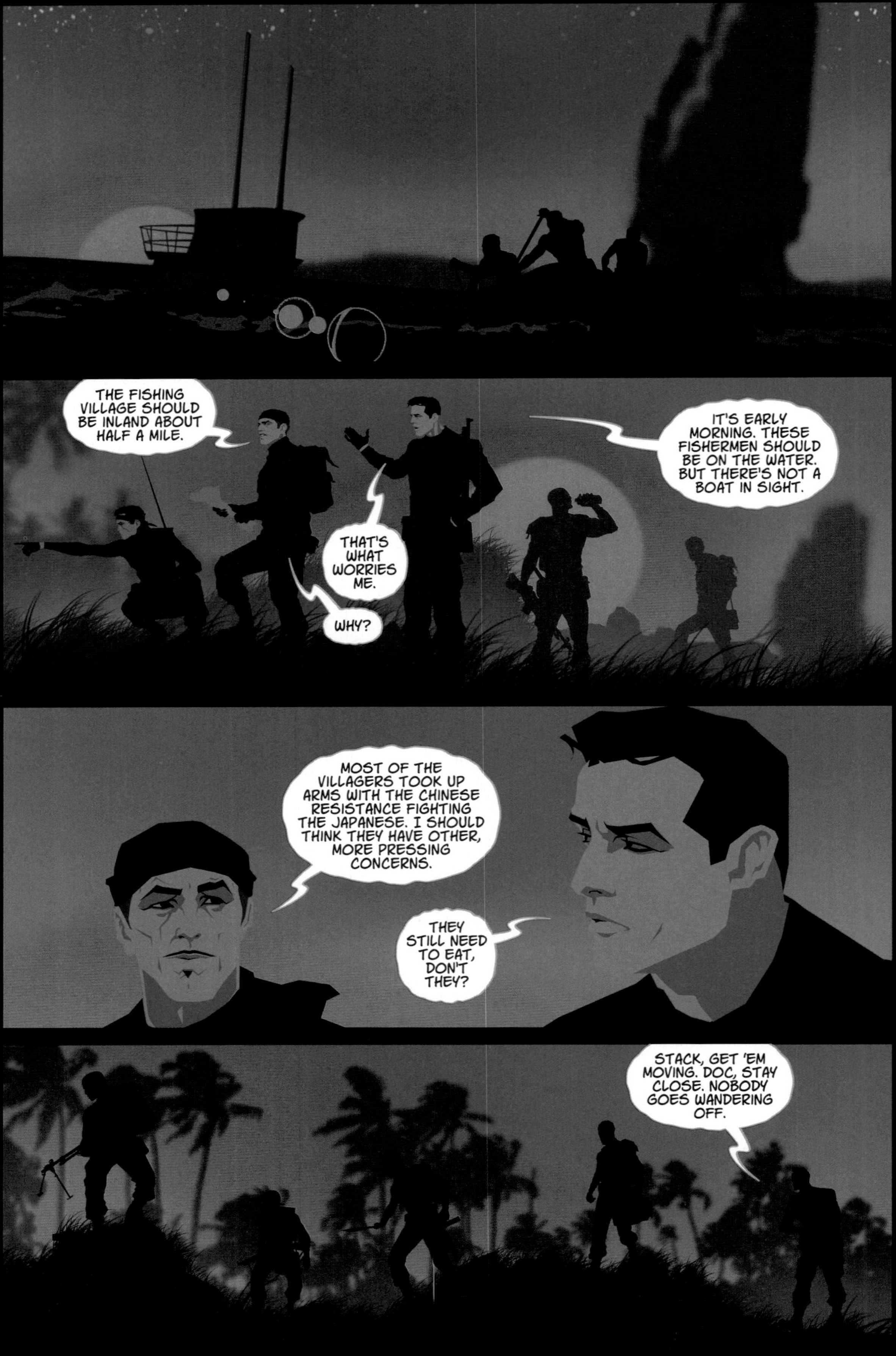
THE FISHING VILLAGE SHOULD BE INLAND ABOUT HALF A MILE.
IT'S EARLY MORNING. THESE FISHERMEN SHOULD BE ON THE WATER. BUT THERE'S NOT A BOAT IN SIGHT.
THAT'S WHAT WORRIES ME.
WHY?
MOST OF THE VILLAGERS TOOK UP ARMS WITH THE CHINESE RESISTANCE FIGHTING THE JAPANESE. I SHOULD THINK THEY HAVE OTHER, MORE PRESSING CONCERNS.
THEY STILL NEED TO EAT, DON'T THEY?
STACK, GET 'EM MOVING. DOC, STAY CLOSE. NOBODY GOES WANDERING OFF.

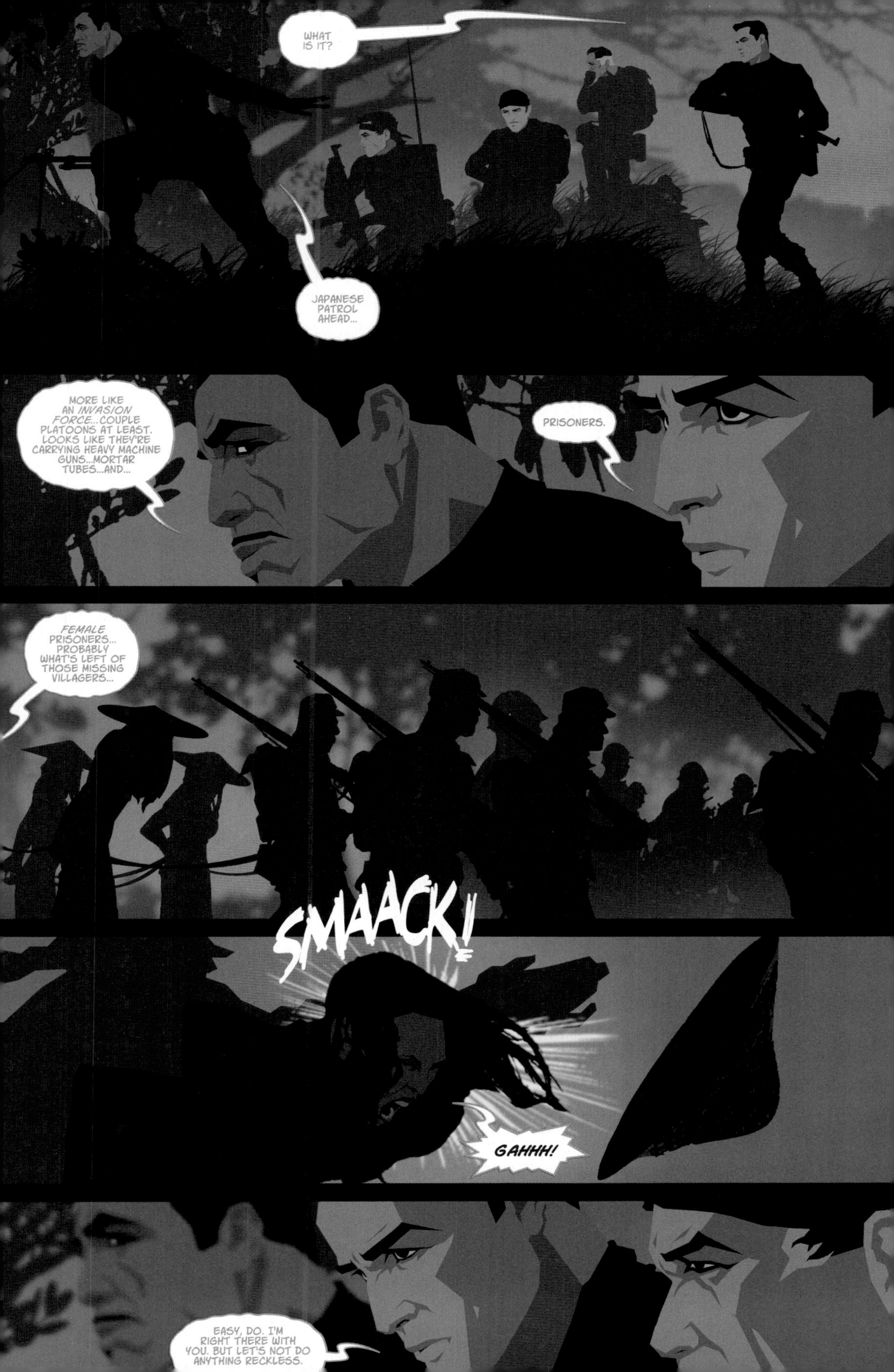
WHAT IS IT?
JAPANESE PATROL AHEAD...
MORE LIKE AN *INVASION FORCE*...COUPLE PLATOONS AT LEAST. LOOKS LIKE THEY'RE CARRYING HEAVY MACHINE GUNS...MORTAR TUBES...AND...
PRISONERS.
FEMALE PRISONERS... PROBABLY WHAT'S LEFT OF THOSE MISSING VILLAGERS...
SMAACK!
GAHHH!
EASY, DO. I'M RIGHT THERE WITH YOU. BUT LET'S NOT DO ANYTHING RECKLESS.

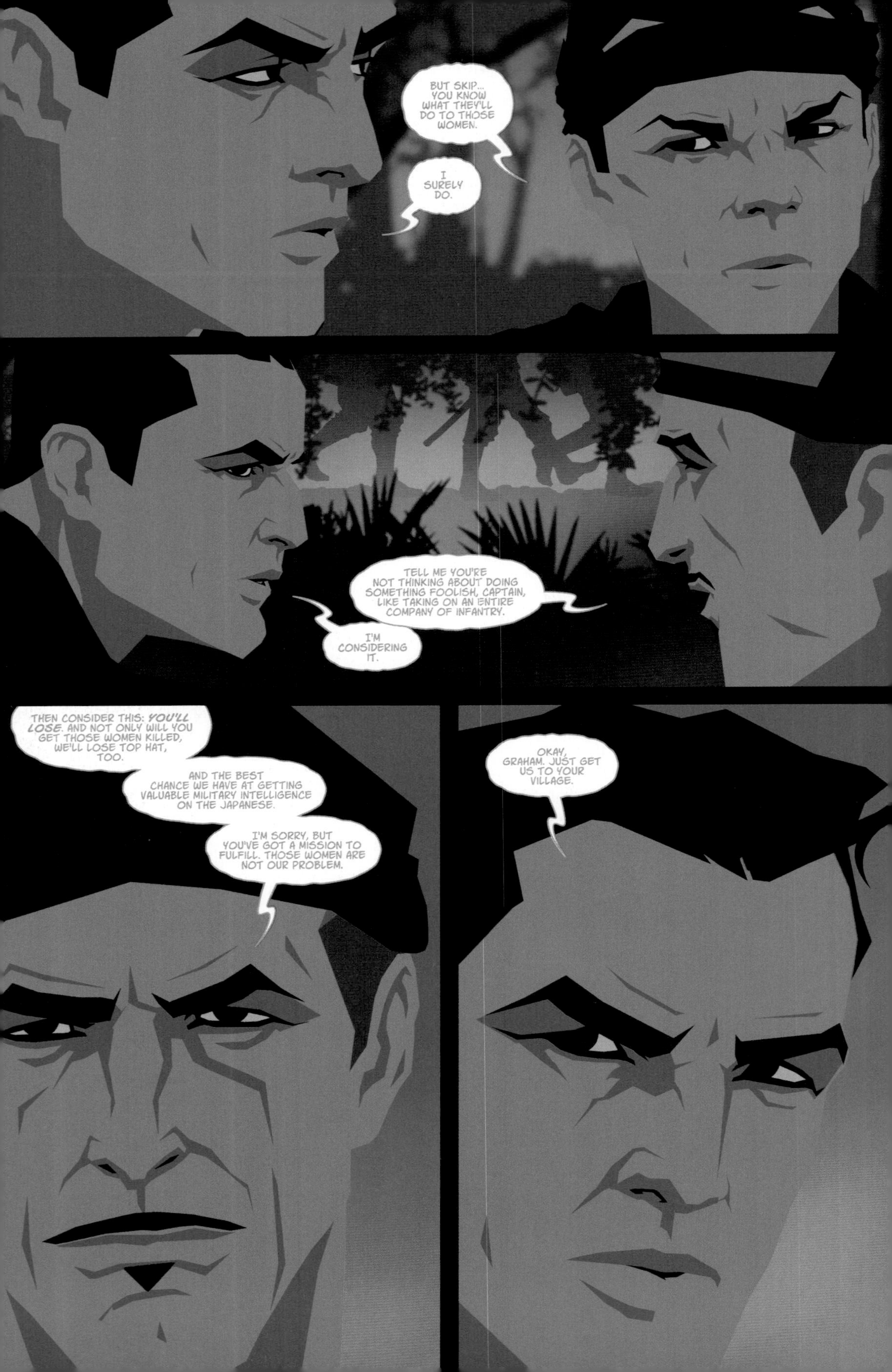
BUT SKIP... YOU KNOW WHAT THEY'LL DO TO THOSE WOMEN.
I SURELY DO.
TELL ME YOU'RE NOT THINKING ABOUT DOING SOMETHING FOOLISH, CAPTAIN, LIKE TAKING ON AN ENTIRE COMPANY OF INFANTRY.
I'M CONSIDERING IT.
THEN CONSIDER THIS: *YOU'LL LOSE*. AND NOT ONLY WILL YOU GET THOSE WOMEN KILLED, WE'LL LOSE TOP HAT, TOO.
AND THE BEST CHANCE WE HAVE AT GETTING VALUABLE MILITARY INTELLIGENCE ON THE JAPANESE.
I'M SORRY, BUT YOU'VE GOT A MISSION TO FULFILL. THOSE WOMEN ARE NOT OUR PROBLEM.
OKAY, GRAHAM. JUST GET US TO YOUR VILLAGE.

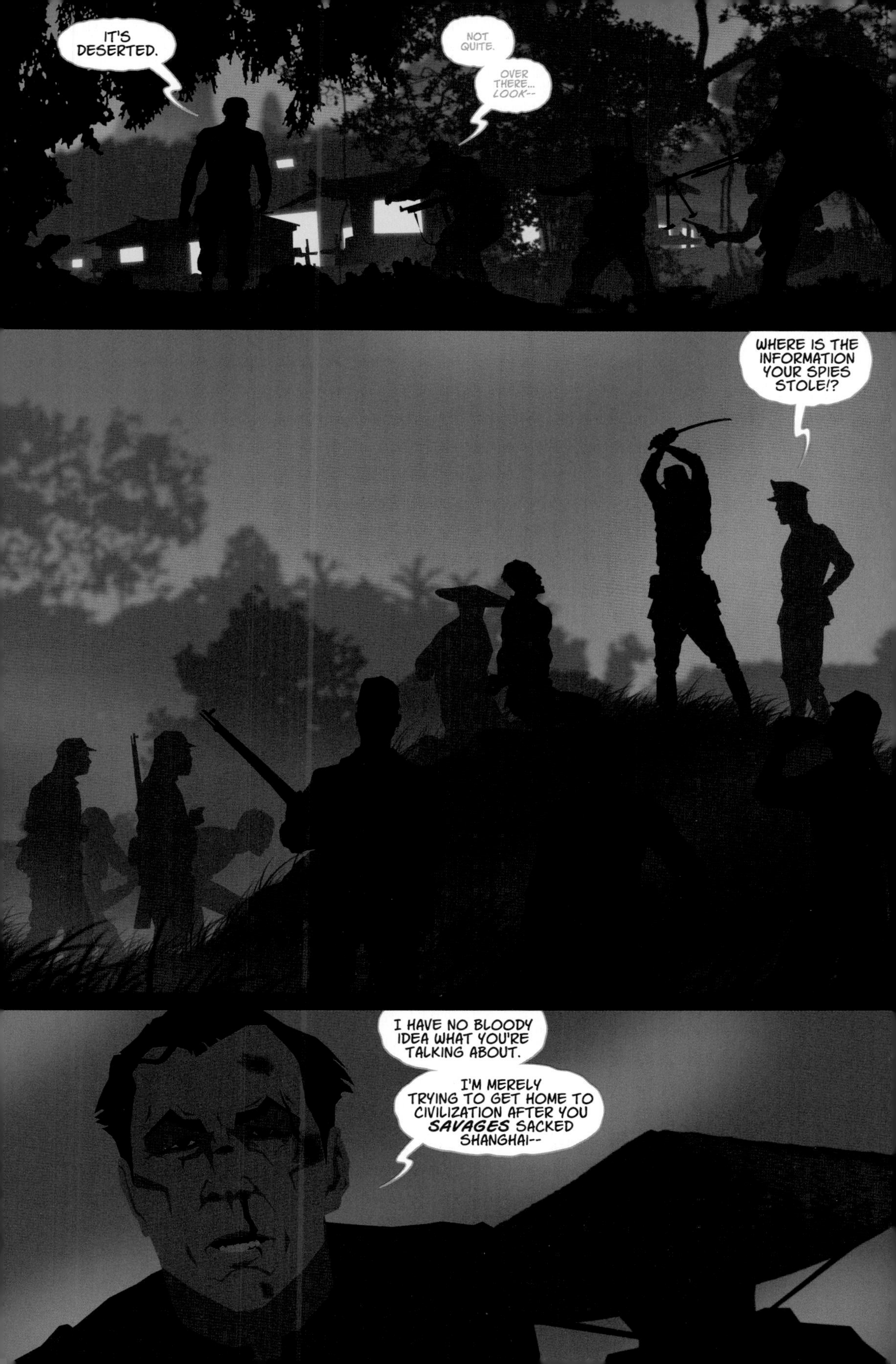
IT'S DESERTED.
NOT QUITE.
OVER THERE... LOOK--
WHERE IS THE INFORMATION YOUR SPIES STOLE!?
I HAVE NO BLOODY IDEA WHAT YOU'RE TALKING ABOUT.
I'M MERELY TRYING TO GET HOME TO CIVILIZATION AFTER YOU SAVAGES SACKED SHANGHAI--

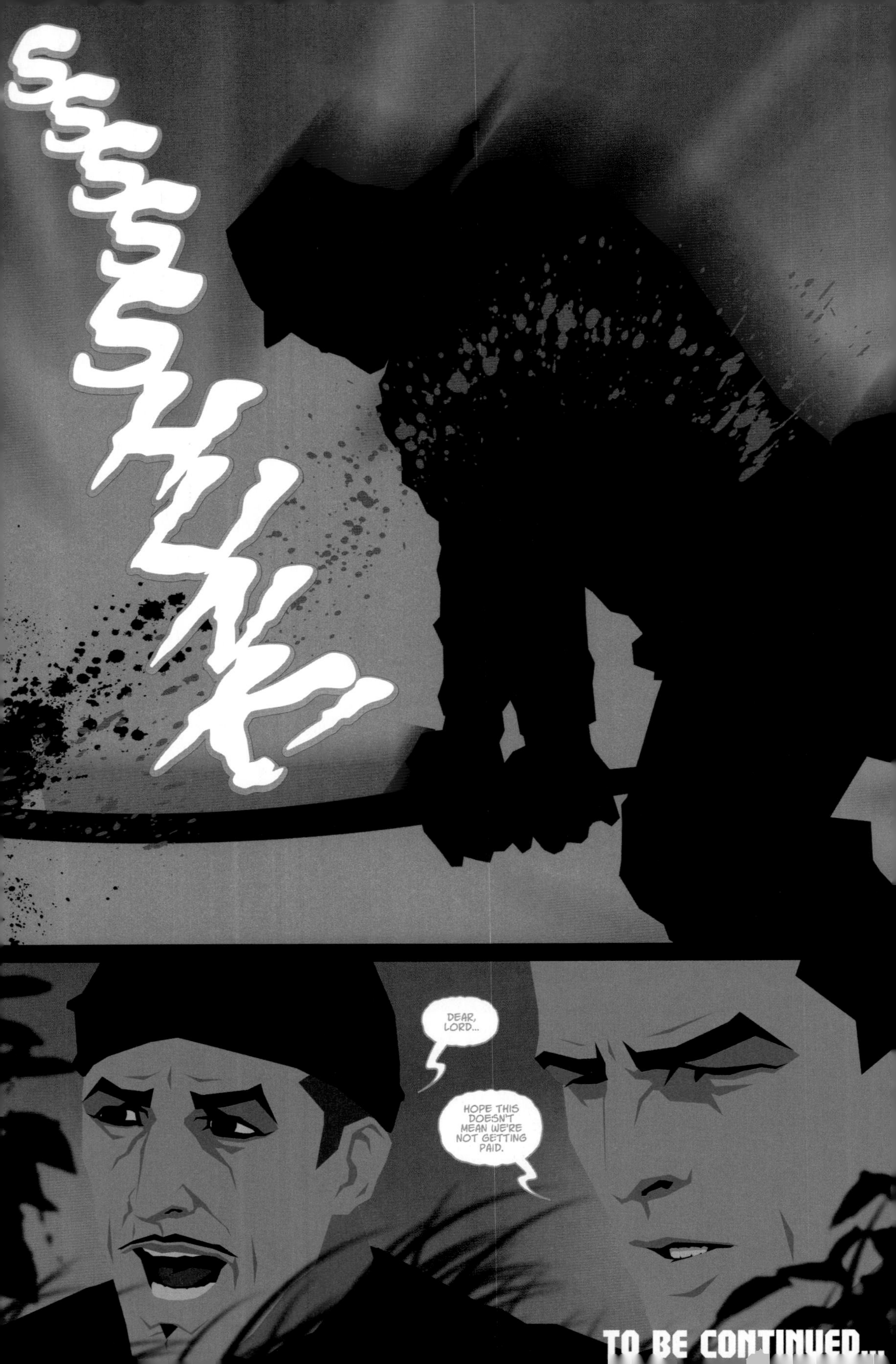
SSSSSHUNK
DEAR, LORD...
HOPE THIS DOESN'T MEAN WE'RE NOT GETTING PAID.
TO BE CONTINUED...

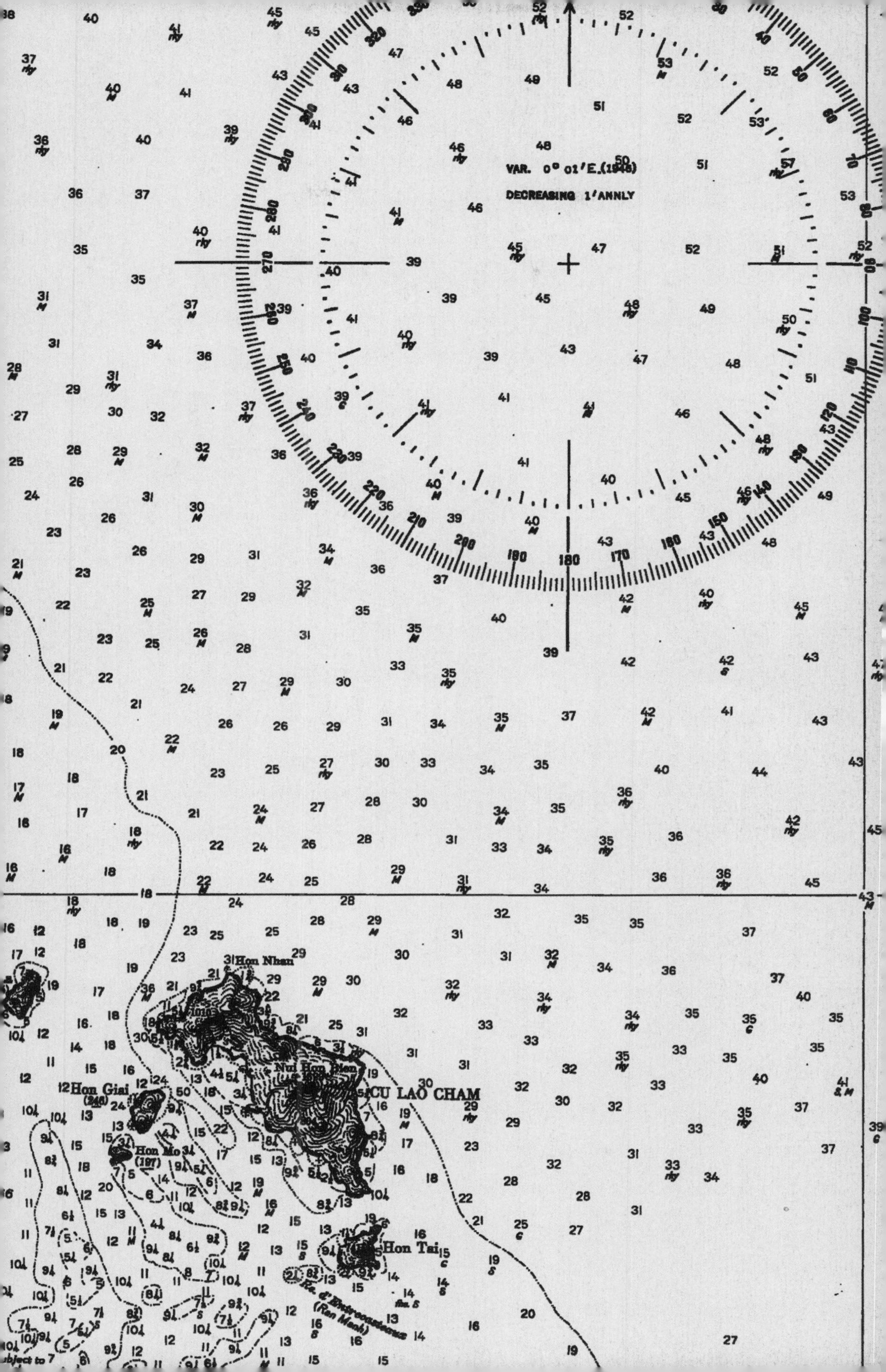
VAR. 0° 01'E.
DECREASING 1'ANNLY
Hon Nhan
CU LAO CHAM
Hon Giai
Hon Mo
Hon Tai

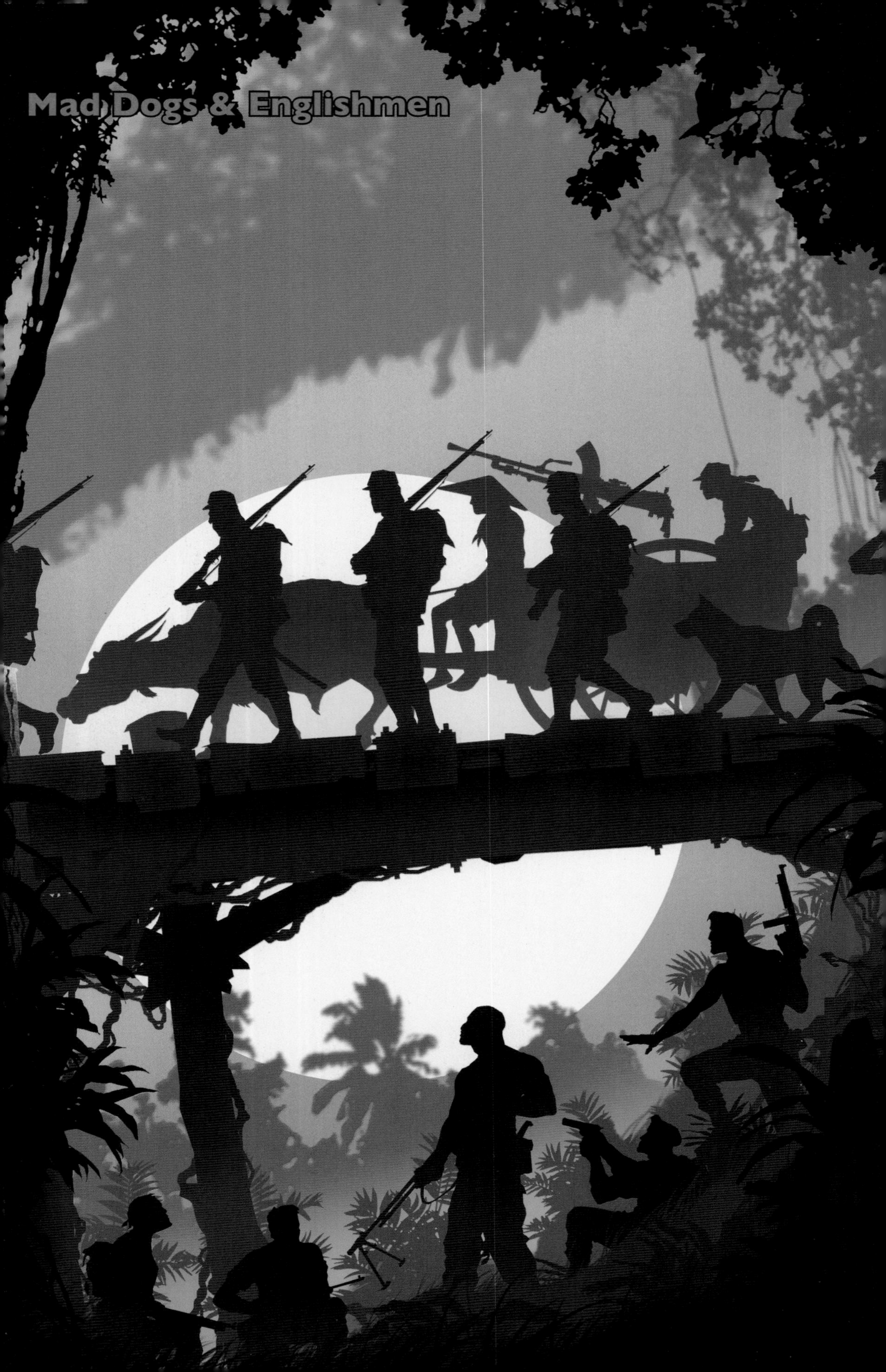
Mad Dogs & Englishmen

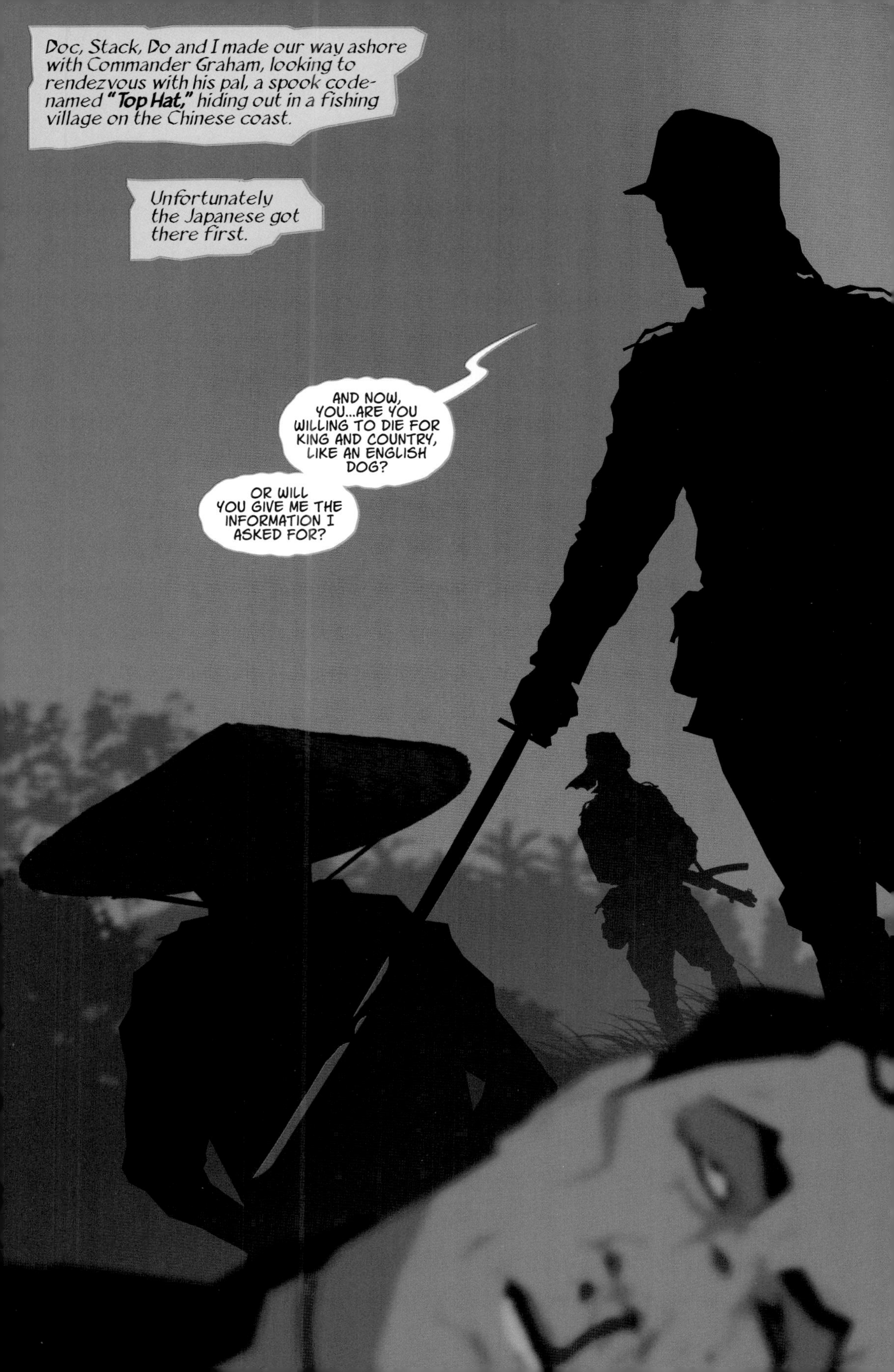

Doc, Stack, Do and I made our way ashore with Commander Graham, looking to rendezvous with his pal, a spook code-named **"Top Hat,"** hiding out in a fishing village on the Chinese coast.
Unfortunately the Japanese got there first.
AND NOW, YOU...ARE YOU WILLING TO DIE FOR KING AND COUNTRY, LIKE AN ENGLISH DOG?
OR WILL YOU GIVE ME THE INFORMATION I ASKED FOR?

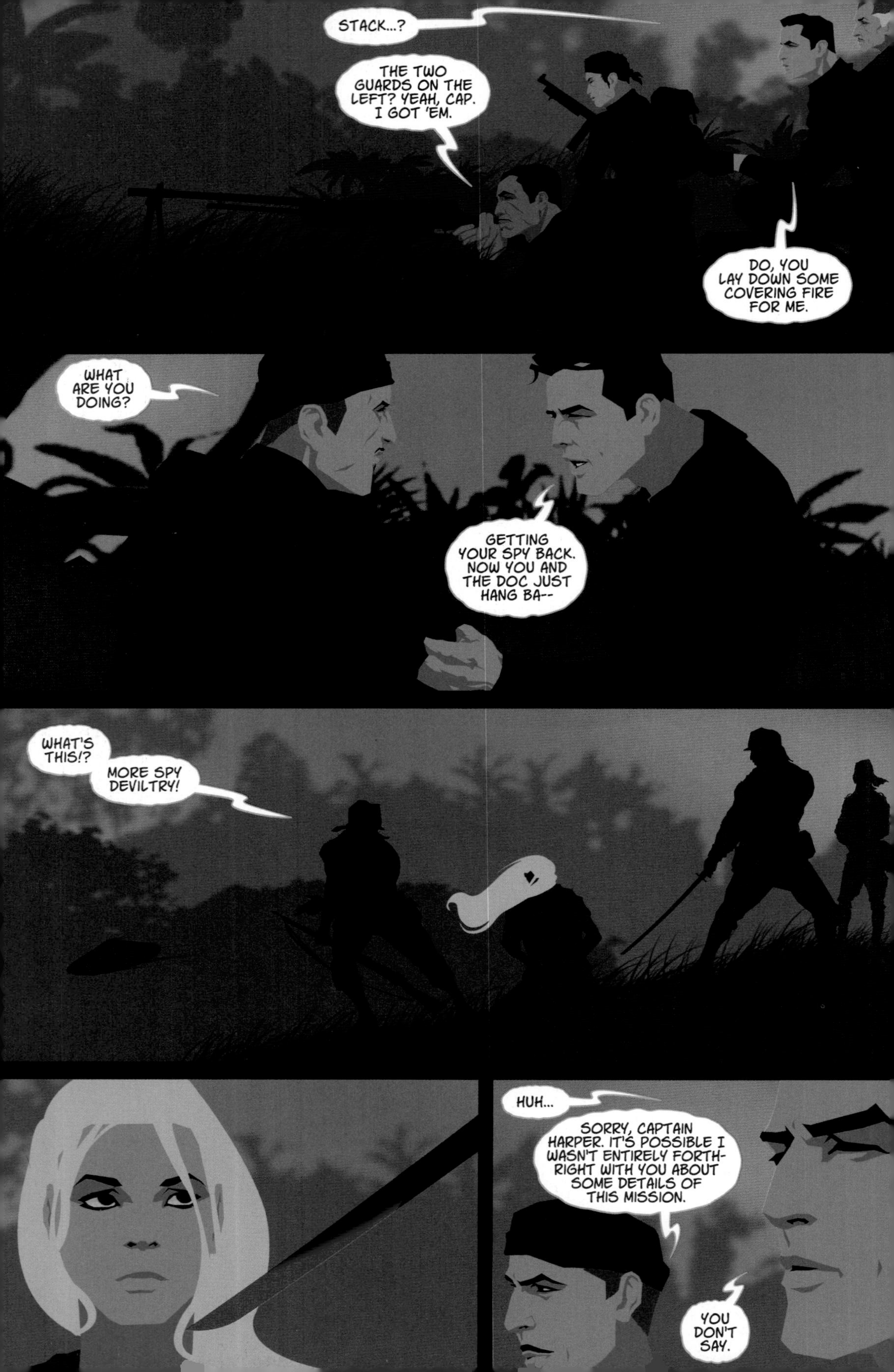
STACK...?
THE TWO GUARDS ON THE LEFT? YEAH, CAP. I GOT 'EM.
DO, YOU LAY DOWN SOME COVERING FIRE FOR ME.
WHAT ARE YOU DOING?
GETTING YOUR SPY BACK. NOW YOU AND THE DOC JUST HANG BA--
WHAT'S THIS!?
MORE SPY DEVILTRY!
HUH...
SORRY, CAPTAIN HARPER. IT'S POSSIBLE I WASN'T ENTIRELY FORTH-RIGHT WITH YOU ABOUT SOME DETAILS OF THIS MISSION.
YOU DON'T SAY.

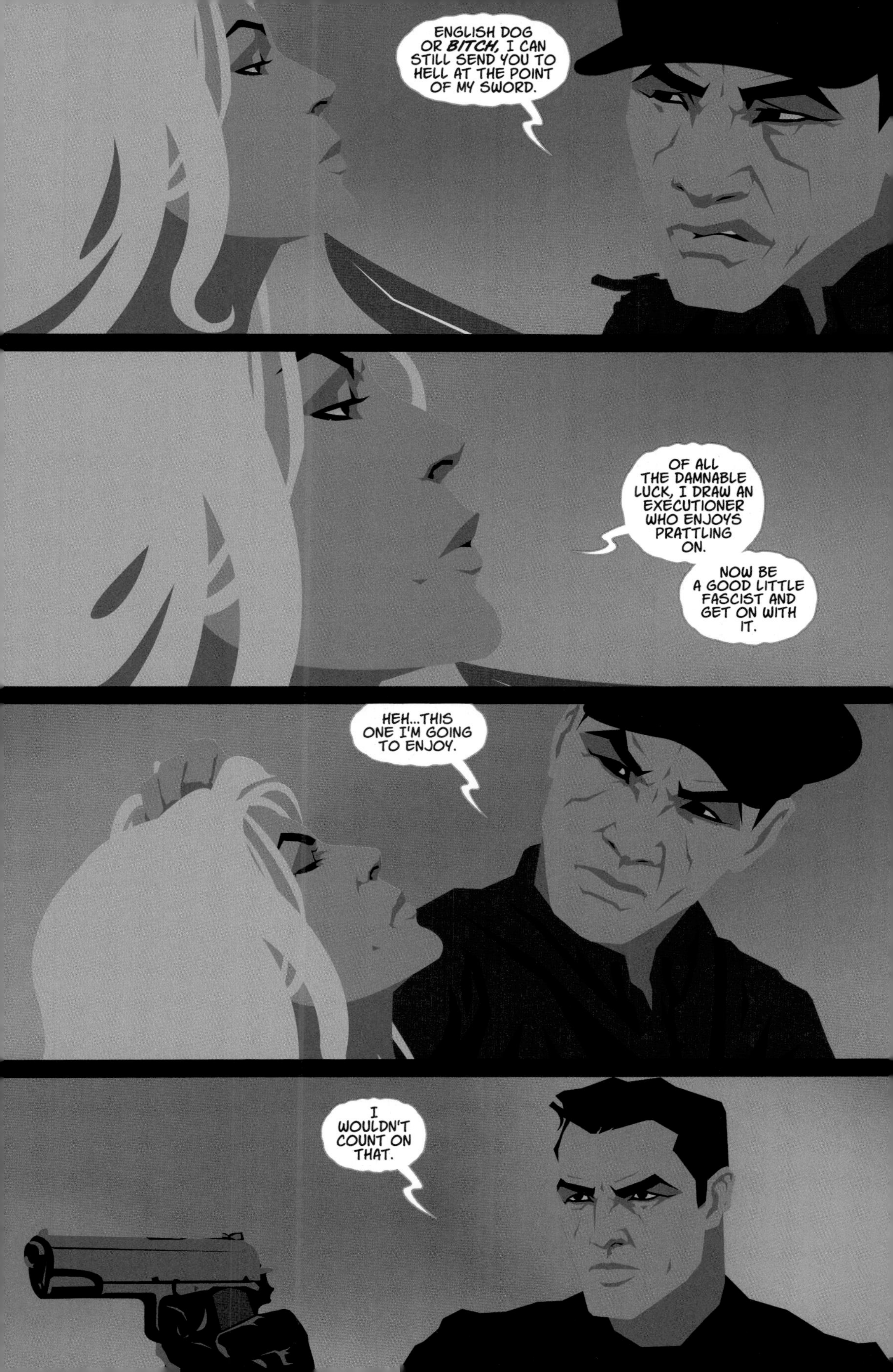
ENGLISH DOG OR BITCH, I CAN STILL SEND YOU TO HELL AT THE POINT OF MY SWORD.
OF ALL THE DAMNABLE LUCK, I DRAW AN EXECUTIONER WHO ENJOYS PRATTLING ON.
NOW BE A GOOD LITTLE FASCIST AND GET ON WITH IT.
HEH...THIS ONE I'M GOING TO ENJOY.
I WOULDN'T COUNT ON THAT.

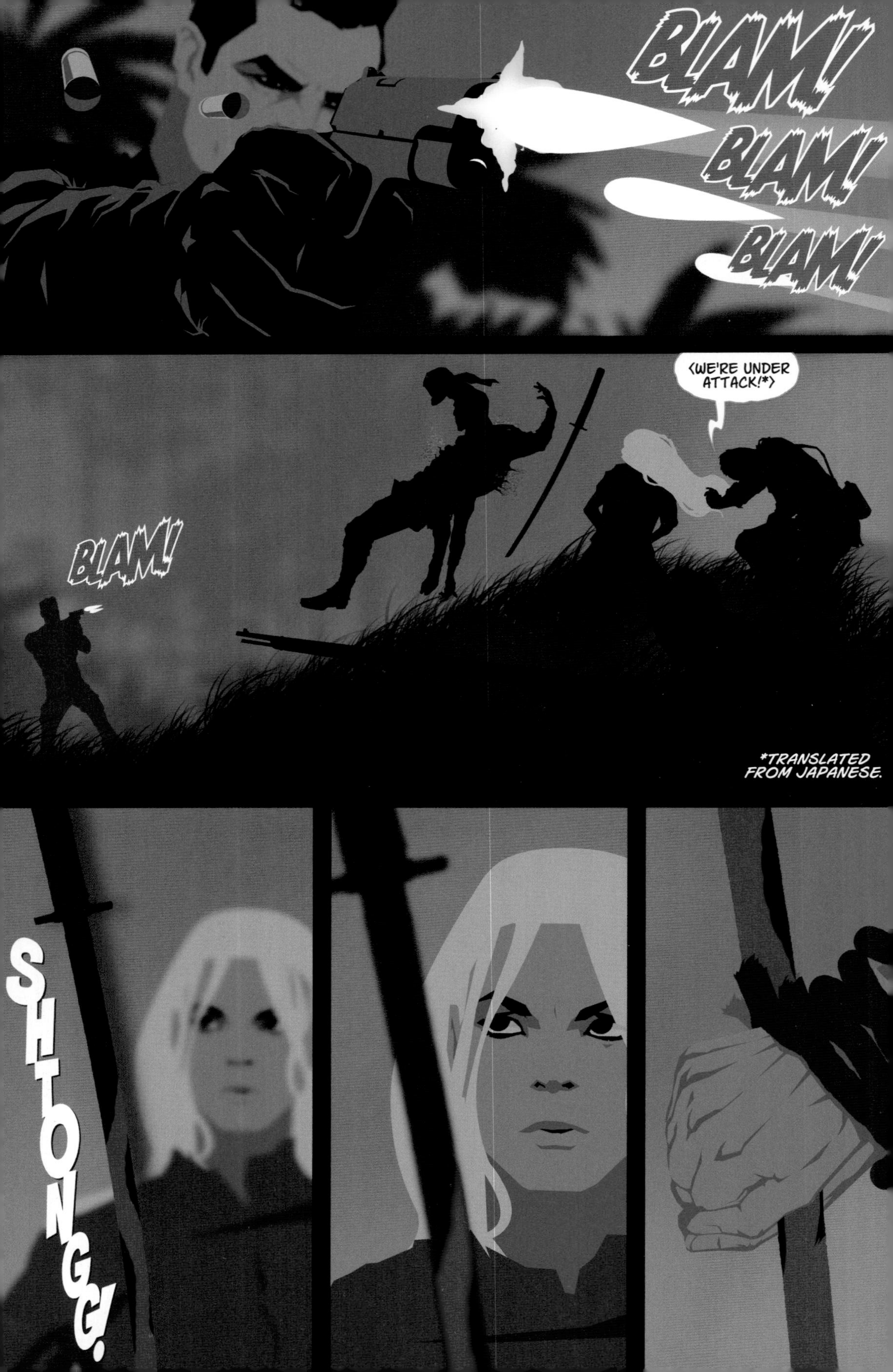
BLAM!
BLAM!
BLAM!
BLAM!
‹WE'RE UNDER ATTACK!*›
*TRANSLATED FROM JAPANESE.
SHTONGG!

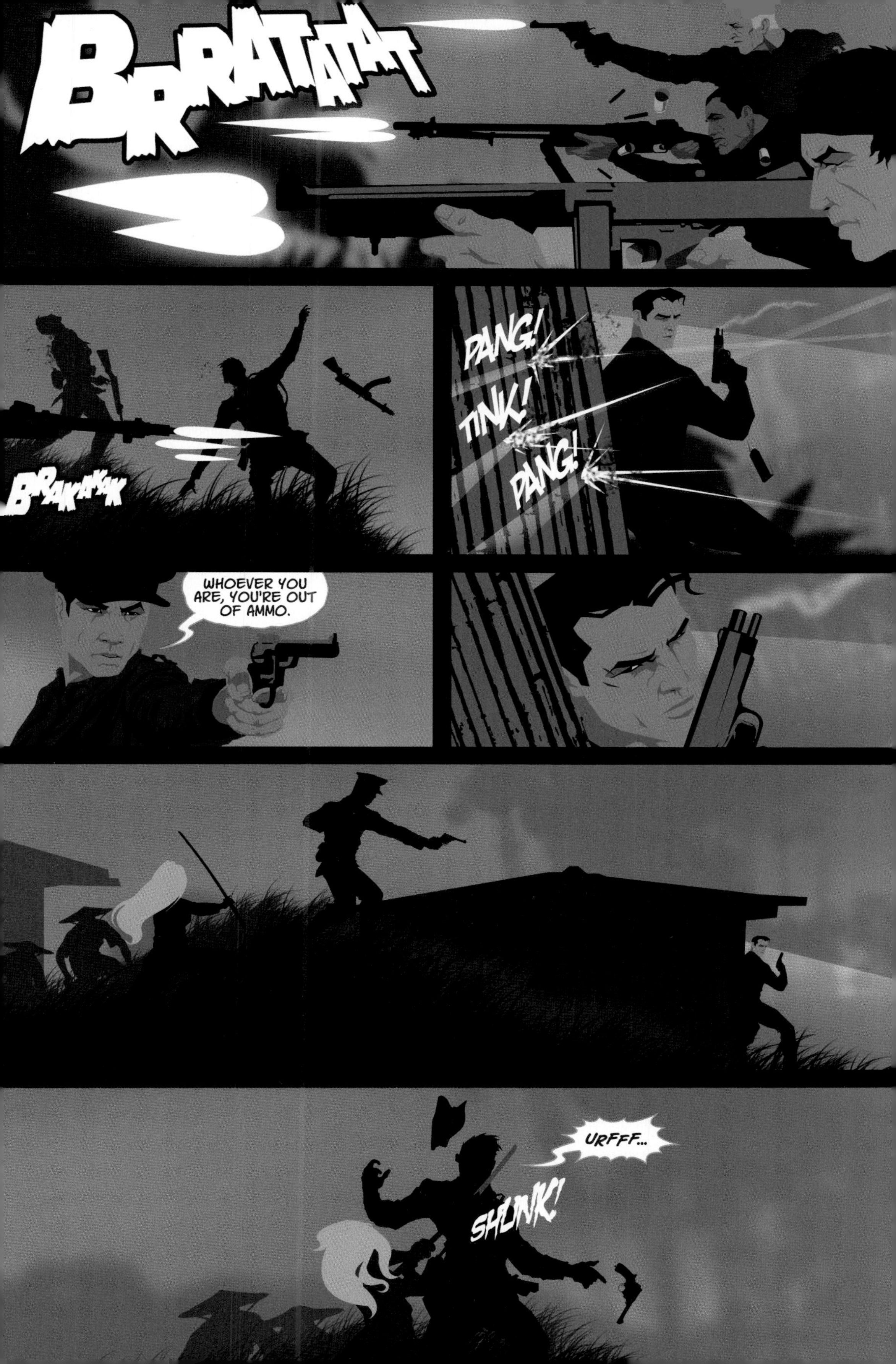
BRRATATAT
BRAKAKAK
PANG!
TINK!
PANG!
WHOEVER YOU ARE, YOU'RE OUT OF AMMO.
URFFF...
SHUNK!

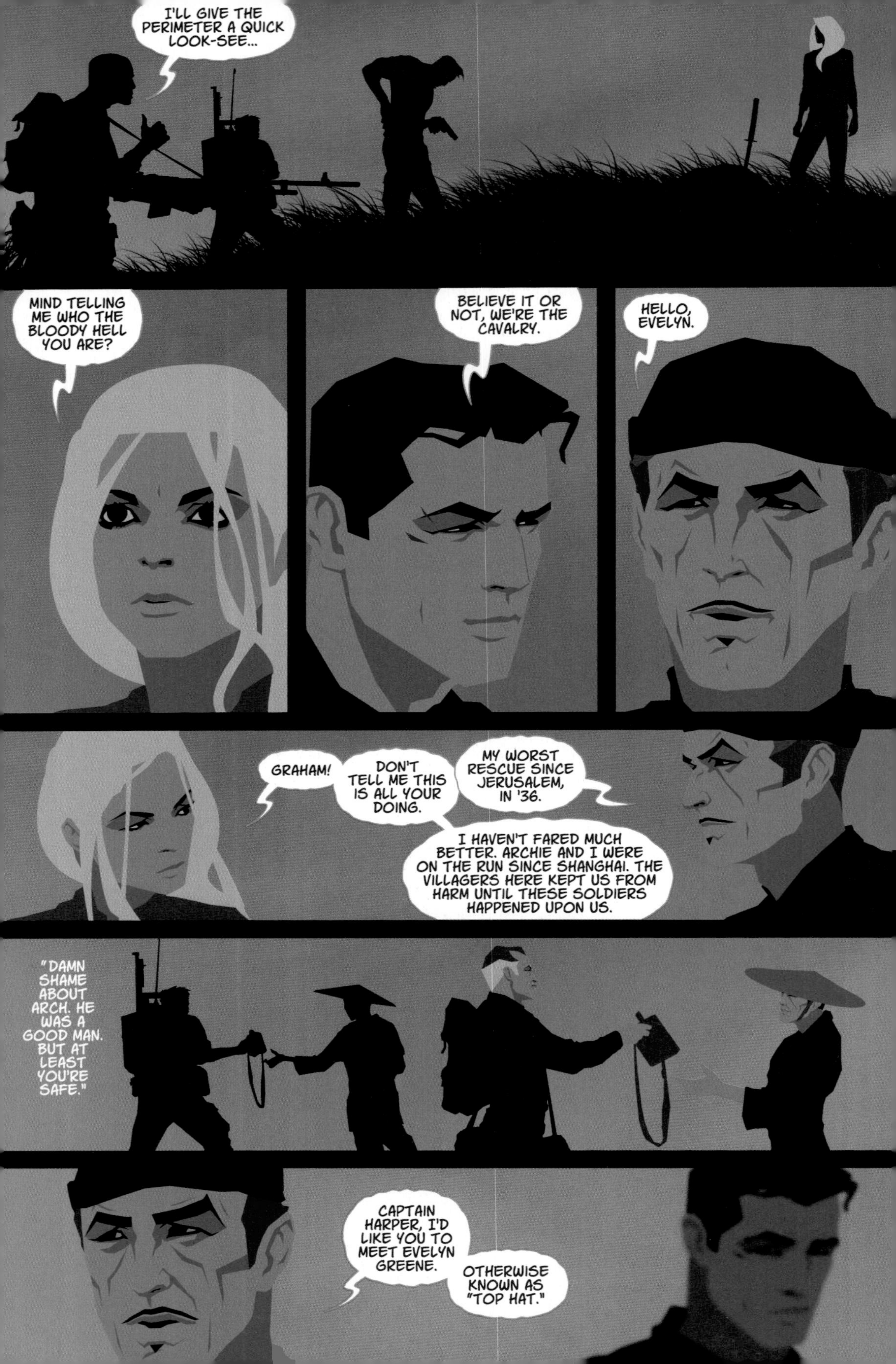
I'LL GIVE THE PERIMETER A QUICK LOOK-SEE...
MIND TELLING ME WHO THE BLOODY HELL YOU ARE?
BELIEVE IT OR NOT, WE'RE THE CAVALRY.
HELLO, EVELYN.
GRAHAM!
DON'T TELL ME THIS IS ALL YOUR DOING.
MY WORST RESCUE SINCE JERUSALEM, IN '36.
I HAVEN'T FARED MUCH BETTER. ARCHIE AND I WERE ON THE RUN SINCE SHANGHAI. THE VILLAGERS HERE KEPT US FROM HARM UNTIL THESE SOLDIERS HAPPENED UPON US.
"DAMN SHAME ABOUT ARCH. HE WAS A GOOD MAN. BUT AT LEAST YOU'RE SAFE."
CAPTAIN HARPER, I'D LIKE YOU TO MEET EVELYN GREENE.
OTHERWISE KNOWN AS "TOP HAT."

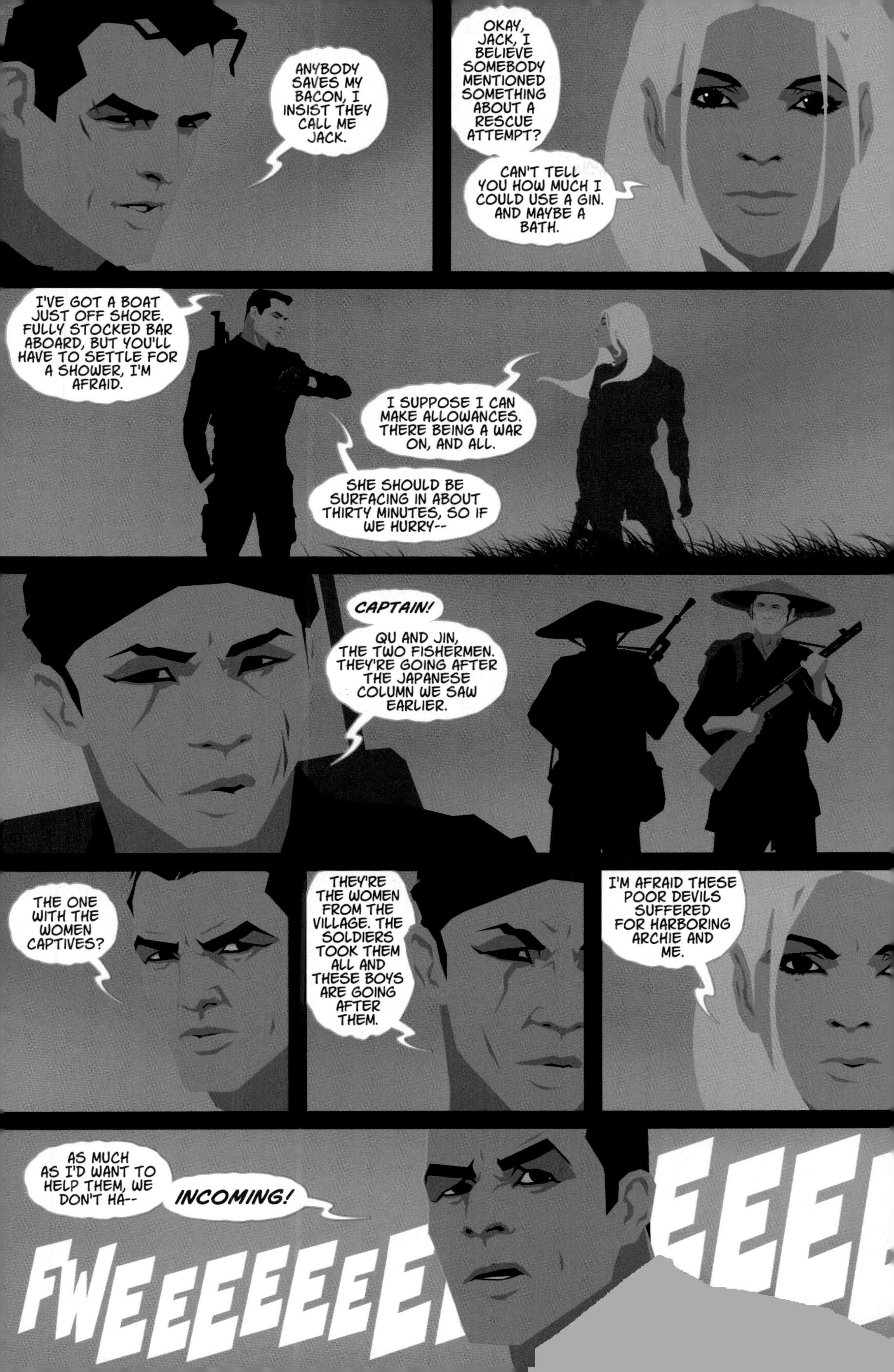

ANYBODY SAVES MY BACON, I INSIST THEY CALL ME JACK.
OKAY, JACK, I BELIEVE SOMEBODY MENTIONED SOMETHING ABOUT A RESCUE ATTEMPT?
CAN'T TELL YOU HOW MUCH I COULD USE A GIN. AND MAYBE A BATH.
I'VE GOT A BOAT JUST OFF SHORE. FULLY STOCKED BAR ABOARD, BUT YOU'LL HAVE TO SETTLE FOR A SHOWER, I'M AFRAID.
I SUPPOSE I CAN MAKE ALLOWANCES. THERE BEING A WAR ON, AND ALL.
SHE SHOULD BE SURFACING IN ABOUT THIRTY MINUTES, SO IF WE HURRY--
CAPTAIN!
QU AND JIN, THE TWO FISHERMEN. THEY'RE GOING AFTER THE JAPANESE COLUMN WE SAW EARLIER.
THE ONE WITH THE WOMEN CAPTIVES?
THEY'RE THE WOMEN FROM THE VILLAGE. THE SOLDIERS TOOK THEM ALL AND THESE BOYS ARE GOING AFTER THEM.
I'M AFRAID THESE POOR DEVILS SUFFERED FOR HARBORING ARCHIE AND ME.
AS MUCH AS I'D WANT TO HELP THEM, WE DON'T HA--
INCOMING!
FWEEEEEEEEEEEEE

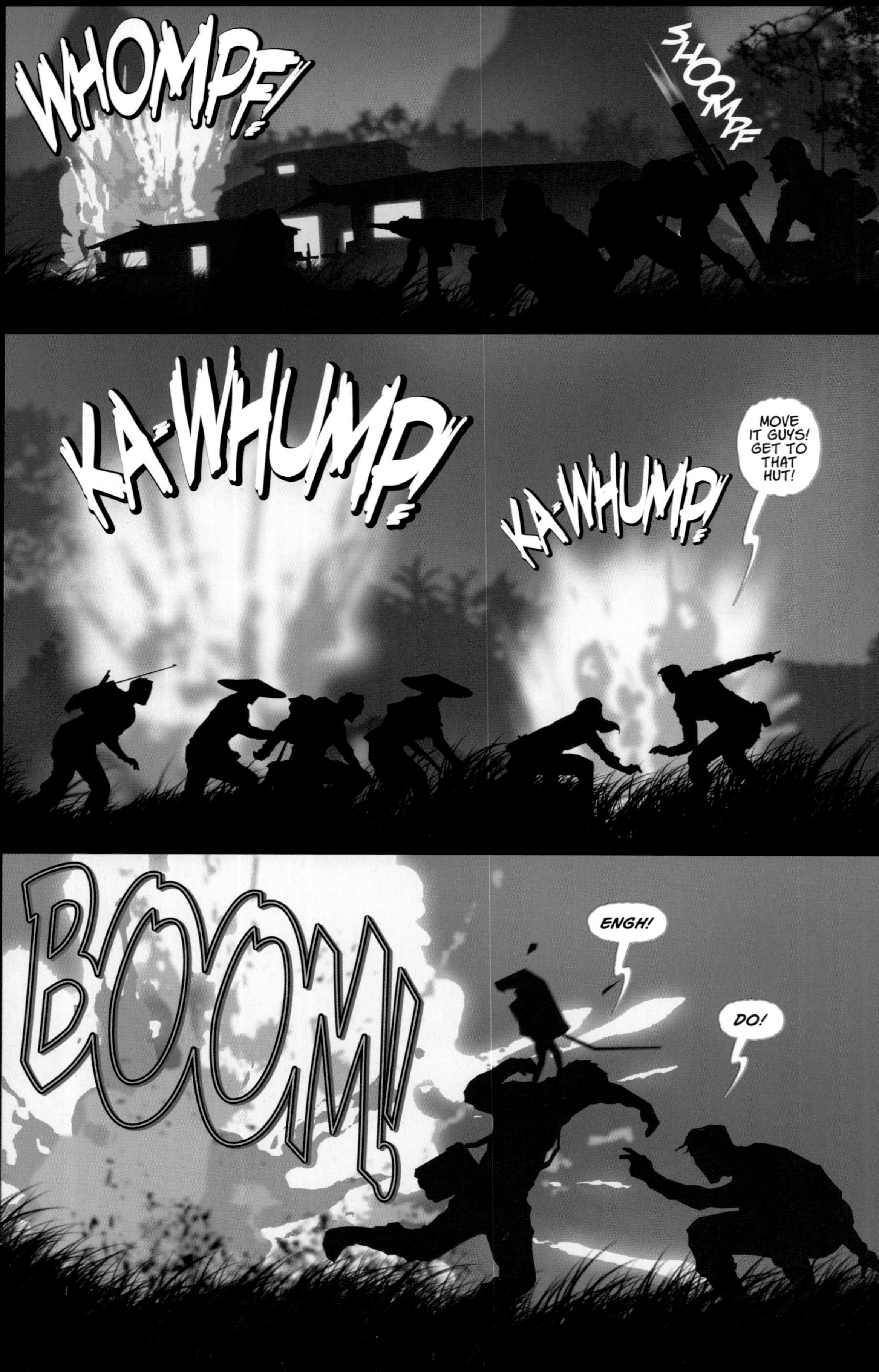
WHOMPF!
SHOOMPF
KA-WHUMP!
KA-WHUMP!
MOVE IT GUYS! GET TO THAT HUT!
BOOM!
ENGH!
DO!

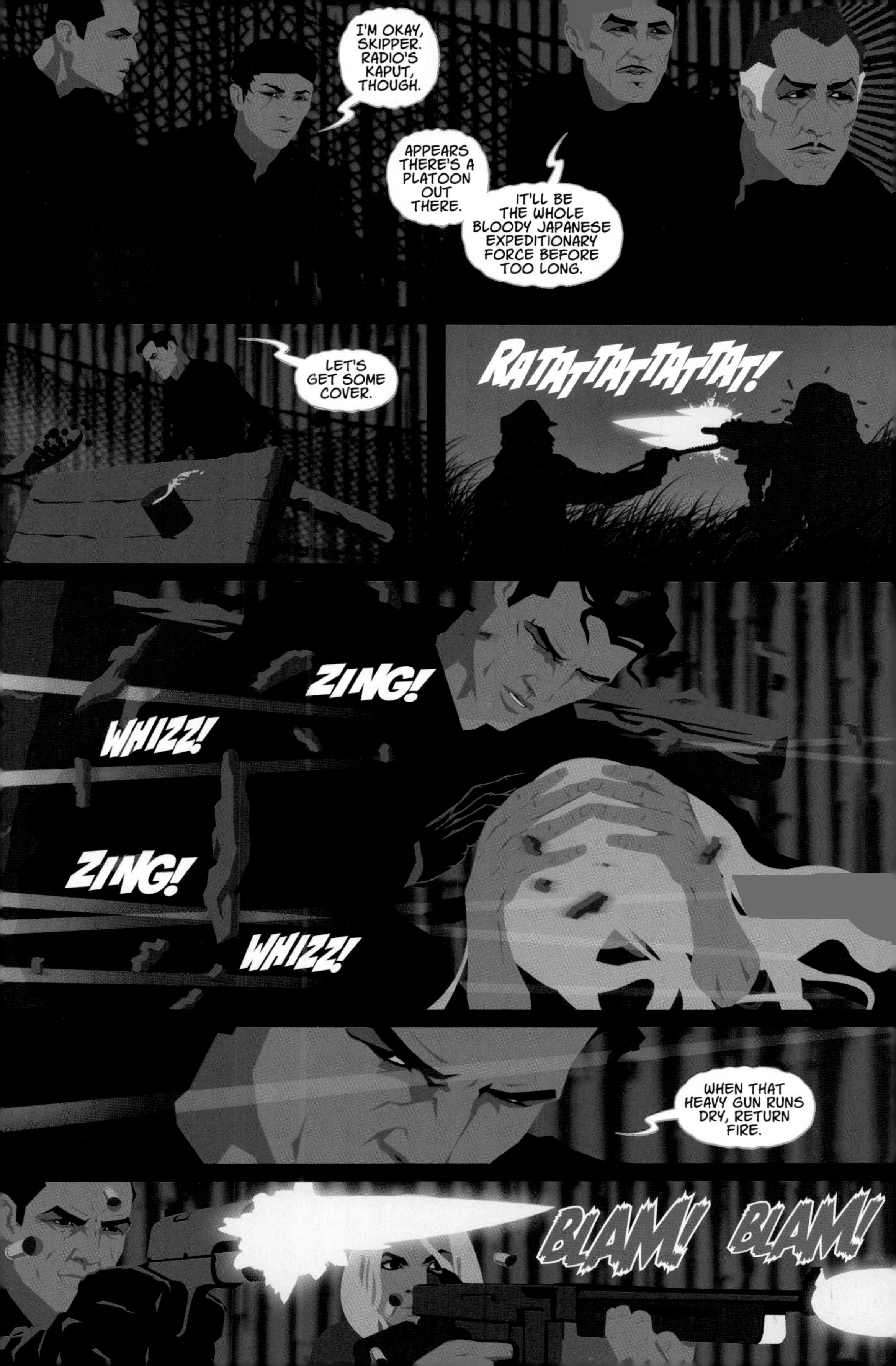
I'M OKAY, SKIPPER. RADIO'S KAPUT, THOUGH.
APPEARS THERE'S A PLATOON OUT THERE.
IT'LL BE THE WHOLE BLOODY JAPANESE EXPEDITIONARY FORCE BEFORE TOO LONG.
LET'S GET SOME COVER.
RATATTATTATTAT!
ZING!
WHIZZ!
ZING!
WHIZZ!
WHEN THAT HEAVY GUN RUNS DRY, RETURN FIRE.
BLAM! BLAM!

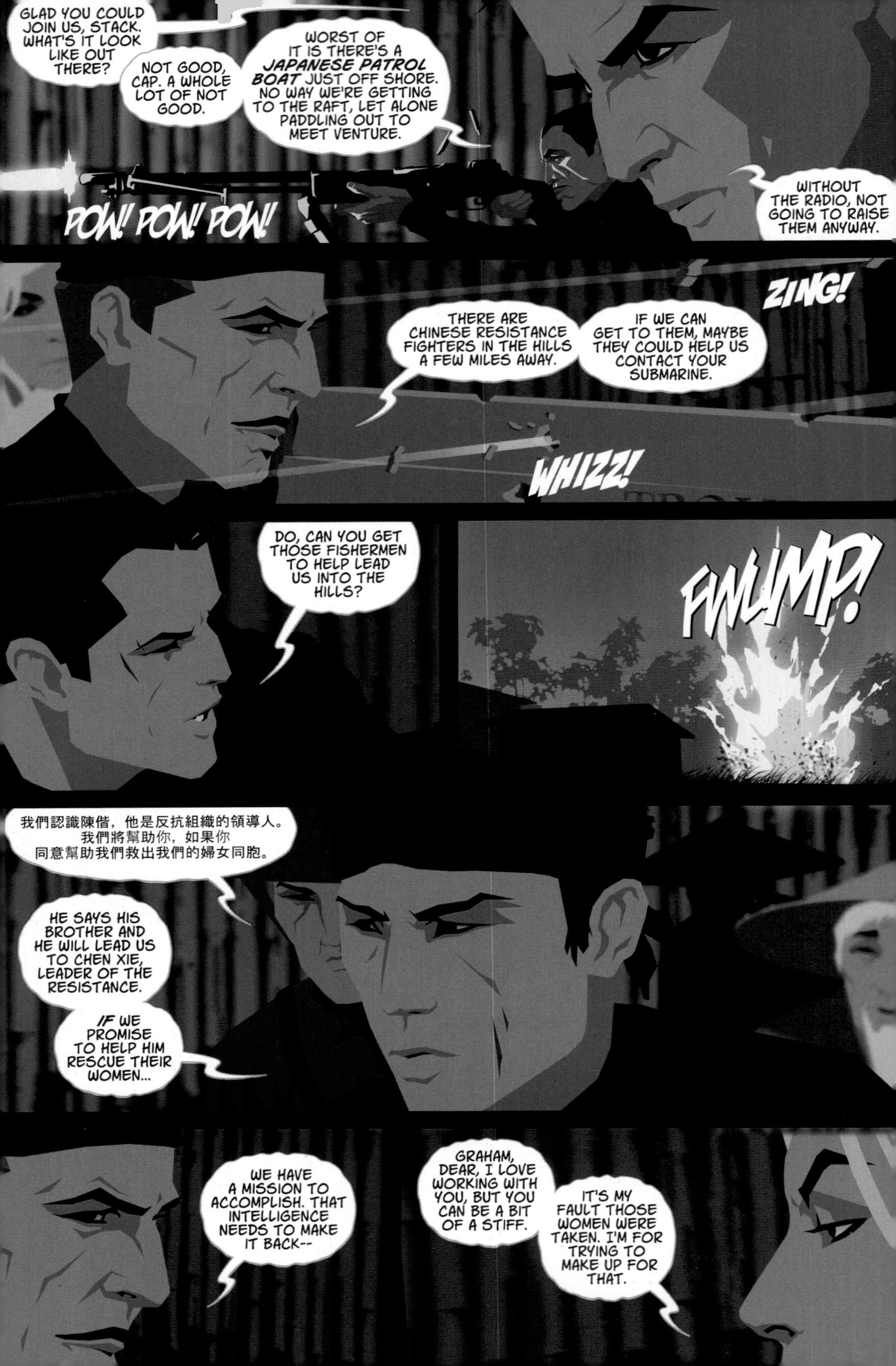
GLAD YOU COULD JOIN US, STACK. WHAT'S IT LOOK LIKE OUT THERE?
NOT GOOD, CAP. A WHOLE LOT OF NOT GOOD.
WORST OF IT IS THERE'S A JAPANESE PATROL BOAT JUST OFF SHORE. NO WAY WE'RE GETTING TO THE RAFT, LET ALONE PADDLING OUT TO MEET VENTURE.
POW! POW! POW!
WITHOUT THE RADIO, NOT GOING TO RAISE THEM ANYWAY.
ZING!
THERE ARE CHINESE RESISTANCE FIGHTERS IN THE HILLS A FEW MILES AWAY.
IF WE CAN GET TO THEM, MAYBE THEY COULD HELP US CONTACT YOUR SUBMARINE.
WHIZZ!
DO, CAN YOU GET THOSE FISHERMEN TO HELP LEAD US INTO THE HILLS?
FWUMP!
我們認識陳偕，他是反抗組織的領導人。我們將幫助你，如果你同意幫助我們救出我們的婦女同胞。
HE SAYS HIS BROTHER AND HE WILL LEAD US TO CHEN XIE, LEADER OF THE RESISTANCE.
IF WE PROMISE TO HELP HIM RESCUE THEIR WOMEN...
WE HAVE A MISSION TO ACCOMPLISH. THAT INTELLIGENCE NEEDS TO MAKE IT BACK--
GRAHAM, DEAR, I LOVE WORKING WITH YOU, BUT YOU CAN BE A BIT OF A STIFF.
IT'S MY FAULT THOSE WOMEN WERE TAKEN. I'M FOR TRYING TO MAKE UP FOR THAT.

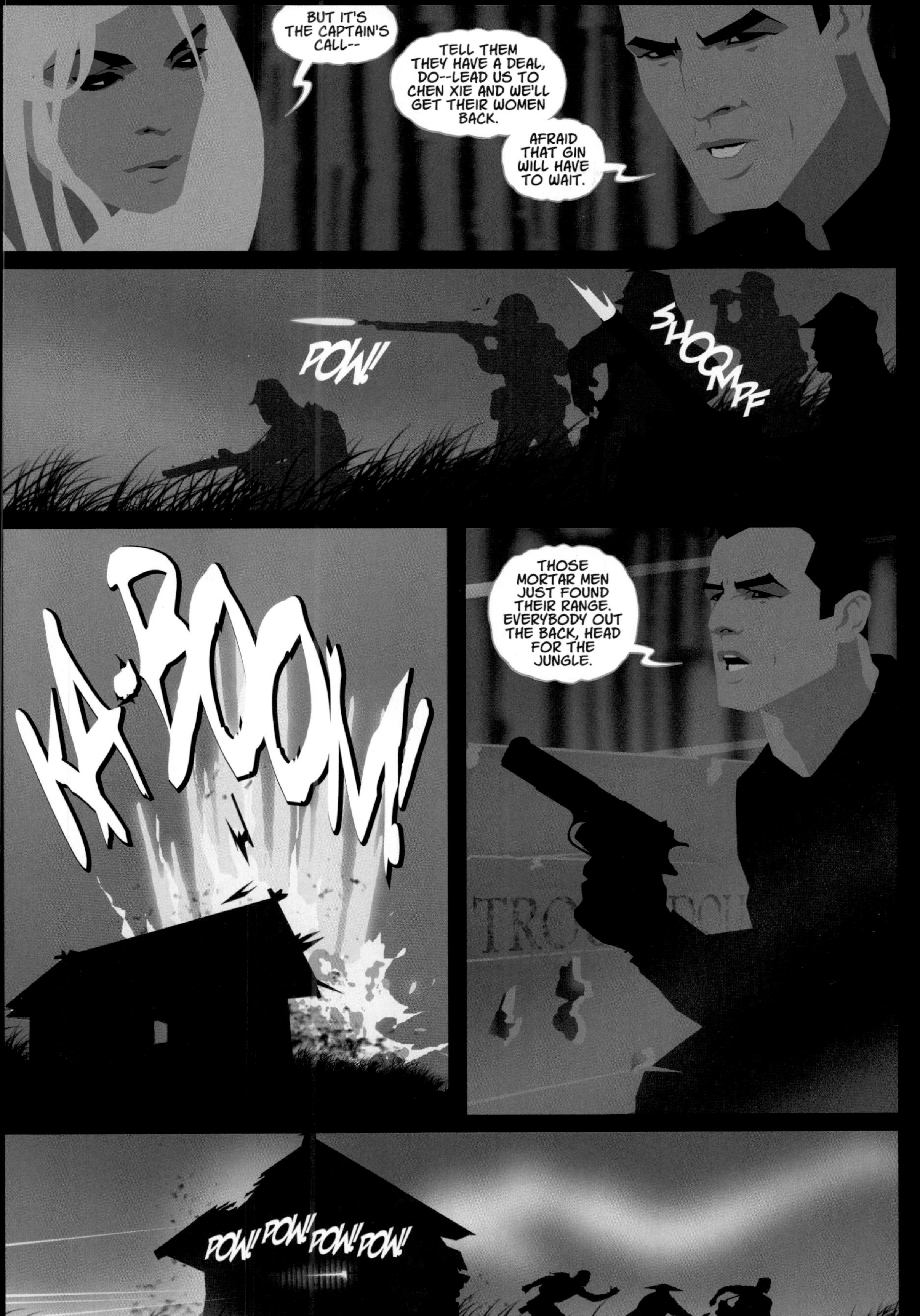
BUT IT'S THE CAPTAIN'S CALL--
TELL THEM THEY HAVE A DEAL, DO--LEAD US TO CHEN XIE AND WE'LL GET THEIR WOMEN BACK.
AFRAID THAT GIN WILL HAVE TO WAIT.
POW!
SHOOMPF
KA-BOOM!
THOSE MORTAR MEN JUST FOUND THEIR RANGE. EVERYBODY OUT THE BACK, HEAD FOR THE JUNGLE.
POW! POW! POW! POW!

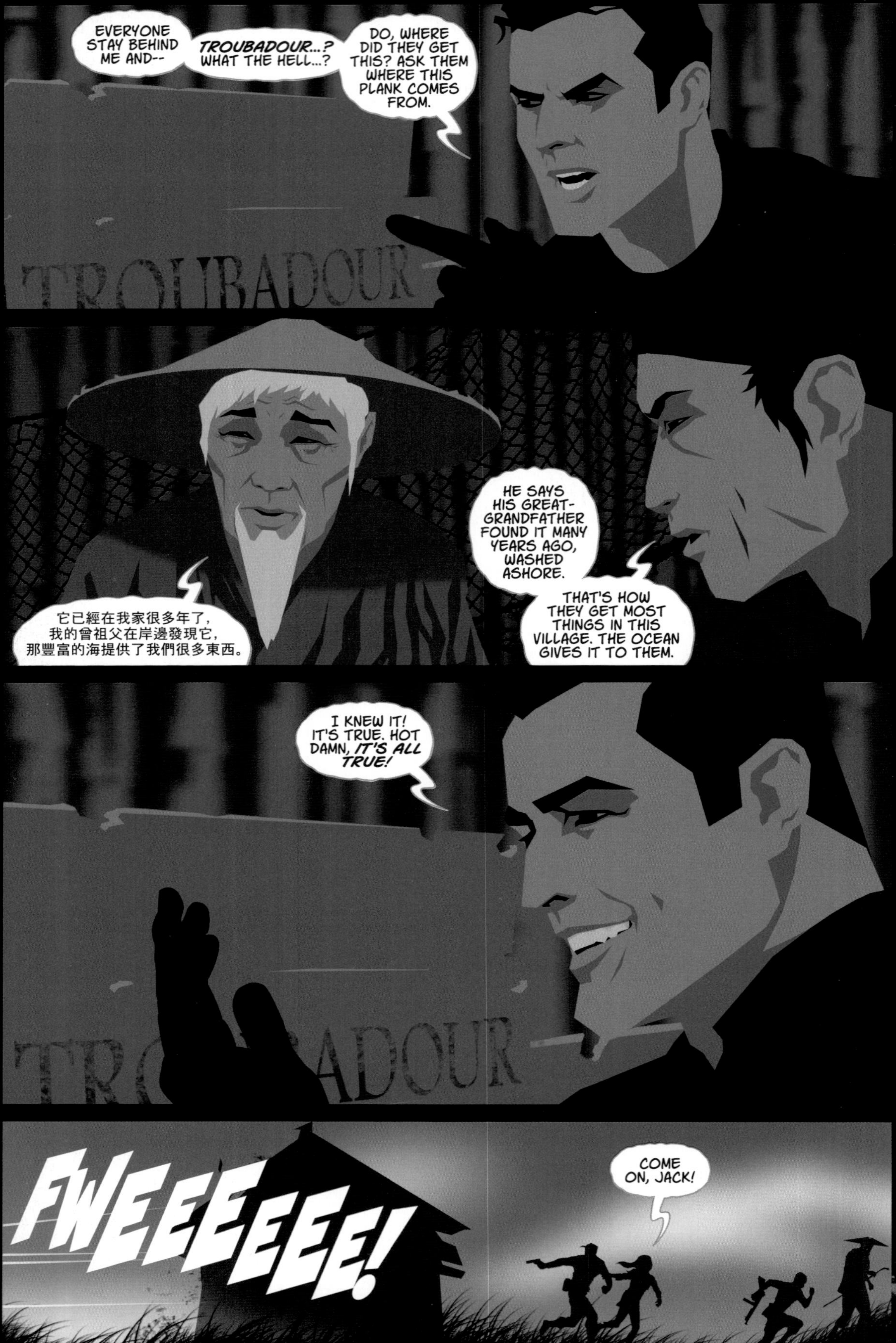
EVERYONE STAY BEHIND ME AND--
TROUBADOUR...? WHAT THE HELL...?
DO, WHERE DID THEY GET THIS? ASK THEM WHERE THIS PLANK COMES FROM.
TROUBADOUR
它已經在我家很多年了,
我的曾祖父在岸邊發現它,
那豐富的海提供了我們很多東西。
HE SAYS HIS GREAT-GRANDFATHER FOUND IT MANY YEARS AGO, WASHED ASHORE.
THAT'S HOW THEY GET MOST THINGS IN THIS VILLAGE. THE OCEAN GIVES IT TO THEM.
I KNEW IT! IT'S TRUE. HOT DAMN, IT'S ALL TRUE!
FWEEEEEE!
COME ON, JACK!

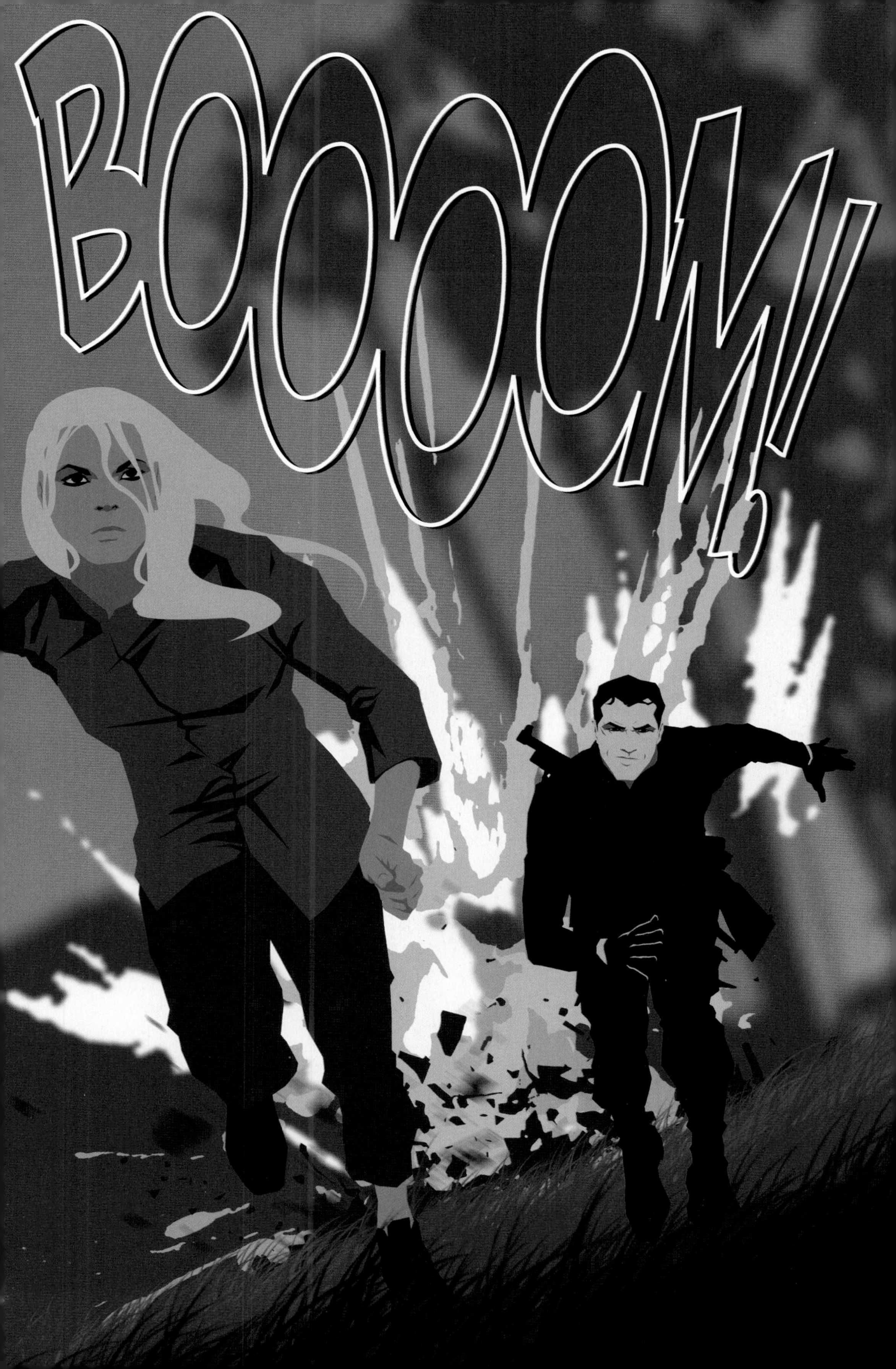
BOOOOM!

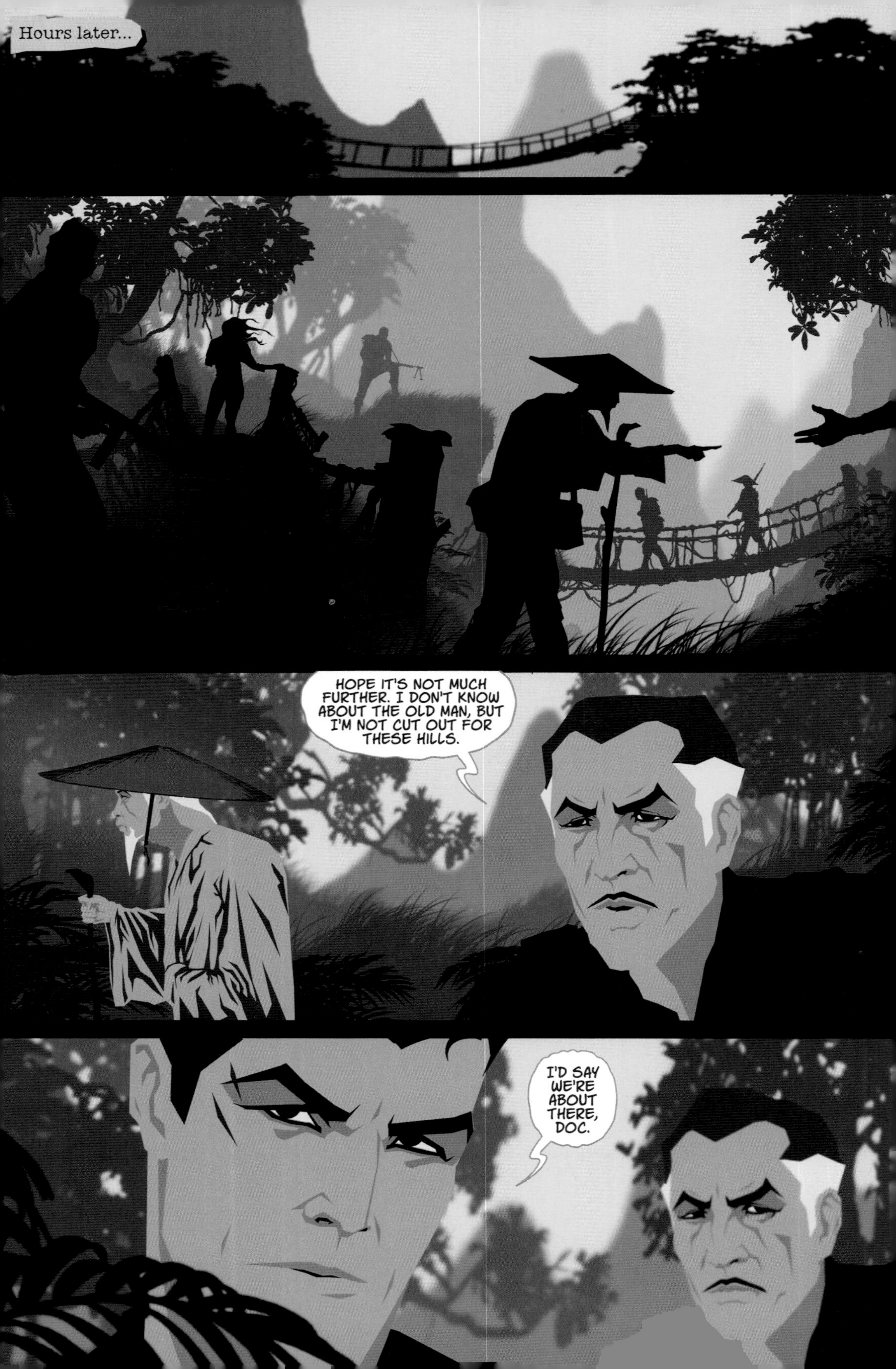

Hours later...
HOPE IT'S NOT MUCH FURTHER. I DON'T KNOW ABOUT THE OLD MAN, BUT I'M NOT CUT OUT FOR THESE HILLS.
I'D SAY WE'RE ABOUT THERE, DOC.

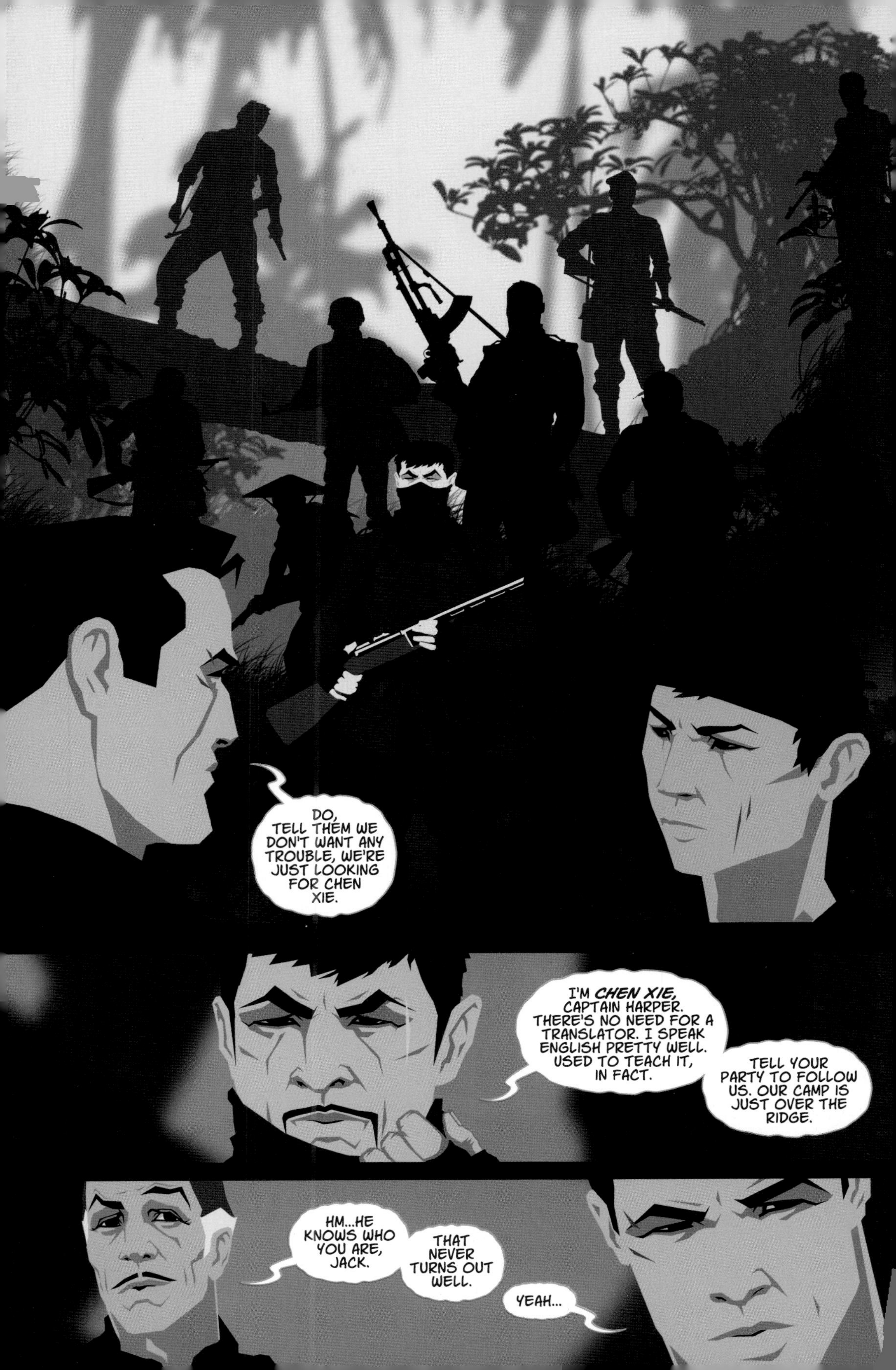
DO, TELL THEM WE DON'T WANT ANY TROUBLE, WE'RE JUST LOOKING FOR CHEN XIE.
I'M *CHEN XIE,* CAPTAIN HARPER. THERE'S NO NEED FOR A TRANSLATOR. I SPEAK ENGLISH PRETTY WELL. USED TO TEACH IT, IN FACT.
TELL YOUR PARTY TO FOLLOW US. OUR CAMP IS JUST OVER THE RIDGE.
HM...HE KNOWS WHO YOU ARE, JACK.
THAT NEVER TURNS OUT WELL.
YEAH...

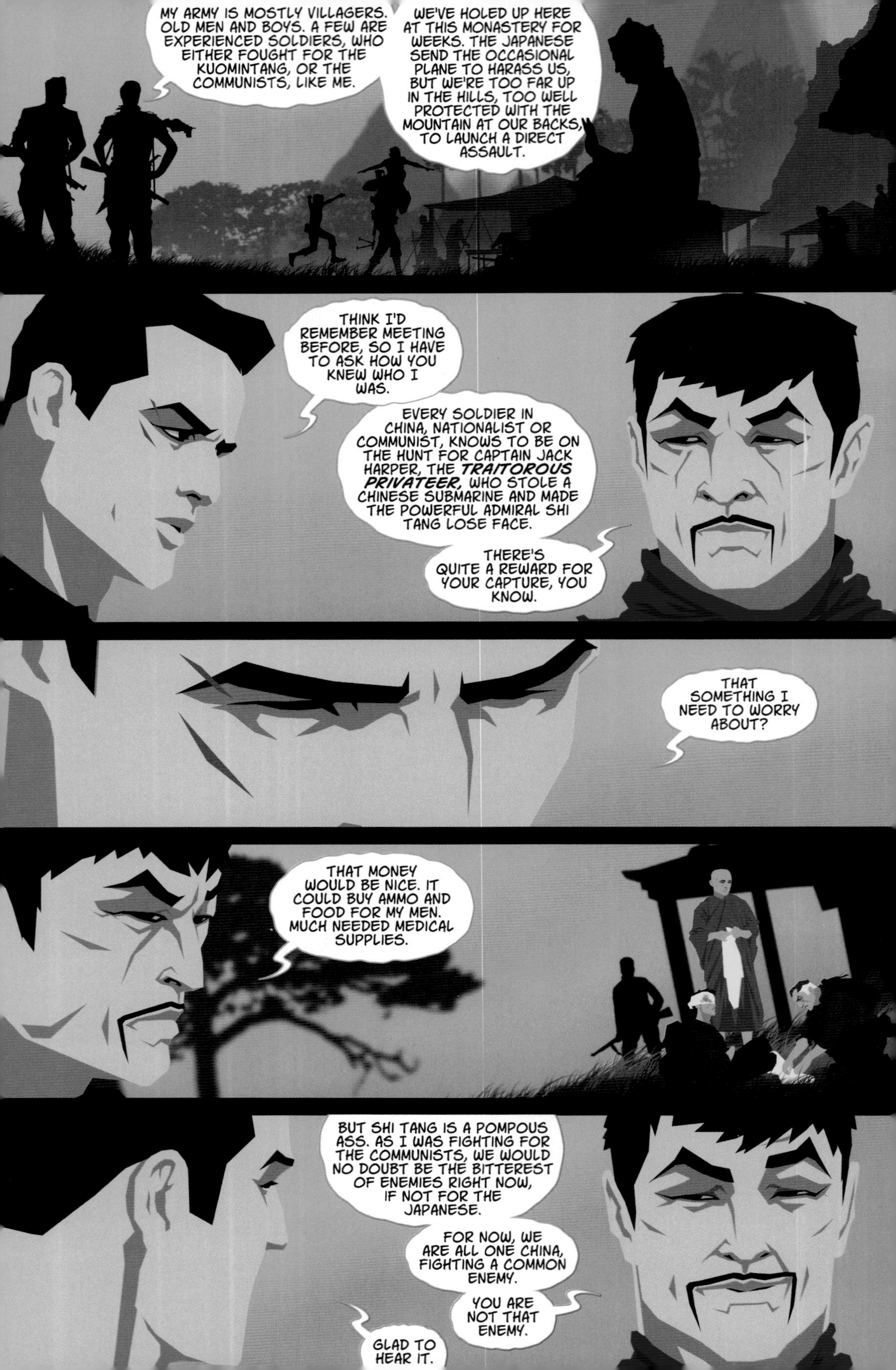
MY ARMY IS MOSTLY VILLAGERS. OLD MEN AND BOYS. A FEW ARE EXPERIENCED SOLDIERS, WHO EITHER FOUGHT FOR THE KUOMINTANG, OR THE COMMUNISTS, LIKE ME.
WE'VE HOLED UP HERE AT THIS MONASTERY FOR WEEKS. THE JAPANESE SEND THE OCCASIONAL PLANE TO HARASS US, BUT WE'RE TOO FAR UP IN THE HILLS, TOO WELL PROTECTED WITH THE MOUNTAIN AT OUR BACKS, TO LAUNCH A DIRECT ASSAULT.
THINK I'D REMEMBER MEETING BEFORE, SO I HAVE TO ASK HOW YOU KNEW WHO I WAS.
EVERY SOLDIER IN CHINA, NATIONALIST OR COMMUNIST, KNOWS TO BE ON THE HUNT FOR CAPTAIN JACK HARPER, THE ***TRAITOROUS PRIVATEER,*** WHO STOLE A CHINESE SUBMARINE AND MADE THE POWERFUL ADMIRAL SHI TANG LOSE FACE.
THERE'S QUITE A REWARD FOR YOUR CAPTURE, YOU KNOW.
THAT SOMETHING I NEED TO WORRY ABOUT?
THAT MONEY WOULD BE NICE. IT COULD BUY AMMO AND FOOD FOR MY MEN. MUCH NEEDED MEDICAL SUPPLIES.
BUT SHI TANG IS A POMPOUS ASS. AS I WAS FIGHTING FOR THE COMMUNISTS, WE WOULD NO DOUBT BE THE BITTEREST OF ENEMIES RIGHT NOW, IF NOT FOR THE JAPANESE.
FOR NOW, WE ARE ALL ONE CHINA, FIGHTING A COMMON ENEMY.
YOU ARE NOT THAT ENEMY.
GLAD TO HEAR IT.

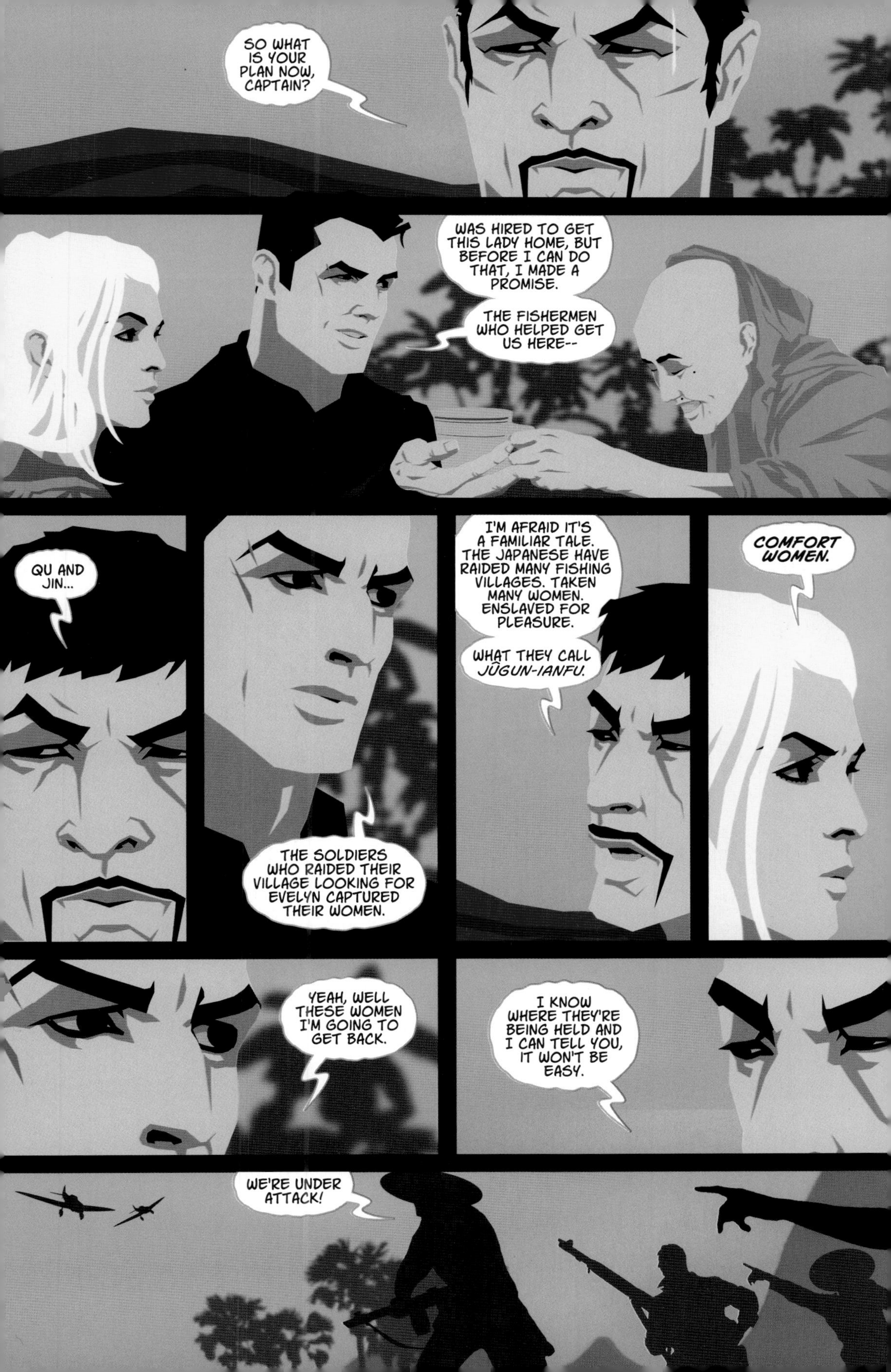
SO WHAT IS YOUR PLAN NOW, CAPTAIN?
WAS HIRED TO GET THIS LADY HOME, BUT BEFORE I CAN DO THAT, I MADE A PROMISE.
THE FISHERMEN WHO HELPED GET US HERE--
QU AND JIN...
THE SOLDIERS WHO RAIDED THEIR VILLAGE LOOKING FOR EVELYN CAPTURED THEIR WOMEN.
I'M AFRAID IT'S A FAMILIAR TALE. THE JAPANESE HAVE RAIDED MANY FISHING VILLAGES. TAKEN MANY WOMEN. ENSLAVED FOR PLEASURE.
WHAT THEY CALL *JŪGUN-IANFU.*
COMFORT WOMEN.
YEAH, WELL THESE WOMEN I'M GOING TO GET BACK.
I KNOW WHERE THEY'RE BEING HELD AND I CAN TELL YOU, IT WON'T BE EASY.
WE'RE UNDER ATTACK!

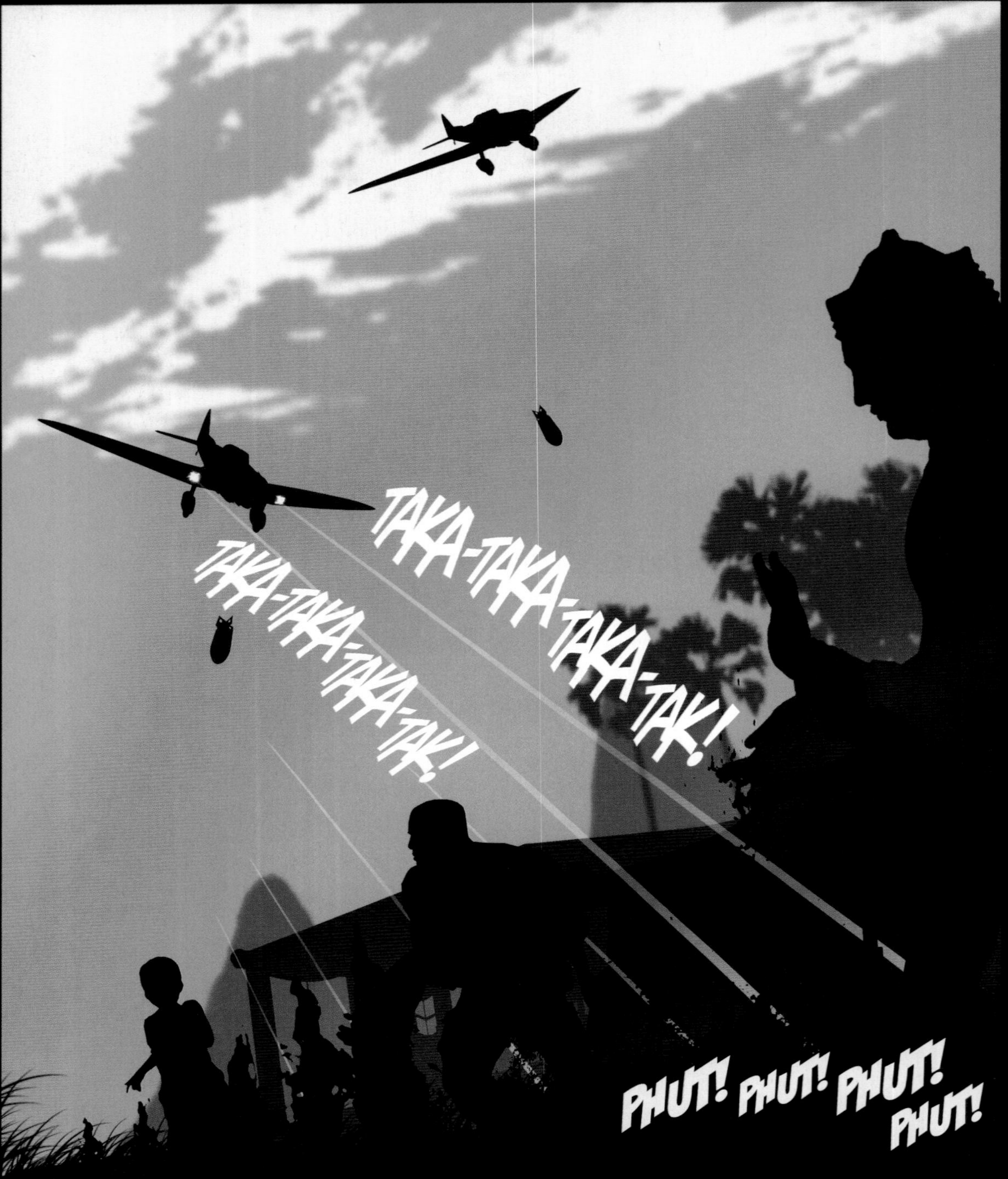
TAKA-TAKA-TAKA-TAK!
TAKA-TAKA-TAKA-TAK!
PHUT! PHUT! PHUT! PHUT!

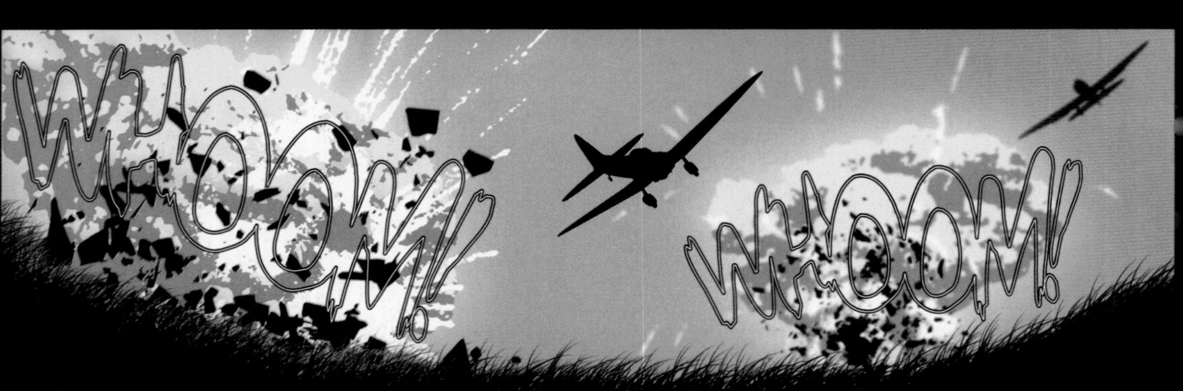
WHOOM!
WHOOM!

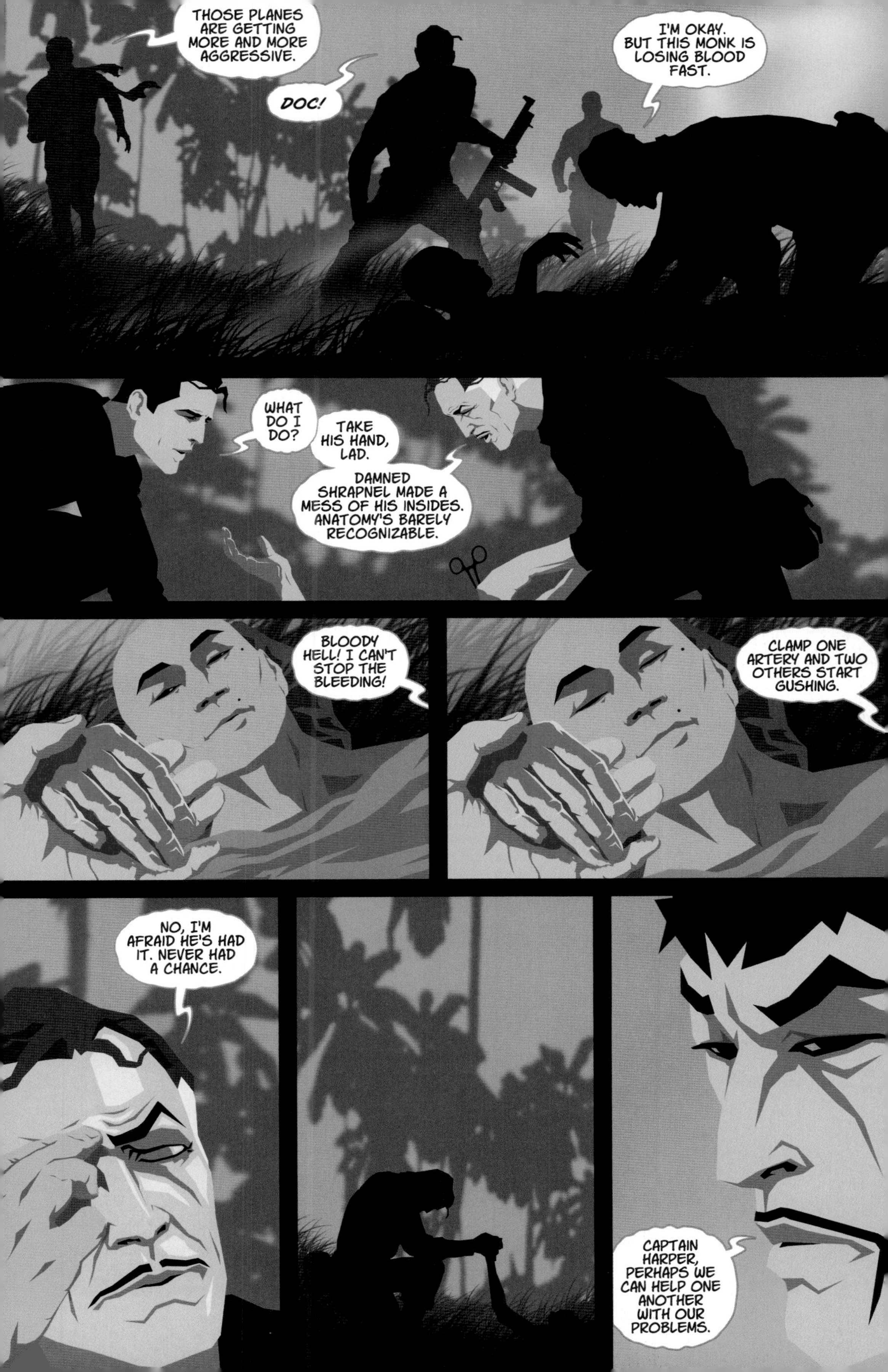
THOSE PLANES ARE GETTING MORE AND MORE AGGRESSIVE.
DOC!
I'M OKAY. BUT THIS MONK IS LOSING BLOOD FAST.
WHAT DO I DO?
TAKE HIS HAND, LAD.
DAMNED SHRAPNEL MADE A MESS OF HIS INSIDES. ANATOMY'S BARELY RECOGNIZABLE.
BLOODY HELL! I CAN'T STOP THE BLEEDING!
CLAMP ONE ARTERY AND TWO OTHERS START GUSHING.
NO, I'M AFRAID HE'S HAD IT. NEVER HAD A CHANCE.
CAPTAIN HARPER, PERHAPS WE CAN HELP ONE ANOTHER WITH OUR PROBLEMS.

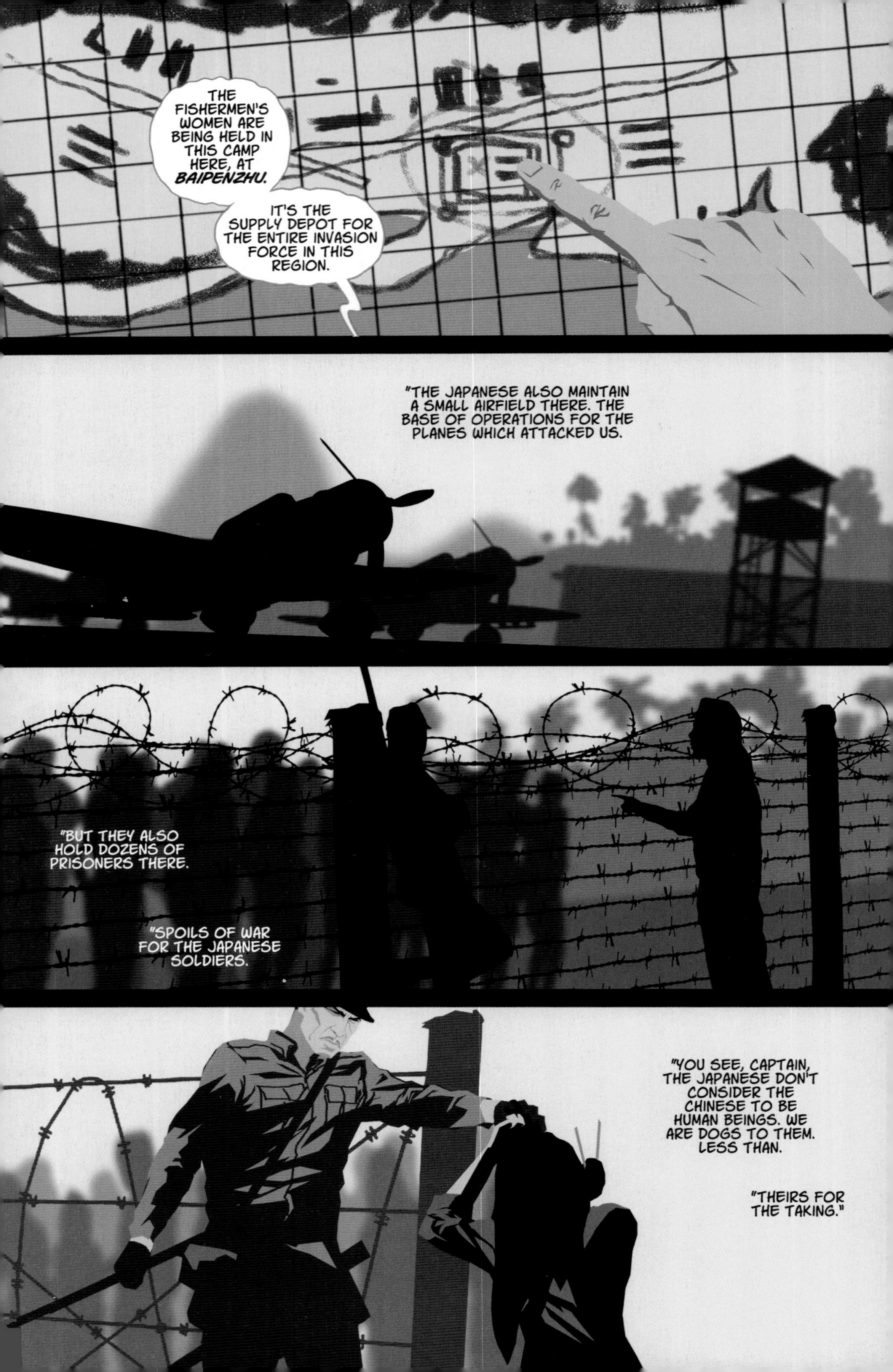
THE FISHERMEN'S WOMEN ARE BEING HELD IN THIS CAMP HERE, AT *BAIPENZHU*.
IT'S THE SUPPLY DEPOT FOR THE ENTIRE INVASION FORCE IN THIS REGION.
"THE JAPANESE ALSO MAINTAIN A SMALL AIRFIELD THERE. THE BASE OF OPERATIONS FOR THE PLANES WHICH ATTACKED US.
"BUT THEY ALSO HOLD DOZENS OF PRISONERS THERE.
"SPOILS OF WAR FOR THE JAPANESE SOLDIERS.
"YOU SEE, CAPTAIN, THE JAPANESE DON'T CONSIDER THE CHINESE TO BE HUMAN BEINGS. WE ARE DOGS TO THEM. LESS THAN.
"THEIRS FOR THE TAKING."

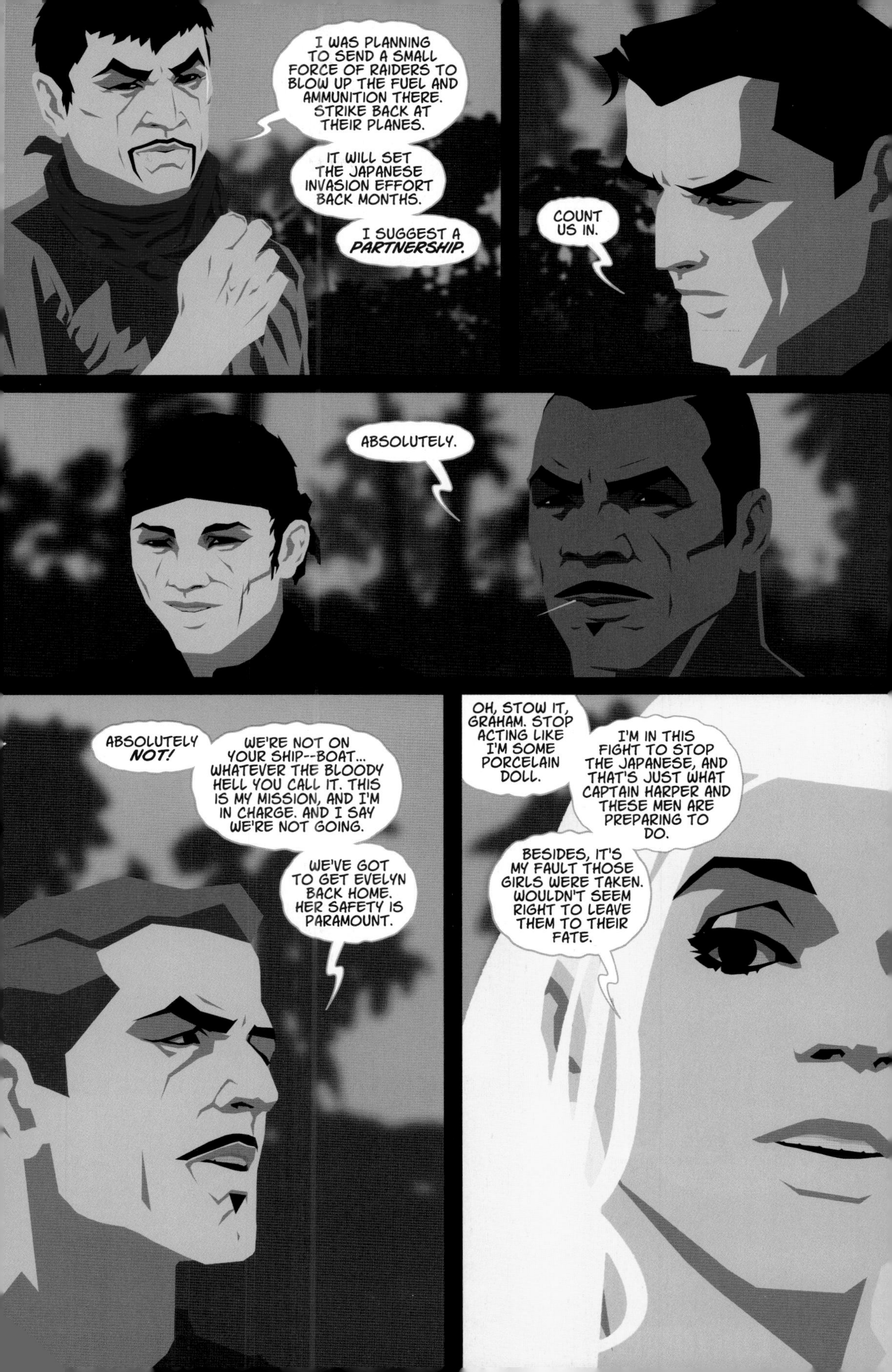

I WAS PLANNING TO SEND A SMALL FORCE OF RAIDERS TO BLOW UP THE FUEL AND AMMUNITION THERE. STRIKE BACK AT THEIR PLANES.
IT WILL SET THE JAPANESE INVASION EFFORT BACK MONTHS.
I SUGGEST A ***PARTNERSHIP***.
COUNT US IN.
ABSOLUTELY.
ABSOLUTELY ***NOT!***
WE'RE NOT ON YOUR SHIP--BOAT... WHATEVER THE BLOODY HELL YOU CALL IT. THIS IS MY MISSION, AND I'M IN CHARGE. AND I SAY WE'RE NOT GOING.
WE'VE GOT TO GET EVELYN BACK HOME. HER SAFETY IS PARAMOUNT.
OH, STOW IT, GRAHAM. STOP ACTING LIKE I'M SOME PORCELAIN DOLL.
I'M IN THIS FIGHT TO STOP THE JAPANESE, AND THAT'S JUST WHAT CAPTAIN HARPER AND THESE MEN ARE PREPARING TO DO.
BESIDES, IT'S MY FAULT THOSE GIRLS WERE TAKEN. WOULDN'T SEEM RIGHT TO LEAVE THEM TO THEIR FATE.

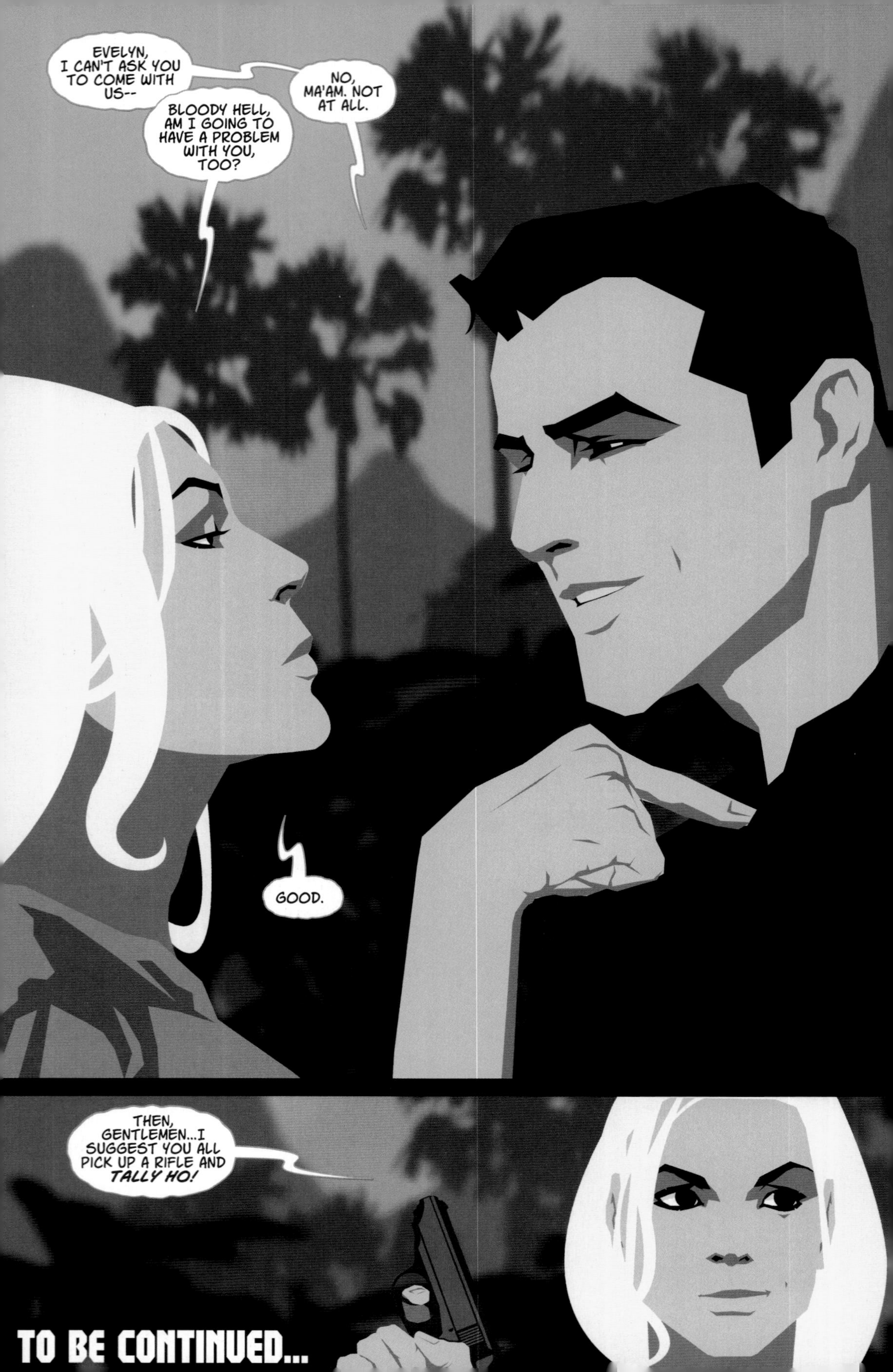
EVELYN, I CAN'T ASK YOU TO COME WITH US--
NO, MA'AM. NOT AT ALL.
BLOODY HELL, AM I GOING TO HAVE A PROBLEM WITH YOU, TOO?
GOOD.
THEN, GENTLEMEN...I SUGGEST YOU ALL PICK UP A RIFLE AND *TALLY HO!*
TO BE CONTINUED...

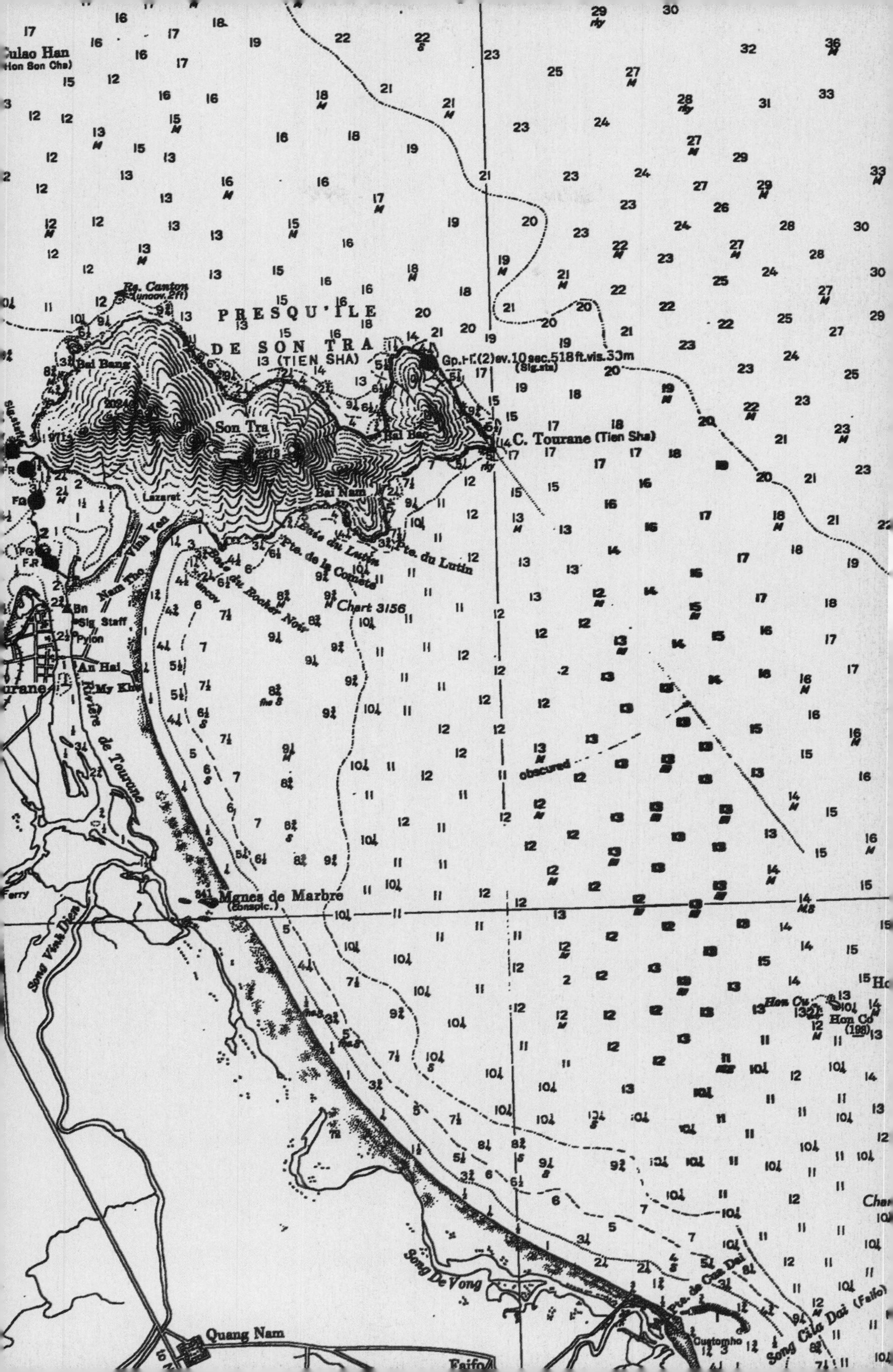

Culao Han
(Hon Son Cha)
PRESQU'ILE
DE SON TRA
(TIEN SHA)
Bai Bang
Son Tra
Bai Bac
Bai Nam
Lazaret
Vinh Yen
Nam Tho
Gp.Fl.(2)ev.10sec.518ft.vis.33m
(Sig.sta)
C. Tourane (Tien Sha)
Pte. du Lutin
Baie du Lutin
Pte. de la Comete
Roche du Rocher Noir
Chart 3156
obscured
Sig Staff
Pylon
An Hai
My Khe
Tourane
Riviere de Tourane
Ferry
Song Vinh Dien
Mgnes de Marbre
Song De Vong
Quang Nam
Faifo
Pte. de Cua Dai
Song Cua Dai (Faifo)
Customho
Hon Cu
Hon Co

March Of The Grenadiers

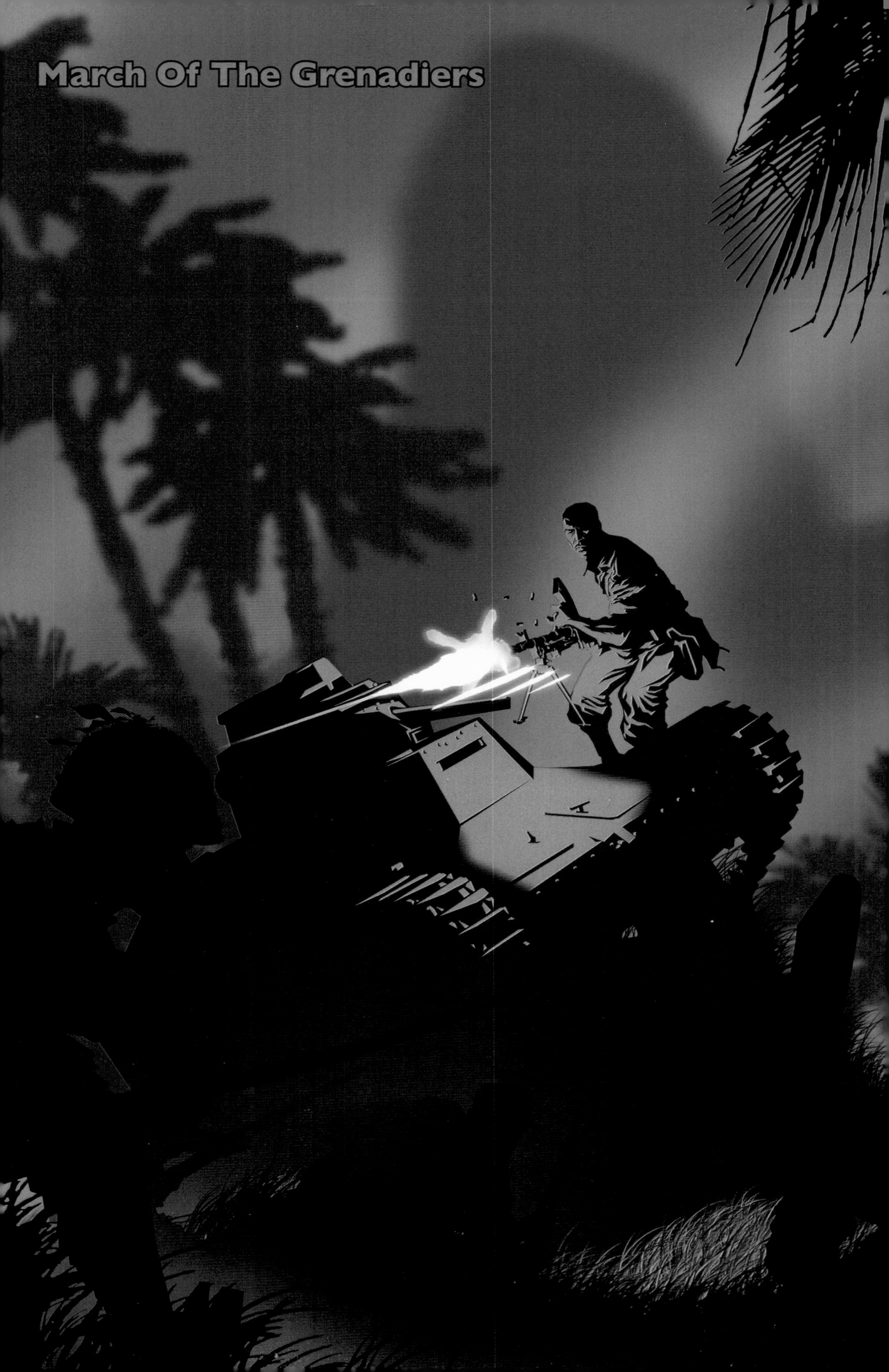

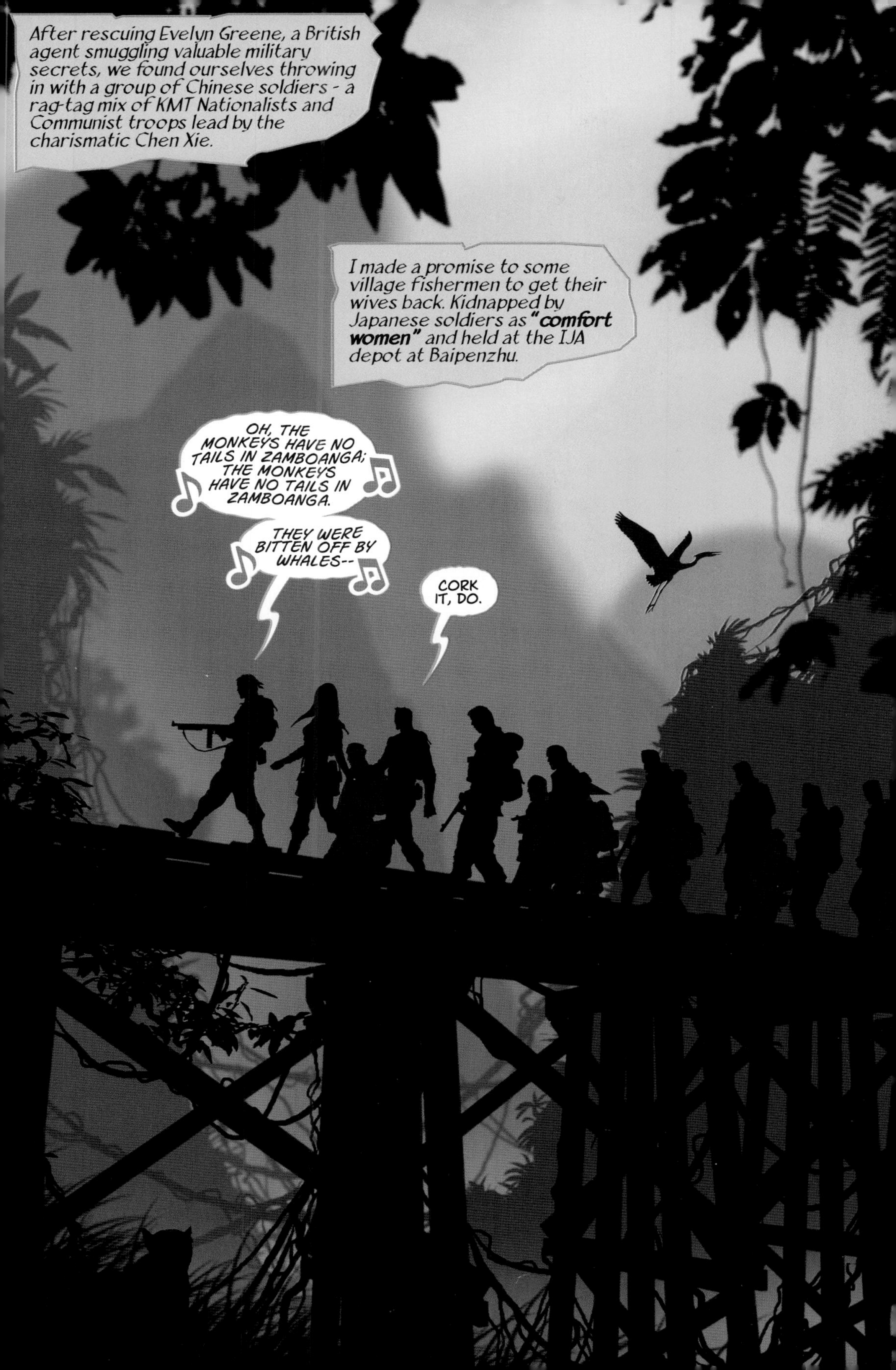
After rescuing Evelyn Greene, a British agent smuggling valuable military secrets, we found ourselves throwing in with a group of Chinese soldiers - a rag-tag mix of KMT Nationalists and Communist troops lead by the charismatic Chen Xie.
I made a promise to some village fishermen to get their wives back. Kidnapped by Japanese soldiers as **"comfort women"** and held at the IJA depot at Baipenzhu.
OH, THE MONKEYS HAVE NO TAILS IN ZAMBOANGA; THE MONKEYS HAVE NO TAILS IN ZAMBOANGA.
THEY WERE BITTEN OFF BY WHALES--
CORK IT, DO.

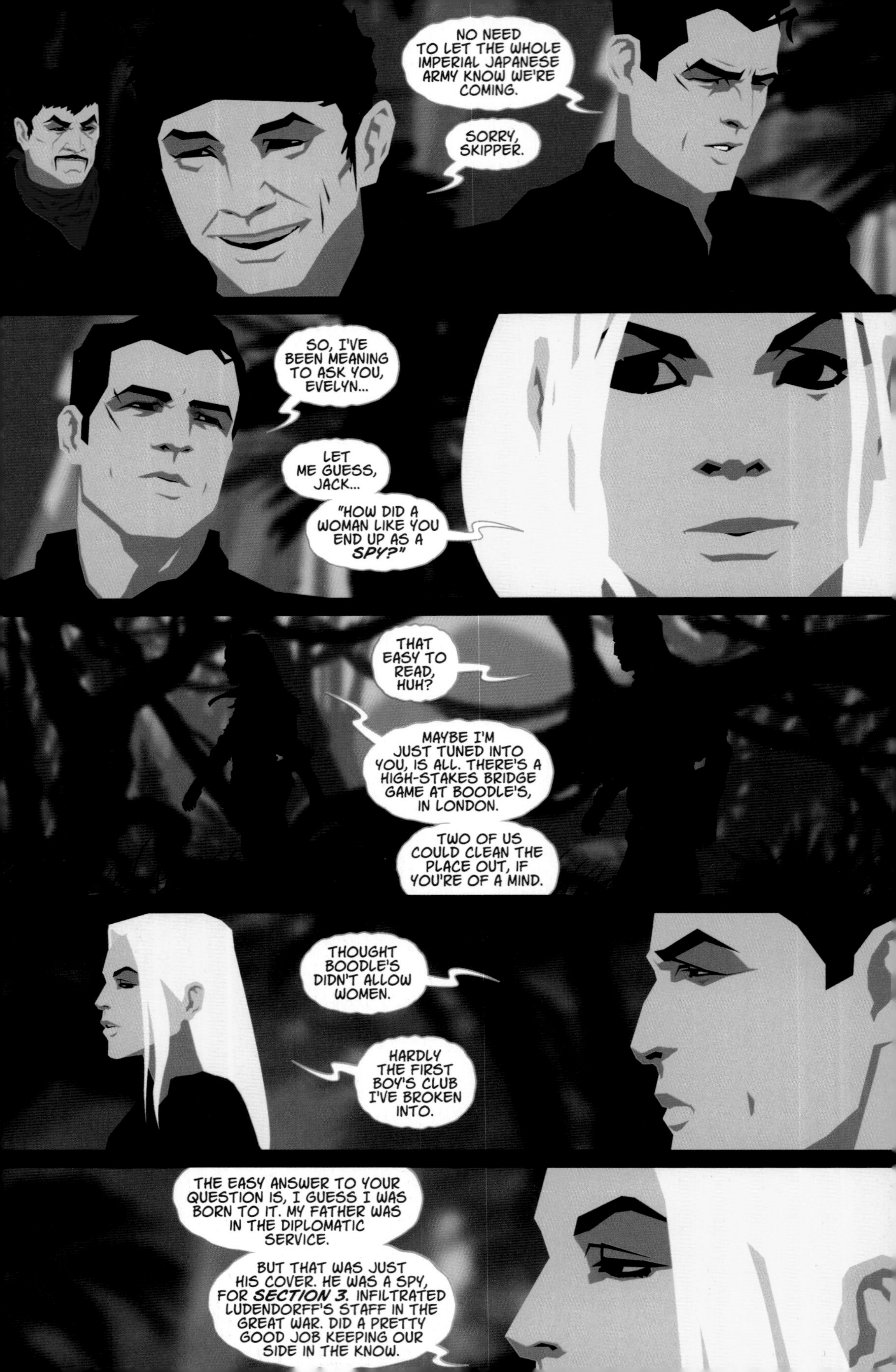
NO NEED TO LET THE WHOLE IMPERIAL JAPANESE ARMY KNOW WE'RE COMING.
SORRY, SKIPPER.
SO, I'VE BEEN MEANING TO ASK YOU, EVELYN...
LET ME GUESS, JACK...
"HOW DID A WOMAN LIKE YOU END UP AS A SPY?"
THAT EASY TO READ, HUH?
MAYBE I'M JUST TUNED INTO YOU, IS ALL. THERE'S A HIGH-STAKES BRIDGE GAME AT BOODLE'S, IN LONDON.
TWO OF US COULD CLEAN THE PLACE OUT, IF YOU'RE OF A MIND.
THOUGHT BOODLE'S DIDN'T ALLOW WOMEN.
HARDLY THE FIRST BOY'S CLUB I'VE BROKEN INTO.
THE EASY ANSWER TO YOUR QUESTION IS, I GUESS I WAS BORN TO IT. MY FATHER WAS IN THE DIPLOMATIC SERVICE.
BUT THAT WAS JUST HIS COVER. HE WAS A SPY, FOR SECTION 3. INFILTRATED LUDENDORFF'S STAFF IN THE GREAT WAR. DID A PRETTY GOOD JOB KEEPING OUR SIDE IN THE KNOW.

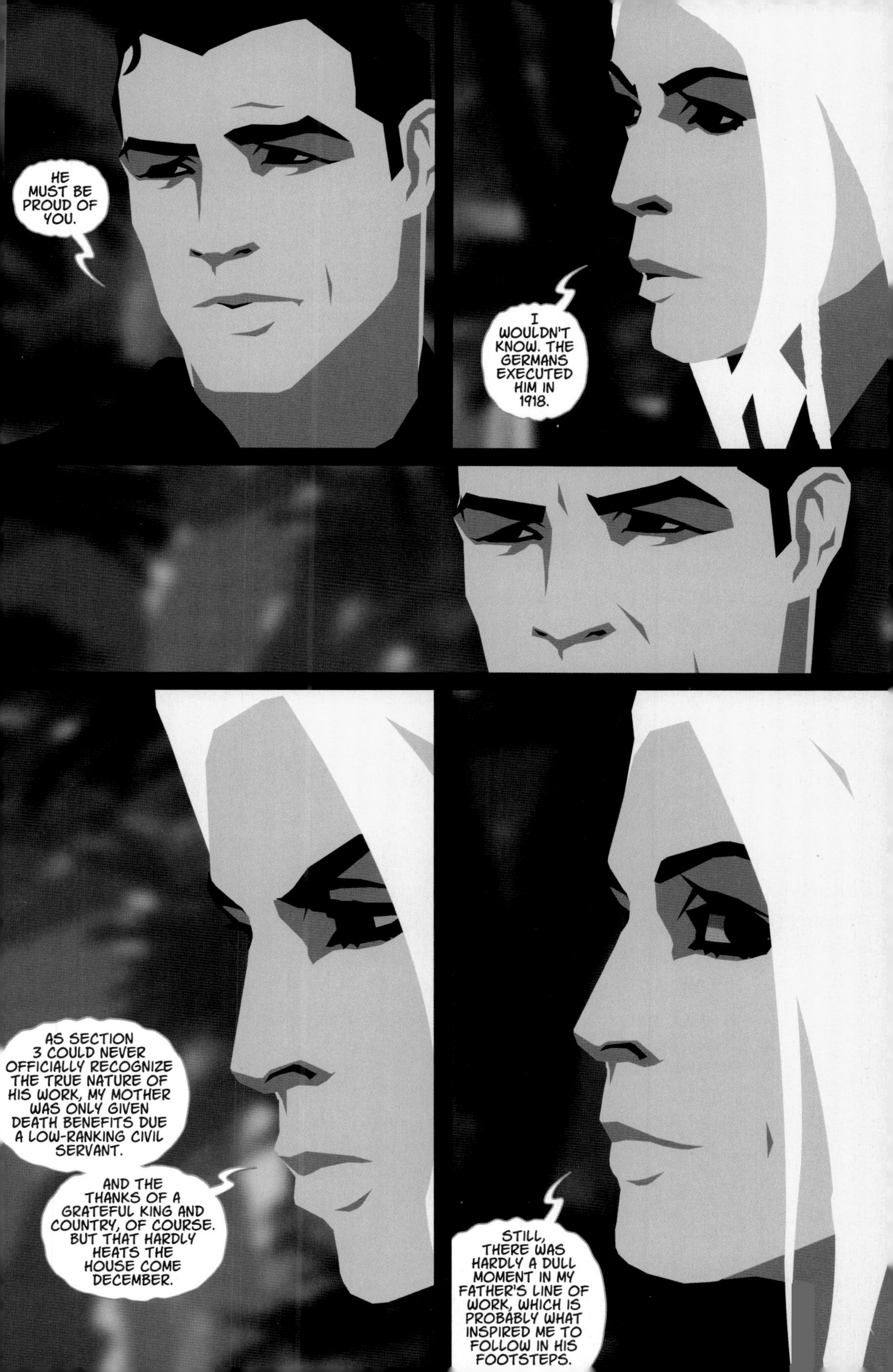
HE MUST BE PROUD OF YOU.
I WOULDN'T KNOW. THE GERMANS EXECUTED HIM IN 1918.
AS SECTION 3 COULD NEVER OFFICIALLY RECOGNIZE THE TRUE NATURE OF HIS WORK, MY MOTHER WAS ONLY GIVEN DEATH BENEFITS DUE A LOW-RANKING CIVIL SERVANT.
AND THE THANKS OF A GRATEFUL KING AND COUNTRY, OF COURSE. BUT THAT HARDLY HEATS THE HOUSE COME DECEMBER.
STILL, THERE WAS HARDLY A DULL MOMENT IN MY FATHER'S LINE OF WORK, WHICH IS PROBABLY WHAT INSPIRED ME TO FOLLOW IN HIS FOOTSTEPS.

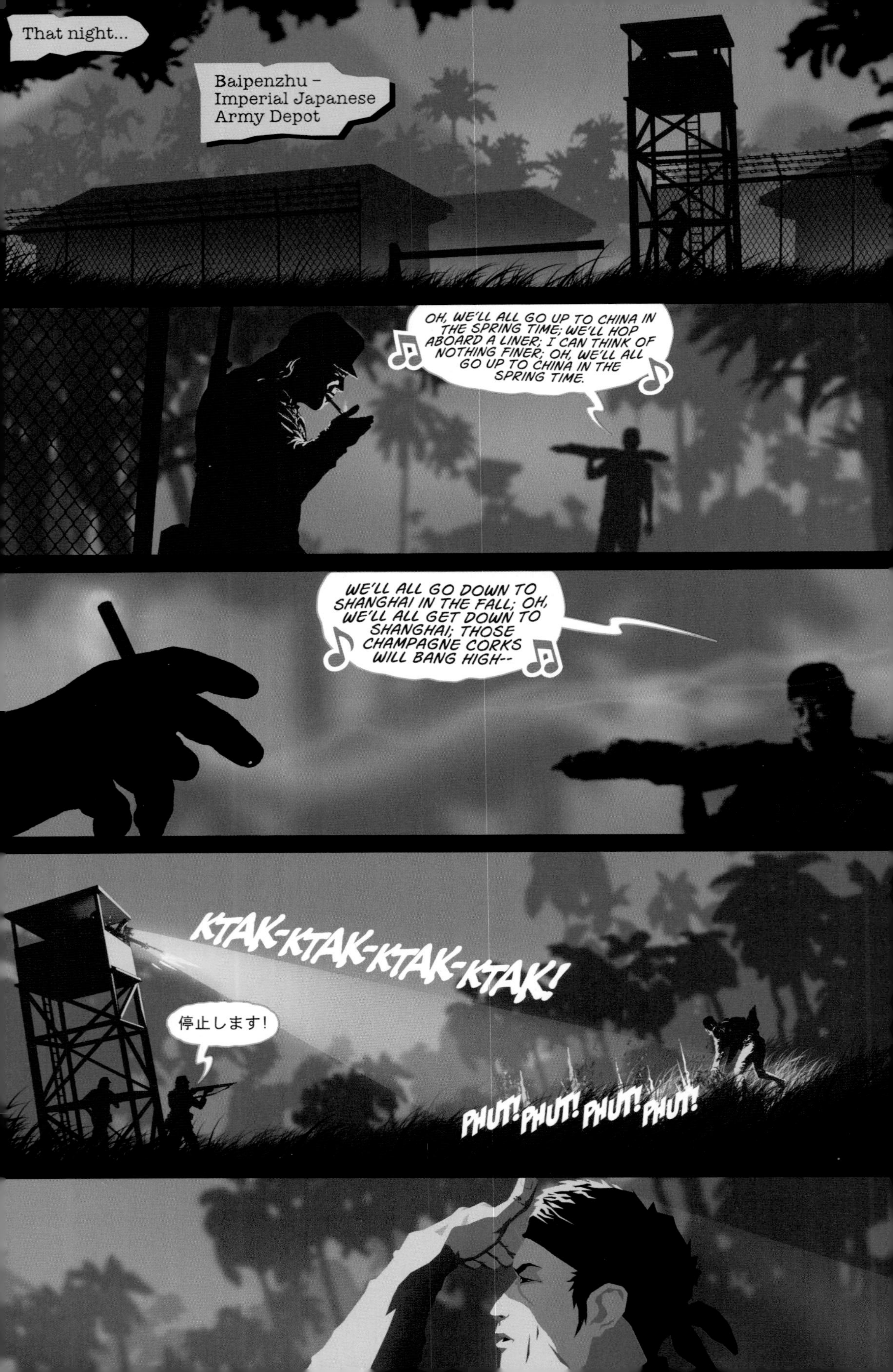
That night...
Baipenzhu – Imperial Japanese Army Depot
OH, WE'LL ALL GO UP TO CHINA IN THE SPRING TIME; WE'LL HOP ABOARD A LINER; I CAN THINK OF NOTHING FINER; OH, WE'LL ALL GO UP TO CHINA IN THE SPRING TIME.
WE'LL ALL GO DOWN TO SHANGHAI IN THE FALL; OH, WE'LL ALL GET DOWN TO SHANGHAI; THOSE CHAMPAGNE CORKS WILL BANG HIGH--
KTAK-KTAK-KTAK-KTAK!
停止します!
PHUT! PHUT! PHUT! PHUT!

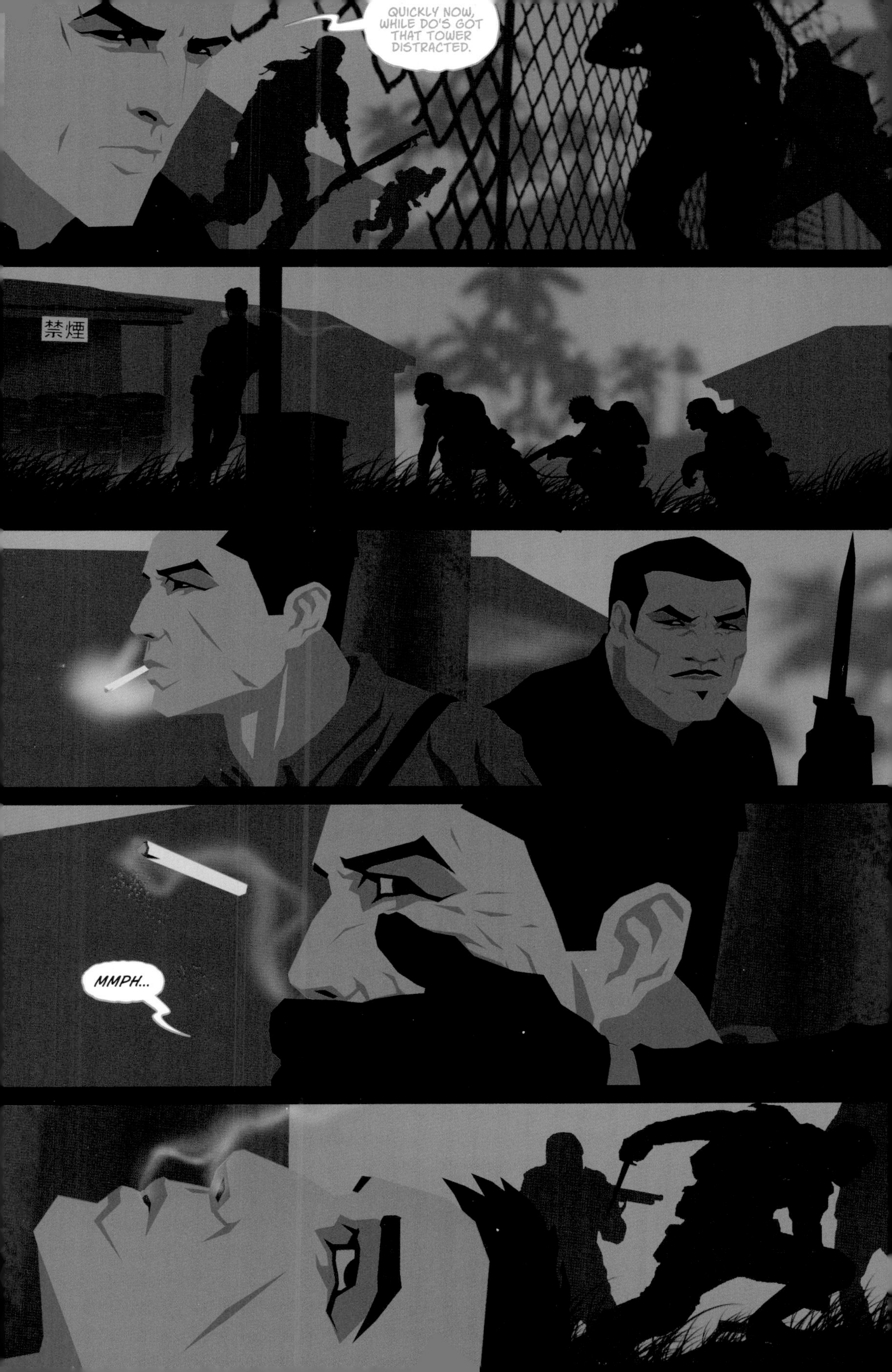
QUICKLY NOW, WHILE DO'S GOT THAT TOWER DISTRACTED.
禁煙
MMPH...

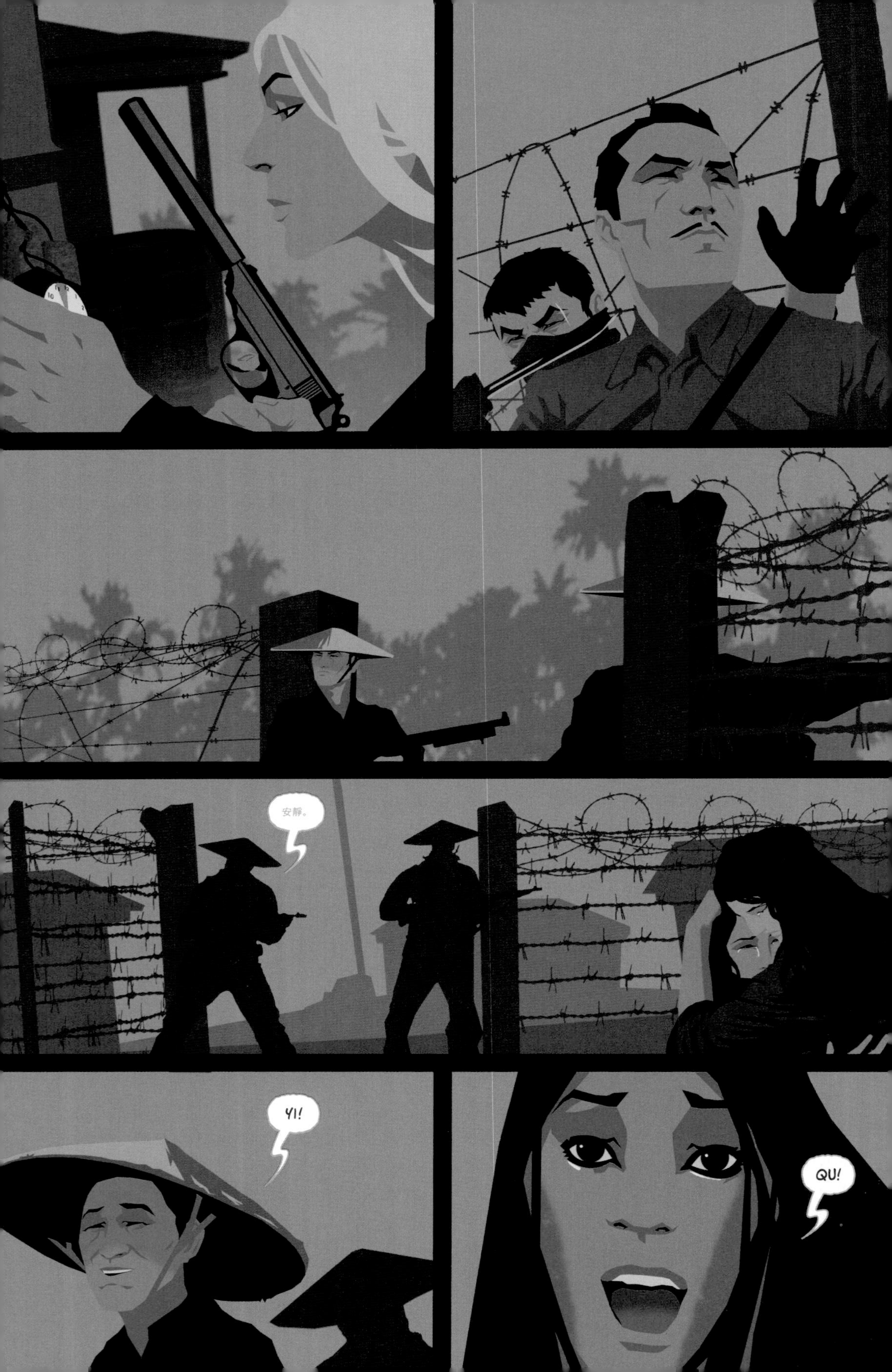
安静。
YI!
QU!

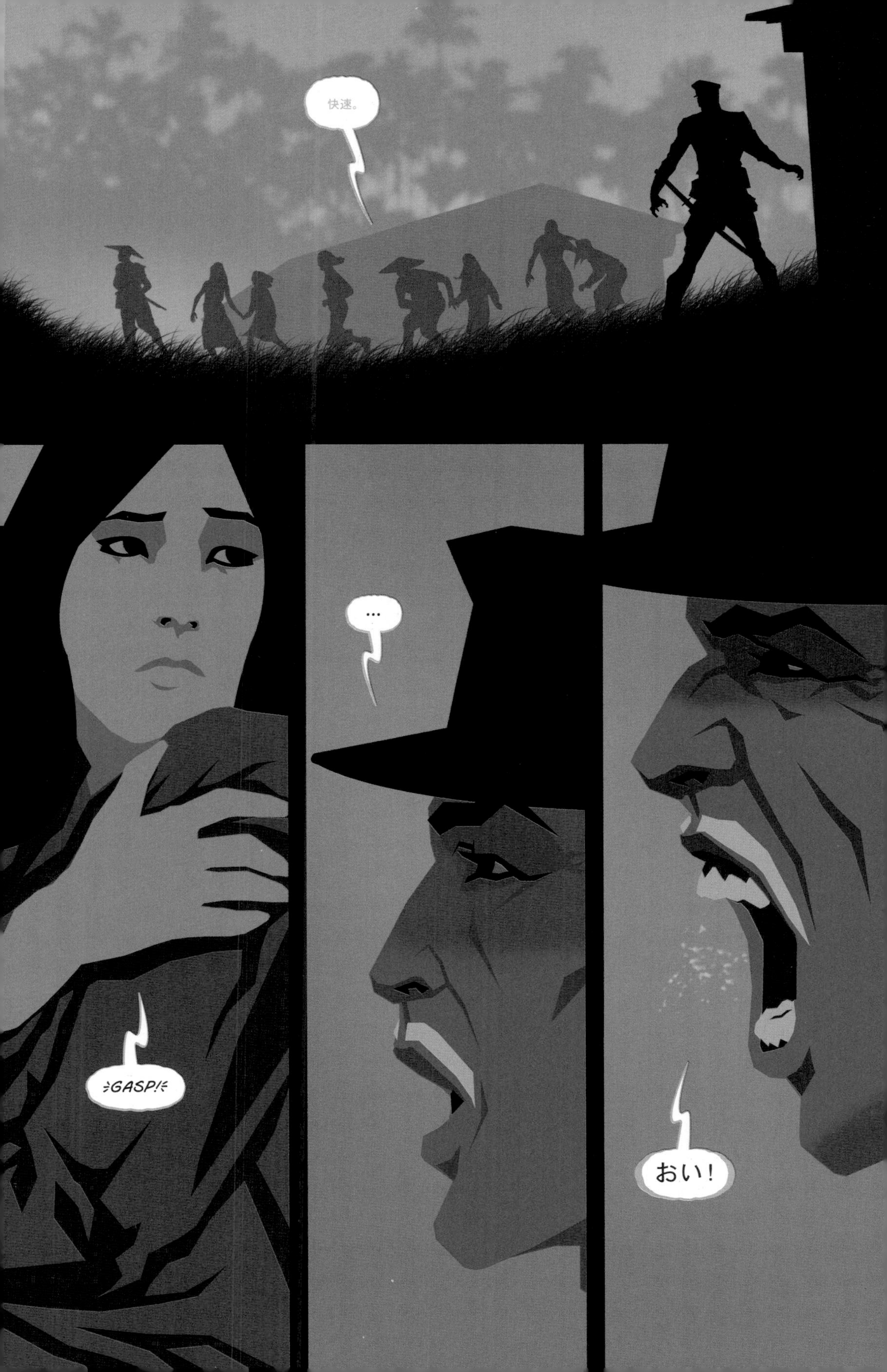
快速。
...
GASP!
おい！

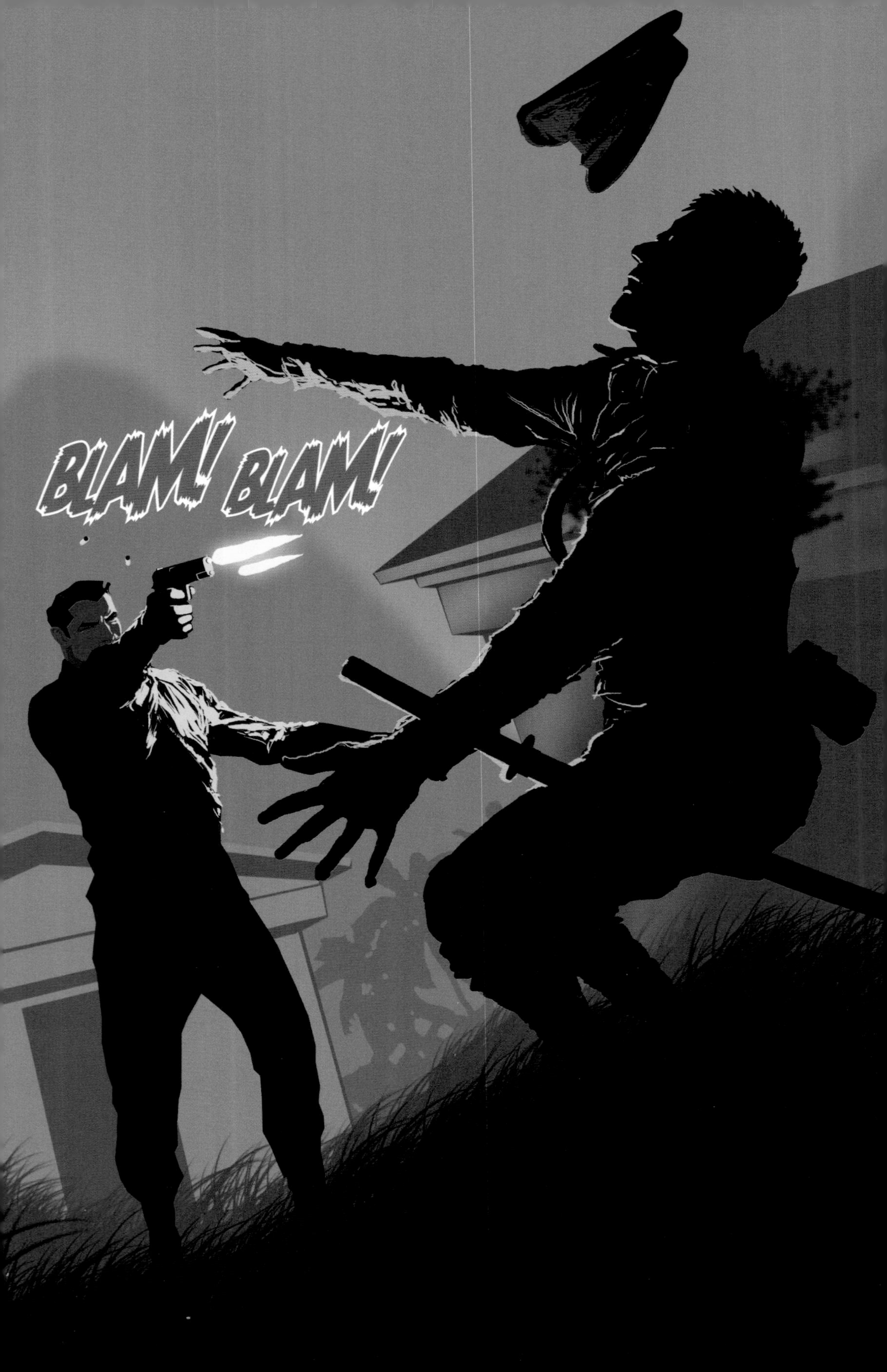
BLAM! BLAM!

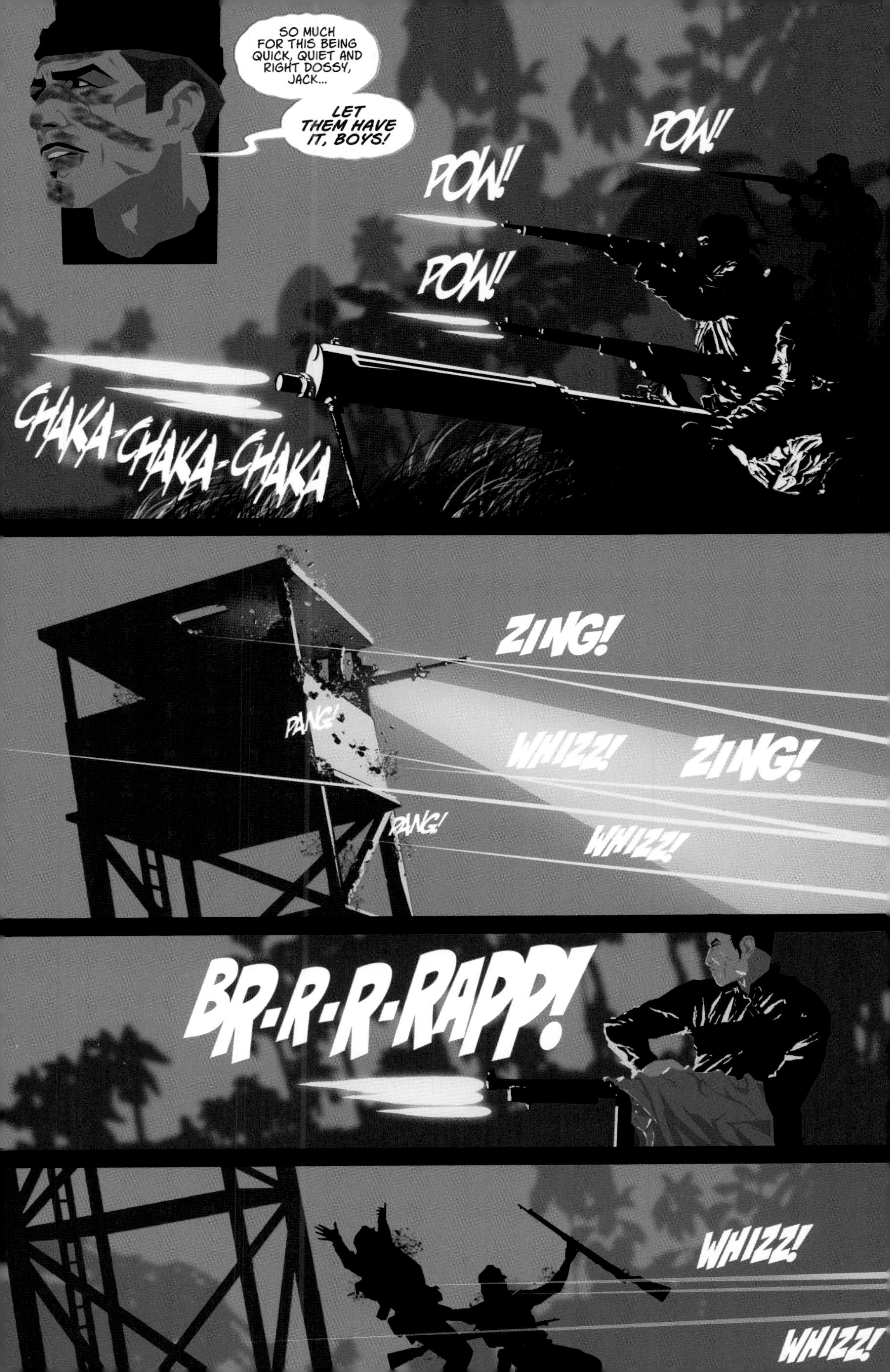
SO MUCH FOR THIS BEING QUICK, QUIET AND RIGHT DOSSY, JACK...
LET THEM HAVE IT, BOYS!
POW!
POW!
POW!
CHAKA-CHAKA-CHAKA
ZING!
PANG!
WHIZZ!
ZING!
PANG!
WHIZZ!
BR-R-R-RAPP!
WHIZZ!
WHIZZ!

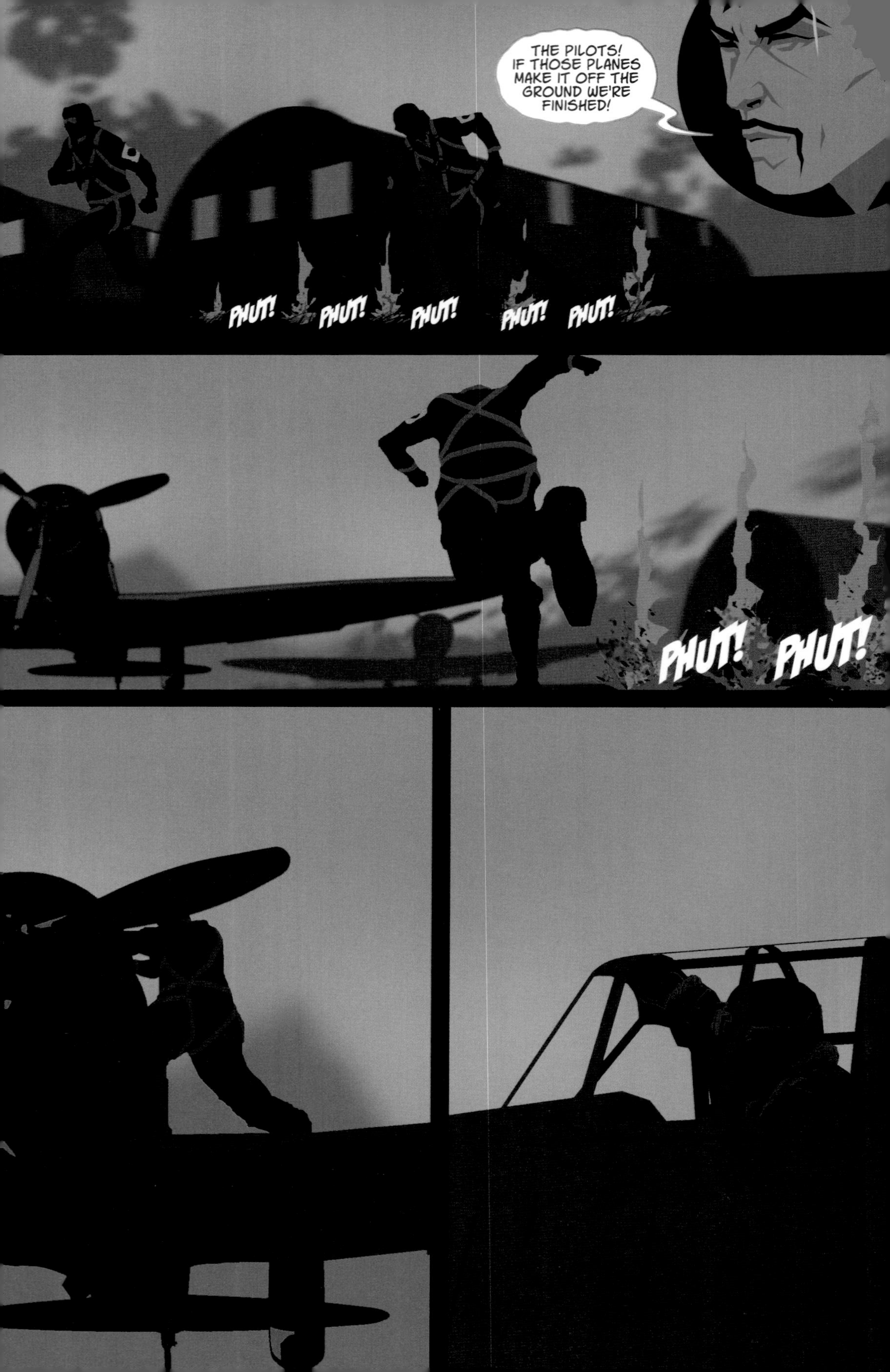

THE PILOTS! IF THOSE PLANES MAKE IT OFF THE GROUND WE'RE FINISHED!
PHUT! PHUT! PHUT! PHUT! PHUT!
PHUT! PHUT!

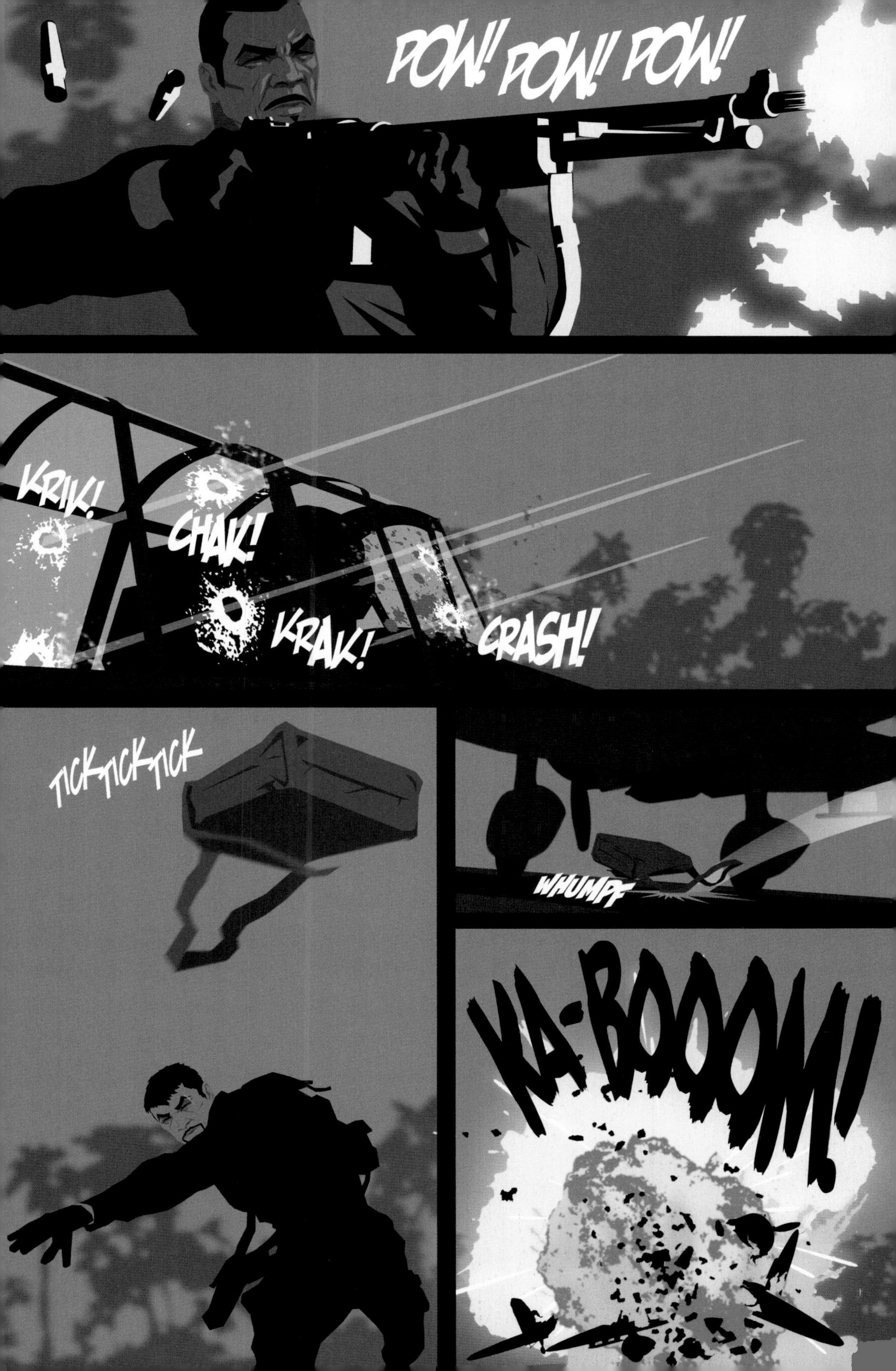
POW! POW! POW!
KRIK!
CHAK!
KRAK!
CRASH!
TICK TICK TICK
WHUMPF
KA-BOOOM!

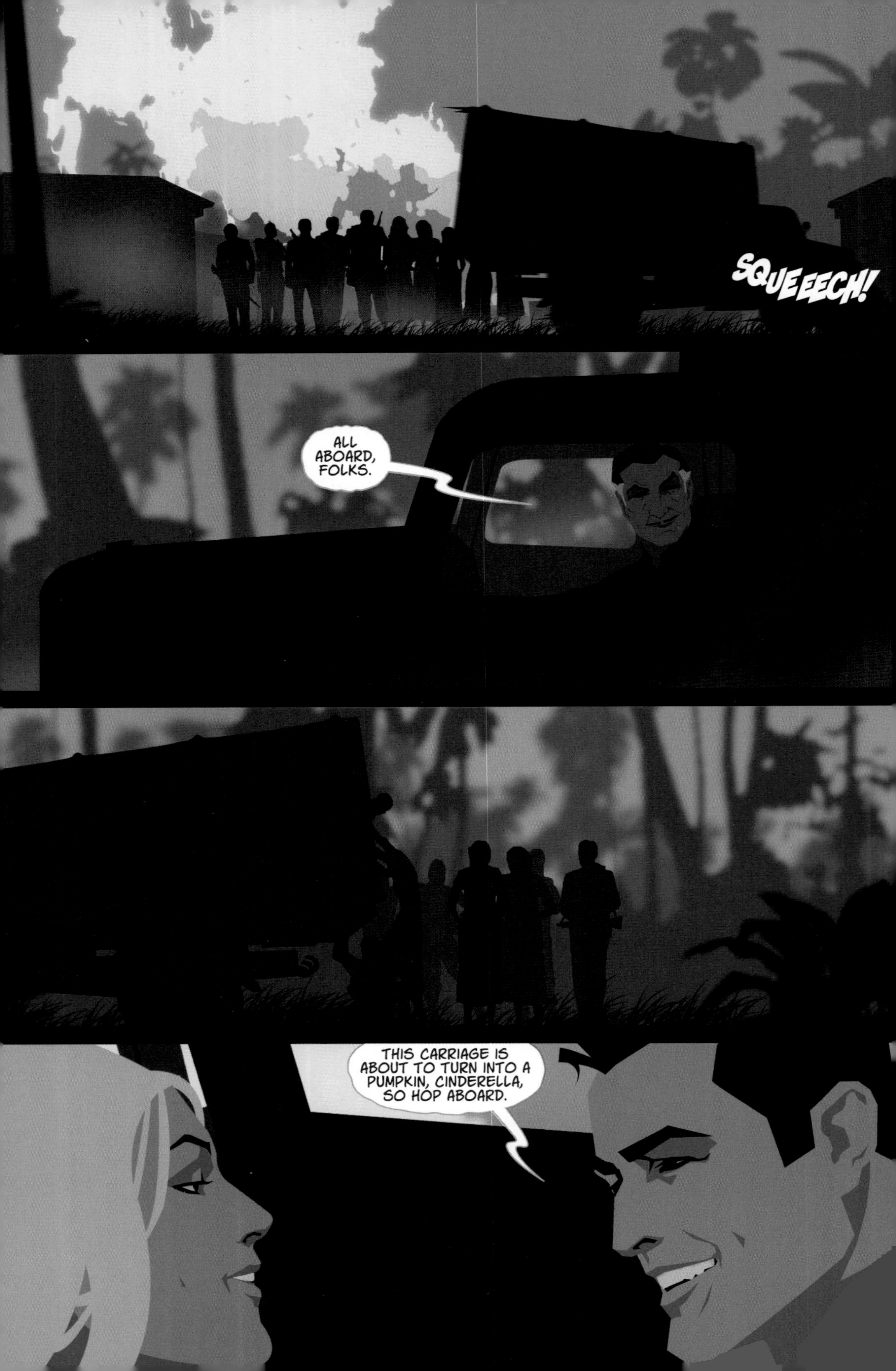
SQUEEECH!
ALL ABOARD, FOLKS.
THIS CARRIAGE IS ABOUT TO TURN INTO A PUMPKIN, CINDERELLA, SO HOP ABOARD.

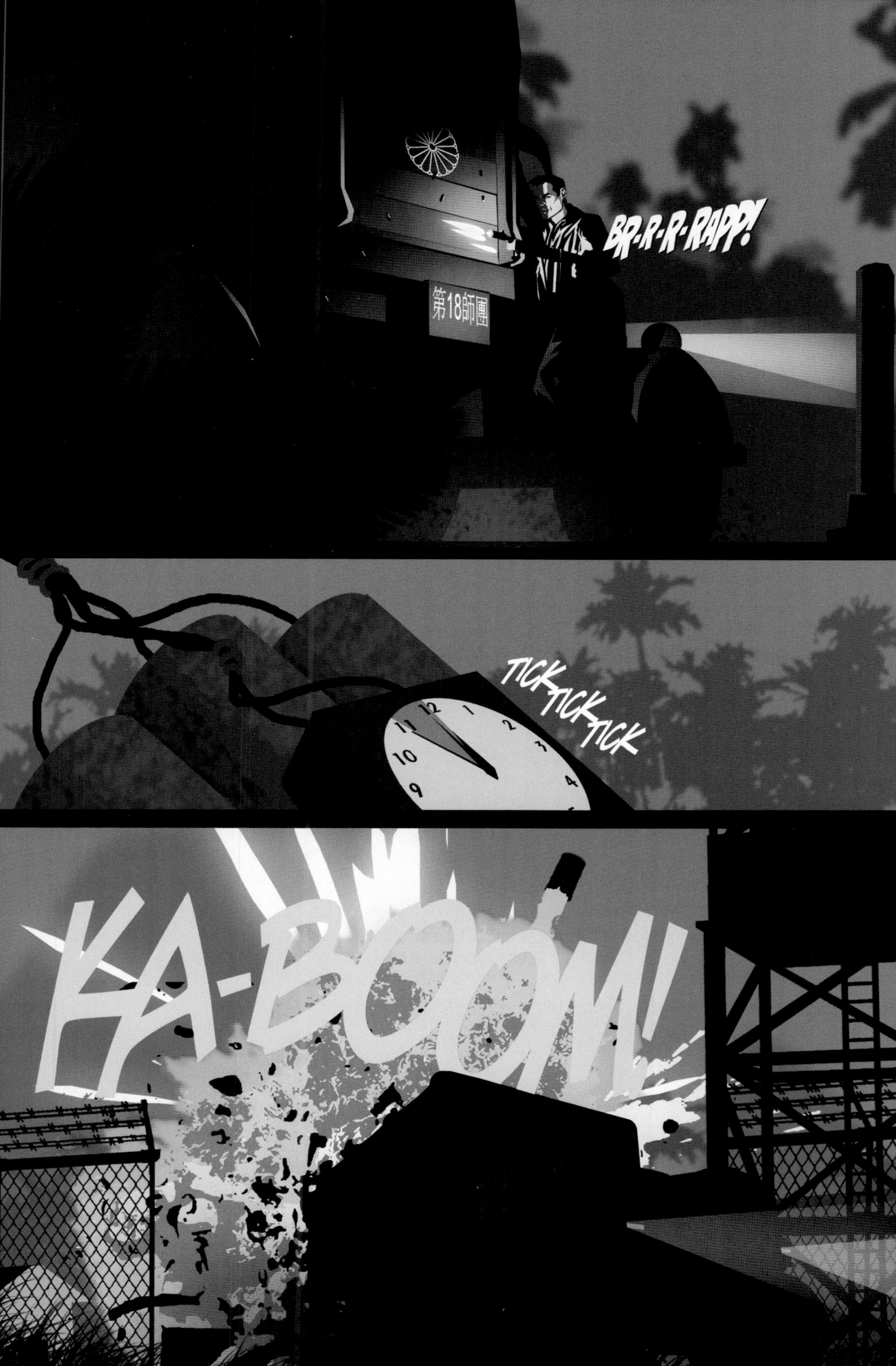
BR-R-R-RAPP!
第18師團
TICK TICK TICK
YA-BOOM!

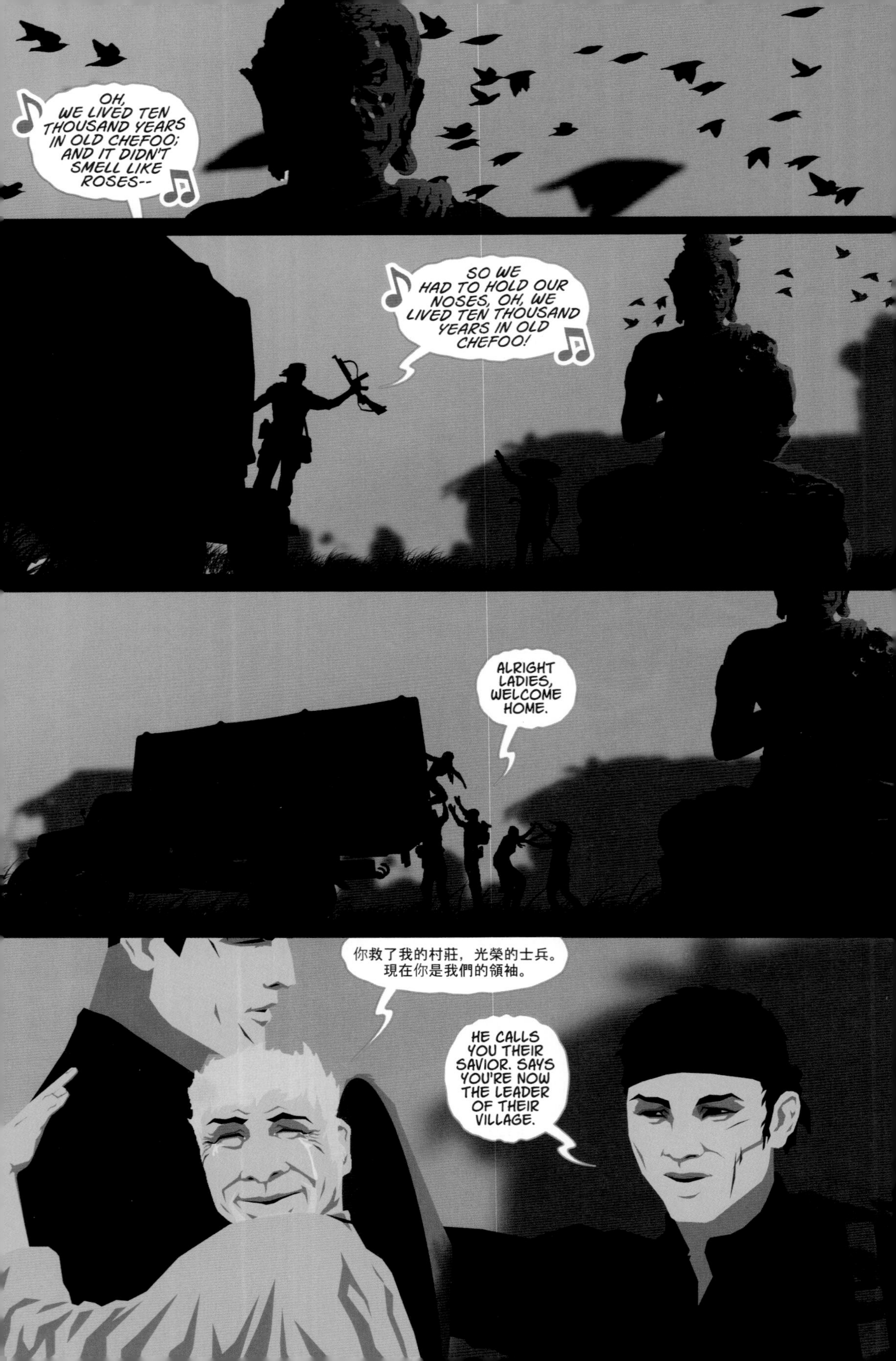
OH, WE LIVED TEN THOUSAND YEARS IN OLD CHEFOO; AND IT DIDN'T SMELL LIKE ROSES--
SO WE HAD TO HOLD OUR NOSES, OH, WE LIVED TEN THOUSAND YEARS IN OLD CHEFOO!
ALRIGHT LADIES, WELCOME HOME.
你救了我的村莊，光榮的士兵。現在你是我們的領袖。
HE CALLS YOU THEIR SAVIOR. SAYS YOU'RE NOW THE LEADER OF THEIR VILLAGE.

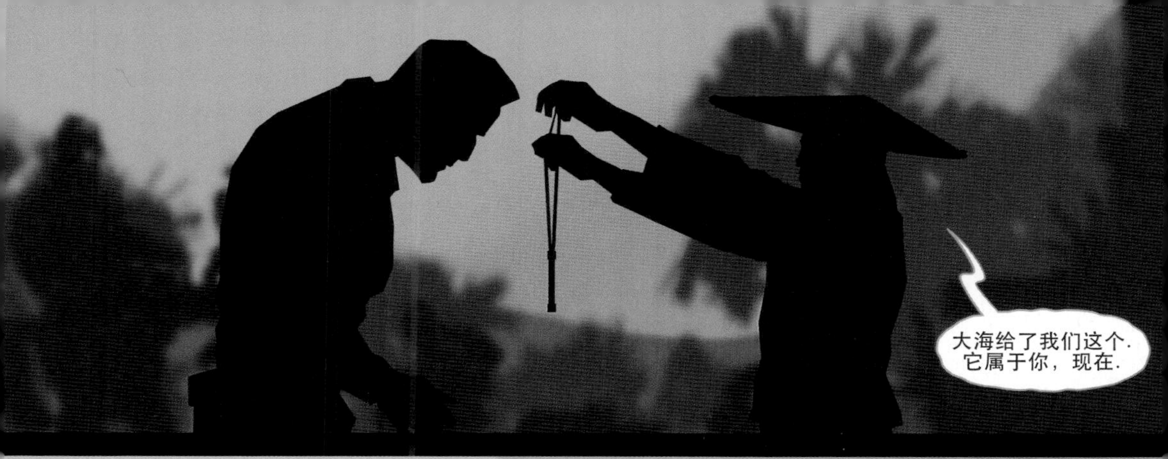
大海给了我们这个.
它属于你，现在.

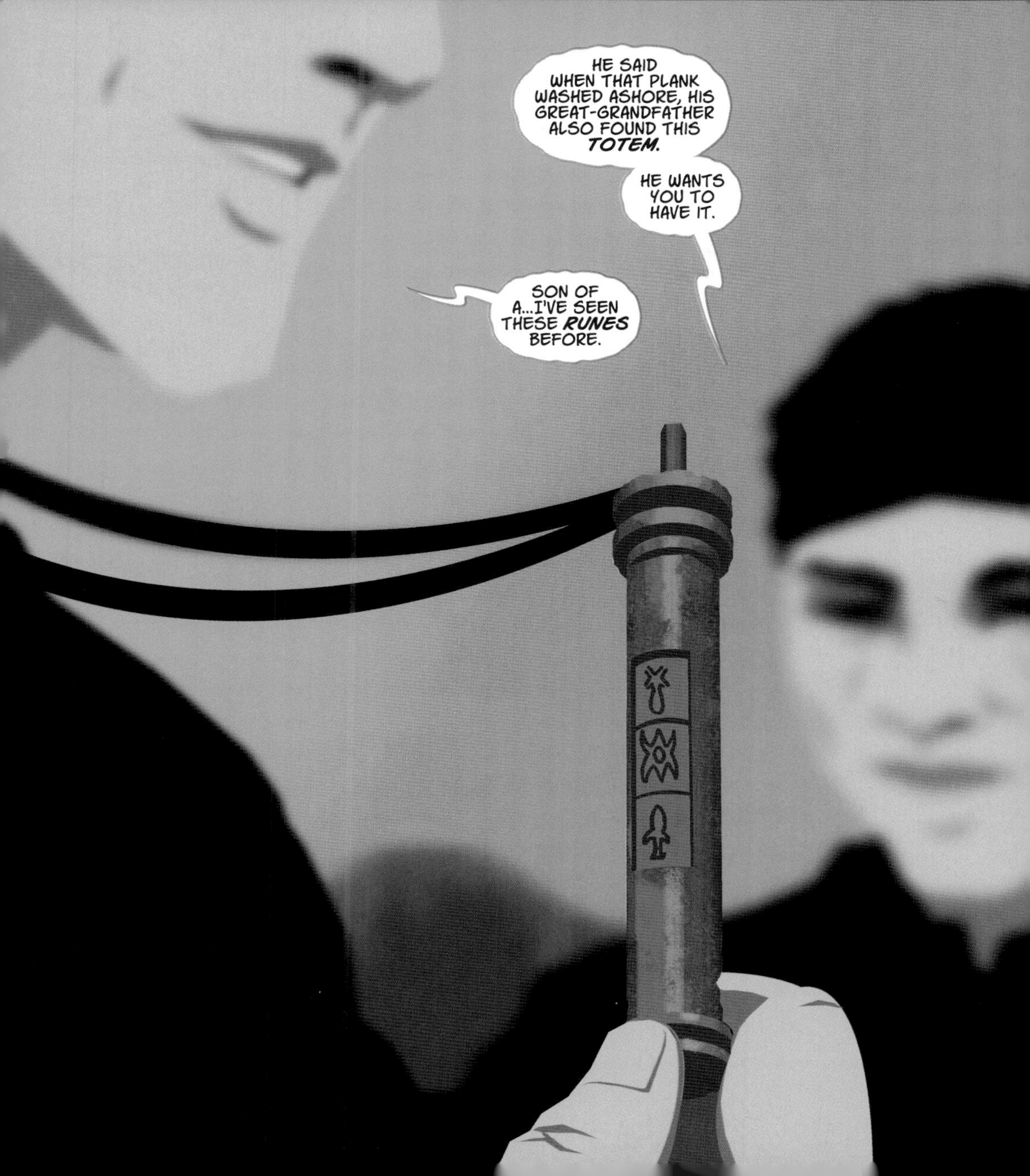
HE SAID WHEN THAT PLANK WASHED ASHORE, HIS GREAT-GRANDFATHER ALSO FOUND THIS TOTEM.
HE WANTS YOU TO HAVE IT.
SON OF A...I'VE SEEN THESE RUNES BEFORE.

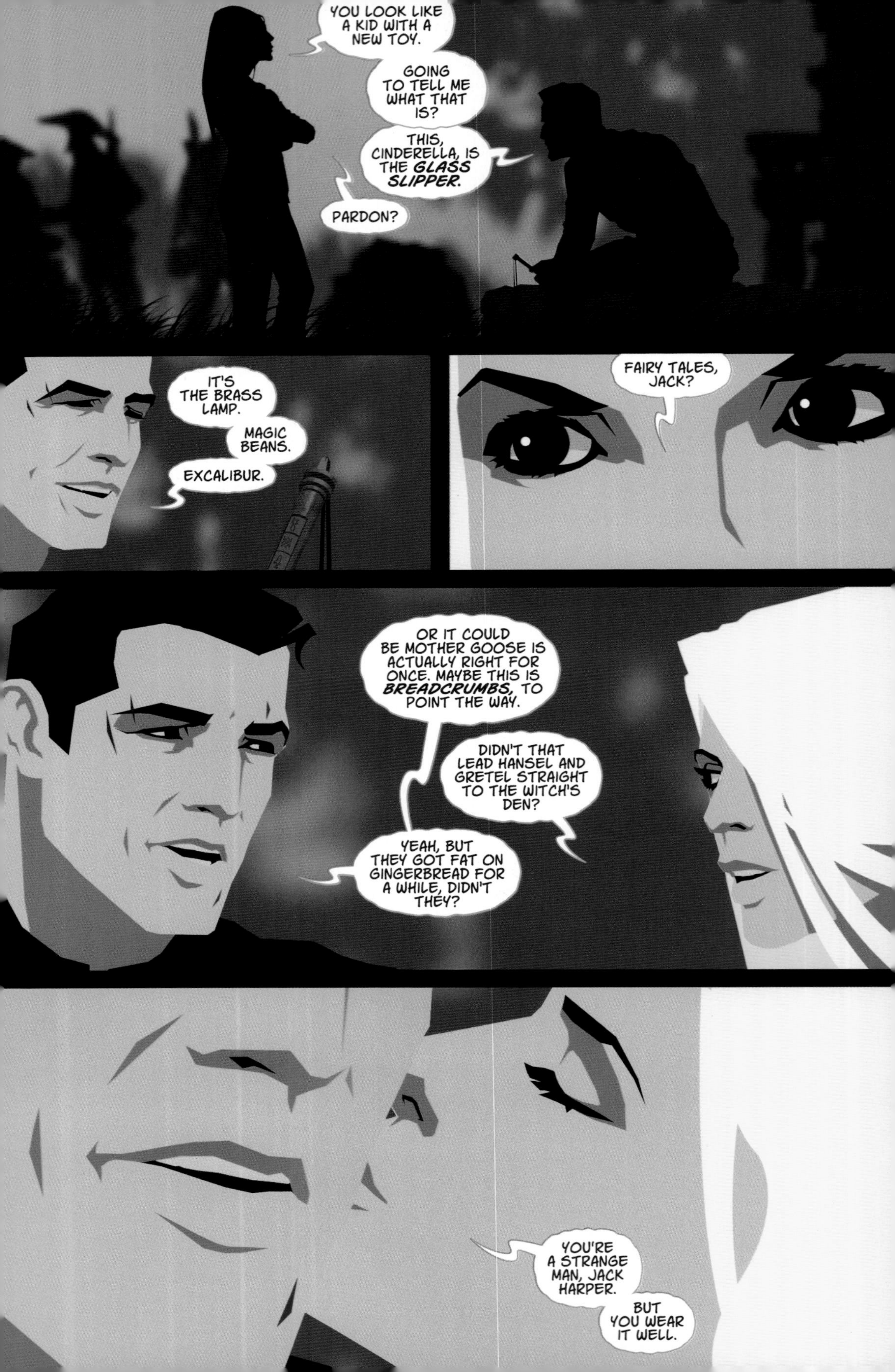
YOU LOOK LIKE A KID WITH A NEW TOY.
GOING TO TELL ME WHAT THAT IS?
THIS, CINDERELLA, IS THE GLASS SLIPPER.
PARDON?
IT'S THE BRASS LAMP.
MAGIC BEANS.
EXCALIBUR.
FAIRY TALES, JACK?
OR IT COULD BE MOTHER GOOSE IS ACTUALLY RIGHT FOR ONCE. MAYBE THIS IS BREADCRUMBS, TO POINT THE WAY.
DIDN'T THAT LEAD HANSEL AND GRETEL STRAIGHT TO THE WITCH'S DEN?
YEAH, BUT THEY GOT FAT ON GINGERBREAD FOR A WHILE, DIDN'T THEY?
YOU'RE A STRANGE MAN, JACK HARPER.
BUT YOU WEAR IT WELL.

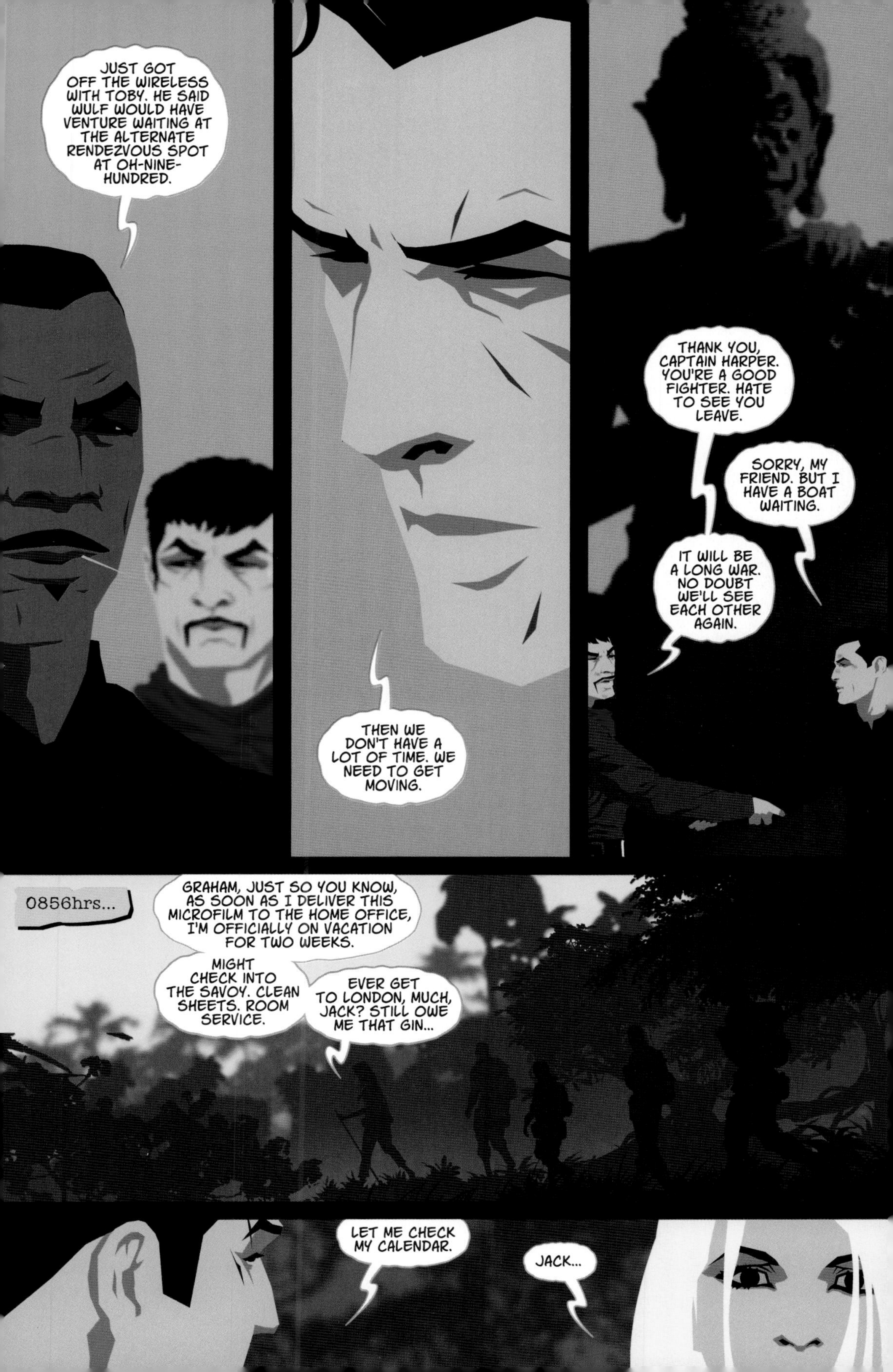
JUST GOT OFF THE WIRELESS WITH TOBY. HE SAID WULF WOULD HAVE VENTURE WAITING AT THE ALTERNATE RENDEZVOUS SPOT AT OH-NINE-HUNDRED.
THEN WE DON'T HAVE A LOT OF TIME. WE NEED TO GET MOVING.
THANK YOU, CAPTAIN HARPER. YOU'RE A GOOD FIGHTER. HATE TO SEE YOU LEAVE.
SORRY, MY FRIEND. BUT I HAVE A BOAT WAITING.
IT WILL BE A LONG WAR. NO DOUBT WE'LL SEE EACH OTHER AGAIN.
0856hrs...
GRAHAM, JUST SO YOU KNOW, AS SOON AS I DELIVER THIS MICROFILM TO THE HOME OFFICE, I'M OFFICIALLY ON VACATION FOR TWO WEEKS.
MIGHT CHECK INTO THE SAVOY. CLEAN SHEETS. ROOM SERVICE.
EVER GET TO LONDON, MUCH, JACK? STILL OWE ME THAT GIN...
LET ME CHECK MY CALENDAR.
JACK...

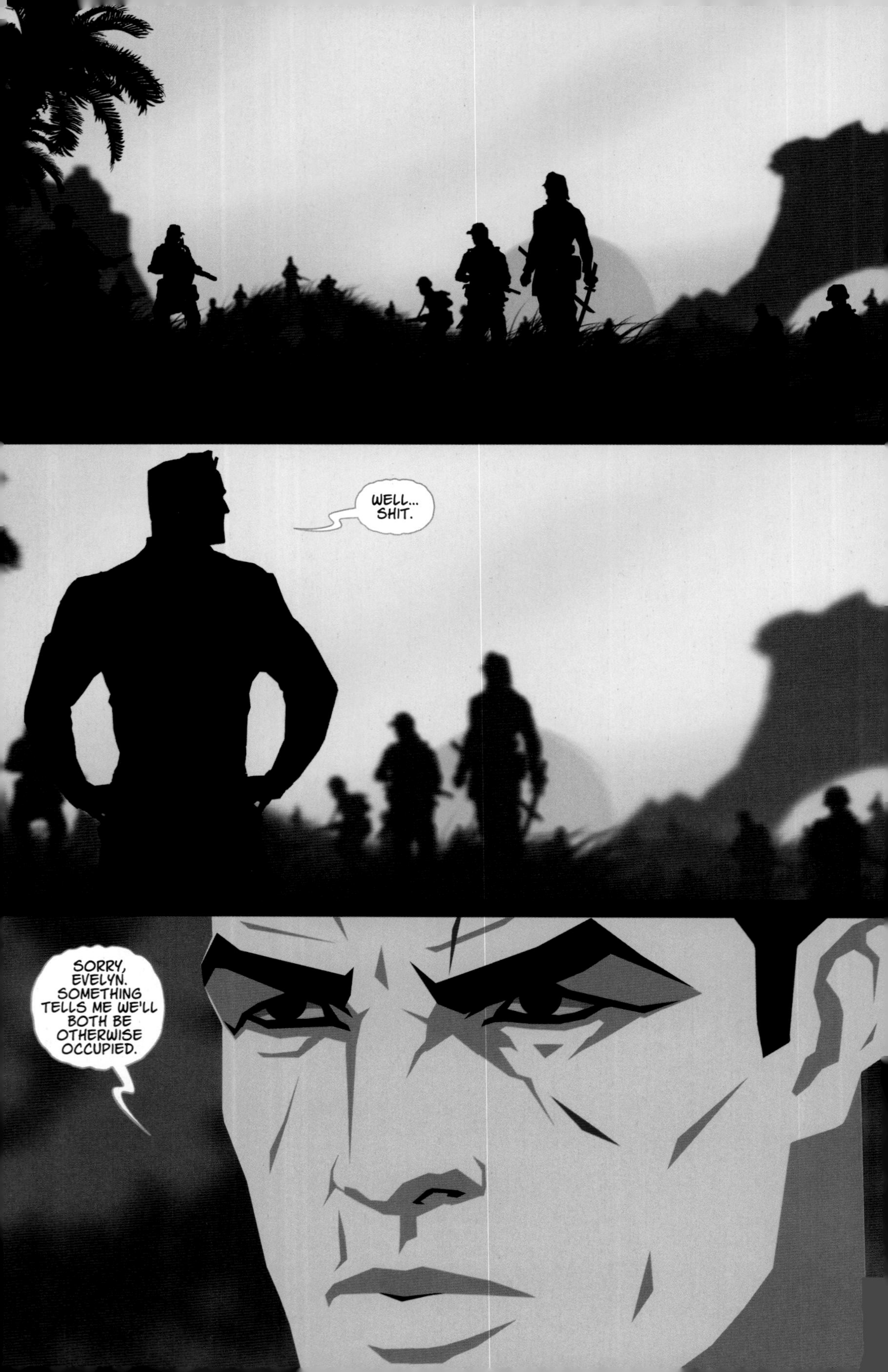
WELL... SHIT.
SORRY, EVELYN. SOMETHING TELLS ME WE'LL BOTH BE OTHERWISE OCCUPIED.

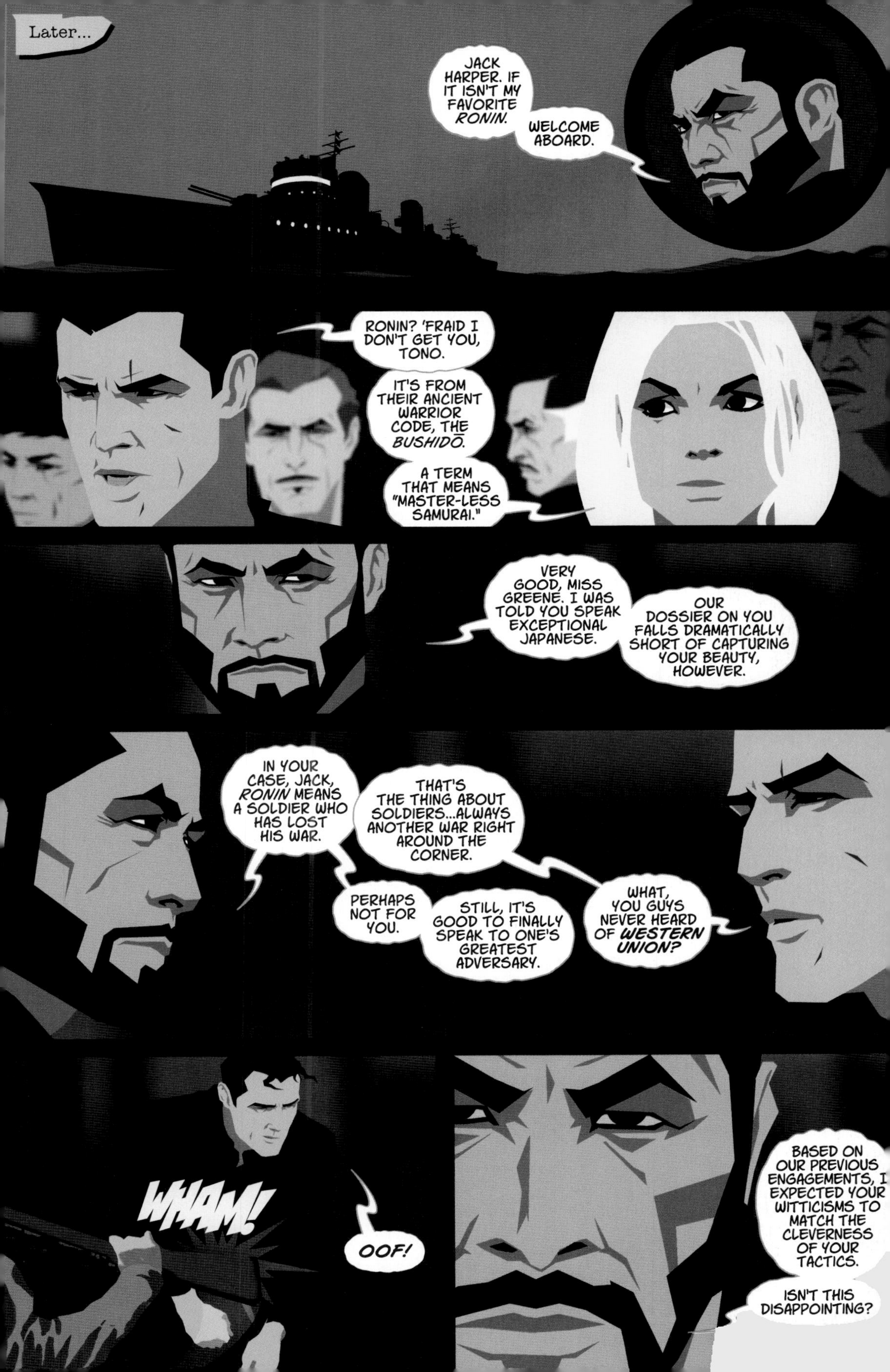
Later...
JACK HARPER. IF IT ISN'T MY FAVORITE RONIN.
WELCOME ABOARD.
RONIN? 'FRAID I DON'T GET YOU, TONO.
IT'S FROM THEIR ANCIENT WARRIOR CODE, THE BUSHIDŌ.
A TERM THAT MEANS "MASTER-LESS SAMURAI."
VERY GOOD, MISS GREENE. I WAS TOLD YOU SPEAK EXCEPTIONAL JAPANESE.
OUR DOSSIER ON YOU FALLS DRAMATICALLY SHORT OF CAPTURING YOUR BEAUTY, HOWEVER.
IN YOUR CASE, JACK, RONIN MEANS A SOLDIER WHO HAS LOST HIS WAR.
THAT'S THE THING ABOUT SOLDIERS...ALWAYS ANOTHER WAR RIGHT AROUND THE CORNER.
PERHAPS NOT FOR YOU.
STILL, IT'S GOOD TO FINALLY SPEAK TO ONE'S GREATEST ADVERSARY.
WHAT, YOU GUYS NEVER HEARD OF WESTERN UNION?
WHAM!
OOF!
BASED ON OUR PREVIOUS ENGAGEMENTS, I EXPECTED YOUR WITTICISMS TO MATCH THE CLEVERNESS OF YOUR TACTICS.
ISN'T THIS DISAPPOINTING?

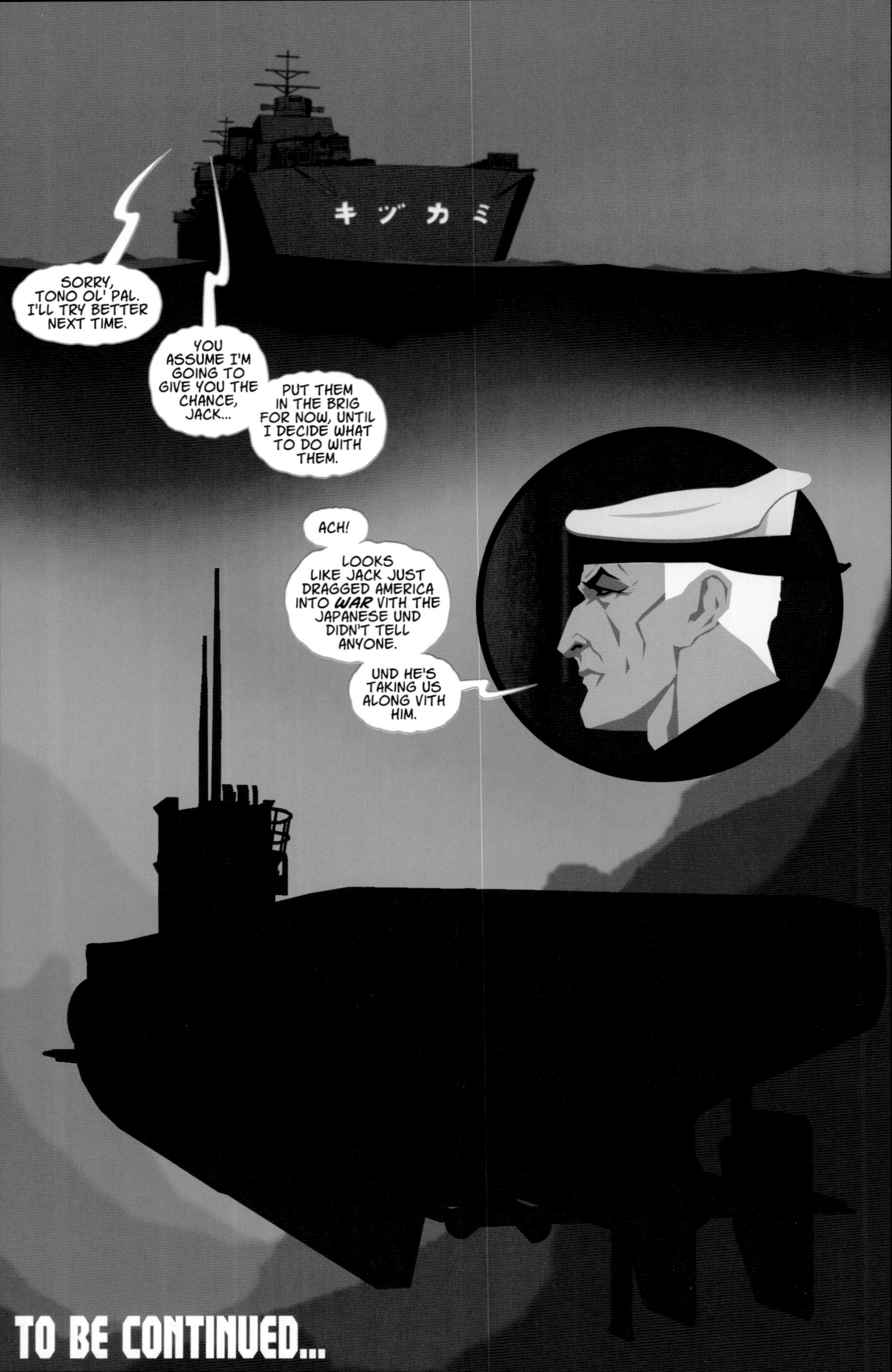
キヅカミ
SORRY, TONO OL' PAL. I'LL TRY BETTER NEXT TIME.
YOU ASSUME I'M GOING TO GIVE YOU THE CHANCE, JACK...
PUT THEM IN THE BRIG FOR NOW, UNTIL I DECIDE WHAT TO DO WITH THEM.
ACH!
LOOKS LIKE JACK JUST DRAGGED AMERICA INTO *WAR* VITH THE JAPANESE UND DIDN'T TELL ANYONE.
UND HE'S TAKING US ALONG VITH HIM.
TO BE CONTINUED...

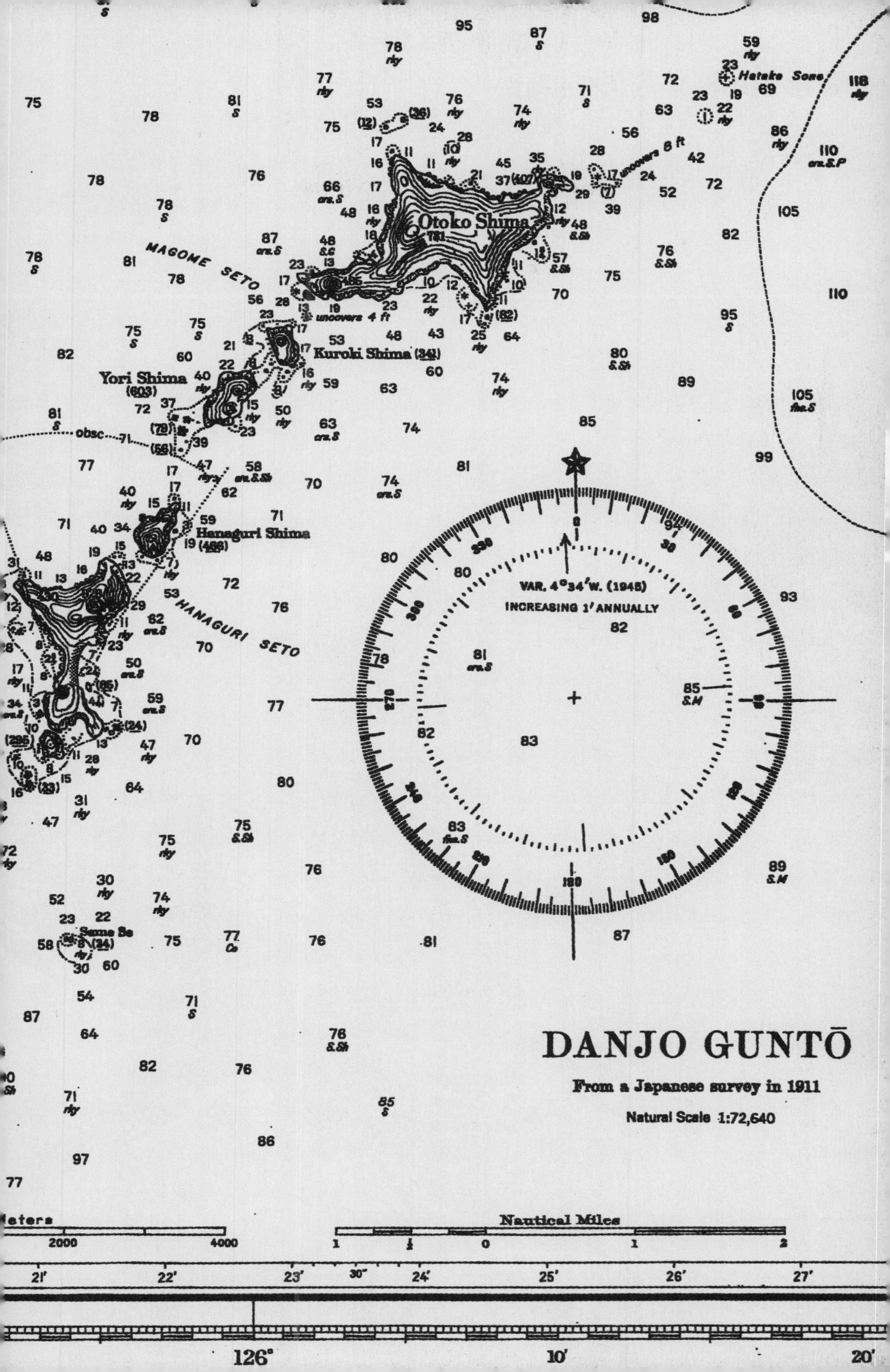

DANJO GUNTŌ
From a Japanese survey in 1911
Natural Scale 1:72,640
Otoko Shima
Kuroki Shima (341)
Yori Shima (603)
Hanaguri Shima (466)
Magome Seto
Hanaguri Seto
Hatake Sone
Same Se
uncovers 4 ft
uncovers 8 ft
obsc
VAR. 4°34′W. (1945)
INCREASING 1′ ANNUALLY
Meters
2000
4000
Nautical Miles
1
½
0
1
2
21′
22′
23′
30″
24′
25′
26′
27′
126°
10′
20′

Top Hat, White Lies, And Tales

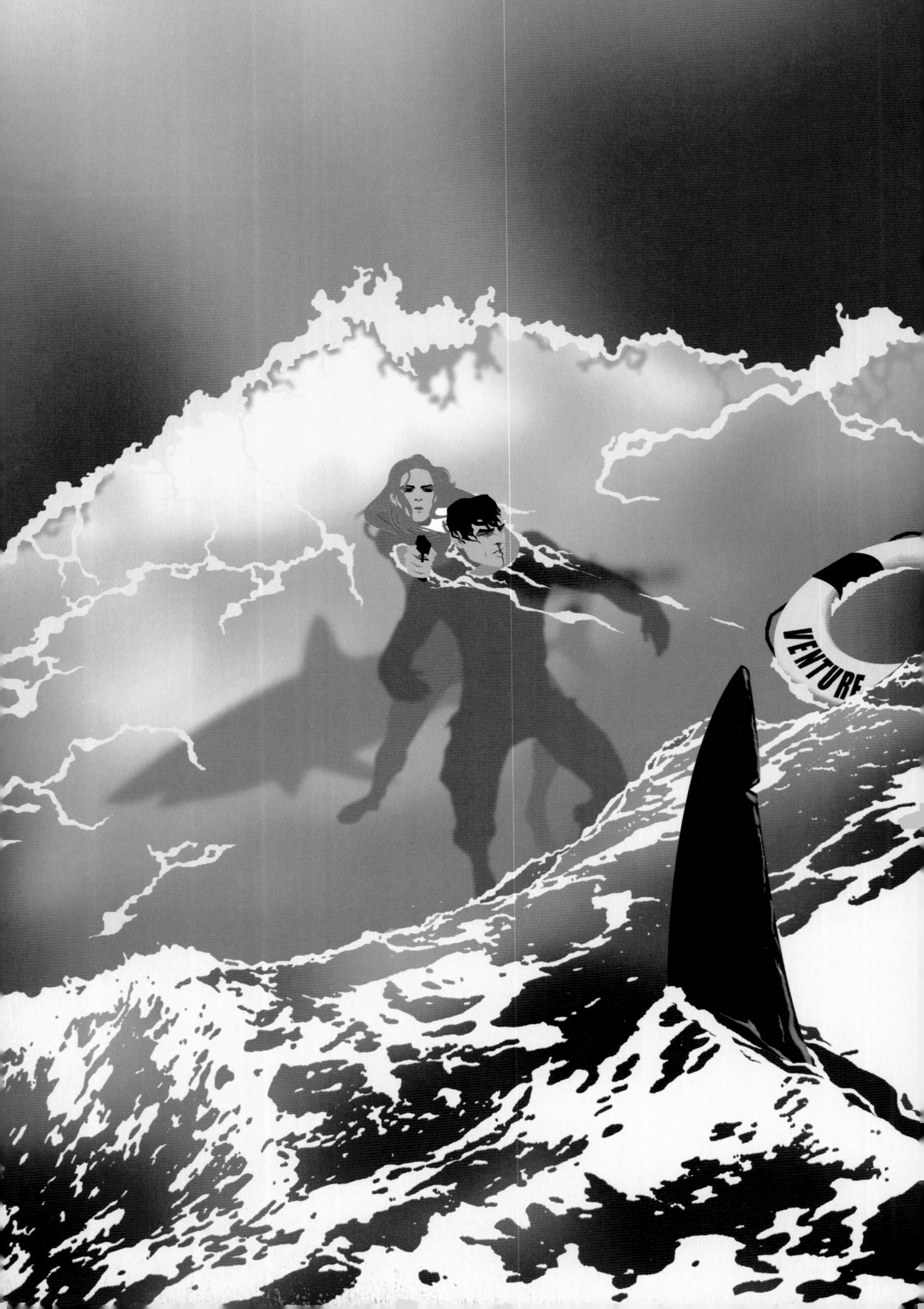
VENTURE

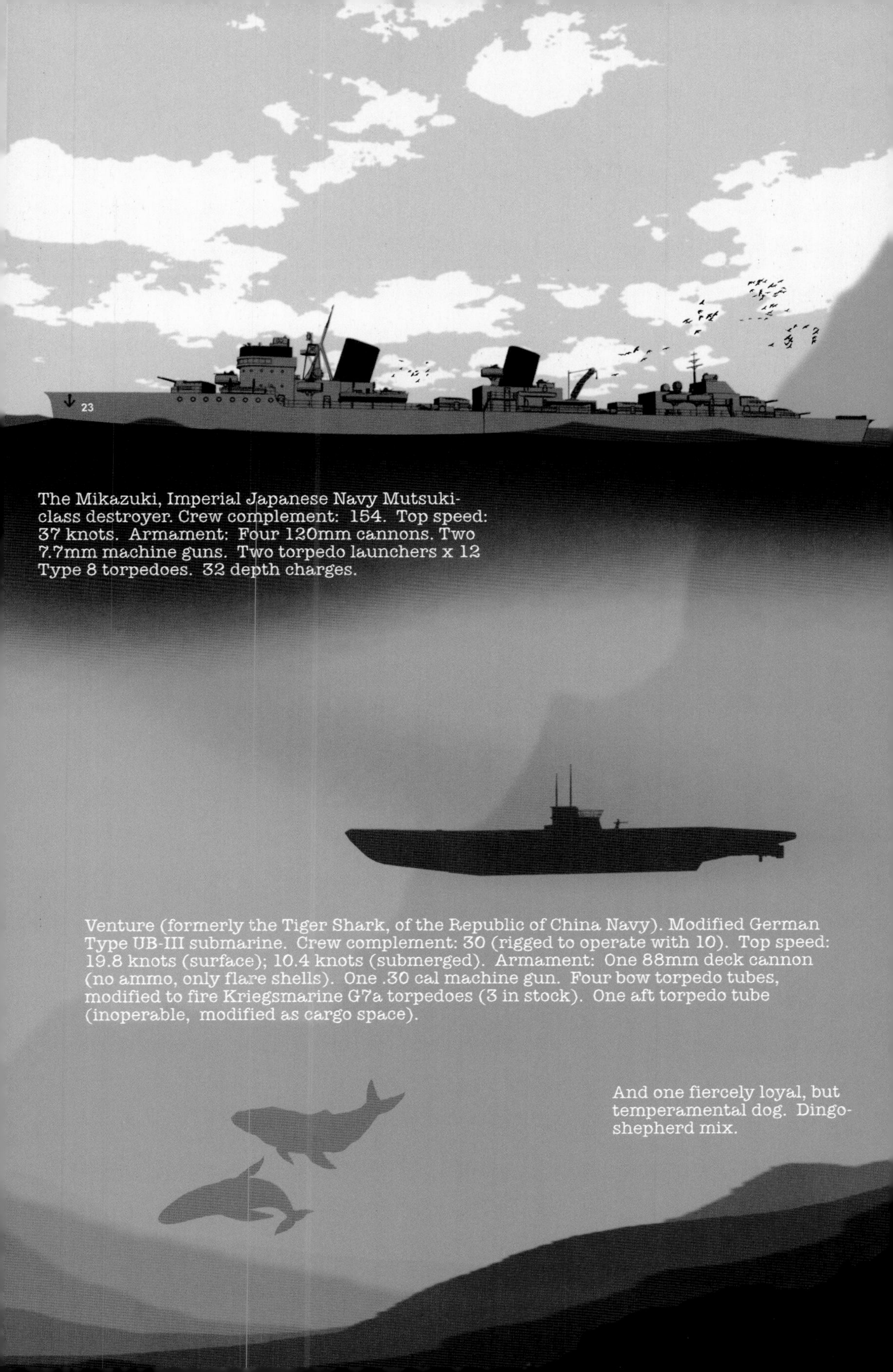
23
The Mikazuki, Imperial Japanese Navy Mutsuki-class destroyer. Crew complement: 154. Top speed: 37 knots. Armament: Four 120mm cannons. Two 7.7mm machine guns. Two torpedo launchers x 12 Type 8 torpedoes. 32 depth charges.
Venture (formerly the Tiger Shark, of the Republic of China Navy). Modified German Type UB-III submarine. Crew complement: 30 (rigged to operate with 10). Top speed: 19.8 knots (surface); 10.4 knots (submerged). Armament: One 88mm deck cannon (no ammo, only flare shells). One .30 cal machine gun. Four bow torpedo tubes, modified to fire Kriegsmarine G7a torpedoes (3 in stock). One aft torpedo tube (inoperable, modified as cargo space).
And one fiercely loyal, but temperamental dog. Dingo-shepherd mix.

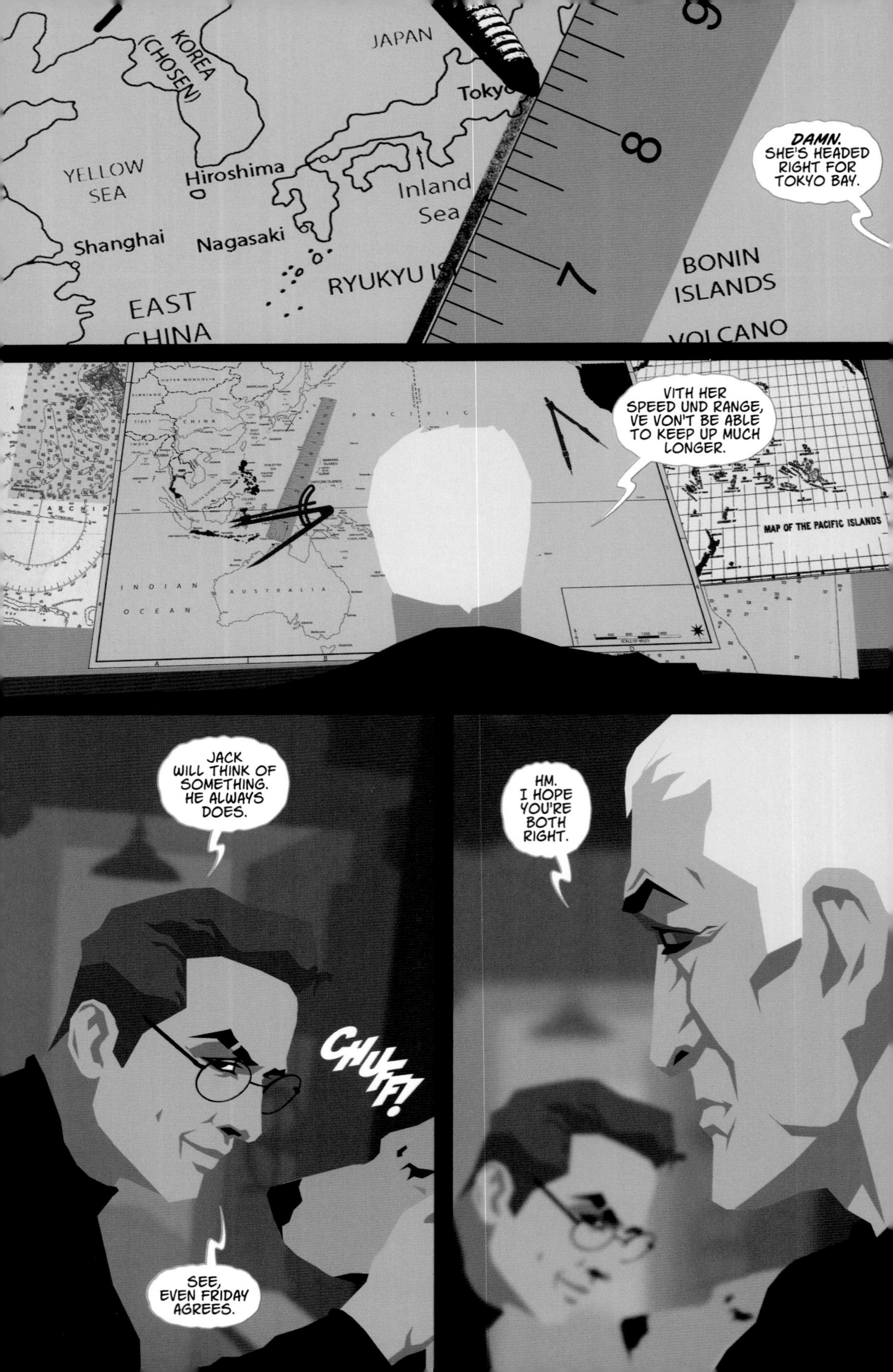

KOREA (CHOSEN)
JAPAN
Tokyo
YELLOW SEA
Hiroshima
Inland Sea
Shanghai
Nagasaki
BONIN ISLANDS
DAMN. SHE'S HEADED RIGHT FOR TOKYO BAY.
MAP OF THE PACIFIC ISLANDS
VITH HER SPEED UND RANGE, VE VON'T BE ABLE TO KEEP UP MUCH LONGER.
JACK WILL THINK OF SOMETHING. HE ALWAYS DOES.
CHUFF!
SEE, EVEN FRIDAY AGREES.
HM. I HOPE YOU'RE BOTH RIGHT.

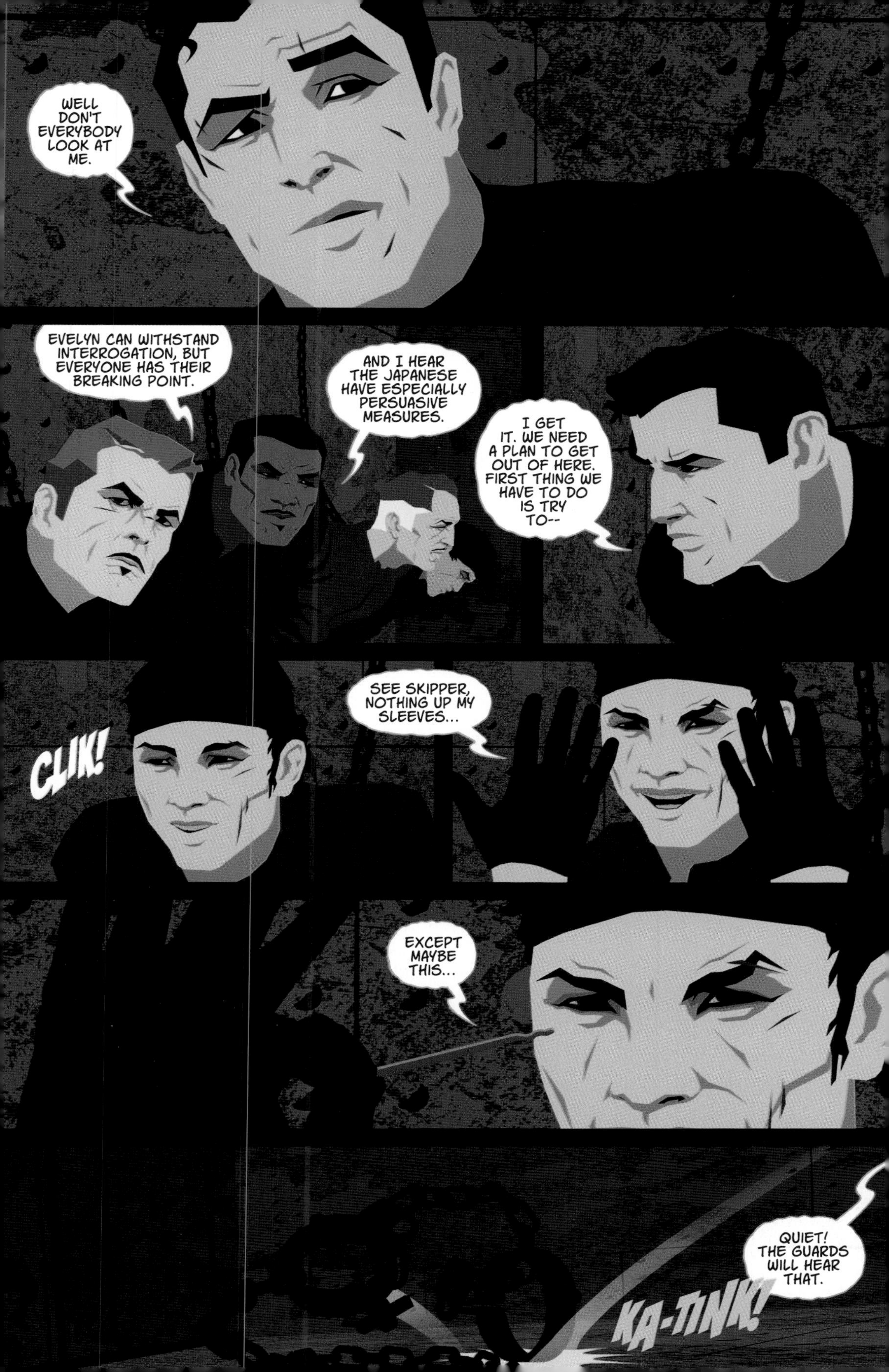
WELL DON'T EVERYBODY LOOK AT ME.
EVELYN CAN WITHSTAND INTERROGATION, BUT EVERYONE HAS THEIR BREAKING POINT.
AND I HEAR THE JAPANESE HAVE ESPECIALLY PERSUASIVE MEASURES.
I GET IT. WE NEED A PLAN TO GET OUT OF HERE. FIRST THING WE HAVE TO DO IS TRY TO--
CLIK!
SEE SKIPPER, NOTHING UP MY SLEEVES...
EXCEPT MAYBE THIS...
QUIET! THE GUARDS WILL HEAR THAT.
KA-TINK!

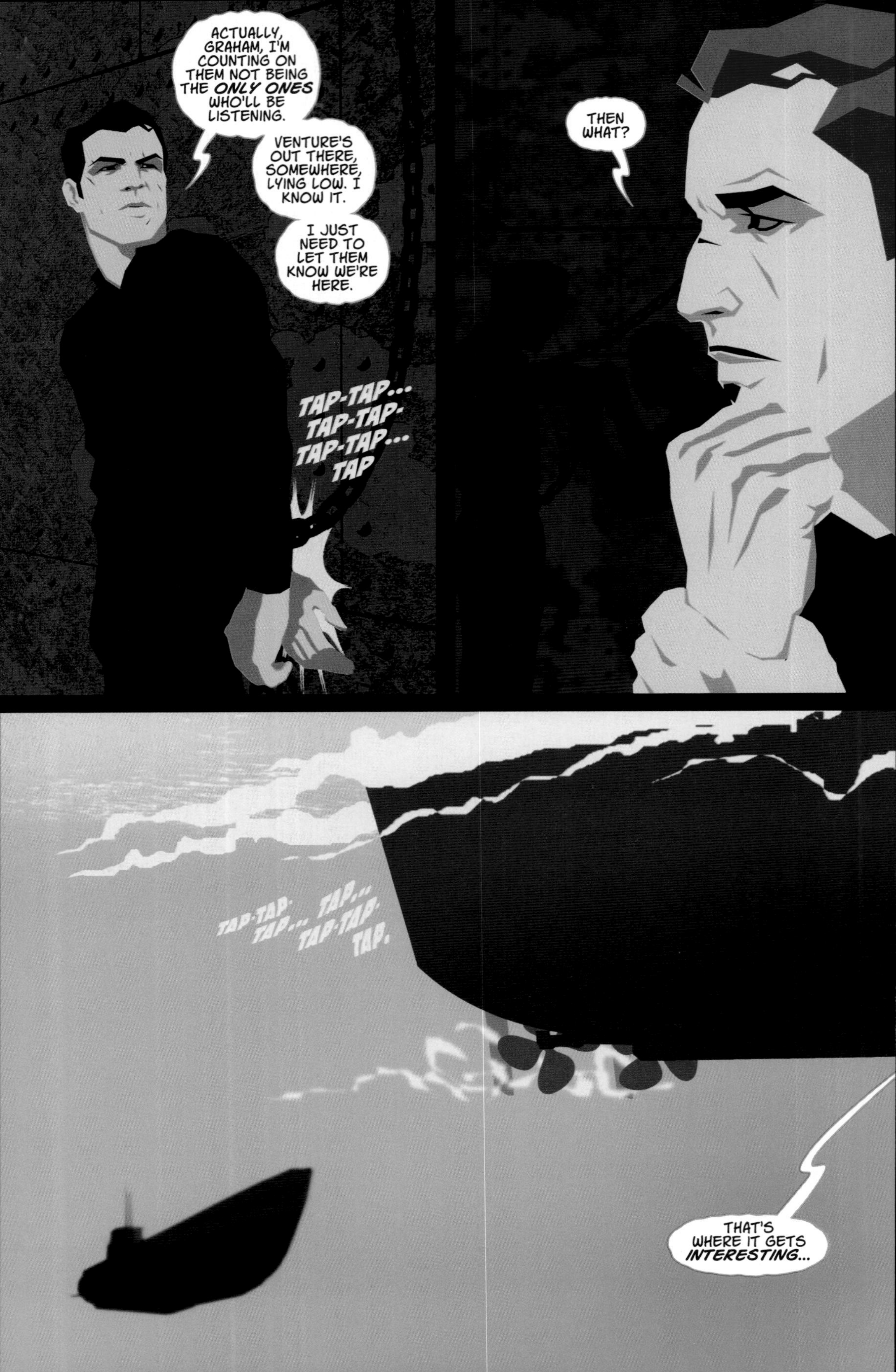
ACTUALLY, GRAHAM, I'M COUNTING ON THEM NOT BEING THE *ONLY ONES* WHO'LL BE LISTENING.
VENTURE'S OUT THERE, SOMEWHERE, LYING LOW. I KNOW IT.
I JUST NEED TO LET THEM KNOW WE'RE HERE.
TAP-TAP... TAP-TAP- TAP-TAP... TAP
THEN WHAT?
TAP-TAP- TAP... TAP... TAP-TAP- TAP.
THAT'S WHERE IT GETS *INTERESTING*...

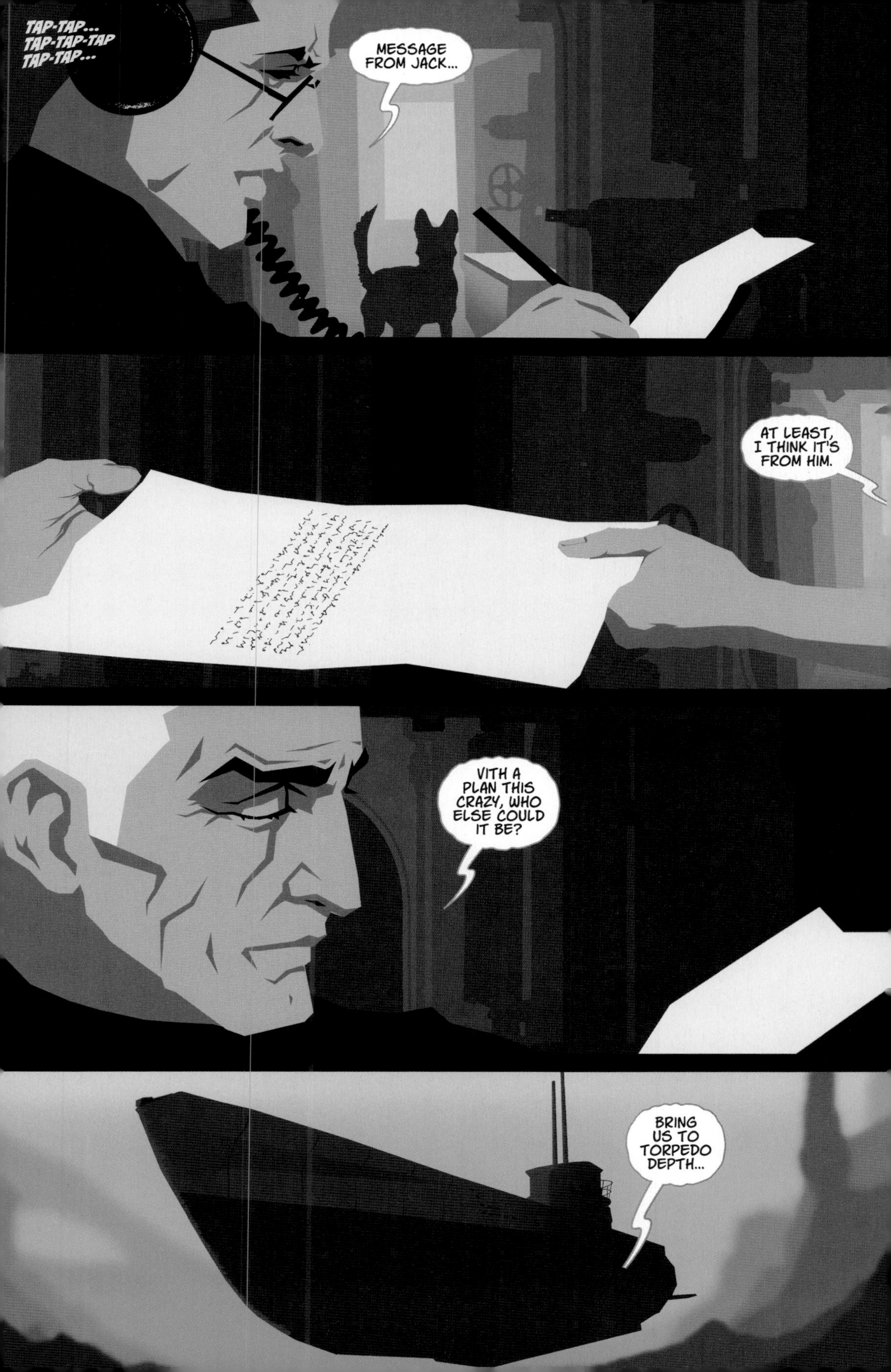
TAP-TAP... TAP-TAP-TAP TAP-TAP...
MESSAGE FROM JACK...
AT LEAST, I THINK IT'S FROM HIM.
VITH A PLAN THIS CRAZY, WHO ELSE COULD IT BE?
BRING US TO TORPEDO DEPTH...

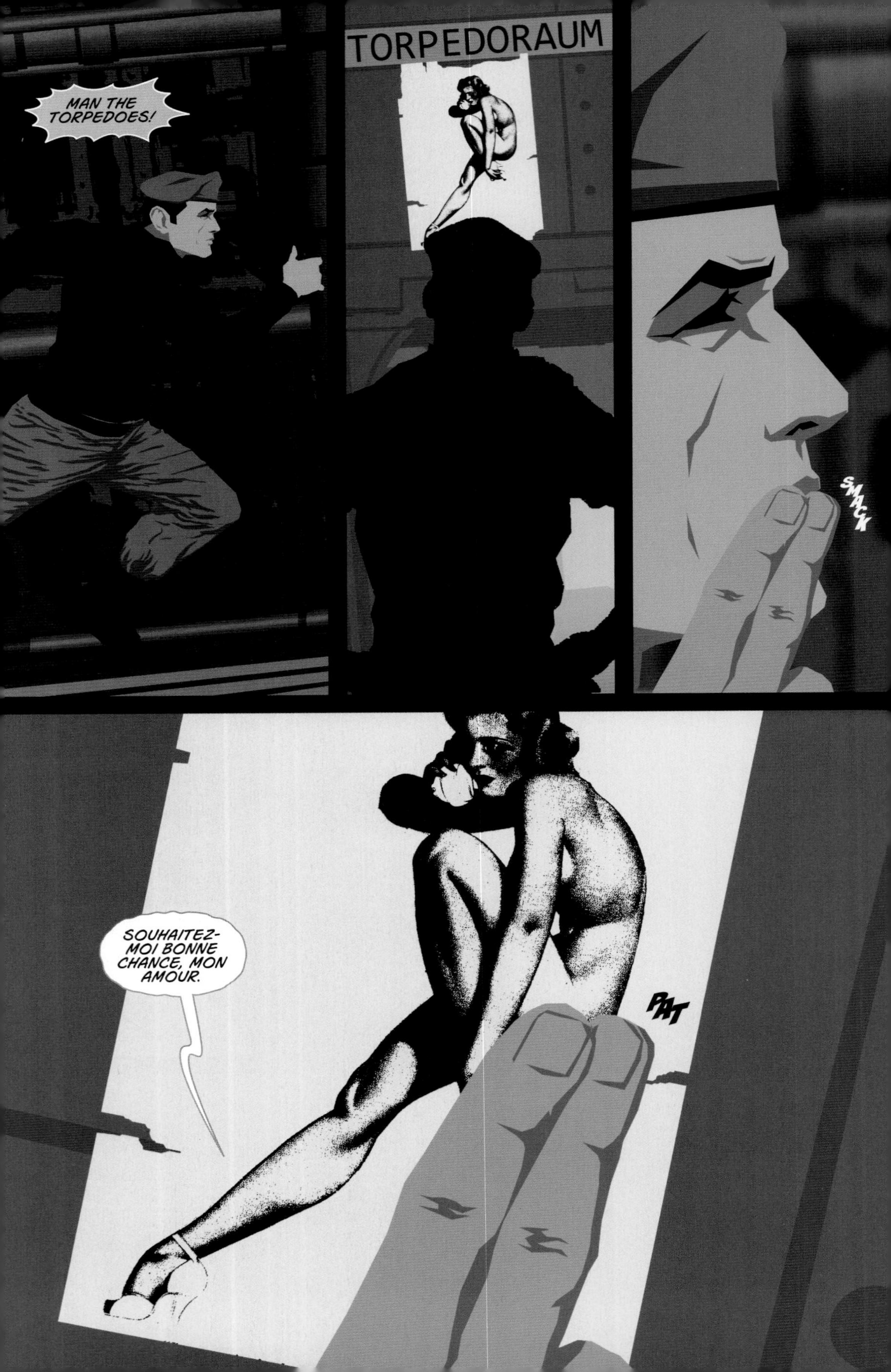
MAN THE TORPEDOES!
TORPEDORAUM
SMACK
SOUHAITEZ-MOI BONNE CHANCE, MON AMOUR.
PAT

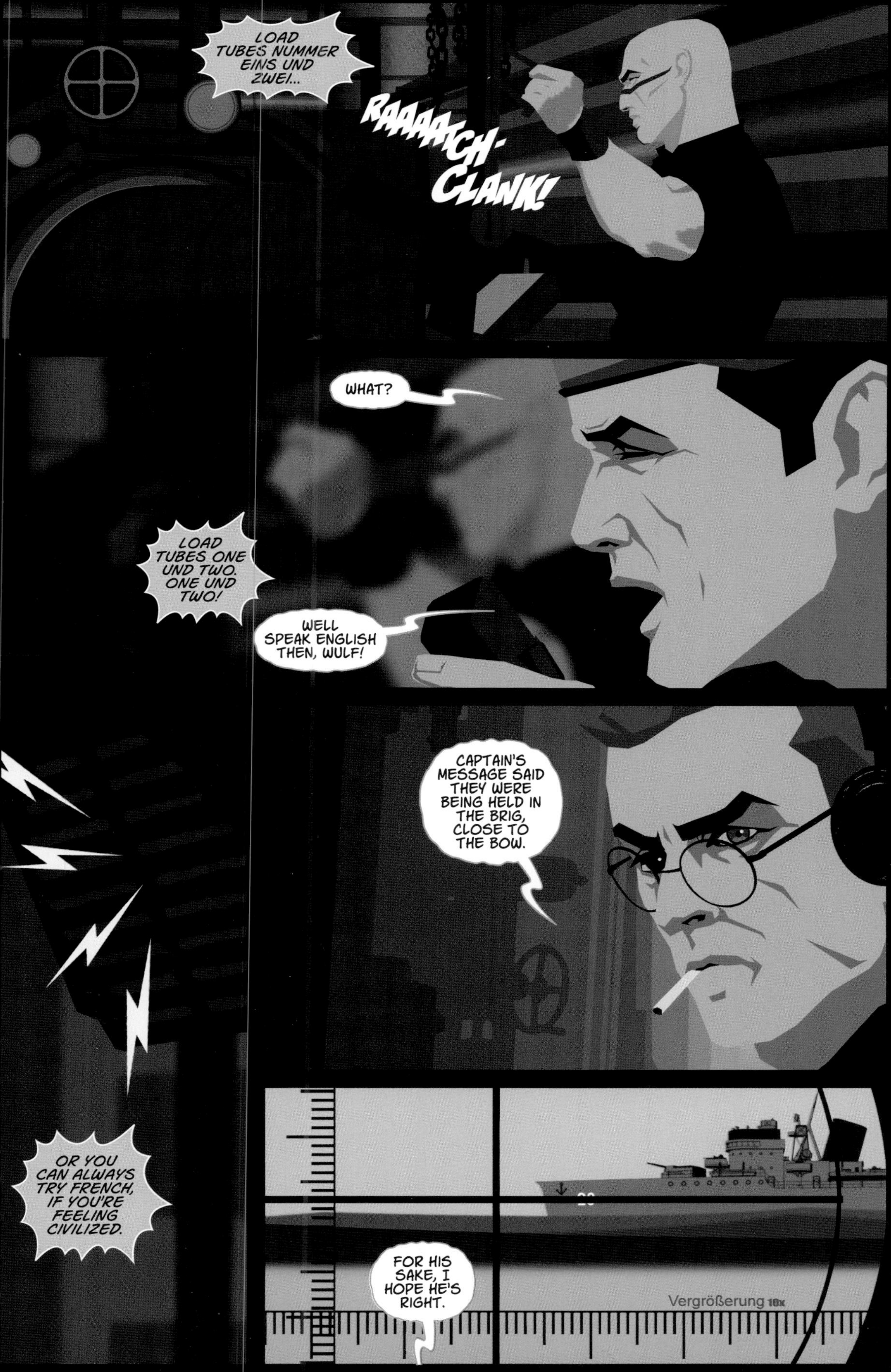
LOAD TUBES NUMMER EINS UND ZWEI...
RAAAATCH-CLANK!
WHAT?
LOAD TUBES ONE UND TWO. ONE UND TWO!
WELL SPEAK ENGLISH THEN, WULF!
CAPTAIN'S MESSAGE SAID THEY WERE BEING HELD IN THE BRIG, CLOSE TO THE BOW.
OR YOU CAN ALWAYS TRY FRENCH, IF YOU'RE FEELING CIVILIZED.
FOR HIS SAKE, I HOPE HE'S RIGHT.
Vergrößerung 10x

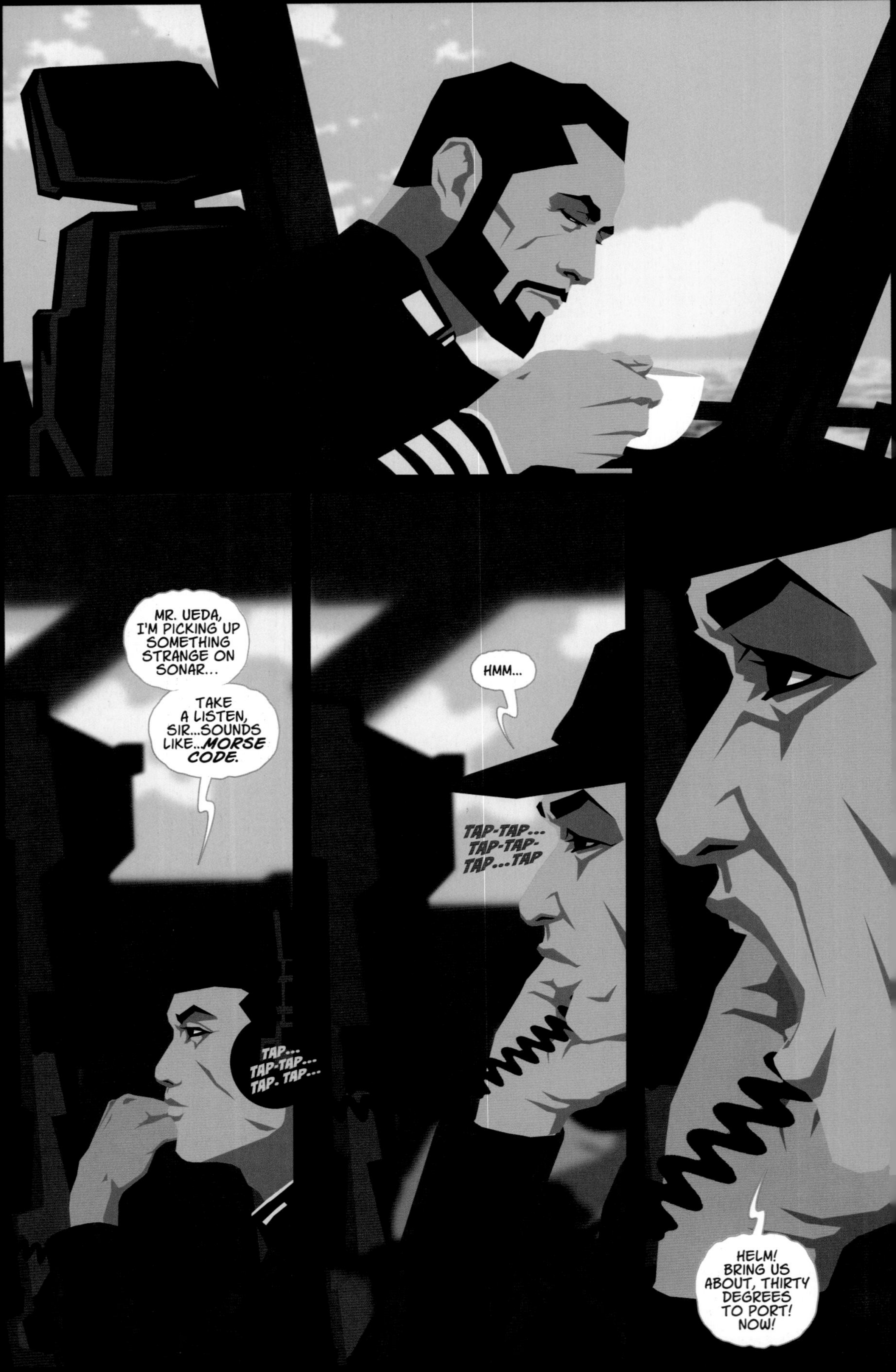

MR. UEDA, I'M PICKING UP SOMETHING STRANGE ON SONAR...
TAKE A LISTEN, SIR...SOUNDS LIKE...MORSE CODE.
TAP... TAP-TAP... TAP. TAP...
HMM...
TAP-TAP... TAP-TAP-TAP...TAP
HELM! BRING US ABOUT, THIRTY DEGREES TO PORT! NOW!

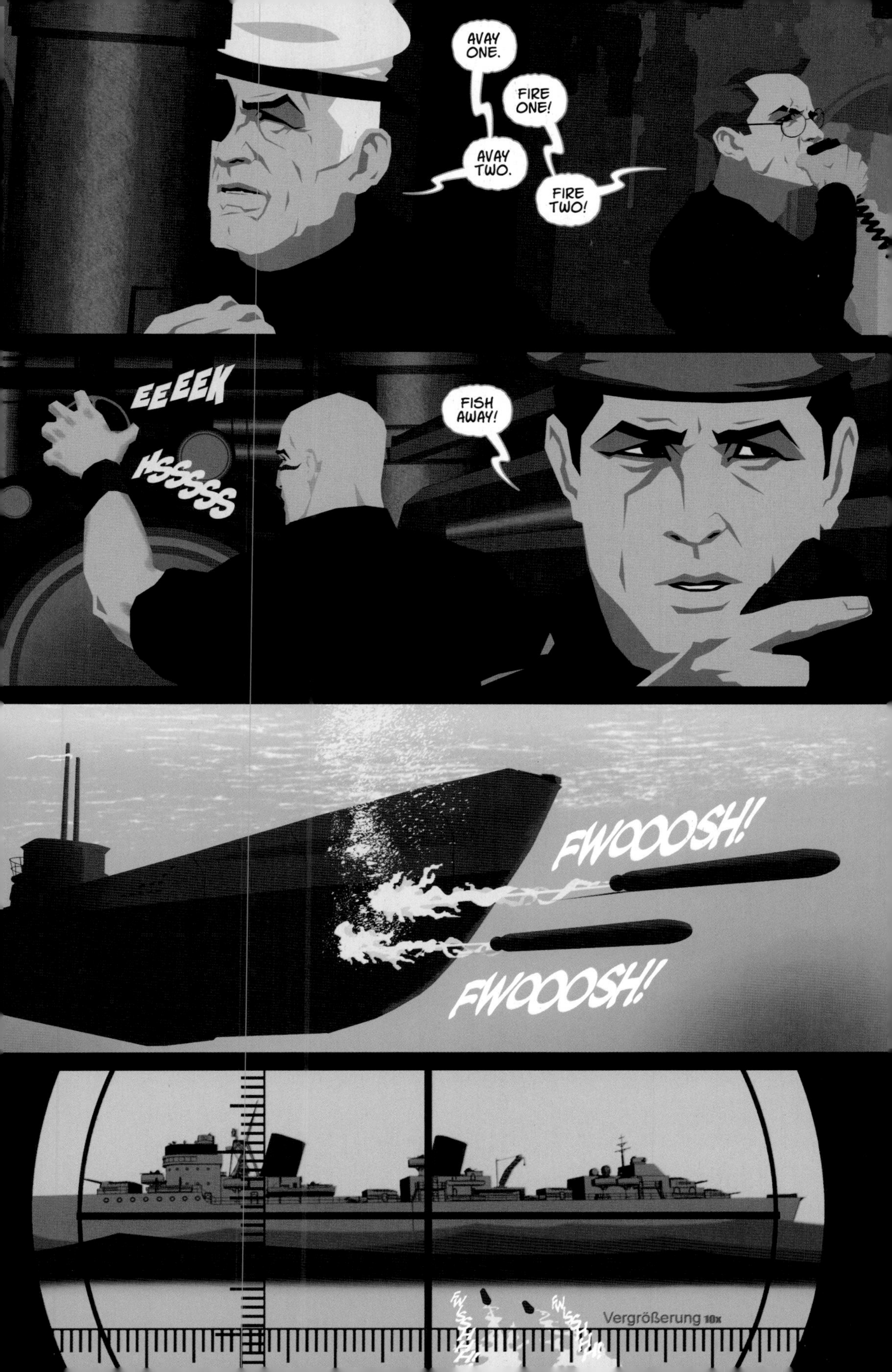
AVAY ONE.
FIRE ONE!
AVAY TWO.
FIRE TWO!
EEEEK
HSSSSS
FISH AWAY!
FWOOOSH!
FWOOOSH!
Vergrößerung 10x

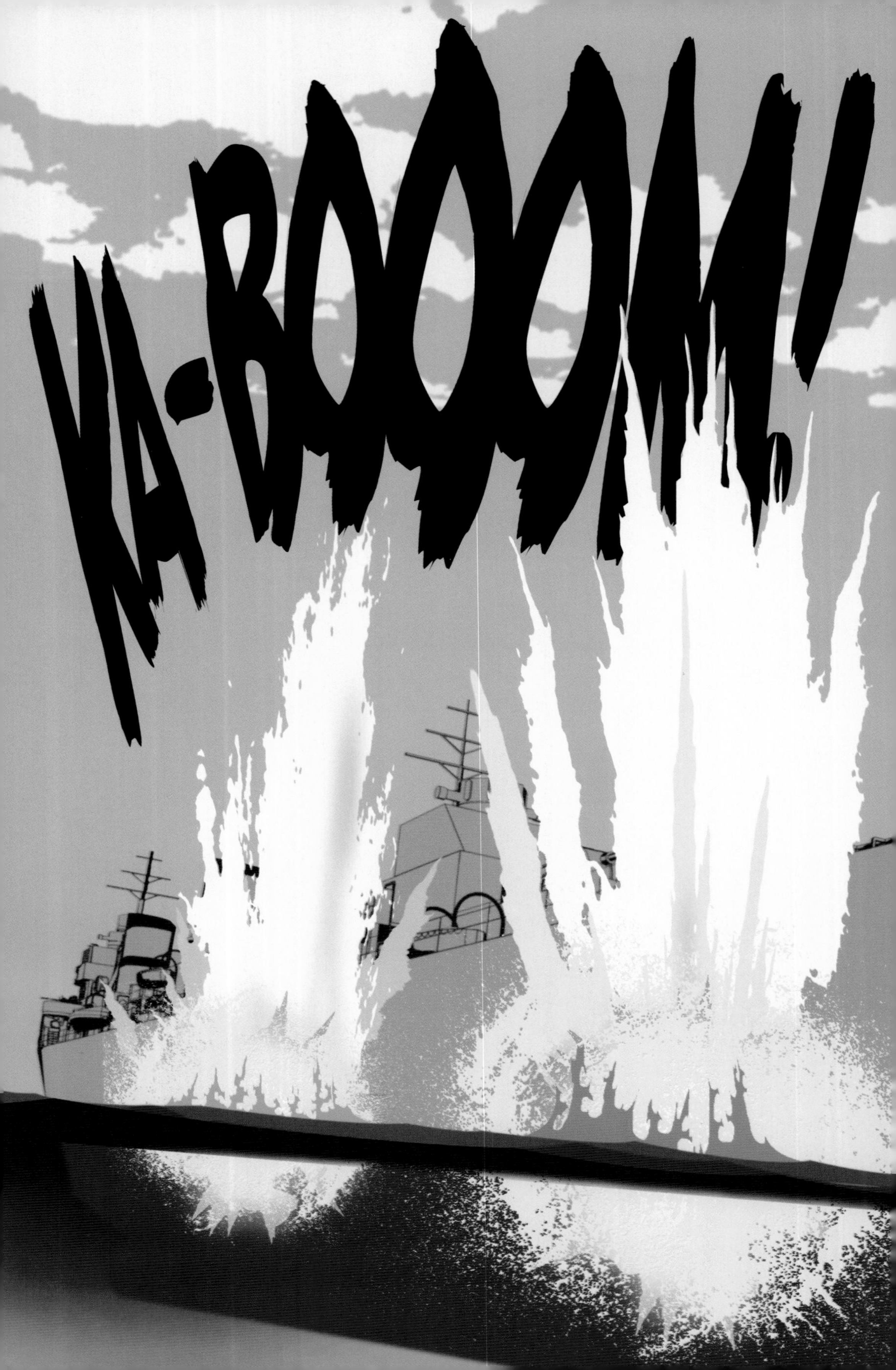
KA-BOOM!

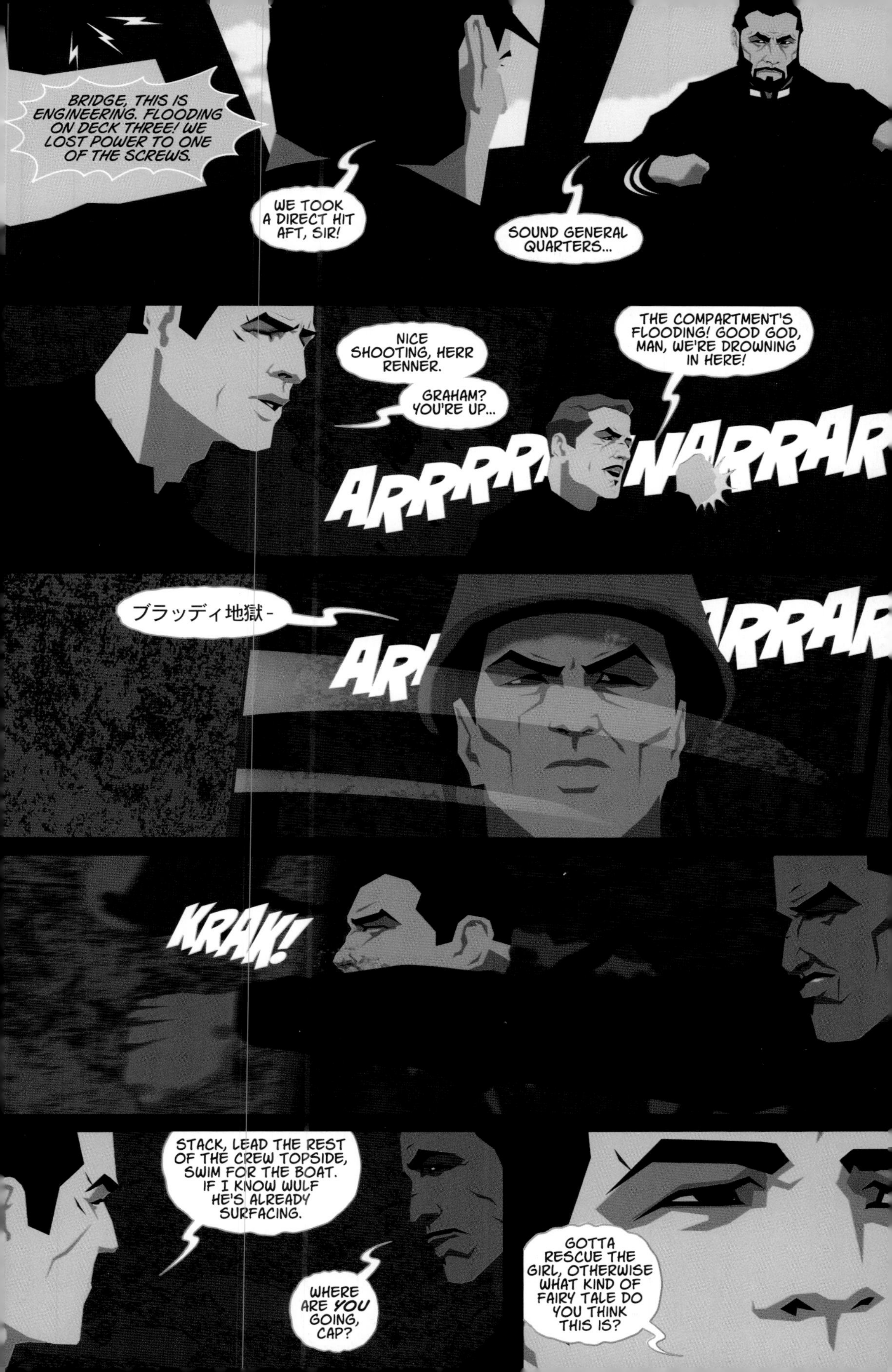
BRIDGE, THIS IS ENGINEERING. FLOODING ON DECK THREE! WE LOST POWER TO ONE OF THE SCREWS.
WE TOOK A DIRECT HIT AFT, SIR!
SOUND GENERAL QUARTERS...
NICE SHOOTING, HERR RENNER.
GRAHAM? YOU'RE UP...
THE COMPARTMENT'S FLOODING! GOOD GOD, MAN, WE'RE DROWNING IN HERE!
ARRRRNARRAR
ブラッディ地獄 -
KRAK!
STACK, LEAD THE REST OF THE CREW TOPSIDE, SWIM FOR THE BOAT. IF I KNOW WULF HE'S ALREADY SURFACING.
WHERE ARE ***YOU*** GOING, CAP?
GOTTA RESCUE THE GIRL, OTHERWISE WHAT KIND OF FAIRY TALE DO YOU THINK THIS IS?

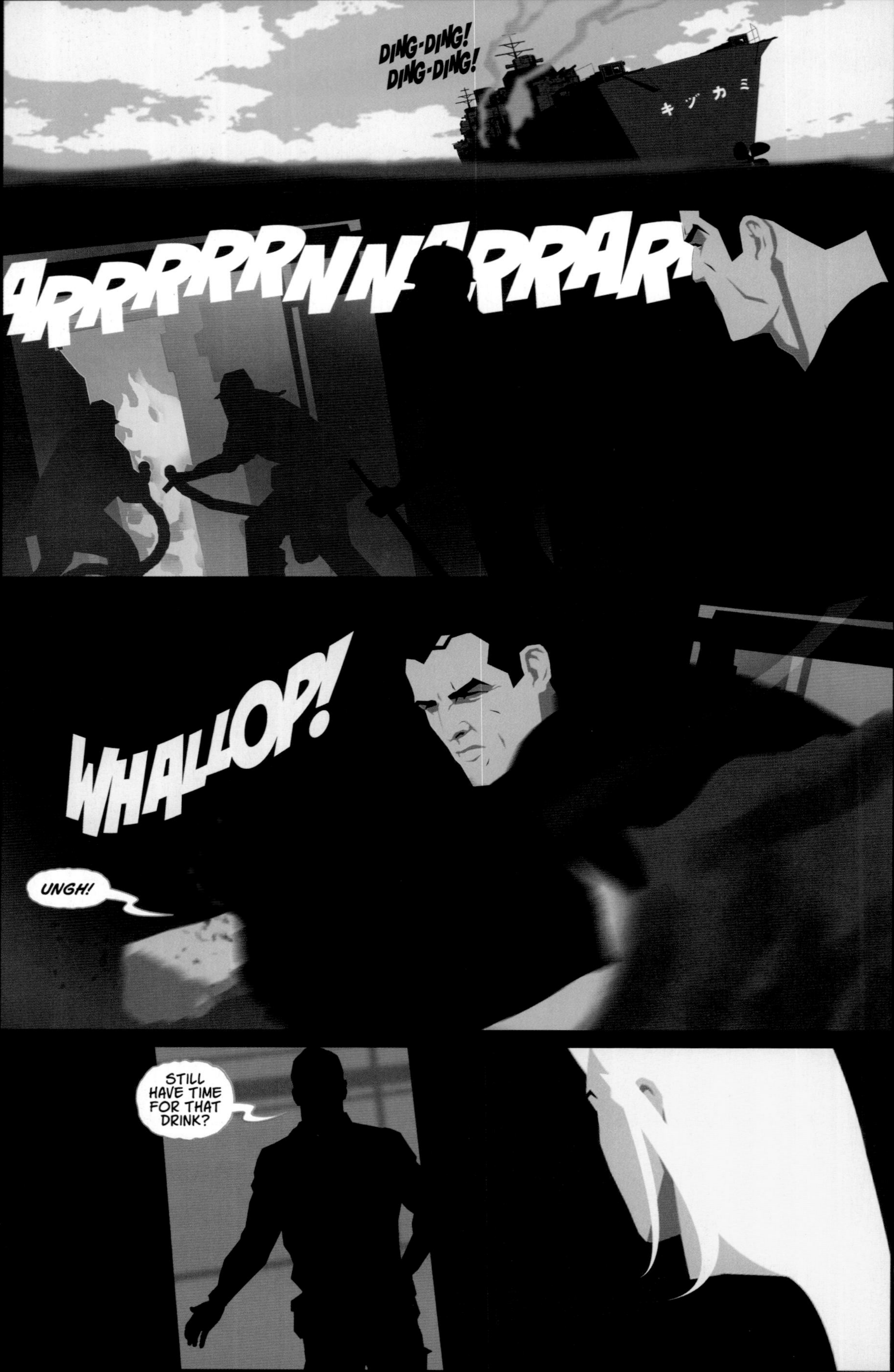
DING-DING!
DING-DING!
ミカヅキ
WHALLOP!
UNGH!
STILL HAVE TIME FOR THAT DRINK?

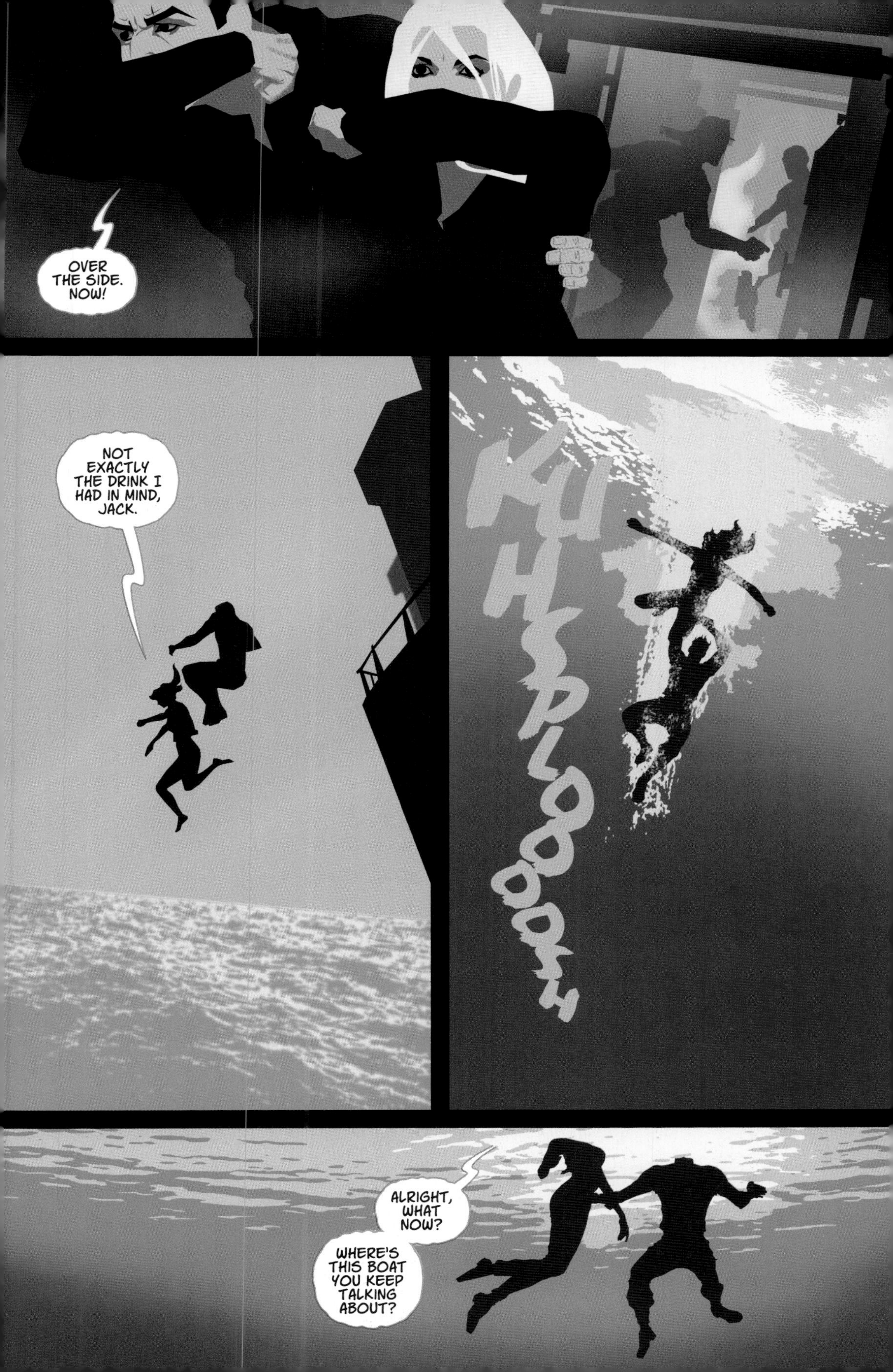
OVER THE SIDE. NOW!
NOT EXACTLY THE DRINK I HAD IN MIND, JACK.
KUHSPLOOOOSH
ALRIGHT, WHAT NOW?
WHERE'S THIS BOAT YOU KEEP TALKING ABOUT?

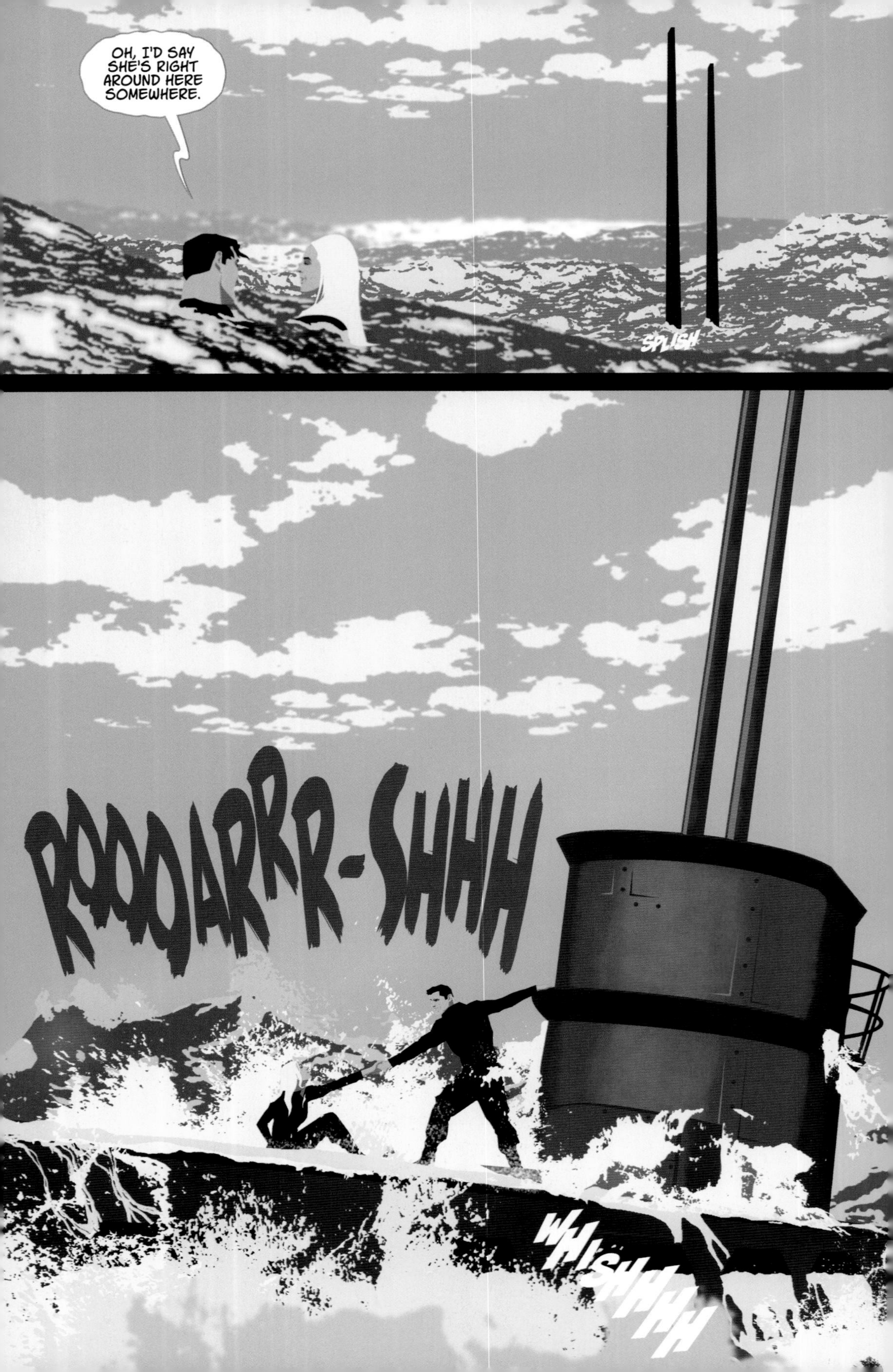
OH, I'D SAY SHE'S RIGHT AROUND HERE SOMEWHERE.
SPLISH
RRROOARRR-SHHH
WHISHHHH

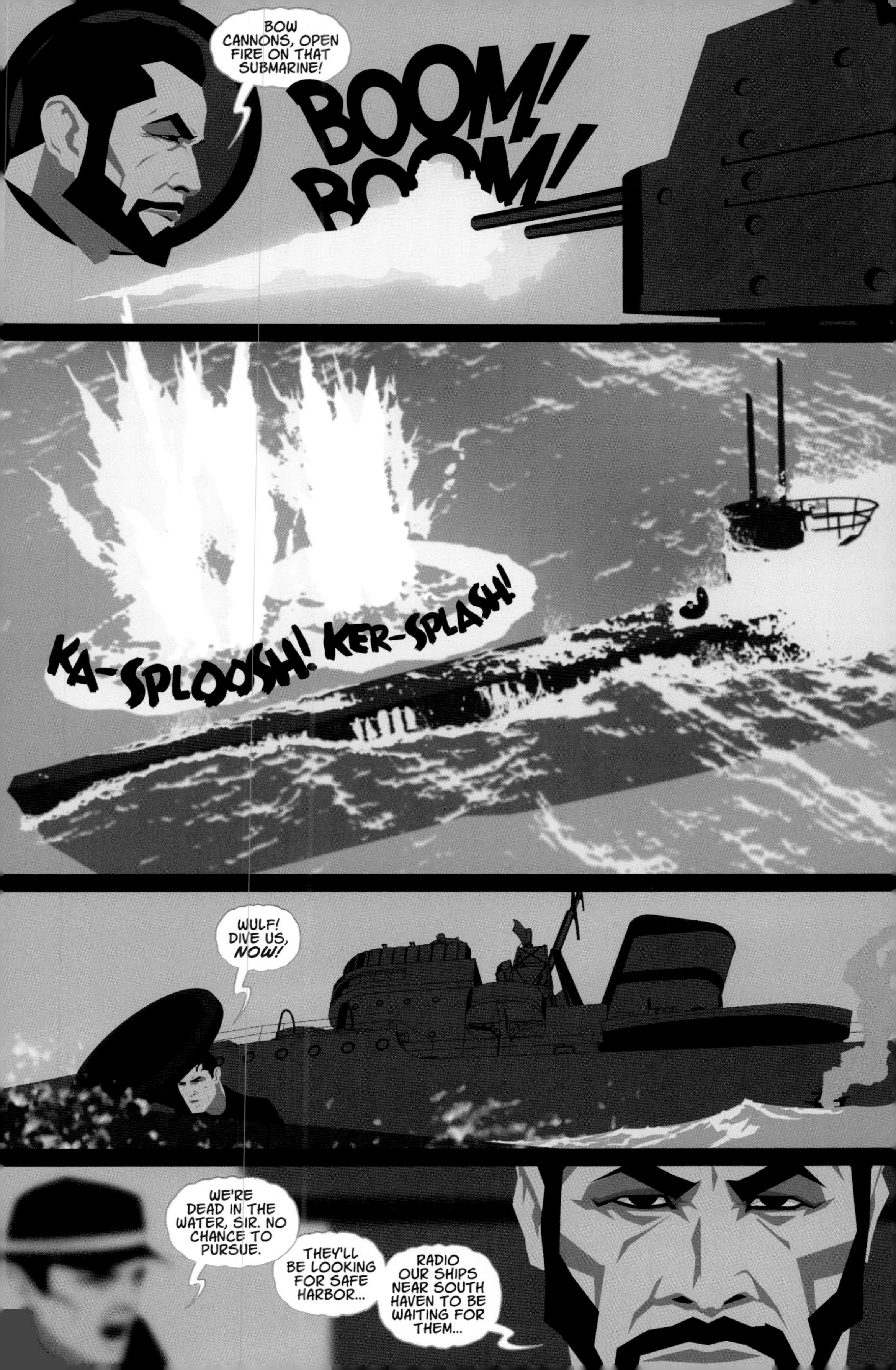

BOW CANNONS, OPEN FIRE ON THAT SUBMARINE!
BOOM! BOOM!
KA-SPLOOSH! KER-SPLASH!
WULF! DIVE US, NOW!
WE'RE DEAD IN THE WATER, SIR. NO CHANCE TO PURSUE.
THEY'LL BE LOOKING FOR SAFE HARBOR...
RADIO OUR SHIPS NEAR SOUTH HAVEN TO BE WAITING FOR THEM...

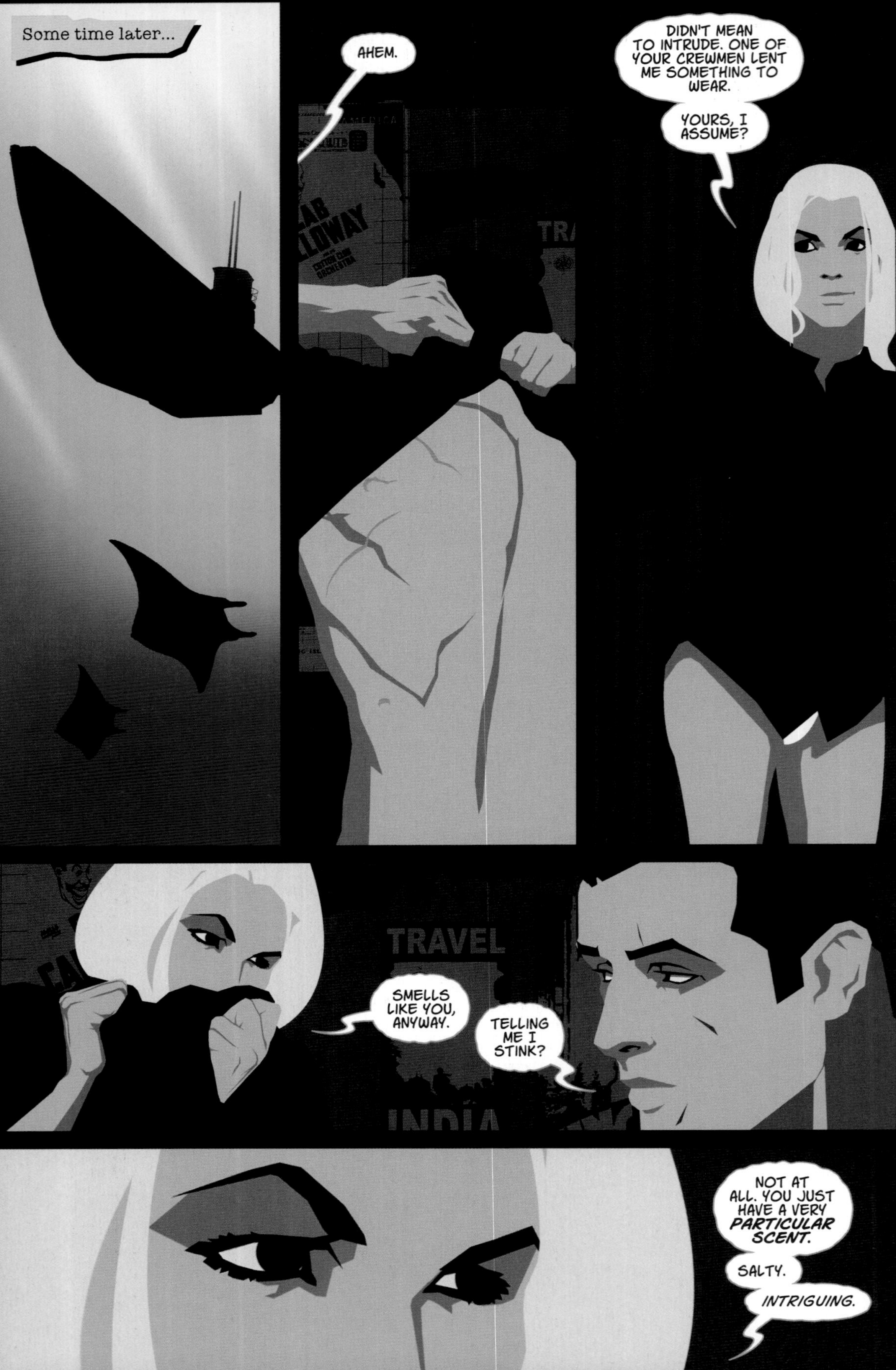
Some time later...
AHEM.
DIDN'T MEAN TO INTRUDE. ONE OF YOUR CREWMEN LENT ME SOMETHING TO WEAR.
YOURS, I ASSUME?
TRAVEL
INDIA
SMELLS LIKE YOU, ANYWAY.
TELLING ME I STINK?
NOT AT ALL. YOU JUST HAVE A VERY *PARTICULAR SCENT.*
SALTY.
INTRIGUING.

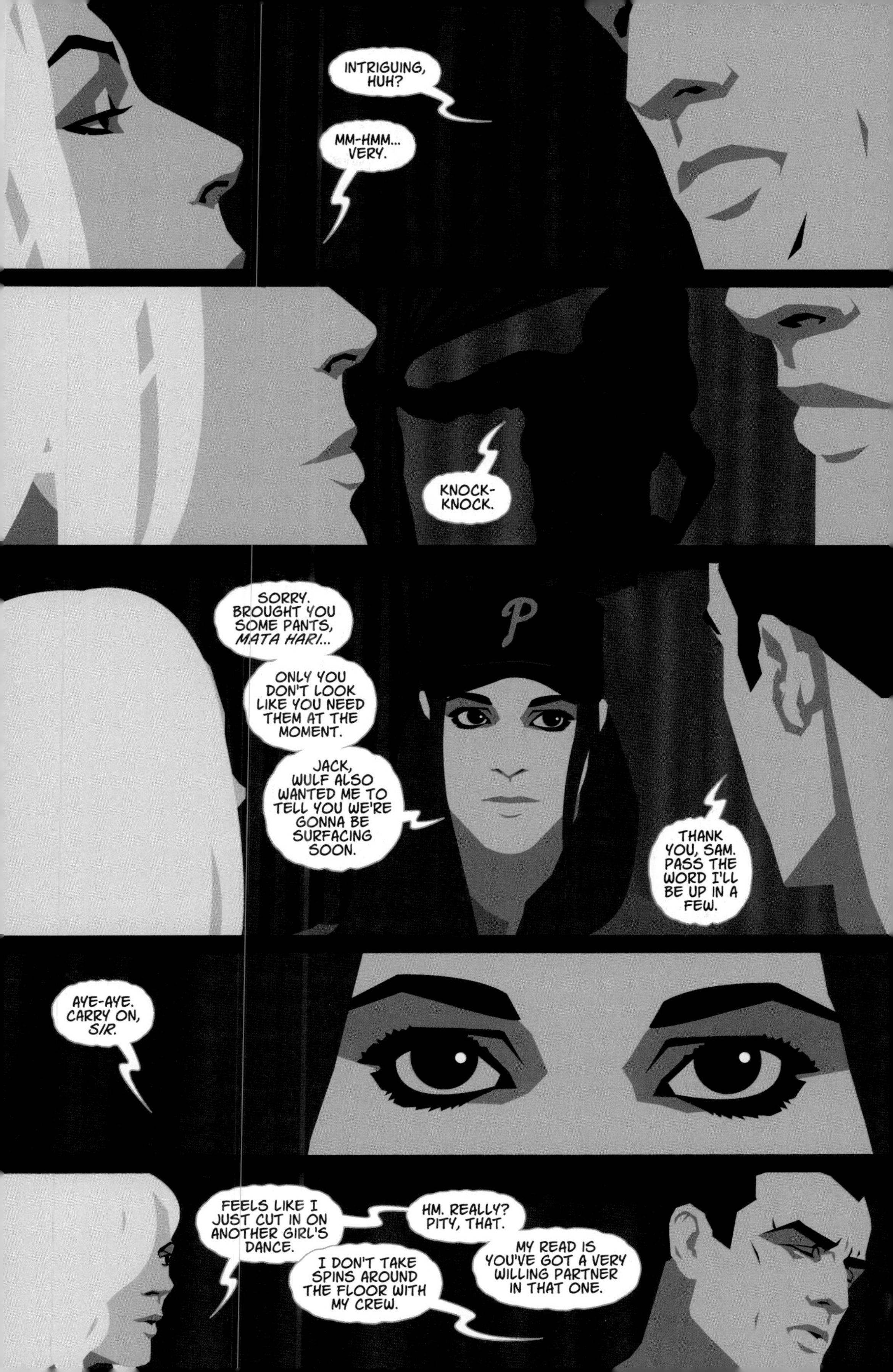
INTRIGUING, HUH?
MM-HMM... VERY.
KNOCK-KNOCK.
SORRY. BROUGHT YOU SOME PANTS, *MATA HARI*...
ONLY YOU DON'T LOOK LIKE YOU NEED THEM AT THE MOMENT.
JACK, WULF ALSO WANTED ME TO TELL YOU WE'RE GONNA BE SURFACING SOON.
THANK YOU, SAM. PASS THE WORD I'LL BE UP IN A FEW.
AYE-AYE. CARRY ON, *SIR*.
FEELS LIKE I JUST CUT IN ON ANOTHER GIRL'S DANCE.
HM. REALLY? PITY, THAT.
I DON'T TAKE SPINS AROUND THE FLOOR WITH MY CREW.
MY READ IS YOU'VE GOT A VERY WILLING PARTNER IN THAT ONE.

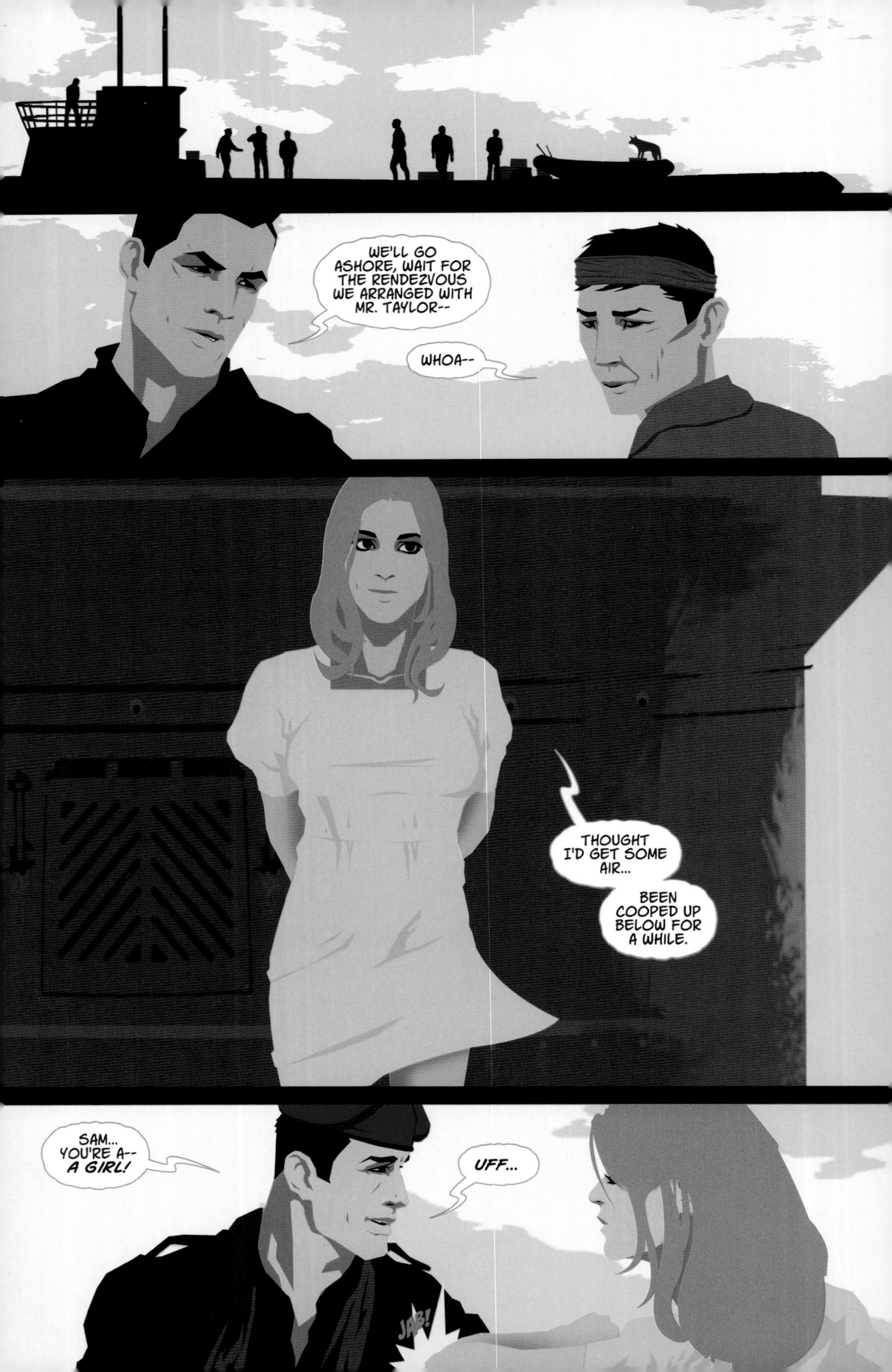
WE'LL GO ASHORE, WAIT FOR THE RENDEZVOUS WE ARRANGED WITH MR. TAYLOR--
WHOA--
THOUGHT I'D GET SOME AIR...
BEEN COOPED UP BELOW FOR A WHILE.
SAM... YOU'RE A-- A GIRL!
UFF...
JAB!

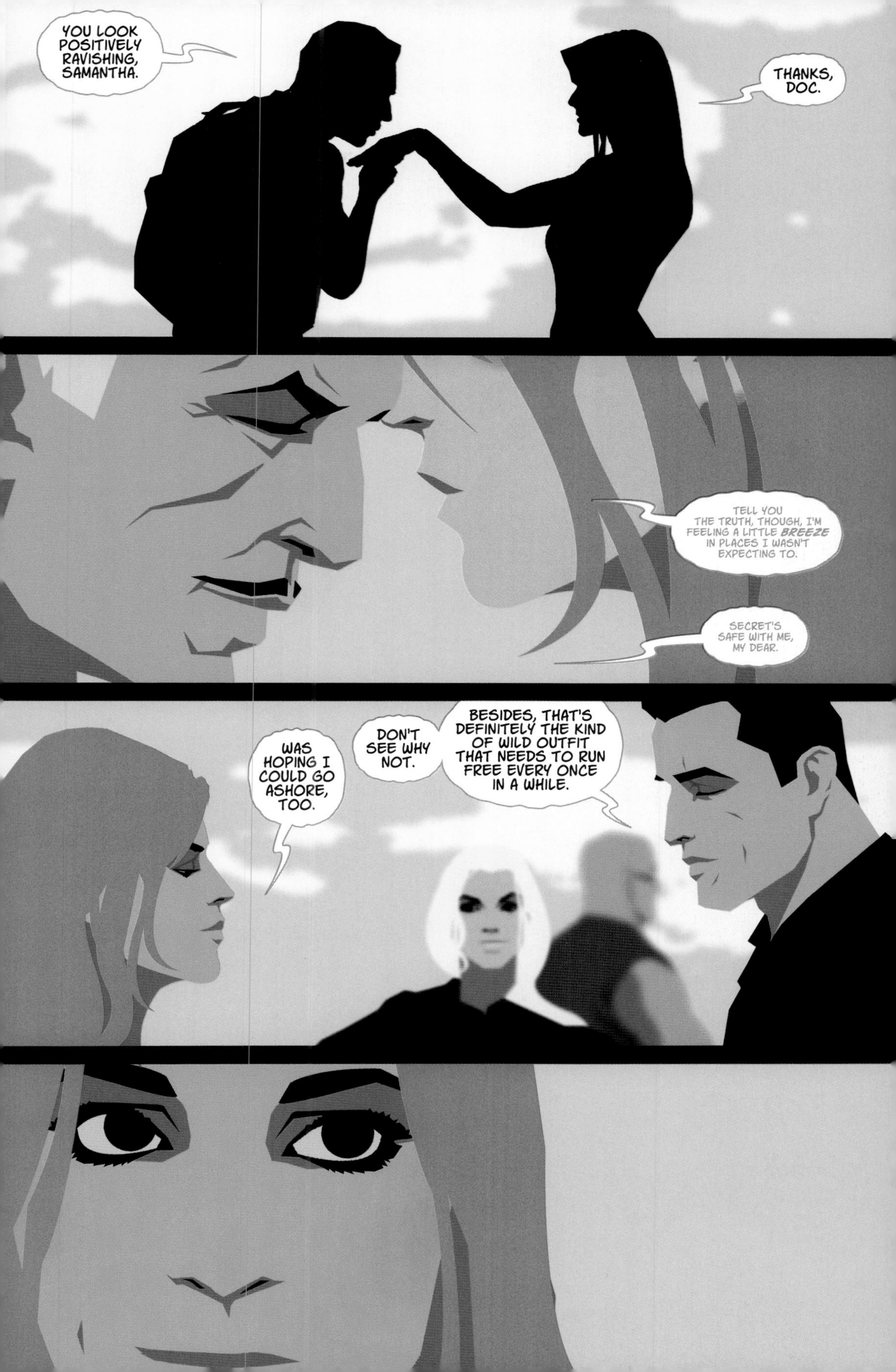
YOU LOOK POSITIVELY RAVISHING, SAMANTHA.
THANKS, DOC.
TELL YOU THE TRUTH, THOUGH, I'M FEELING A LITTLE BREEZE IN PLACES I WASN'T EXPECTING TO.
SECRET'S SAFE WITH ME, MY DEAR.
WAS HOPING I COULD GO ASHORE, TOO.
DON'T SEE WHY NOT.
BESIDES, THAT'S DEFINITELY THE KIND OF WILD OUTFIT THAT NEEDS TO RUN FREE EVERY ONCE IN A WHILE.

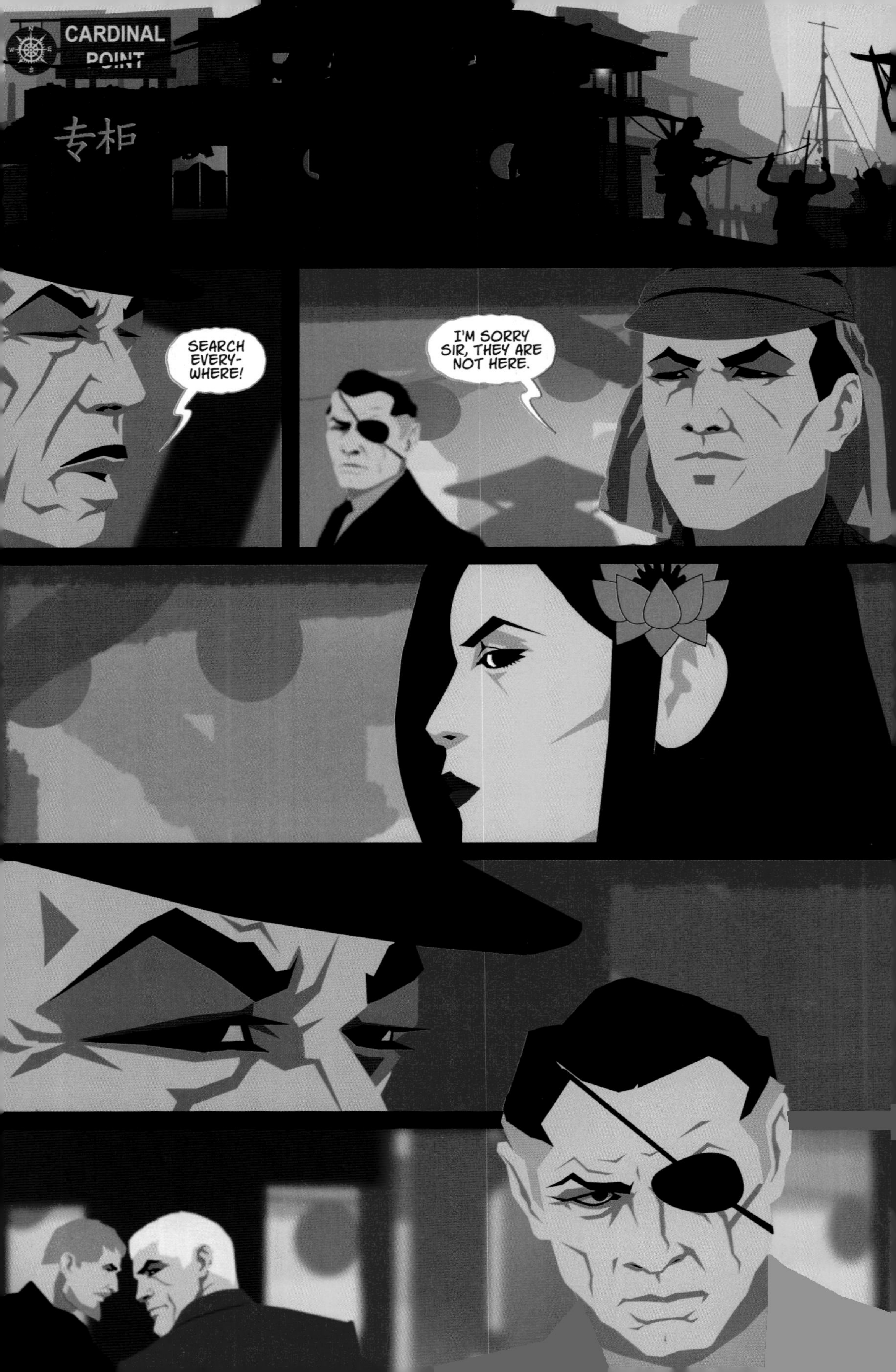
CARDINAL POINT
专柜
SEARCH EVERY-WHERE!
I'M SORRY SIR, THEY ARE NOT HERE.

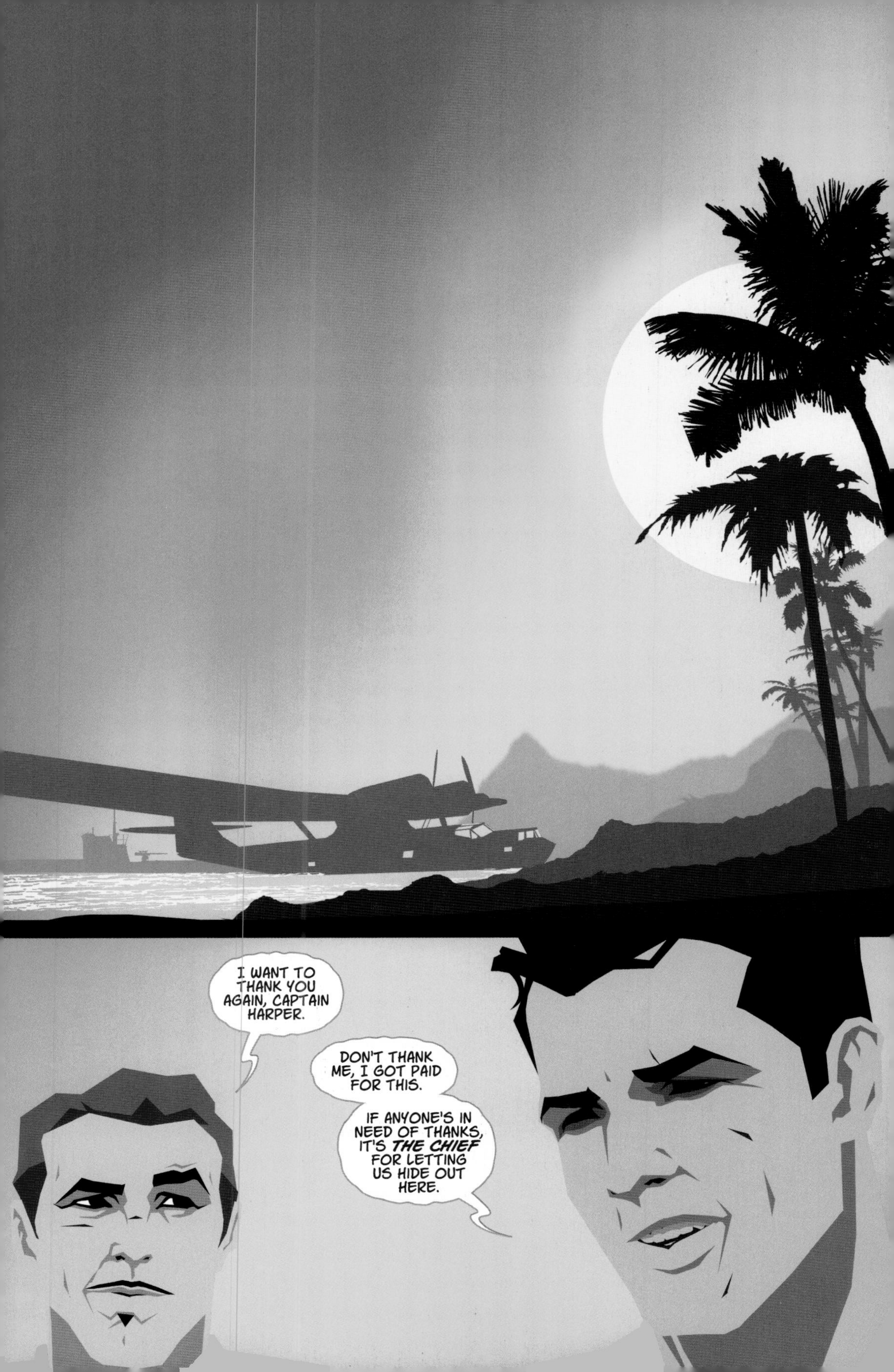
I WANT TO THANK YOU AGAIN, CAPTAIN HARPER.
DON'T THANK ME, I GOT PAID FOR THIS.
IF ANYONE'S IN NEED OF THANKS, IT'S *THE CHIEF* FOR LETTING US HIDE OUT HERE.

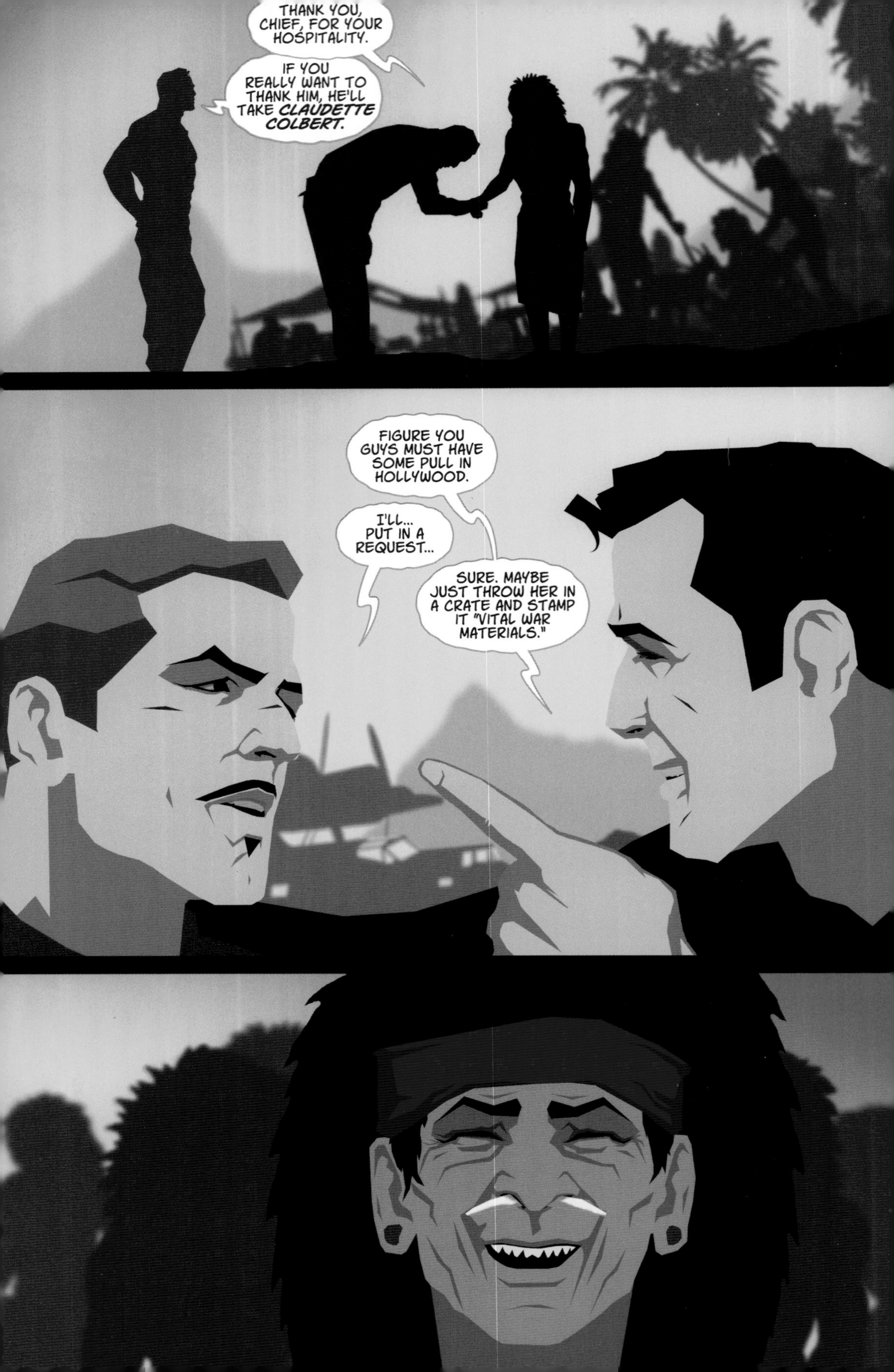
THANK YOU, CHIEF, FOR YOUR HOSPITALITY.
IF YOU REALLY WANT TO THANK HIM, HE'LL TAKE *CLAUDETTE COLBERT.*
FIGURE YOU GUYS MUST HAVE SOME PULL IN HOLLYWOOD.
I'LL... PUT IN A REQUEST...
SURE. MAYBE JUST THROW HER IN A CRATE AND STAMP IT "VITAL WAR MATERIALS."

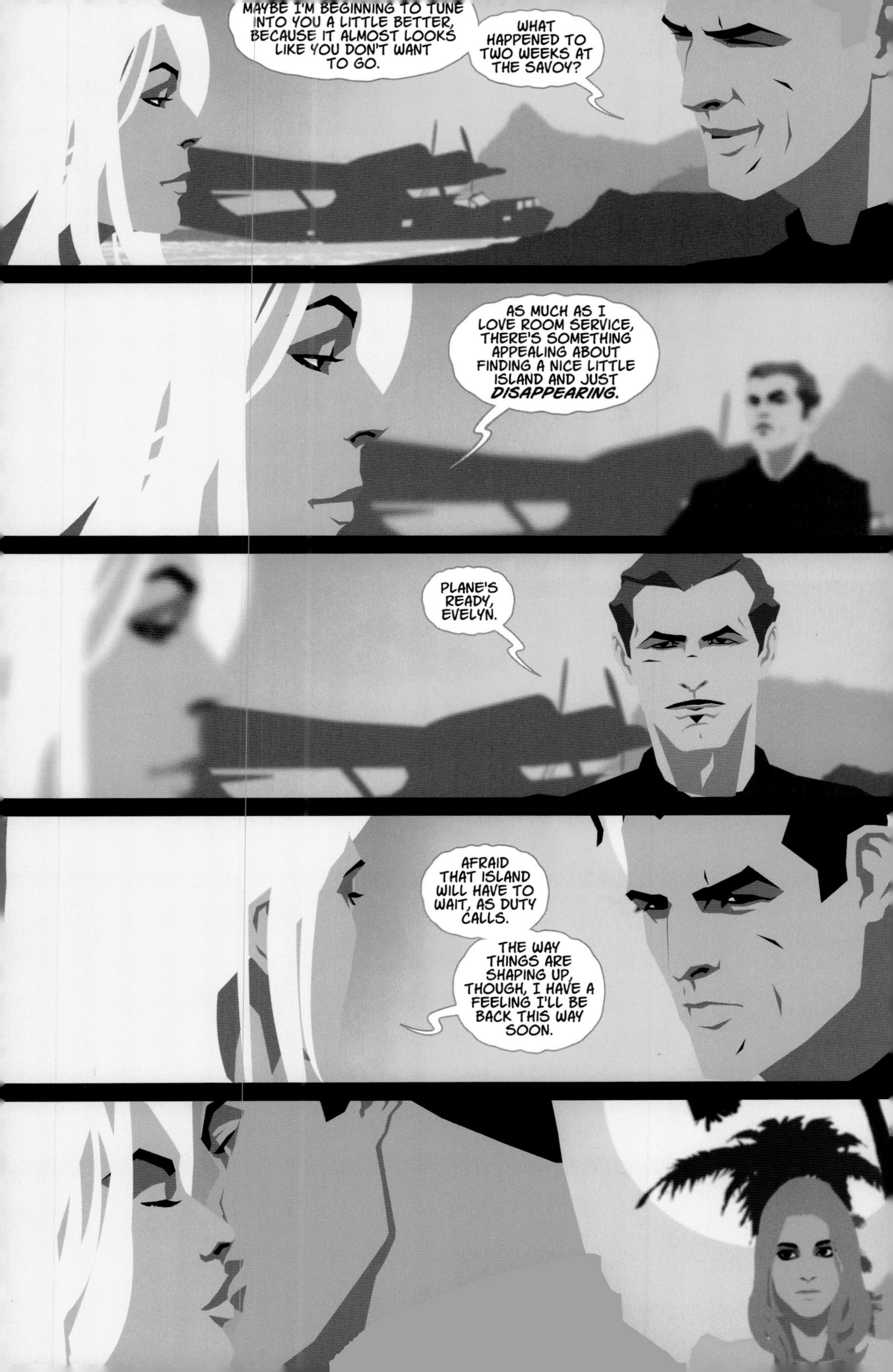
MAYBE I'M BEGINNING TO TUNE INTO YOU A LITTLE BETTER, BECAUSE IT ALMOST LOOKS LIKE YOU DON'T WANT TO GO.
WHAT HAPPENED TO TWO WEEKS AT THE SAVOY?
AS MUCH AS I LOVE ROOM SERVICE, THERE'S SOMETHING APPEALING ABOUT FINDING A NICE LITTLE ISLAND AND JUST ***DISAPPEARING***.
PLANE'S READY, EVELYN.
AFRAID THAT ISLAND WILL HAVE TO WAIT, AS DUTY CALLS.
THE WAY THINGS ARE SHAPING UP, THOUGH, I HAVE A FEELING I'LL BE BACK THIS WAY SOON.

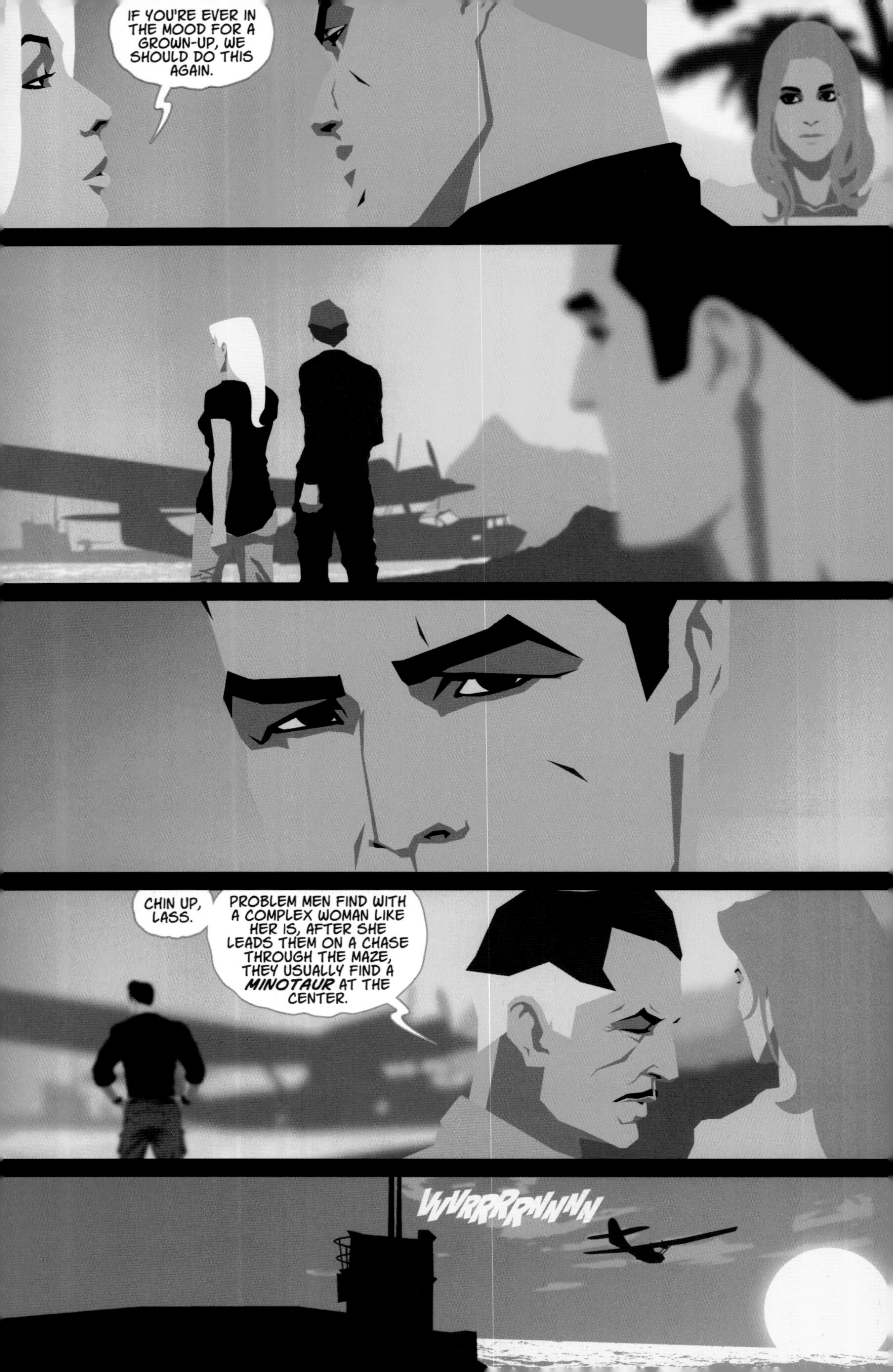
IF YOU'RE EVER IN THE MOOD FOR A GROWN-UP, WE SHOULD DO THIS AGAIN.
CHIN UP, LASS.
PROBLEM MEN FIND WITH A COMPLEX WOMAN LIKE HER IS, AFTER SHE LEADS THEM ON A CHASE THROUGH THE MAZE, THEY USUALLY FIND A MINOTAUR AT THE CENTER.
VVVRRRRNNNN

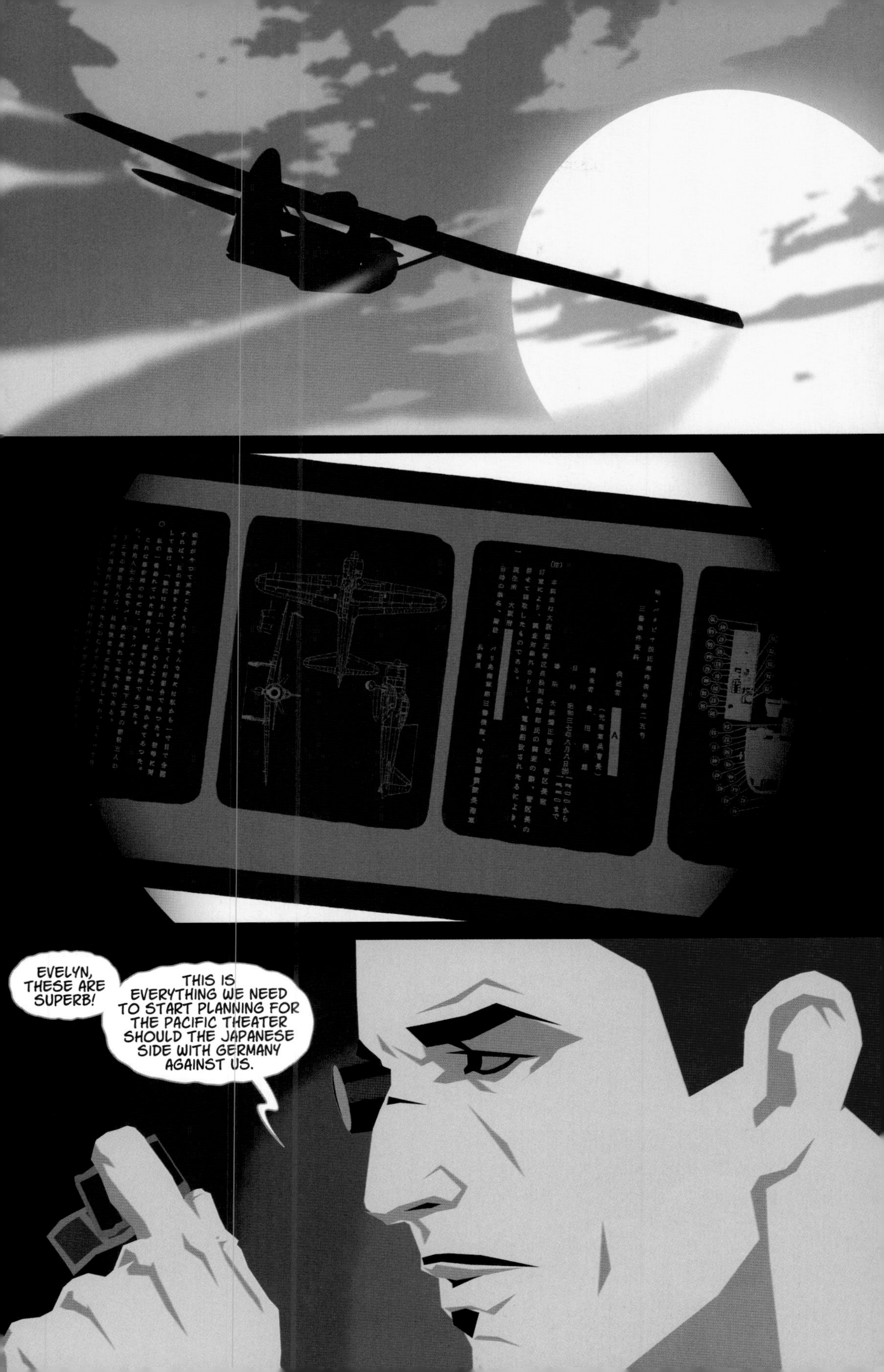

EVELYN, THESE ARE SUPERB!
THIS IS EVERYTHING WE NEED TO START PLANNING FOR THE PACIFIC THEATER SHOULD THE JAPANESE SIDE WITH GERMANY AGAINST US.

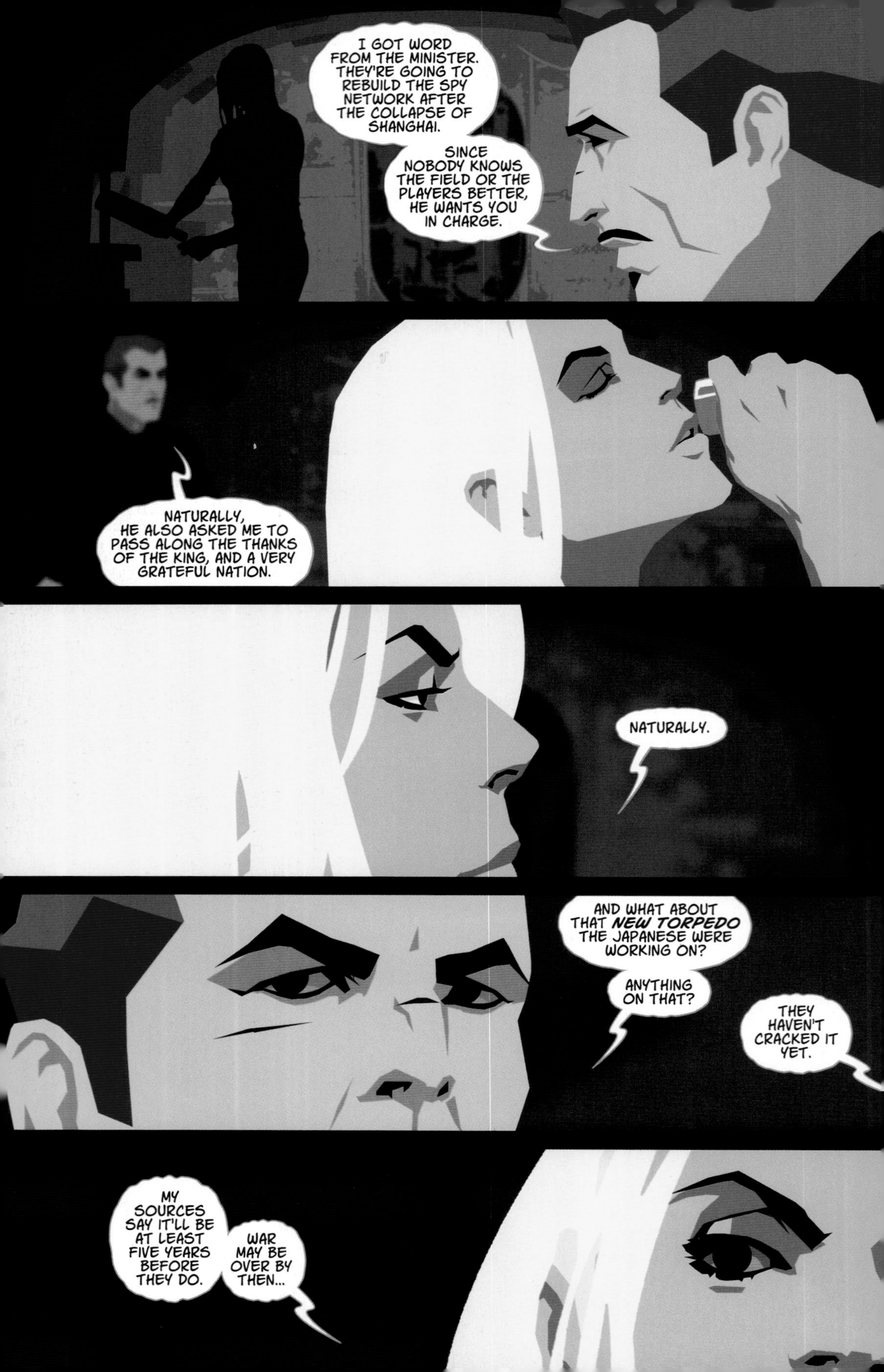
I GOT WORD FROM THE MINISTER. THEY'RE GOING TO REBUILD THE SPY NETWORK AFTER THE COLLAPSE OF SHANGHAI.
SINCE NOBODY KNOWS THE FIELD OR THE PLAYERS BETTER, HE WANTS YOU IN CHARGE.
NATURALLY, HE ALSO ASKED ME TO PASS ALONG THE THANKS OF THE KING, AND A VERY GRATEFUL NATION.
NATURALLY.
AND WHAT ABOUT THAT *NEW TORPEDO* THE JAPANESE WERE WORKING ON?
ANYTHING ON THAT?
THEY HAVEN'T CRACKED IT YET.
MY SOURCES SAY IT'LL BE AT LEAST FIVE YEARS BEFORE THEY DO.
WAR MAY BE OVER BY THEN...

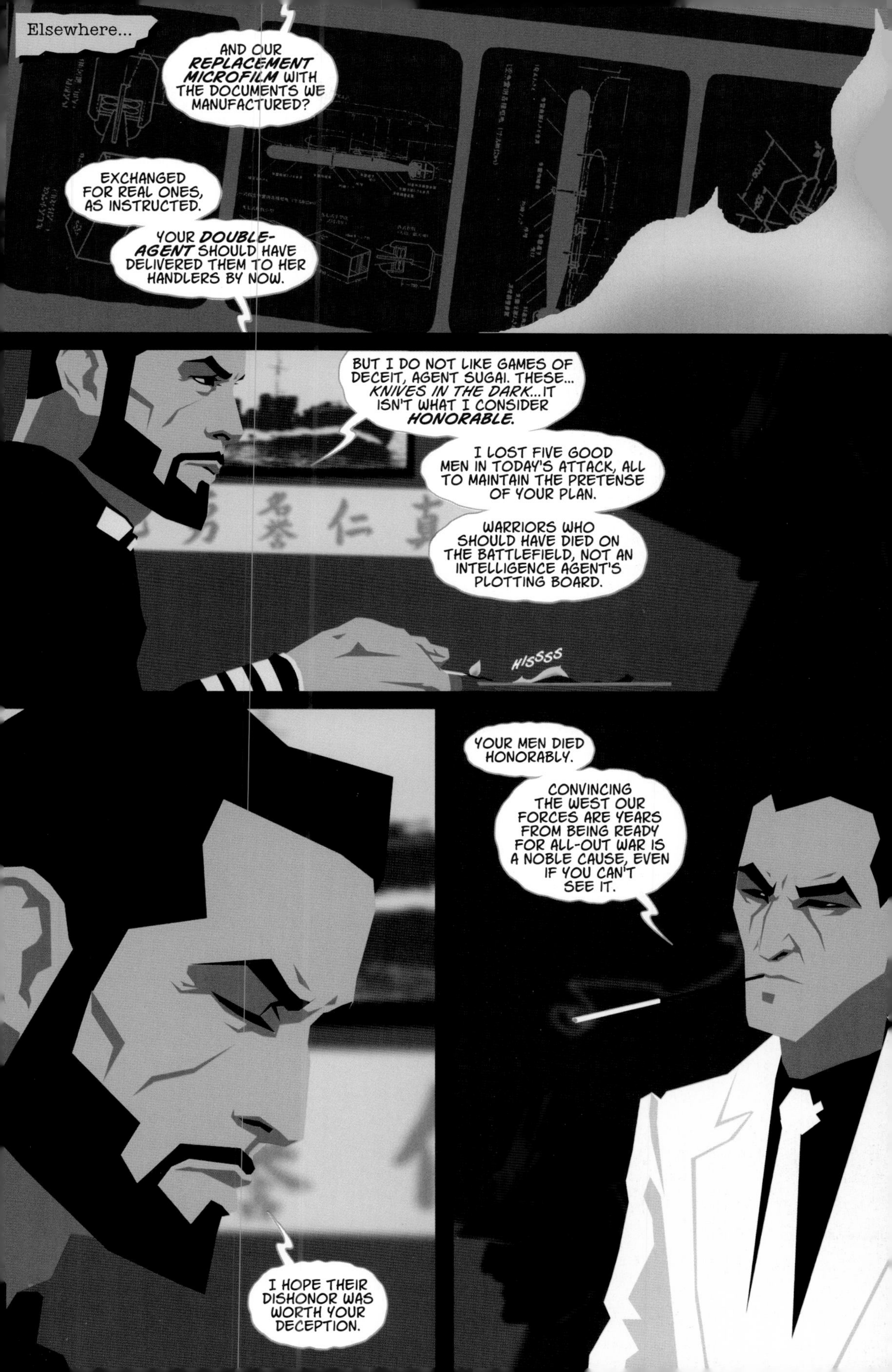
Elsewhere...
AND OUR REPLACEMENT MICROFILM WITH THE DOCUMENTS WE MANUFACTURED?
EXCHANGED FOR REAL ONES, AS INSTRUCTED.
YOUR DOUBLE-AGENT SHOULD HAVE DELIVERED THEM TO HER HANDLERS BY NOW.
BUT I DO NOT LIKE GAMES OF DECEIT, AGENT SUGAI. THESE... KNIVES IN THE DARK...IT ISN'T WHAT I CONSIDER HONORABLE.
I LOST FIVE GOOD MEN IN TODAY'S ATTACK, ALL TO MAINTAIN THE PRETENSE OF YOUR PLAN.
WARRIORS WHO SHOULD HAVE DIED ON THE BATTLEFIELD, NOT AN INTELLIGENCE AGENT'S PLOTTING BOARD.
HISSSS
YOUR MEN DIED HONORABLY.
CONVINCING THE WEST OUR FORCES ARE YEARS FROM BEING READY FOR ALL-OUT WAR IS A NOBLE CAUSE, EVEN IF YOU CAN'T SEE IT.
I HOPE THEIR DISHONOR WAS WORTH YOUR DECEPTION.

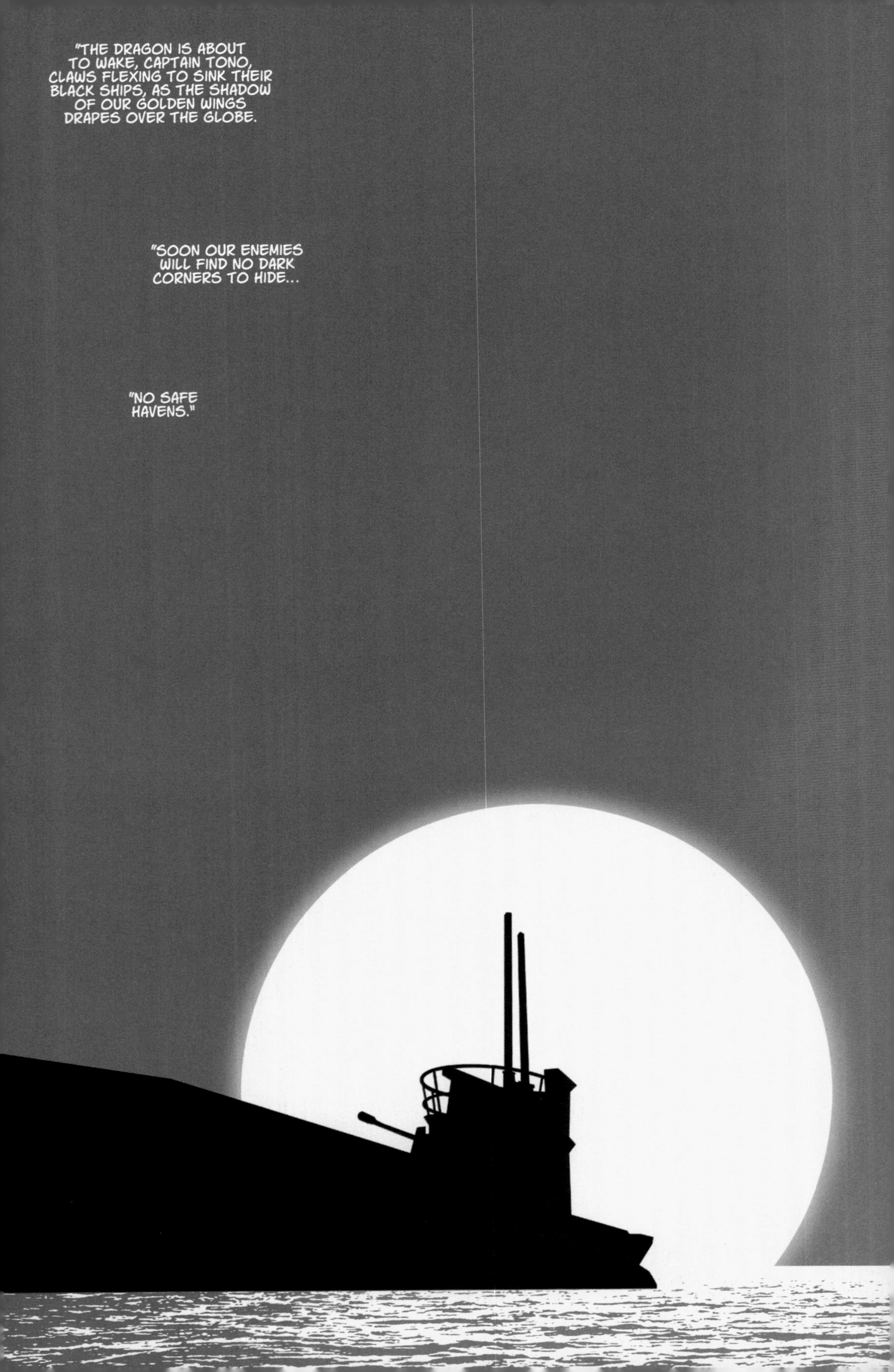
"THE DRAGON IS ABOUT TO WAKE, CAPTAIN TONO, CLAWS FLEXING TO SINK THEIR BLACK SHIPS, AS THE SHADOW OF OUR GOLDEN WINGS DRAPES OVER THE GLOBE.
"SOON OUR ENEMIES WILL FIND NO DARK CORNERS TO HIDE...
"NO SAFE HAVENS."

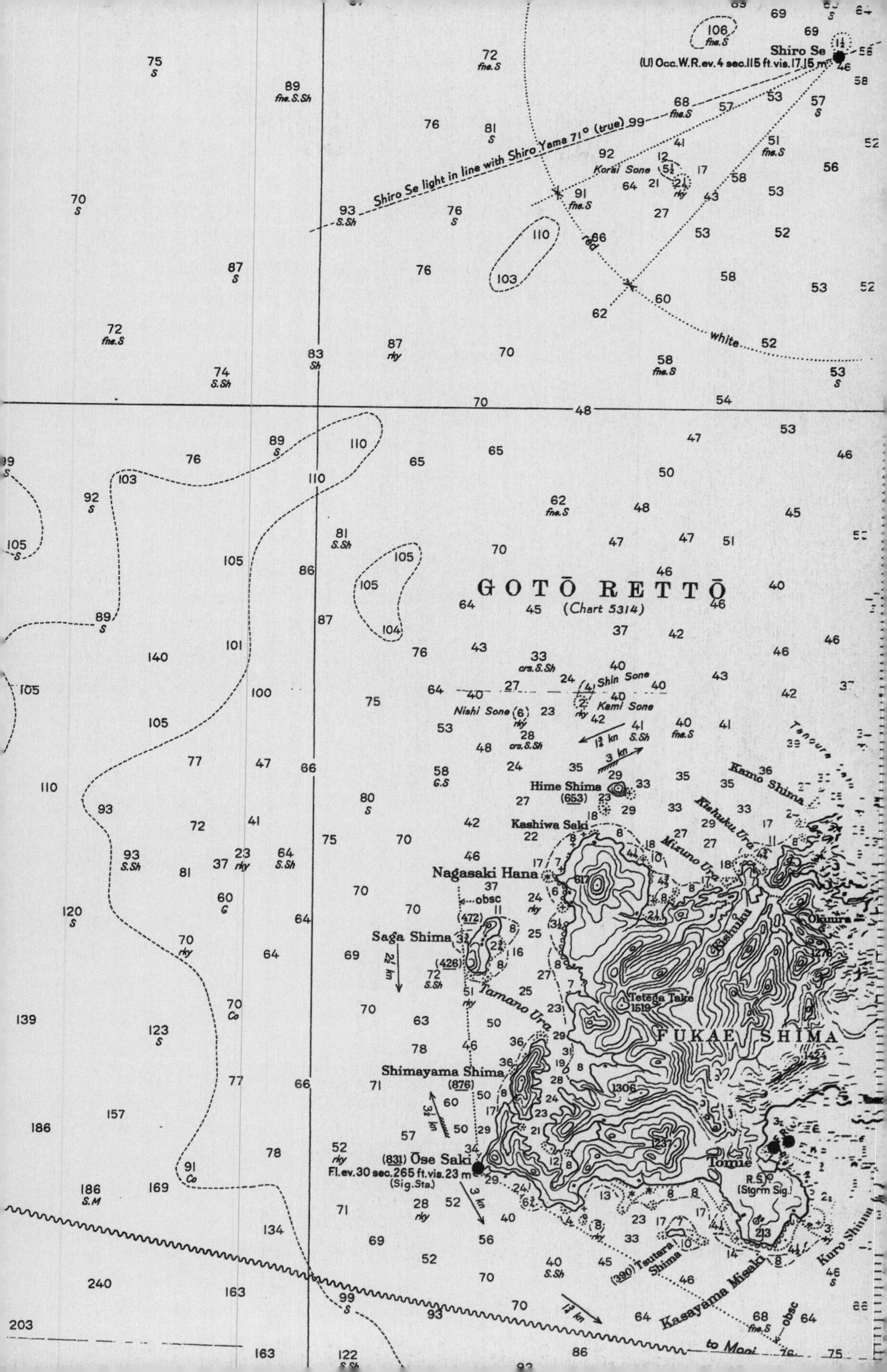

Shiro Se
(U) Occ. W.R. ev. 4 sec. 115 ft. vis. 17.15 m
Shiro Se light in line with Shiro Yama 71° (true)
Korai Sone
red
white
GOTŌ RETTŌ
(Chart 5314)
Shin Sone
Kami Sone
Nishi Sone
Hime Shima
Kashiwa Saki
Nagasaki Hana
obsc
Saga Shima
Tamano Ura
Mizuno Ura
Kishuku Ura
Kishuku
Kamo Shima
Tanoura Seto
Okuura
Tetega Take
FUKAE SHIMA
Shimayama Shima
Ōse Saki
Fl. ev. 30 sec. 265 ft. vis. 23 m
(Sig. Sta.)
Tomie
R.S.
(Stgrm Sig.)
Tsutara Shima
Kasayama Misaki
Kuro Shima
to Mogi

Jack Harper - Captain
Born: August 13, 1902 (37)
Gloucester, MA

At 16, Jack ran away from home, leaving behind his "bayman" father, who had taught Jack everything he knew about the sea. But, Jack didn't want to be a fisherman. After knocking around the streets of South Boston, Jack found work with the local Irish mob. During Prohibition, Jack, who knew the coast from Portsmouth to Cape Cod like the back of his hand, became a rumrunner, landing Canadian booze by the boatload. That is, until a rival mobster dimed him out to the T-men, and Jack was forced to leave the country, with nothing more than the shirt on his back, or face arrest and decades in prison.

After bumming around the globe for a number of years, Jack wound up in Asia, running a mail service and passenger boat, until he found high-paying mercenary work with the Chinese Navy. It was during this time he teamed up with many of the crewmembers of the Venture, then known as the Tiger Shark, a converted UB-III submarine, to fight the Japanese invaders.

Jack ran afoul of his superior in the Chinese Navy, Admiral Shi Tang, who eventually set Jack and his crew up to be killed or captured. Surviving the trap, and learning of their betrayal, they decided to part ways with Shi Tang, taking the boat as compensation, and have been freelancing in the South Pacific ever since.

Wulfric Renner - First Mate
Born: October 22, 1889 (50)
Bremerhaven, Germany

Served with the Imperial German Navy during the Great War. After briefly serving aboard UB-65 as young officer, Wulf transferred to UB-107, where he won distinction in combat, and eventual command as its captain. UB-107 was a terror in the North Atlantic, sinking eight enemy vessels, the last of which was the H.M.S. Foster. Renner, however, was relieved of duty shortly after the Foster's sinking, and when UB-107 went out again under the command of another officer, it was sunk in July, 1918. Renner resigned from the Navy, sailing aboard a variety of civilian steamers and freighters, until being recruited by the Chinese to fight the Japanese.

Samantha "Sam" Blair - Engineer
Born: December 28, 1919 (20)
Feasterville, PA

Samantha's father, Richard Blair, was a former stock car racer and genius mechanic, able to soup up any engine. Blair plied his trade with mobsters running Canadian whiskey dropped ashore by bootleggers. This is where he became a close friend and associate of Jack Harper. After his wife succumbed to cancer, Richard would often bring young Samantha along on these runs, and she picked up more than a few tricks from her old man. When Richard Blair was finally caught, convicted and sentenced to life in the Eastern State Penitentiary, Samantha was made a ward of the state. After Sam turned 18, she left the U.S. looking for adventure, hoping to find work with Jack (whom she'd also developed a crush on).

Jarreau - Cook & Quartermaster
Born: July 26, 1906 (32)
Dijon, France

Arrested, and facing serious jail time for a series of thefts he
committed as a youth, Jarreau opted to join the French Foreign Legion
instead. His first service was in Morocco with the Spanish against
the Rifs. After two years of combat, seeing more than his fair share
of bloodshed, Jarreau deserted the Legion. He fell in with a group
of thieves and pirates working the South Seas, until he ended up in
China, serving aboard what was then, the Tiger Shark. His dream is to
earn enough money to one day retire from a life of war and violence,
and buy a plantation in French Indochina - maybe raise dairy cows.

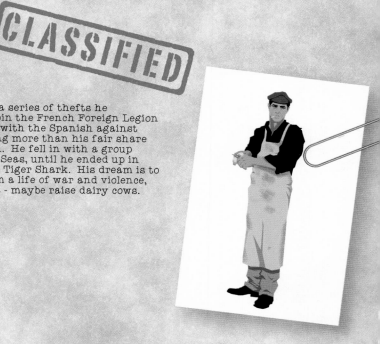

Milton "Doc" Weatherborne, III - Surgeon
Born: 1882 (56)
Maidstone, England

From a family with a long history of military doctors, he served
with the Queen's Own Royal West Kent Regiment, as a prominent
field surgeon in Afghanistan and later India. However, Major
Weatherborne was charged with misconduct and deemed unfit to
serve, after he botched a routine surgery of a soldier while intoxicated.
Stripped of rank and medical license, he served two years in military
prison before leaving the continent permanently, signing on as a
ship's doctor with a string of dubious merchant vessels running trade
routes through the Mediterranean and Indian Ocean, until he met
Jack in Hong Kong and came aboard Venture.

John "Stack" Jackson - Boatswain
Born: April 4, 1904 (34)
Chicago, IL

A heavyweight fighter who fought under the name "Smokestack
Jackson." Undefeated, with a winning record of 19 fights, four by KO.
Stack was headed for big things, until a crooked bookie pressed him to
throw an upcoming fight he was heavily favored to win. When Stack
refused, the bookie had his trainer killed, and cops on the take framed
Jackson for his murder. Stack ran, first to Canada, then worked his
way West, and then overseas, until he found himself back in the ring,
as a fighter in underground matches in Hong Kong and Macao. He
and Jack met up during this time, and when Jack found employment
with the Chinese, he sent word for Stack to join him.

Toby Silver - Electrician
Born: October 20, 1909 (29)
Brooklyn, NY

Toby grew up working in his family's radio and appliance repair shop, proving quite adept with any electronics or technology. A bright student, Toby eventually enrolled in college (the first in his family) after earning an engineering scholarship at Cornell. In his second year, however, the family shop was robbed by local hoodlums, and his father was beaten within an inch of his life. Toby left school, ostensibly to keep the shop running with his younger brother. For reasons unknown, he left the U.S. at the end of 1935, eventually ending up in China, where he signed aboard the Venture (then the Tiger Shark) as electrician, radioman and sonar operator.

Kevahitua-kahiali "Kevin" - a'Moko Boatswain's Mate
Born: Unknown, but thought to be 30

Kevin, as the crew of the Venture know him (mostly because no one can pronounce his given name) is a bit of an enigma. He was found adrift, apparently lost at sea for months, dehydrated and suffering from a limited form of amnesia. His tattoos and boat, while distinct, did little to identify which island tribe he may have hailed from. And though he did not speak English, Kevin was a quick study, picking up the language, as well as a number of tasks aboard the boat, becoming a valuable crew member.

Do - pronounced "Dough" Machinist's Mate
Born: June 18, 1921 (17)
Lianshang Prefecture

He grew up in the hills of Sichuan, his parents farmers, like their parents before them, and theirs before that. But after a season of torrential rains washed his family's holdings away, Do said his spirit wanted to wander south, and he had no choice but to follow. Hanging around coastal towns and forced to find work to survive, young Do picked up his trade operating diesel engines for fishing vessels. When the Japanese invaded, he was pressed into service with the Republic of China's Navy, eventually assigned to the Tiger Shark, an old German U-Boat the Chinese picked up cheap, and crewed by mostly Western sailors and mercenaries. Do is the only Chinese national that served under Jack who opted to stay aboard, rather than return home to China after Jack took the boat and ran.

Friday

Shepherd-dingo mix. Not a fan of bounty hunters. Or cats.

Original Description for Jack:

"Something like Clark Gable in Gone with the Wind or Cary Grant in Only Angels Have Wings. Though he might be closer to Humphrey Bogart in To Have and Have Not.

He may not be the best looking guy you've ever met, but his rugged charm pegs him as a ladies man. He's also something of an idealist – he's not afraid to fight for a losing cause, just as long as it's a worthy one.

Jack is a hopeless romantic. Lining the shelves of his rack are pulp fantasy and adventure tales, like Tarzan, Call of the Wild, Moby Dick, Robinson Crusoe, Treasure Island, 20,000 Leagues Under the Sea, etc. Often seen with a perpetual 5 o'clock shadow, wearing a Navy watch sweater, khakis, combat boots and his trusty .45 strapped in a shoulder holster modified for quick-draw."

When I saw these first few sketches from Mathew, it immediately brought to mind Ian Fleming's description of James Bond in the books, his having "dark, cruel good looks." I knew this was our man.

Original description for Wulf:

"An experienced but taciturn former U-boat captain in his 50s. Why he wound up in the Pacific, and a member of the Venture's crew, is a mystery even Jack doesn't know the answer to. Picture him like a stoic Yul Brynner in Morituri. He always wears his old beaten captain's hat and uniform jacket, visibly stripped of any rank or insignia."

As you can see, he turned out to be a little more like an older, seasoned Race Bannon. But he's also sort of the boat's "mother" to Jack's father. Only he doesn't have a lot of patience for nonsensical matters like treasure hunting – instead, he's always got his eye on the bottom line.

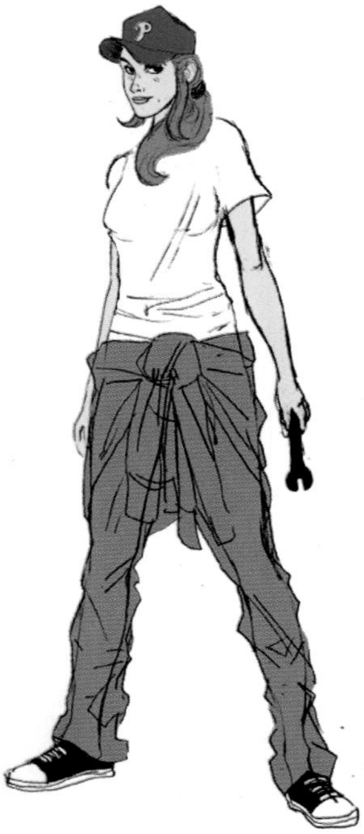

Original description for Sam:
"Barely 20, she's a genius with tools and machinery. Her father worked with Jack back in the day, and as a freckle-faced girl, Sam always harbored a crush on Jack. When her father is arrested and imprisoned, she takes off for the Pacific, all grown up and looking for work. She keeps the boat running, and there's sexual tension between her and Jack always. He feels like her older brother, but can't help but notice she's all woman now. Only he's too honorable to act on it, which drives Sam nuts. Like a much cuter Katherine Hepburn (sorry Kate!), I see her dressed as a tomboy, wearing greasy coveralls and an old Phillies ball cap most of the time. Though occasionally she will dress to impress, especially when Jack is tempted by other female company."

When Mathew turned in his first couple of sketches, I asked him to bring down the lips a bit, saying she looked like "a grease monkey version of Kim Bassinger."

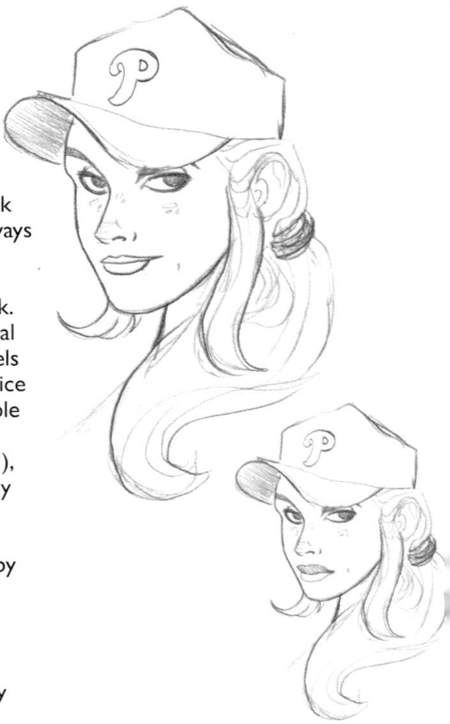

Original description for Doc:
"While his medical skills are unparalleled, he drinks to excess. As he says, he's a functioning alcoholic – without booze, he can't function. He looks like George Peppard, but he acts like George Sanders."

Though I think you can see here that he has a little Vincent Price and Peter Cushing in him.

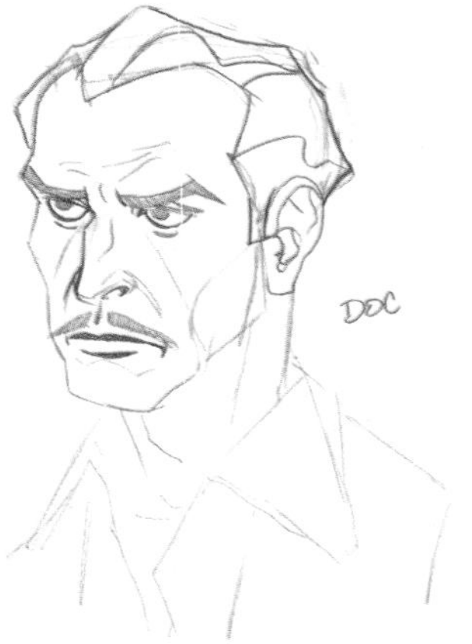
DOC

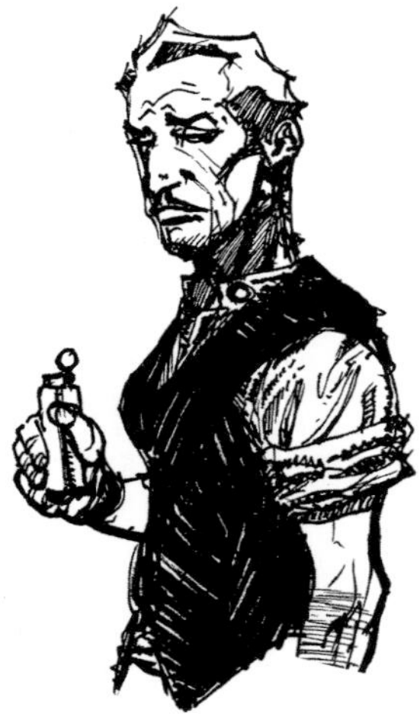

Original description for Stack:
"Picture him as a muscular Idris Elba, always in a tank top and fingerless gloves, chomping on a cigar. Or maybe he looks like "Roadblock" from GI Joe."

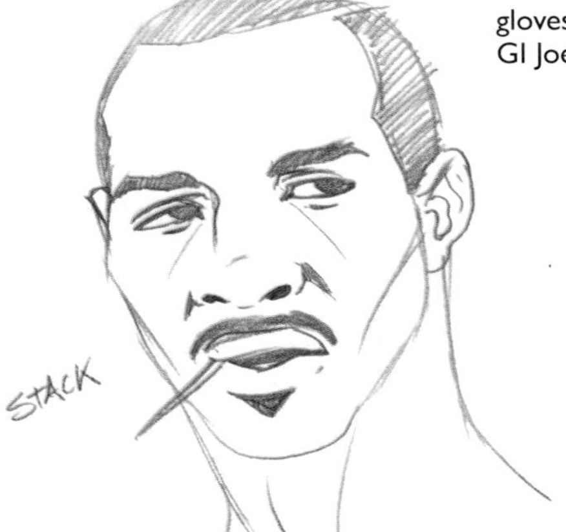
STACK

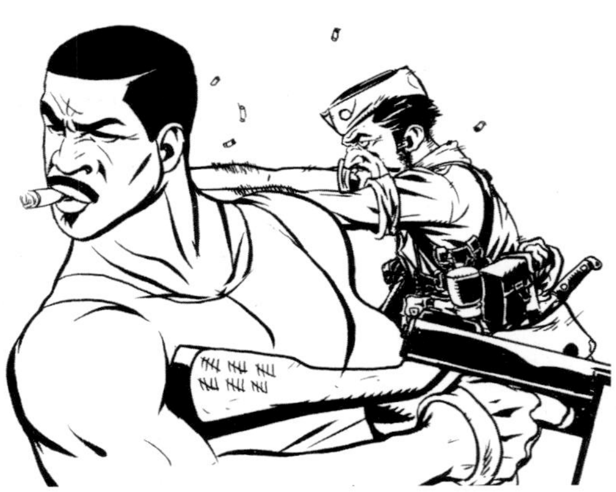

Original description for Jarreau:
"So smooth, he could sell suntan oil to the natives. As the boat's scrounger, he's always got his ear to the ground, looking to pick up the latest rumors of lost tribal treasure or pirate booty. And real butter – the captain may be on the hunt for Koji Ra, but the only gold Jarreau will be satisfied with is honest-to-God artisanal butter from France. Think Yves Montand in The Wages of Fear."

Original description for Kevin:
"A massive South Seas islander. With his piercings and powerful arms covered in tribal tattoos, he looks like he might fit in with the alternative crowds in present day L.A., San Francisco or New York. Visually he should resemble actor Robert Tessier from The Deep."

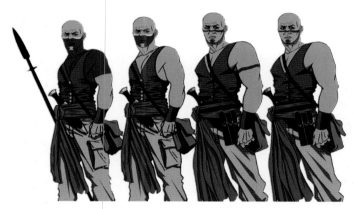

Original description for Captain Tono:
"He faced Harper and his crew many times during their brief career with Chinese navy, and Tono always got the short end of the engagement. But, the Japanese captain has a begrudging respect for Jack and his crew; honoring the code of Bushido, Tono considers Jack to be a ronin, betrayed by his masters and roaming the sea in search of retribution. Think of Toshiro Mifune."

Original description for Evelyn "Top Hat" Greene:
"She's a proud Englishwoman, who is dressed in Chinese peasant garb, her hair done up under a cap, made to look like a man. Her stiff upper lip is quaking now having seen her friend just gutted."

I described her to Mathew as being beautiful, whereas Sam was "girl next door cute;" blonde, a bit cold, and looking a little like Honor Blackman in Goldfinger. Her eventual turn as a double-agent wasn't originally planned, and surprised me as much as anyone.

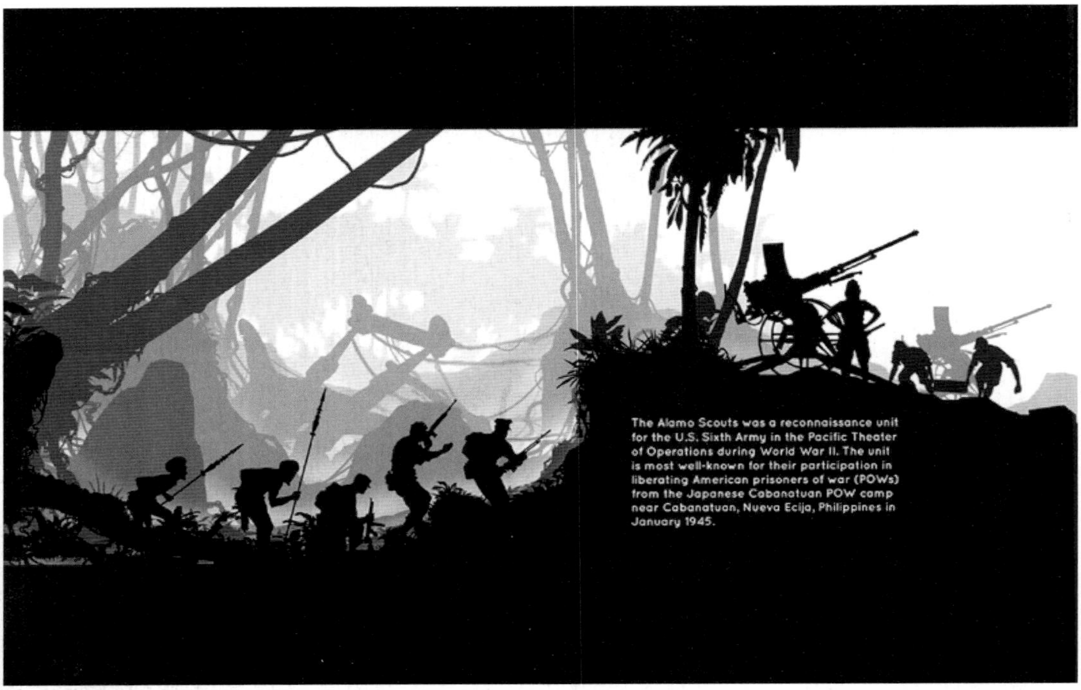
The Alamo Scouts was a reconnaissance unit for the U.S. Sixth Army in the Pacific Theater of Operations during World War II. The unit is most well-known for their participation in liberating American prisoners of war (POWs) from the Japanese Cabanatuan POW camp near Cabanatuan, Nueva Ecija, Philippines in January 1945.

An early piece by Mathew. When I saw his work online – the first thing I'd seen was a series of adventure scenes starring everybody's favorite archeologist – I was duly impressed. His use of depth of field, silhouette and cinematic focus created art that looked like two-dimensional dioramas. I loved it.

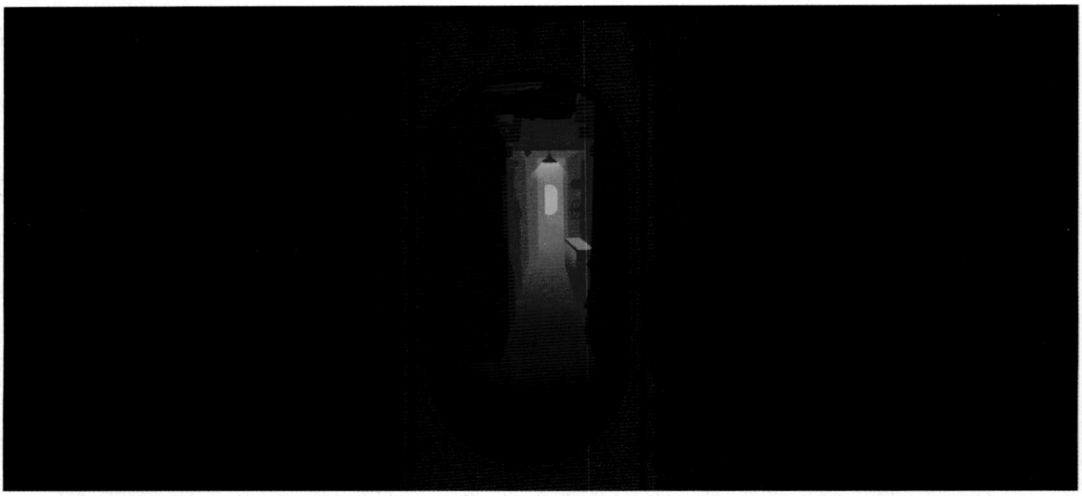

Some of the early interior layouts Mathew did for the Venture. We knew life aboard a World War I era U-boat would be a tight squeeze, but we wanted the Venture to have some personality, especially because we knew we'd be spending a lot of time there.

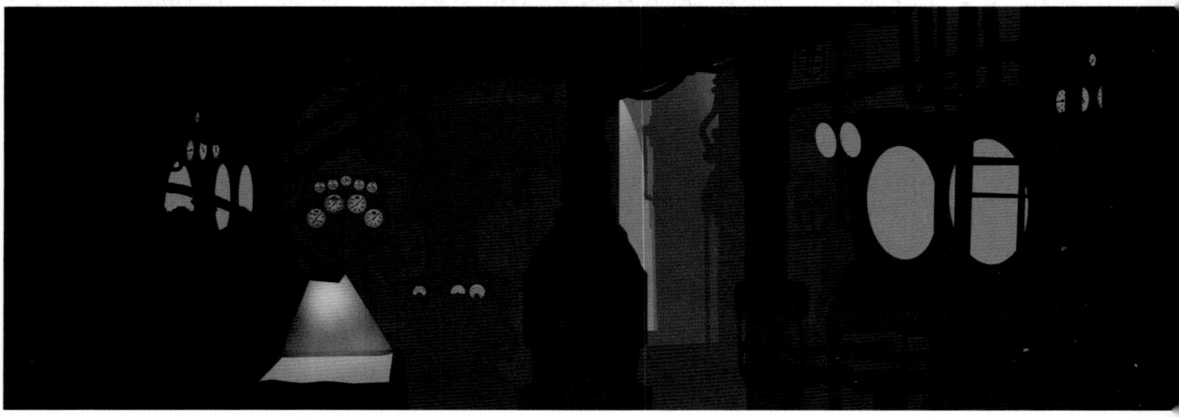